THE PARKS OF NASHVILLE
1897–1984

THE PARKS OF NASHVILLE
1897–1984

*A History of the
Board of Parks and Recreation*

Leland R. Johnson

1986, 2025
Metro Nashville Board of Parks and Recreation

Copyright © 1986, 2025 by Metro Nashville Board of Parks and Recreation
Nashville, Tennessee
All rights reserved

Second edition, 2025

All rights reserved. No part of this publication may be reproduced, distributed, or transmitted in any form or by any means, including photocopying, recording, or other electronic or mechanical methods, without the prior written permission of the publisher, except as permitted by US copyright law.

ISBN: 9798218694067
Library of Congress Control Number: 2025940905

The disposition to forget history, or the crime of not knowing it, eternally confronts and hampers Nashville.
Eugene Castner Lewis, 1913

FOREWORD

Recreation and leisure-time activities have been a part of my life for as long as I can remember. The DuPont Company, with whom my father was employed, had plenty of organized recreational activities and I was fortunate to grow up in a physically and mentally healthy atmosphere. I remember vividly a company picnic that was held in Shelby Park and even at that time I was grateful to have a great place to get together with family and friends.

As I look back on the 22 years I have spent in the employ of Nashville's Department of Parks and Recreation, I am amazed at the growth and vital role this department has played in the shaping of Nashville. And though I have spent a lifetime involved with parks in one way or the other, it is still just a fraction of the life of the parks themselves.

I have always been intrigued by the rich history of Nashville's park system and was consequently very excited when the prospect of putting it in book form was presented to me.

The successful fruition of this project is due to many hours of hard work from Historian Leland Johnson and various members of our park staff. I must also express my gratitude to Mayor Richard Fulton, the Metropolitan Council, and our Park Board members for their unflagging support of all that we do.

It is with great pride that we offer this history to lifelong Nashvillians as well as newcomers of our rapidly growing community. There is, however, a great deal of history yet to be made.

James H. Fyke, Director

1912 selfie at the Parthenon. Metro Nashville Archives, Nashville Public Library

CONTENTS

Preface	xi
1. The Centennial Exposition and Parks	21
2. Nashville Parks before 1901	33
3. The First Nashville Park Board	43
4. Managing the First Parks	53
5. The Playground Movement	63
6. Park Expansion, 1910–1916	73
7. Recreational and Cultural Emphasis	84
8. Management and Expansion, 1917–1930	94
9. Boom to Bust in the Parks	106
10. Federal Assistance Begins	117
11. The Parks During Wartime	128
12. Parks in the West Administration	140
13. Ending the City System	151
14. The Metropolitan Park Challenge	162
15. Parks for an Affluent Society	173
16. Park Management in the 70's	185
17. Park Management in the Golden Age	194
Notes	205
Bibliography	223
Appendix A: Historical Resources Inventory of Parks	232
Appendix B: Monuments, Memorials and Markers in the Parks	261
Appendix C: Members of the Park Boards	289
Appendix D: Biographical Sketches of Board Members in the 1980s	291

Shelby Park. Metro Nashville Archives, Nashville Public Library

PREFACE

Seventy parks adorned Nashville like green jewels in 1985, ranging in size from tiny Bass Park to Warner Parks—the largest municipal park in Tennessee—and totaling 6,644 acres in area. Filled with golf courses, swimming pools, ball diamonds, community centers, and unique features such as an ice rink, sailboat marina, steeplechase, and wave pool, those parks were operated with an annual budget of nearly $10 million by about 900 permanent and seasonal personnel under supervision of the Director of Parks and Recreation and his staff who reported to the Metropolitan Board of Parks and Recreation appointed by the Mayor and confirmed by the Metropolitan Council. The Nashville urban area had in 1985 a large, diverse, and enviable park system, second to none in the nation among cities of comparable size. Yet, those parks along with the funds and personnel needed to operate them have all been acquired during the 20th century, starting in 1901 with a single park, one mule, and a few seasonal employees.

This study of the history of the Metropolitan Nashville and Davidson County parks and recreation system necessarily is a record of growth, of continuing efforts to expand the number and size of parks, to increase and diversify recreational opportunities, and to secure the funding and personnel required for proper operation of the system. For ease of understanding, the park system history may be divided into three major phases: the 19th century formulative period when Nashvillians, stimulated by the success of their 1897 Centennial Exposition, sought and obtained the creation of a municipal park system; the years from 1901 to 1962 when Nashville's Board of Park Commissioners nursed a toddling park system to maturity, increasing the number of parks from one in 1901 to thirty-three in 1962; and the modern period of Metropolitan government since 1963 during which the number of parks more than doubled and their funding and personnel registered corresponding increases, and in which the system, as Director James H. Fyke expressed it, moved beyond "ball and bat" recreation to a highly diversified program.

After observing the deterioration of Park Board records and noting the gradual loss of oral traditions concerning park history, the Committee on Historical Perspectives of Mayor Richard H. Fulton's Commission on Community Excellence recommended in 1983 that the records be microfilmed and a narrative history of the park system written. This study therefore is an outgrowth of the work of that committee, chaired by B. R. Allison and including Robert McGaw, Ben Page, Ann Reynolds, Lallie Richter, and Wilbur F. Creighton, Jr. The study was authorized in 1984 by the Metropolitan Council, performed under the aegis of the Metropolitan Board of Parks and Recreation, and supervised by Director James H. Fyke and his administrative assistant Pauline Rigsby, to whom the author expresses his thanks.

The author is grateful to the Board of Parks and Recreation for their support of this project, especially to George Reichardt, Isaac Northern, and Fred Russell who reviewed the manuscript. Special thanks are due to Pauline Rigsby for her guidance, to Florence Becton who handled interoffice communications, and to Lallie Richter, Bill Dunaway, and Larry Cockerham of the Research and Planning Division who made available the records at their disposal. Mary Glenn Hearne, Laura H. Rehmert, and Frances C. Steele eased access to municipal park records at the Nashville Room of the Metropolitan Public Library, while Professors Don Doyle of Vanderbilt University and Bobby Lovett of Tennessee State University provided specialized information. The author, and in fact all Nashvillians, owe a debt of gratitude to Louise Davis, Hugh Walker, Margaret L. Warden and other news reporters and columnists who have preserved park history in scores of fine news articles, and to the publishers of Nashville's newspapers who have, since the days of Major E. C. Lewis, Major E. B. Stahlman, and Colonel Luke Lea, not only helped preserve park history but also created it by sponsoring innumerable activities and public events in the parks.

The author sought to provide both information about individual park history for the reference use of the park system staff and a cohesive narrative for the general reader. Leaders of the park system since 1901 have normally defined progress in terms of the number of parks, the amount of park acreage, and the quantity of recreation facilities, and the author accepted that definition as his central theme, although applying it became difficult when the number of parks proliferated during modern park history; therefore, appendices were added concerning the history of individual parks and the historic features found in the system. A secondary theme concerned assessment of the value of park services to the urban area, and it became apparent during the study that parks contribute to the city in many ways, notably by enhancing and stablizing property values and consequently reimbursing the public investment in the system. In addition, the author was impressed by the fact that the park system has not been created through municipal taxes alone, but also by hundreds of individual Nashvillians who as members of the Park Board or simply as civic-spirited citizens gave generously of their personal time and property to establish the park and recreation facilities Nashvillians enjoyed in 1985. A large part of the park system expansion has occurred in response to the population growth experienced in the Nashville area, and that expansion will no doubt continue to the end of the 20th century and beyond, for Dr. George Reichardt once observed that, while population increases may at last level off, the recreation needs of people will continue to increase.

Leland R. Johnson

1897 Centennial Exposition. Courtesy of the Tennessee State Library & Archives

1897 Centennial Exposition. Courtesy of the Tennessee State Library & Archives

The Giant Seesaw was the centerpiece of the Midway at the Centennial Exposition, shown in this picture from Spiral Hill looking east. Left of the seesaw is the Spanish Palace, to the right is the Commerce Building, and in the center is the Education Building with the Memphis Pyramid behind it. The State Capitol is visible on the horizon to the left. Courtesy of the Tennessee State Library & Archives

1897 Centennial Exposition. Metro Nashville Archives, Nashville Public Library

Horse-drawn carriages line the walk at the 1897 Centennial Exposition. Metro Nashville Archives, Nashville Public Library

Hadley Park. Metro Nashville Archives, Nashville Public Library

Hadley Park. Metro Nashville Archives, Nashville Public Library

Lake Watauga. Metro Nashville Archives, Nashville Public Library

Centennial Park. Metro Nashville Archives, Nashville Public Library

Centennial Park, 1912. Metro Nashville Archives, Nashville Public Library

Eighth Avenue Reservoir failure of 1912. Some of this stone and/or the stone used in the repairs likely came from Fort Negley. Metro Nashville Archives, Nashville Public Library

Eighth Avenue Reservoir failure of 1912. Some of this stone and/or the stone used in the repairs likely came from Fort Negley. Metro Nashville Archives, Nashville Public Library

Woodmont Boulevard, Nashville's first concrete road, under construction in 1914, near what would become Woodmont Park. Metro ITS Photographic Services

This pavilion stood in East Park from 1926–1956. Warner School visible in background. Metro Nashville Archives, Nashville Public Library

Elizabeth Park. Metro Nashville Archives, Nashville Public Library

Lindauer Park. Metro Nashville Archives, Nashville Public Library

Morgan Park. Metro Nashville Archives, Nashville Public Library

Morgan Park. Metro Nashville Archives, Nashville Public Library

Napier Park. Metro Nashville Archives, Nashville Public Library

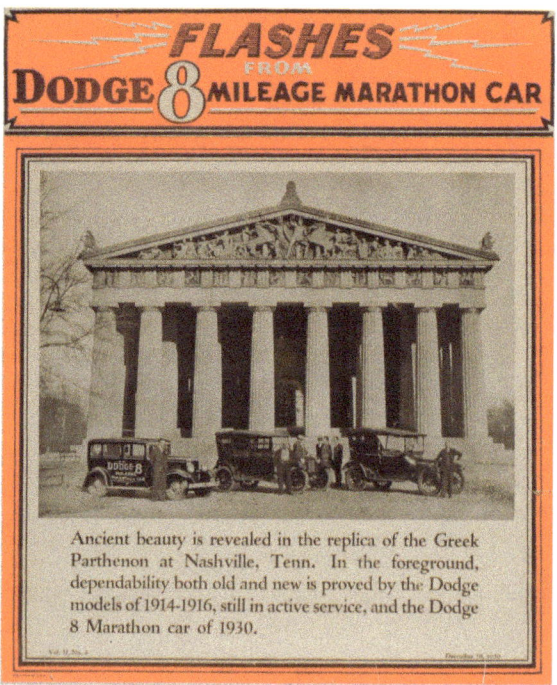

Metro ITS Photographic Services

Steeplechase. Metro Nashville Archives, Nashville Public Library

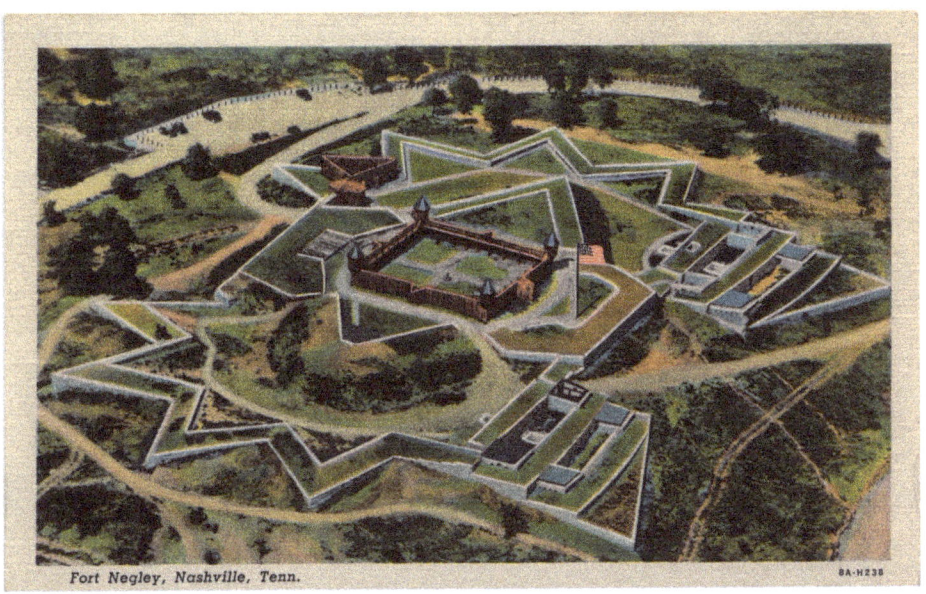
Courtesy of the Tennessee State Library & Archives

Planning Seven Oaks Park. Metro Nashville Archives, Nashville Public Library

Metro Nashville Archives, Nashville Public Library

Metro Nashville Archives, Nashville Public Library

Shelby Park, 1959. Metro Nashville Archives, Nashville Public Library

Future Charlotte Park. Metro Nashville Archives, Nashville Public Library

Steeplechase. Metro Nashville Archives, Nashville Public Library

Metro Nashville Archives, Nashville Public Library

Mayor Fulton at Buena Vista Park. Metro Nashville Archives, Nashville Public Library

Metro Nashville Archives, Nashville Public Library

Metro Nashville Archives, Nashville Public Library

Coleman Wheel Cats basketball team. Coleman Park, 1970. Metro Nashville Archives, Nashville Public Library

Constructing the dragon in Fannie Mae Dees Park. Metro Nashville Archives, Nashville Public Library

Fannie Mae Dees Park soon after the completion of the dragon. Metro Nashville Archives, Nashville Public Library

Antigone performed at the Parthenon, 1985. Metro Nashville Archives, Nashville Public Library

Hamilton Creek Sailboat Marina. Metro ITS Photographic Services. Photo by Shane Potter

Wave Country, 1983. Metro Nashville Archives, Nashville Public Library

Metro ITS Photographic Services

1 THE CENTENNIAL EXPOSITION AND PARKS

Last days are better or worse than most all others, and so it was on the final day of the Tennessee Centennial Exposition of 1897. The Thirtieth of October 1897 dawned painfully brilliant, a cool golden sun and autumn-tinted trees blazing over still emerald grass. Festive crowds thronging the streets of the magnificent Centennial City for a last fling enjoyed one more ride on the Giant Seesaw, another plunge down the boat chute at the side of Flagpole Hill, a final tour of the myriad exhibits, and at nine that evening, exhausted, they collected around Lake Watauga near the Parthenon as sputtering rockets blasted skyward and burst. When the dazzling fireworks display died, the throng streamed into the Auditorium, packing it for the concluding concert and closing ceremony.[1]

The last day of a grand adventure often is the first of the next, and thus it was at the end of the 1897 Centennial celebration. The planning and organization required of a city with a population of less than a hundred thousand, caught up moreover in the coils of an economic anaconda, to stage such a six-month extravaganza as the Centennial Exposition had united, if but temporarily, all elements of Nashville's body civic, and that euphoria of accomplishment, that confidence of purpose, was to endure into the 20th century. Serving in 1897 as a great stage where Nashville and Tennessee displayed their talents and resources to all the world, the Centennial grounds were to become a grand park in a city where none before had existed. That poignant Thirtieth of October in 1897 marked not just the last day of Tennessee's Centennial Exposition but also the genesis of Nashville's public parks system and indeed of municipal park systems throughout the state.[2]

At the capo of the Centennial's final concert, about ten in the evening of October 30, John W. Thomas, imposing president of the Centennial Exposition Company and also of the Nashville, Chattanooga and St. Louis Railway, strode center stage to introduce the orator for the occasion. It was only appropriate, President Thomas declared, that the Centennial's final oration be delivered by the man who in 1895 had kindled with his golden tongue a new fire in the hearts of despairing Nashvillians, when it seemed their dream of conducting a Centennial Exposition was evaporating—by the man whose fiery defiance of the many obstacles in the path had stimulated the formation of the company which "carried out the Tennessee Centennial today, the Honorable Tully Brown."[3]

Applause filled the Auditorium as Tully Brown stepped to the podium. The son of a governor of Tennessee, Brown served as Nashville's United States District Attorney in 1897 and was the finest orator in the "Athens of the South," if not in the state, in a day when public declamation remained a prized art. "It is with great pain, my fellow countrymen, that we close the gates of this beautiful Exposition, and yet there is pleasure in the great triumph we have achieved," he proclaimed: "In its physical proportions it has challenged the admiration of the intelligent world. From all parts of the country the most distinguished citizens, from the President down, have visited us, and but one word, and that of approval, of enthusiastic approval, has been given. Of its other features, its higher features, its spiritual and soul features, they will live with us, my fellow citizens, for many years to come." And so they did, indelibly printed on the memory of every citizen who had the privilege of seeing the White City of 1897 until their deaths; and so they do, in the hearts of every citizen who today enjoys the Parthenon and Centennial Park.[4]

Tully Brown regaled the crowd in the Auditorium that last evening with a brief account of the Centennial's planning and construction, of the obstacles encountered and overcome, and of the herculean efforts required of those sitting behind him on the stage. Because the Centennial celebration formed the historical cornerstone for the building of Nashville's park system, a synoptic recounting of its planning and construction is also appropriate here, with specific notice of the civic leadership and organization which made both it and the city park system possible.

Douglas Anderson, a Nashville attorney, in letters to newspaper editors first proposed a Centennial celebration of Tennessee's entry in the Union, and in 1894 Colonel William C. Smith, an architect and head of Tennessee's National Guard, recommended that Nashville's Commercial Club—subsequently merged with its Chamber of Commerce—undertake such a celebration. Both men probably were inspired, perhaps through personal visits to Chicago, by the memorable Columbian Exposition of 1893 at the Windy City, an exposition generally remembered today for the giant ferris wheel which was its centerpiece. Colonel Smith appealed to the business acumen of Nashville's commercial leaders by emphasizing the economic boost such an exposition could provide the city, which like the remainder of the nation was in the throes of the depression following the Panic of '93. As Tully Brown graphically described it to his audience: "We had little money, we had great courage; times were as hard as flint, banks were popping and cracking all over the Union; every day newspaper columns were but records of bank failures and business enterprises being thrown into the hands of receivers." In the face of those economic handicaps and the fact that Nashville was merely a tenth the size of Chicago, the Commercial Club approved Smith's recommendation and appointed an executive planning committee with James M. Head, former member of the state legislature and publisher of the Nashville *American*, as its director.[5]

Because the proposed exposition was to celebrate Tennessee's history, the Commercial Club initially expected it to be a statewide endeavor, supported by major funding from state government and from the federal government. James Head called together a convention of representatives from throughout Tennessee in June 1894 where plans for the celebration were devised, a public corporation to organize and supervise it formed, and the first stock subscriptions to finance it taken. The convention selected Major Andrew W. Wills as the Director General for the Centennial. A Union Army officer who had settled in Nashville after the Civil War and had become its

Republican postmaster, Major Wills concentrated on securing federal funding for the celebration. James Head and his law partner Samuel A. Champion, who both had served in the state legislature, undertook to obtain state funding. But, with an economy devastated by depression, the Tennessee General Assembly showed little interest in funding an exposition; and in Washington Major Wills was courteously informed that his requests would receive sincere consideration. That consideration continued more than a year while the 1896 centennial of Tennessee's entry into Union drew ever nearer.[6]

Nashville's hope that a Centennial Exposition might be conducted was dissipating by June 1895. Economic conditions slowed the sale of stock in the exposition to individuals and firms, neither federal nor state funding was offered, and government aid came only from Davidson County, which in December 1894 had loaned the Exposition $50,000. In mid-1895 it therefore seemed unlikely that the Exposition could open in 1896, and the question arose whether it should open at all. At a mass meeting of Nashvillians interested in the Exposition on June 8, whether to continue with the planning was debated and District Attorney Tully Brown delivered his stirring exhortation on behalf of continuing. After his speech, and some people who heard it said as a direct result thereof, Nashville's city council decided to ask the voters whether they would approve issuing $100,000 worth of bond subscriptions to the Exposition company, thereby indicating their desire to conduct the Exposition even without state or federal assistance. At that meeting, the Exposition company also reorganized, evidently to establish a broader community base and attract more stock subscriptions. Famed railroad man John W. Thomas became president of the company, and he selected Major E. C. Lewis as the new Director General. Major Andrew Wills became Commissioner General, in which position he continued his lobbying for federal funding. The company decided to make no effort to open the Exposition in the disruptive presidential election year of 1896 and to aim for its opening in the spring of 1897.[7]

In October 1895, 7,256 of the approximately 13,000 eligible voters in Nashville went to the polls, and only 488 opposed subscribing $100,000 of their taxes toward the Exposition; in all Nashville history, seldom has there been such unity of purpose expressed by its citizens, especially on pocketbook issues. Purchasing stock in the Exposition became nearly a patriotic duty in the city: businessmen and workingmen associations subscribed, wealthy individuals purchased, and both major railroads serving the city contributed substantial sums and, moreover, agreed to deliver construction materials to the Exposition site without charge. Once Nashville made it evident that it was fully committed to the Exposition, the efforts to secure state and federal assistance met better success. Major Wills, with support from Tennessee's congressmen, wrangled $130,000 from Congress toward the development of national exhibits, and, after what was described as a "bitter struggle," James Head, Samuel Champion, and Tully Brown extracted a $50,000 pledge from state government.[8]

Even before funding arrangements were completed, the Exposition company selected a site and began construction, perhaps to prove to potential stock subscribers that their investment was wise. Nashville then had two racetracks, Cumberland Park on Nolensville Road (now the State Fair Grounds) and West Side Park at the end of Church Street, and the company chose West Side Park, leasing it from the Tennessee Fair Association which had used it as the state fair grounds until converting it into a racetrack in 1884. Director General E. C. Lewis chose the prominent engineer Wilbur F. Foster as Director of Works and Foster's business partner Robert T. Creighton as chief of engineering. The engineers began digging at West Side racetrack, excavating lakes, mounding the earth as foundation for the Exposition's central building, building the roads, and laying five miles of sewer. Casting about for a central theme to highlight the cultural history of Nashville as the "Athens of the South," Major Lewis hit upon the happy concept of centering the Exposition around a full-scale replica of the Parthenon of Ancient Greece, won instant approval for his idea from the company directorate, and employed Colonel William Smith as its architect. On October 8, 1895, as Nashville voters polled their approval of the $100,000 bond subscription, the cornerstone of the Parthenon was laid with appropriate Masonic rites, initiating construction of what was to become known as the "White City."[9]

Construction went on at a frantic pace throughout 1896 and into 1897. Buildings to house displays of agricultural, forest, and mineral resources, of industrial and mechanical arts, and of Tennessee's history went up in a rush. All were of economical, temporary construction, of wooden lathing covered with white plaster designed for removal at the end of the celebration—the replica of the Parthenon, for instance, cost only $34,611.75. Art Dyer, a Nashville engineer, designed and built the Giant Seesaw, centerpiece of the Midway, and W. F. Josolyne, chief landscape architect, planted the shrubbery and flowers, recruiting George B. Moulder as the aquatic plant specialist. To demonstrate the progessiveness of the state and community, chief electrician J. W. Braid installed ten thousand electric lights, even outlining the buildings with light to make them truly a White City even at night.[10]

As construction accelerated and opening day approached, one major legal hurdle remained: the sale of alcohol. Tennessee then was in the midst of an acrid conflict between "wets" and "drys" over prohibition, and while Nashville was thoroughly "wet" the remainder of the state raised objections to the sale of liquor at the Exposition. The question therefore had a bearing on whether state government would contribute any funding whatsoever to the celebration. Samuel Champion, General Counsel for the Exposition, ushered through the state legislature a bill chartering Centennial City, a town with mayor, alderman, and law-making powers with its town limits being the Exposition grounds and its charter to expire at the end of the Centennial. The new town government enacted an ordinance permitting the sale of beer and wine with meals at the Exposition but forbidding hard liquor on the grounds; and to enforce that and other ordinances the town hired a 138-man police force called the Centennial Guard and headed by Captain Eastman Currey. During the six-months of the Centennial, the Guard arrested about about a hundred rascals a month, maintaining excellent order among the huge crowds; the only serious incident of record occurred when the Guard knocked soldiers from the Louisville Legion in the head when they disrupted one of the "girlie" shows on the Midway.[11]

President William McKinley in Washington on May 1, 1897, moved the control setting the machinery in motion and officially opening the Centennial Exposition, and there followed the busiest, if not the most glorious, summer in Nashville's history, an endless round of pageants, concerts, parades, and receptions that taxed the city's resources. On one day, more people attended the Exposition than lived in Nashville. Nashville's leaders welcomed a daily procession of dignitaries from the President down, and the city's grande dames—especially Mrs. Van Leer "Kate" Kirkman and Mrs. John H. Eakin—conducted receptions to their hearts' content. While most buildings on the grounds exhibited Tennessee's resources and economic activities, Tennessee's women had their own building housing various historical displays, a library of books by and about women, and an exhibit of inventions patented by women. Banker J. C. Napier, teacher Richard Hill, minister Preston Taylor, and a dozen other leaders of Tennessee's black citizens directed the black achievement exhibits and welcomed such prominent national leaders as Booker T. Washington.[12]

Throughout the summer of 1897, trains into Nashville were at capacity, all hotels and rental property in the city were occupied, and anyone who wanted work found it in the construction and operation of the Exposition, or in providing the services needed by the 1.8 million people who visited the Exposition. In relieving the effects of the economic depression, the Exposition proved even more successful than its proponents had predicted; and at the end the Director General reported the Exposition was completed with a cash balance remaining on hand of $39.44, plus the salvage value of the structures on the grounds, an achievement as rare for world's fairs then as it has been in the 20th century. Some Nashvillians, in view of the prosperity and excitement generated by the celebration, clamored for extending it additional months, as had been done at earlier expositions in Atlanta and Louisville, but the summer's efforts had exhausted the community's leaders and they wisely decided to close it on October 39, 1897.[13]

"What good has the Exposition done?" asked Tully Brown as he recapitulated the herculean work of the summer and the two years preceding it. Tennessee's history had been writ large, he asserted, and the attention of the state's people fixed thereon; that alone made the Exposition worthwhile, in his opinion. He perceived that out of the Exposition had come a renewed hope and cheerfulness, a new unity, among the people of the state and especially of Nashville. Nashville was an "unknown" city when the Exposition commenced, but at its end the city had the respect of the nation, and news reporters from New York or Boston no longer lamented about "Poor Old Nashville." Those were ephemeral achievements, however, and Brown urged the crowd in the Auditorium that last evening to consider the city's future, declaring:[14]

The question comes up, my fellow citizens of the city of Nashville, are you going to stay out of these grounds forever? Are we to have them, are we to own them, are they to be a monument of this glorious Exposition, or are they to be sold in lots by the people who own them? [Applause.] Are we going to make this a public park [cheers and cries of "yes, yes"] that the people of Nashville may come here and enjoy this for all time to come? Are we to throw away the hundred thousand dollars that has been expended to make it a beautiful landscape and do without a beautiful park? [Cries of "No, never!"] Will the people of Nashville submit, I ask; will this great audience, will Nashville people submit to the ignominy of not, upon these grounds, building a suitable monument to their courage and energy? [Applause.] Who will be the man that will strike the first blow at the Parthenon? It seems to me he will be a bold man who does. That glorious temple as Voltaire said, "the *ne plus ultra* of architectural genius," for ages and ages by arms, architecture, history, astrology, and all the brain of man could give, has been poured in wild and rich profusion in praise of that majestic temple. [Applause.] The most artistic race in its most artistic time builded that temple, the highest reach of their art. It has never been reached since, and the greatest thing that has been done since was the suggestion of our Director General that we, in the city of Nashville, in the State of Tennessee—a country that was not discovered for more than two thousand years after that was built—that we should rebuild the Parthenon. [Applause.] I desire in person, for myself, to think him warmly for his idea. [Applause.] I never dreamed that it would be my great good fortune to gaze upon the Parthenon, but here it stands, and here it has stood in the blaze of day, and in the beautiful light of the stars at night for six long months, the light and glory of the Exposition and of the world. [Applause.]

Tully Brown at that moment, near midnight on October 30, 1897, launched Nashville's public park system, for he voiced a sentiment that had arisen among Nashvillians that it would be tragic to lose such a central recreation center crowned by the Parthenon which had brought the city such fame. As the reception to his remarks indicated, Brown touched a responsive chord within the hearts of his fellow Nashvillians in that auditorium, which included the majority of the city's political, economic, and social leaders. The masterpiece of the Centennial Exposition, the replica of the Parthenon would become the centerpiece of the municipal park system and remain its crowning glory throughout the 20th century.

Major E. B. Stahlman and James M. Head, publishers of

Nashville's major newspapers, lent their influential support to the campaign following the Exposition to preserve the Parthenon and make the Exposition grounds the Centennial Park. Noting that public sentiment strongly favored such a park, Major Stahlman in the *Banner* encouraged the park movement, but questioned the wisdom of the purchase and operation of the park by the city, suggesting it might be best for an independent public corporation headed by unpaid civic leaders to undertake that task. The *American* urged that a public park should be one of the "many glorious results" of the Exposition and the first step in a broad civic improvement program. "The wonderful work that Nashville has accomplished, with practically no assistance, other than that of her own people and of her own resources has led Nashvillians to a proper conception of their power," the *American's* editor asserted, "and they will now leave nothing undone that tends towards making her the metropolitan city that she can be."[15]

When the executive directorate of the Exposition met on November 10, 1897, Major E. B. Stahlman declared that Nashvillians clearly supported the creation of Centennial Park and urged the directors to consider establishing and operating the park on their own with minimal municipal tax assistance. Samuel Champion, the General Counsel, pointed out it would be necessary for the Exposition company to purchase the park land, but "we must not stop here, but we should push forward." President John W. Thomas reminded the other directors that they had taken an option to buy the land for $175,000 when they leased it for the Exposition. He estimated that the state fair association which owned it had invested at least $150,000 in the property: to raise that large sum for the purchase would be very difficult.[16]

Tully Brown warned the directorate that it would be positively humiliating to have all the buildings on the grounds demolished and the land subdivided for the construction of housing. Director General E. C. Lewis therefore described the condition of the structures, recommending that the Parthenon, History Building, and arbors and bridges be preserved, and the directors concurred, placing Robert Creighton in charge of the grounds and of dismantling and selling the structures before the lease expired in late 1898. Creighton actually retained more structures than the directorate had approved, for when the lease expired there remained—in addition to the Parthenon and History Building—the Auditorium, the Mexican building, two bandstands, a pagoda, the small emergency hospital, the children's nursery, and other minor structures.[17]

The directors of the Centennial proved unable to organize a campaign to secure the $175,000 needed to exercise their option and convert the Centennial grounds into a public park. Perhaps the efforts required to stage the Exposition had exhausted their initiative; they met for a lavish banquet annually for years after 1897, but the meetings seem to have borne no fruit. The fact that several of their number entered politics or took public appointments after 1897 may also have disrupted the unity of the group.

Leadership of the Exposition proved a stepping stone to public office for some, yet fate intervened in other cases. Orator Tully Brown seemed destined in 1897 for very high office, but he had been appointed U.S. District Attorney in the Democratic administration of President Grover Cleveland and left that post under Republican William McKinley in 1898; he resumed his law practice and never was elected to a major public office. Major Andrew Wills, on the other hand, had been Nashville's postmaster under Republican President Benjamin Harrison, had lost that post when Democrat Grover Cleveland took office, but was reappointed in 1898 by Republican William McKinley; he remained the city's postmaster throughout the succeeding Republican administrations until Democrat Woodrow Wilson became President. The most politically successful of the directors was James M. Head, the skilled lobbyist, attorney, and newspaper publisher.[18]

The son of a surgeon in Nathan B. Forrest's Confederate cavalry, James M. Head grew up in Sumner County, graduated from the law school at Harvard University in 1876, practiced law at Gallatin, and moved to Nashville in 1881 to serve in the state legislature. Leaving the legislature in 1884, he became a partner in the Champion, Head, and Brown law firm and publisher of the Nashville *American*. As chairman of the Exposition's executive committee, he organized state conventions supporting the Centennial celebration and lobbied in the General Assembly for state support, earning a statewide reputation for administrative talent. He received serious consideration in 1898 as the Democratic nominee for state governor, but lost to Benton McMillin.[19]

Head's candidacy in 1898 gubernatorial election certainly must have made Benton McMillin, the winner, aware of the widespread public support in Nashville, and also in Memphis and Knoxville, for the creation of municipal park systems. In his first message to the General Assembly in 1899, Governor McMillin expressed his support for city parks, declaring that such parks would easily reimburse the public investment by permitting people to remain in the cities during the heat of summer instead of fleeing to cooler climes. Recommending that the General Assembly enact legislation authorizing Tennessee cities to create urban parks, he said:[20]

> Whilst this is not a reform to be forced upon our urban population against their wishes, I feel so keenly its importance that I am constrained to recommend to you the passage of a general law authorizing the appointment or selection in such ways as you deem best, of Park Commissioners for all cities and towns desiring them, to serve without pay. I doubt not home loving and enterprising citizens would, in many instances, accept such a trust even without pay. If in only a few cities a spirit can be aroused, or increased, of beautifying and making them more comfortable and healthful, the effort will have been well made.

The General Assembly made that effort in 1899, enacting a bill permitting Tennessee cities to appoint park commissioners who would serve five-year terms without pay. It provided no state funding to assist with park development, but granted permission to municipal governments to issue bonds of up to $250,000 for the purchase of park lands, if the bonds were approved by voter referendum. The Governor vetoed that bill because he thought it improperly, or unconstitutionally, worded, and the General Assembly again took up the subject in 1900. Governor McMillin signed an act authorizing Memphis in 1900 to establish a public park system, but none for Nashville.[21]

Having lost the gubernatorial nomination, James M. Head entered the race and was elected Mayor of Nashville in 1899. During his first year in office, he concentrated upon erasing a deficit under which the city had been operating, and after he balanced the budget in early 1901 he initiated renewed efforts to obtain public parks for Nashville. "There can be no doubt, however, that the time has come when something should be done looking to the establishment of an extensive park system for this city," Mayor Head proclaimed: "Its population demands it, and every consideration of policy and humanity requires that some source of recreation and innocent amusement be provided for that class of our population which cannot leave the city during the summer months, and which must have some recreation and fresh air during the warm summer nights."[22]

In his efforts to secure a municipal park system, Mayor Head enjoyed support from both major Nashville newspapers, of Major Stahlman at the *Banner* and of Major E. C. Lewis, to whom Head had sold the *American*. He had enthusiastic support from the Governor and apparently won the support of the General Assembly through the expert liaison of Samuel Champion, his law partner who had been the Exposition's General Counsel. Governor McMillin signed a bill on April 3, 1901, allowing Nashville to create public parks not only within its corporate limits but also adjacent thereto. The city parks were to be in charge of an independent board of five commissioners, all serving without pay during five-year terms and each taking the required oath of allegiance and executing $10,000 bonds to assure the faithful performance of their duties. The Board was given the power to enact ordinances governing the use of the parks, to employ park police to enforce those rules, and to employ workmen needed to maintain the parks. It was directed to submit its annual budget request to the city council, and the council had the authority to levy taxes for the support of the park system, with the tax revenues to be placed in a separate fund for parks and not in the general revenue fund.[23]

The origins of Nashville's public park system thus may be traced to the Centennial Exposition of 1897, and although Centennial Park did not become the city's first public park, its preservation for public use was the fundamental motivation behind the formation of Nashville's park system. Though his efforts were ably supported by Major E. C. Lewis and other civic leaders, to Mayor James Head belongs the principal credit for creating a public park system in Nashville. The combination of Mayor Head's political acumen with the public spirit of Nashville's commercial leadership, which had overcome all obstacles to make the Centennial Exposition a success, created the city's park system and carried it during the 20th century toward full "metropolitan" status among America's cities.

2 NASHVILLE PARKS BEFORE 1901

While Nashville's municipal park system was not established until 1901, the city did not entirely lack parks and open spaces during the 19th century. Its citizens enjoyed several well known and fondly remembered private amusement parks and some open spaces generally referred to as the "commons." Some Nashvillians, after they became aware at the time of the Centennial Exposition of the potential of municipal parks, complained that the city had lagged behind others of its size in park development, but that idea was more illusory than real. It was true that the founders of the city had not included in their plat of the town several open city blocks to serve as public commons, as was done for instance at Memphis when it was platted in 1819, but the nationwide movement in support of urban parks had developed chiefly during the late 19th century. Of the 159 American cities with populations exceeding 25,000 in 1900, 37 had no public parks, 43 had less than fifty acres of parks, and 79 had more than fifty acres. The majority of those existing municipal park systems then were less than ten years old, created during the 1890s. Nor was the park development record better at the state and federal levels: Tennessee in 1901 had not a single state park, and the half dozen national parks were located in the Far West. A brief discussion of Nashville's 19th century parks and of the national movement on behalf of public parks is necessary to place the Nashville experience in perspective.[1]

Though the idea that federal, state, and municipal governments should acquire and develop parks for public use was essentially a late 19th century concept, the perception that cities needed some sort of open spaces was as ancient as urban civilization. Many residents of ancient cities enjoyed nearby "sacred groves," and the idea that communion with nature in a park constitutes a purifying spiritual experience has survived even unto today. Frederick Law Olmsted, the father of city park planning in America, remarked in 1880: "There are woody resorts in Rome which have been woody resorts from the time of the Caesars. The Mount of Olives still serves as a place of retreat from the confinement and bristle of the streets of Jerusalem, and its present groves are believed to have sprung from the roots of trees planted centuries before the summer days when the humble friends of a certain unpractical Jew were apt to look for him among the afternoon strollers under their shade." There are Nashvillians today who recall their principal Sunday afternoon recreation when they were young consisted of a trip with their parents to the Mount Olivet, Greenwood, or City cemeteries to enjoy cool shade while visiting the graves of their forebears. And, though somewhat less sedate, the concept that wilderness encounters have a spiritual connotation undergirded the national environmental preservation movement of recent American history.[2]

In addition to spiritual benefits, parks near urban centers also had utilitarian values until the late 19th century. Before the advent of such modern amenities as electrical heat and appliances, living conditions required that even the wealthiest urban denizens have some access to forests as a firewood supply and to open fields for the pasturage of dairy cattle and livestock. Medieval cities had "greens" or commons set aside for the gathering of firewood and the subsistence of livestock which served also as space for drill by the militia and play by the children; and the custom of demarcating town commons for the joint use of urban populations continued in American colonial towns, especially in New England. Nashville had no publicly owned commons, but the open fields around the town served the same purpose. In 1825, for instance, the Marquis de Lafayette reviewed the Nashville militia on what was called the South

Field on the outskirts of town (in the southeast corner of present Eighth and Broad streets).[3]

Real estate developers in Nashville learned at an early date that reserving part of their subdivision plat as a "park" stimulated lot sales around the park and enhanced the value of the remainder of their property, and the description of those and other open spaces adjacent to a community as the "commons" survived in Nashville's folk culture into the 20th century. George Boyles, who grew up in the Sylvan Park neighborhood of Nashville at the turn of the century, recalled in 1984 the folk definition of "commons":[4]

> The Commons was also the place for pasturing milk-cows, some horses and ponies, chickens (mostly hens), ducks, geese and guineas. It was a romping place for stray dogs, cats and barefoot boys. The wild grasses were never mowed and the prickly-pears never bothered anyone except when bare feet stepped on them. Daisies, rag-weed, and milk-weed grew shoulder high in places, and a multitude of sweet odors filled the air.
>
> Mothers who wanted to be free from bother told children to "go out and play in the commons," or, for punishment of misdeeds, would cry, "Don't you dare go out in the commons."

Surrounded by open countryside, early Nashvillians had little need for either public commons or public parks as we know them today. The city's population at the time of the War Between the States was less than 20,000 or, for comparison, smaller than the 1985 populations of the nearby Columbia and Murfreesboro communities. Its citizens could easily walk or ride horseback into the open rural areas around the city for fresh air and exercise and often did. Randall McGavock, Nashville's mayor in 1858, frequently walked out of the city with his friends to attend political barbeques, picnics, and the like at Watkins grove, which apparently became known as Watkins Park and became Nashville's first city park.[5]

Nashville's wealthier families during the 19th century generally escaped summer heat by fleeing the city, taking refuge in the shade at one of their plantations or "taking the waters" at one of the thirty-one mineral water spas dotting Middle Tennessee. At the spas, they drank and bathed in mineral water from springs, then thought to have curative powers. Very often they found their cures, if not as a result of the water, then through the palliative effects of a change of social and natural scenery, of strolling in the shade, or of rocking and complete rest on the verandas of the hotels. The popularity of the spas continued well into the 20th century, notably Horn Springs on the Tennessee Central Railroad east of Nashville which was the chosen spa of Nashville's First Presbyterian Church and Vanderbilt University's sororities until the 1950s. With the opening of railroad lines, well-to-do Nashvillians also refreshed themselves with summer vacations at Monteagle, Beersheba Springs, and other resorts at the cooler mountain elevations, a practice that remained common even in 1985.[6]

Under those conditions, Nashvillians during the 19th century felt little need for a public park system; yet, there were a few far-sighted individuals who perceived that public park space should be reserved as a hedge against the city's future growth. The first proposal that the city acquire public park lands apparently was voiced in 1856, when a Nashville newspaper editor noted that London had Hyde Park, Paris its Champs Elysées, Berlin the Unterden-Linden, and that New York City had begun the development of Central Park. Though admitting the vacant pastures around the city's perimeter adequately served the park needs of 1856, the editor predicted urban growth would continue, buildings proliferate, and the time would come when no open recreational space remained for the pleasure and health of future generations. "It is our duty as good citizens," he enjoined, "not only to promote such improvements as may tend to beautify and adorn our city, but also to take care that compact blocks of brick and mortar do not usurp the whole of the land." It seemed to him short-sighted for the city to neglect purchasing public park lands in 1856 that might become prohibitively expensive in later years.[7]

The editor received only a single unsigned letter of support for his idea. It urged the city to purchase fifty acres surrounding Sulphur Springs—formerly known as French Lick in the valley north of Capitol Hill—and there build a public bath, or swimming pool, where Nashvillians could take the mineral water amidst forest, shrubbery, and flowers. "A Parisian would go into ecstasy over such a Champs Elysees," the letter concluded, "with its rustic bridges and mossy banks, its cool shades and balmy breezes, for be it remembered it is the coolest spot in Nashville in summer."[8]

Though the city purchased neither Sulphur Springs, nor any other public park land during the 19th century, Sulphur Springs was developed by a private firm. During the Civil War, Union soldiers played baseball in a field at Sulphur Springs, and on September 11, 1866, the first organized baseball game in Nashville took place there. (The Flynns defeated the Burns, 25 to 16.) The Sulphur Springs Company, headed by John M. Thompson, built a bathhouse and ballpark at the springs, leased the park to the Nashville Base Ball Association, and marketed sulphur water from the spring, selling several hundred gallons daily of the bottled water which was valued for its laxative and diuretic properties. Known during the 19th century as the Athletic Park at Sulphur Springs Bottom, it was renamed Sulphur Dell by sportswriter Grantland Rice and served as the home of professional baseball in the city until 1963. The park, however, never became sufficiently attractive to excite the envy of a Parisian.[9]

Before the advent of baseball and other team sports, horse racing was the most popular spectator sport in Nashville, and the racetracks served as parks of a sort. Clover Bottom racetrack at Stone's River near the Hermitage attracted the largest crowds during the city's early history, and after 1828 the most popular racetrack was the Island Track operated by Lysander McGavock and located near the modern Metro Center. When the Island Track closed in 1884, West Side Park opened on land that previously had been the site of the Tennessee State Fair and which became Centennial Park. As a footnote to Centennial Park history, it might be mentioned that Frank James, the brother of Jesse James who resided in Davidson County for a time, entered horses and won races at the West Side track. Cumberland Park opened in 1891 on Nolensville Road chiefly for harness or trotting races, and operated until the state legislature in 1906 enacted laws against wagering and killed organized racing in the state for the time being. At a time when horses were the principal means of transportation, horse racing was not only the sport of kings but in Nashville the sport of practically everyone; and 19th century horse races in Nashville attracted both the sort of crowds which in 1985 attended the Iroquois Steeplechase and those which gathered for the automobile races at the Fair Grounds.[10]

The immediate predecessors of Nashville's public parks were the "trolley parks," which as their name implied were established by the streetcar lines during the 1880s for several purposes. People traveling to and from the parks increased the traffic on the streetcar lines, and the parks produced other and perhaps more important benefits for the owners of the streetcar companies. Most owners of the lines also engaged in real estate development in subdivisions located along and at the end of the lines. The "trolley parks" created an open, park atmosphere within the new suburbs which could enhance the sales of adjoining real estate, and the amusements they offered attracted potential customers from older sections of town who thereby became accustomed to riding the streetcars and had an opportunity to see what the new subdivisions had to offer. Families who visited an amusement park on a weekend might return the following week to investigate buying a new home in the suburb building around the perimeter of the park. Streetcar lines not only facilitated the expansion of Nashville's urban population out from the central business district, they promoted it as good business.[11]

According to a Nashville civic booster publication of 1885, the first "trolley park" in Nashville, and the only site in town worthy of the name "park," was Spring Park in East Nashville on Fatherland Street at Thirteenth Street. Built by one of the first streetcar lines in the city, which had mules pulling the streetcars, Spring Park had a small spring-fed lake, a bandstand, a monkey cage, and shady walkways lined with shrubbery and flowers. "Spring Park is the only resort for the people of Nashville for recreation and change of air and water," proclaimed the brochure, "and is a beautiful spot, but so small as to suggest the establishment of a park by the city, a need which is sorely felt and which is the one thing waiting to make the Rock City attractive in every regard as a place of residence."[12]

A second "trolley park" opened in 1887 on sixty-four acres south of the city at the end of the Overland Railway, a "dummy" streetcar line which had a small steam locomotive pulling its cars. James E. Caldwell and Oscar Noel, Sr., headed the Waverly Land Development Company which directed construction of the line, the opening of the park, and the development of the adjacent suburb known as Waverly. Initially known as Woodstock Park, it was renamed Glendale Park in 1890 and became the most popular amusement park in the city. With amusement rides, concerts, various special events, a zoo, and an attractive natural setting, Glendale Park proved so successful that Nashvillians still spoke of the pleasures of visiting it a half century after it had closed.[13]

The builders of the West Nashville community in the 1880s

planned parks for their subdivisions on a much larger scale than had been done by previous developers, laying out Richland, Clifton, and Cherokee parks. Of the three, Cherokee Park was the largest at eighty-three acres, and it lay at the terminus of a streetcar line built in 1889 by Mark S. Cockrill, L. H. Davis, and James Yarbrough who also were the principals of the West Nashville Development Company. Running north from the Public Square on trestles over Sulphur Spring Bottom, the line turned west parallel to Jefferson and Charlotte streets to its terminal at Cherokee Park. While Clifton and Richland parks served West Nashvillians as "commons," Cherokee Park like Glendale Park had amusements, concerts, dances, and in addition four sulphur springs valued for their mineral waters. An electric streetcar line and a railroad spur track entered West Nashville in the 1890s and put the original "dummy" streetcar line out of business, and Cherokee Park subsequently was subdivided and sold with the exception of a few acres that in 1909 became one of the city's public parks. As a footnote to Cherokee Park history, it might be mentioned that in 1898 the First Tennessee Regiment commanded by Colonel William C. Smith used the park as training camp for service in the Philippines.[14]

Owners of the streetcar lines expected the parks to stimulate business but were astonished by the number of people, even hanging out the car windows and riding atop the cars, who flocked to the parks during holidays and summer weekends. Lacking public parks, Nashvillians during the 1890s were desperate for open spaces, amusements, and escape from city heat. "Summer has come upon us once more," lamented a Nashville newspaperman in June 1890, "and that numerous class that must stay through the heat and dust and mental and physical strain super-induced by the summer months in town, is faced with the problem of how to get through the summer."[15]

Nashville's population of about 17,000 in 1860 doubled by 1880 and redoubled by 1890 when it reached 76,000. Crowding strained available urban services, and by 1890 the urban area had expanded outward to the extent that walking to the rural areas surrounding the city was no longer feasible for most citizens. They therefore paid the five-cent fare for streetcar travel to the trolley parks, providing the streetcar lines with revenue on weekends when the usual commuter traffic to and from the downtown district was slack and providing land developers in the vicinity of the parks with a ready-made flow of potential buyers of their real estate.[16]

Nashville's population doubled from 43,000 in 1880 to 95,000 at the turn of the century, and similar urban growth, crowding, and expansion occurred throughout the United States during that score of years. The total population of all American cities climbed from fourteen million in 1880 to thirty million in 1900. Though their working hours were long and their pay generally low, city folk in the United States became increasingly eager for respite at least one day a week from the crowding and accompanying irritations of urban life. Increased city population, decreased access to rural areas, and visits to trolley parks contributed to growing appreciation of the value of parks, but there also were other elements influencing the broad public support for city parks which developed during the 1890s.[17]

The nationwide city parks movement of the late 19th century had its origin in New York City's Central Park, created in 1853 and widely recognized as the first major public park in America. Among the principal planners of Central Park was Frederick Law Olmsted, a landscape architect and author of several interesting travel journals, who as a result of the success of Central Park enjoyed a strong demand for his services during the late 19th century to plan parks in other American cities. He and his firm planned parks in thirty-seven cities, in practically all the large cities of the northeast and in Indianapolis and Louisville nearer to Nashville. Olmsted also published dozens of articles concerning the value of public parks and their planning, bringing the subject to the attention of literate Americans everywhere. His success brought competing landscape architect firms into the park planning field, and after 1890 the firms had all the business they could handle.[18]

While New York City had the first major public park, the honor of having the first city-wide park system goes to Boston and Kansas City, both of which established their systems in 1893. From 1893 to 1905, Kansas City acquired 2,000 acres of parks as part of a comprehensive system, while Boston expended $11 million purchasing a 15,175-acre metropolitan park system, including the Blue Hills Park which at 4,857 acres became the largest city park in the United States. Chicago began issuing bonds in 1899 to finance an elaborate park system. Olmsted's firm participated in planning the District of Columbia's park system, including the Mall west of the Capitol, in

1901, and planned Baltimore's park system in 1905. While those large cities had owned a few large parks before 1890, it was near the turn of the century that they began comprehensive park systems funded by bond issues and taxes.[19]

Similar park development began at the turn of the century in cities nearer Nashville in size. Madison, Wisconsin, bought its first park in 1899 and approved a small city tax for its operation. Cincinnati, Ohio, had about 400 acres of park land at the turn of the century and in 1904 enacted a $1 million bond issue to buy more. Frederick Olmsted planned Louisville's park system between 1891 and 1894, and the "Falls City" issued bonds to purchase the lands, opening in 1901 one of the first public playgrounds for children in the nation. Mayor James Head of Nashville took special interest in the park system at Indianapolis, designed by Olmsted in 1896, because the capital of Indiana had used a tax on streetcar fares to finance its park system. Memphis received a state charter for its three-member park commission in 1900, and in 1901 purchased Overton and Riverside parks with the proceeds of a $250,000 bond issue. A comparison of these dates with those marking the origins of Nashville's park system indicates the city was not, as its park boosters often declared, laggard in its initial park development program, but rather participated in the general city parks movement which swept the nation at the end of the century.[20]

Part of an upheaval in the social consciousness of the American urban middle class, the nationwide parks movement at the turn of the century reflected a popular return to nature as a wellspring of inspiration. While visions of great cities and industries—a "New South"—had galvanized the American middle class after the Civil War, by 1890 a reaction had occurred as the less desirable results of urbanization and industrialization became fully apparent. Coal-blackened and grimy cities, corrupt municipal politics, extreme poverty and crime-ridden slums offended the sensibilities of the urban middle class, and they began their exodus to greener suburbs, founding country clubs, sending their children to summer camps, reading Henry David Thoreau, taking interest in historian Frederick Jackson Turner's idea that the roots of American democracy lay in the vanishing frontier rather than in urban experience. They voted for Theodore Roosevelt, that famous advocate of the vigorous outdoor life, and they listened to ministers preaching the gospel of social progress. They supported the creation of national parks to preserve America's scenic wilderness, joined wholeheartedly in the Boy Scout and Girl Scout movements, and provided the leadership which established municipal park systems.[21]

Though Nashville, with a population of less than 100,000 in 1900, was spared some of the serious problems afflicting larger cities at the time, its middle class read the popular journals, heard the ministers of the social gospel, saw park systems developing in other cities, were familiar with Olmsted's writings, and participated fully in the nationwide parks movement. Based upon their experiences with trolley parks, Nashville's commercial leaders learned that parks were good for business, not only stimulating streetcar traffic but also enhancing real estate values. The city's commercial middle class were also its principal civic boosters, and they asked if other cities were developing parks and presenting them as concrete evidence of civic progress, should Nashville lag behind, perhaps at the risk of losing industry to "more progressive" neighboring cities?

Broadspread public support for city parks in Nashville developed largely as a result of the success of the trolley parks and of the Tennessee Centennial Exposition of 1897. None of Nashville's trolley parks survived to become public parks; Spring Park was subdivided and sold in the 1890s, and Cherokee Park was subdivided and, except a two-acre plot, sold by 1909. Only Glendale Park remained in operation thereafter, surviving until 1932 when it also was subdivided. But their apparent success, not only as sources of entertaining recreation but also as business propositions, planted the idea in Nashville's consciousness that perhaps parks and recreation were not wasteful of tax dollars. It was during the Centennial celebration that Nashville's commercial middle class learned how to cooperate, politically and otherwise, to achieve major civic improvements, and in that grand Exposition lie the roots of Nashville's modern park system. The desire of the leaders who planned and conducted the 1897 Exposition to preserve the Parthenon as a symbol of the city's civic triumph and the Exposition grounds as a Centennial Park meshed well with the popular idea that Nashville should get on the city park bandwagon, or be left behind.

3 THE FIRST NASHVILLE PARK BOARD

Park management, personnel, and funding did not trouble Nashville's Park Commissioners when they first met in 1901. They had none: no parks, no personnel, no funds. Efforts by the Exposition Company and the city to acquire Centennial Park had not succeeded, and the Tennessee legislature had blundered when writing the act of April 3, 1901, chartering Nashville's park system. Instead of approving a one-mill-per-dollar tax levy for city parks, the act had mistakenly authorized only one-mill-per-hundred-dollars, a rate so inadequate as to be useless. Lacking funding, the Park Commissioners could accomplish little until the authorizing act was rewritten; yet, they hd prospects, enthusiasm, and challenges in abundance, and they proceeded to establish a park system for the city as best they could, relying upon financial support from Nashville's business and civic leadership and upon their own initiative and hard work to develop the first city park.[1]

A week after Governor Benton McMillin had signed the 1901 park act, Mayor James M. Head had selected the five men who would constitute the independent Board of Park Commissioners, and most of the appointees had served on the committees which directed the Centennial Exposition. Three were businessmen, the fourth the engineer who had been the Centennial's Director General, and the fifth the attorney who had served as Consul General for the Centennial Exposition. Because they were the charter members of Nashville's Board of Park Commissioners, and also the last to be appointed by a mayor until 1963, their character is of interest.

The three businessmen included Major Fountain P. McWhirter, Benjamin Lindauer, and Robert Dudley. McWhirter, a Confederate veteran and Methodist church leader born in McWhirtersville (now named Donelson), was owner of Harris, McWhirter and Company, a dry goods firm; he also owned property in Florida and his brother was the Tennessee Commissioner of Agriculture. Ben Lindauer was a partner in the Herman and Lindauer wholesale dry goods firm, the largest of its kind in the South; he also was president of the Nashville City Council and an urbane world traveler. Robert M. Dudley was a leading Baptist layman and a well-known hardware merchant, having served as president of the National Hardware Association; he also was president or director of a half dozen other firms such as the Pioneer Water Company, Dudley Gum Company, and Foster & Creighton Construction Company.[2]

Eugene C. Lewis, the engineer, was invariably addressed in the best Southern tradition with the honorary rank of "Major." Son of a Pennsylvania ironmaster, he was raised at the Cumberland ironworks near Nashville, educated in Pennsylvania, and served as engineer for the Louisville and Nashville Railway and the DuPont Company. He developed the Sycamore Powder Works near Ashland City, planned Union Station in Nashville for the railroad, and selected the Old Hickory plant site for the DuPont Company. He had been Director General of the Centennial and had purchased the Nashville *American* from Mayor Head. A remarkably inventive and original engineer, the Major also was impatient and blunt to the extent that some of his contemporaries thought him eccentric.[3]

Samuel A. Champion, an attorney from Henry County, moved to Nashville to serve in the State Senate and afterwards formed a law partnership with James Head and James S. Brown, both of whom became mayor of Nashville. Champion attended every National Democratic Party convention during the late 19th century, became politically powerful, and served as General Counsel for the Centennial Exposition. He was largely responsible for securing from the state legislature a charter for Centennial City and state funding assistance for the Exposition.[4]

The first Park Board therefore consisted of well-to-do white males, leaders of Nashville's aggressive commercial middle class. Lewis, Champion, and Lindauer had moved to the city after the Civil War, and Dudley and McWhirter were Davidson County natives. The majority were devoutly religious men and Freemasons, and their religion may have been significant in their selection. Ben Lindauer was a leader of the city's Jewish community, and that set a precedent followed thereafter: the Board always had at least one representative of the Jewish community among its membership. Nashville's large Roman Catholic community was not represented, but that neglect was remedied with the first appointment of a successor to one of the charter members. The economic status of the commissioners was to prove advantageous to the park system, for they gave not only their time but also gave of their personal funds and property toward the success of the system.

In retrospect, it appears that Mayor Head could have selected no more distinguished and capable commissioners from the leadership of the city. The Board's representation of the Nashville population could perhaps have been improved by expanding its membership to seven and adding philanthropist Preston Taylor for the black community and Sarah (Mrs. J. C.) Bradford, the recognized leader of Nashville's cultural activities at the time, but in view of the social prejudices of 1901 the appointment of women and minorities to the Board might have been politically difficult for Mayor Head.

The first Park Commissioners assembled at four in the afternoon of April 16, 1901, in Mayor Head's city hall office, presented to the mayor a $10,000 bond to assure the faithful performance of their duties, and subscribed to an oath of allegiance to the constitutions of Tennessee and the United States. Samuel Champion nominated Major Lewis as chairman of the Board, and he was duly elected. The Board had no funds with which to acquire park lands, but Mayor Head offered a small plot of city property called Watkins Park and the Board accepted it, also requesting the mayor to provide it with a list of all unused property owned by the city which might be converted into parks.

At the suggestion of Ben Lindauer, the Board elected Harwood

Wilson, the stenographer and secretary to the Mayor, to serve also as secretary to the Board but without compensation because the Board had no funds at its disposal. It then requested its chairman to visit Watkins Park, determine the work needed to convert it from a common pasture and unofficial dump into a real park, and submit an estimate of the cost of the work. Having acquired the first city park and employed its first secretary, the Board adjourned to await a report from Major Lewis.[5]

Samuel Watkins, wealthy brick-manufacturer and building contractor, had given the 8.2-acre Watkins Park to the city in 1870. He owned stone quarries in the park vicinity that had supplied stone for construction of the state capitol building during the 1840s, and in the 1850s the land, called Watkins grove, had served Nashvillians as an unofficial park. Mayor Randall McGavock had attended high school graduation exercises in the grove in 1856 and also a celebration of Nashville's founding conducted at the grove in 1858. During the Civil War, however, the Union Army had cut the trees and pastured mules on the land, ruining it for use as a park. It was commonly used by residents of the area in 1901 as pasture and an illicit dump when Major Lewis inspected it. The Major saw that with some work, however, it could be converted into a respectable public park, and he drew up plans for building a central shelter house, fencing the grounds, building walkways, planting flower beds and shrubbery, and installing water and lighting systems.[6]

At its second meeting, the Board approved the Major's plans for Watkins Park but lacked the wherewithal to implement them. They took up the matter with the Mayor and with civic leaders with remarkable success. The Mayor supplied $1,400 of the public works budget to build the shelter house and labor from the public works department to do the work, while public-spirited businesses donated the remainder of the materials needed. Foster & Creighton Company donated the stone needed for the shelter's foundation and the fountains; Nashville Roofing and Paving Company donated paving materials and the Nashville, Chattanooga and St. Louis Railway gave the gravel needed for walkways. J. H. Fall Hardware donated wire fence; Cumberland Electric Company installed lighting and furnished power without charge; and several city florists planted flower beds. A combination of city financing and private contributions thus made development of Nashville's first park a reality.[7]

The Board also won its first federal assistance through coordination with Major Andrew W. Wills, the postmaster and former Commissioner General of the Centennial. Many Nashvillians in 1901 picked up their mail once a week on Sunday afternoons at the Federal Customs House built in 1877 at Eighth and Broad streets, and for that reason the Board thought a park there desirable. The wings of the Customs House were not added until 1917, and the building in 1901 had a lawn surrounded by a fence. At the request of the Board, Major Wills obtained permission from the Treasury Department to convert the lawn into a public park. Naming it Federal Park, the Board arranged through the Mayor to place a few simple improvements on the lawn of the Customs House: walkways, flower beds, benches, and a fountain. Postmaster Wills had the custodians at the Customs House maintain the little "resting place," and he subsequently became the first Nashvillian to make a cash contribution of sorts to the city park system. He was owed $900 back pay by the Centennial Exposition Company, was suing to collect it, and he dropped the litigation and assigned his claim to the Park Board.[8]

Having determined to proceed with development of Watkins and Federal parks, the commissioners at their second meeting on April 25, 1901, decided they should not embark on a haphazard program and instead would devise a definite plan for a city-wide park system. They therefore wrote and adopted a two-point plan:[9]

> 1. There shall be a system of large parks, consisting each of fifty or more acres, one in each section or quarter of the city or adjacent thereto. The number of large parks shall be not less than four nor more than five.
>
> 2. There shall be a system of small parks, consisting of a number of lots, plots, squares or tracts, all to be within the city limits, as said limits may be now or hereafter defined. The location of said interior parks to be evenly distributed over the entire city as a wise consideration of the conditions of the topography, geography, populosity and economy may determine to be desirable.

The Commissioners published their comprehensive plan in the newspapers, much to their subsequent regret. They had hoped thereby to reassure Nashvillians that no section of the city would be neglected, but most of their meetings during the following year were consumed by real estate agents seeking to sell them property for parks when they had not a cent to purchase one. The development of Watkins and Federal parks also lagged because the donated materials were not always available when needed and the city's public works department performed the construction at its own convenience. Neither park could be opened to the public in 1901, and by the end of the year public discontent was growing. Major E. B. Stahlman at the *Banner* fumed at the delay. "Nashville is certainly behind the times in the matter of parks, and the need of these ornamental places for public recreation becomes more apparent every year," one *Banner* editorial declared: "Nashville must have parks someday or fall behind in the progress of cities, and the longer the delay the costlier will be the work of park establishment."[10]

Hoping to arrange a purchase by the city, the board in early 1902 initiated negotiations with the owners of Centennial Park who had announced their plans to subdivide and sell that seventy-two acres of historic property. The land had once been part of a 640-acre farm, including part of the present Vanderbilt University campus, acquired in 1783 by pioneer John Cockrill for sixty-four pounds currency, or about fifty cents an acre. Cockrill's wife was Ann, the sister of James Robertson. The land had been a terminal of the Natchez Trace and had served as an assembly and staging area for Tennessee troops during the War of 1812 and the Civil War. Its successive use as state fair grounds, racing park, and site of the Centennial Exposition had preserved it from housing development, and the board desired to make it a park for continued public use.[11]

Present at the Board meeting of February 4, 1902, were representatives of the Centennial Land Company: Samuel J. Keith, Johnson Bransford, Joseph H. Thompson, V. E. Shwab, and F. O. Watts. Major Lewis told them the Board was anxious to preserve the park but lacked funds for the purpose. F. O. Watts replied the company expected to sell it for $150,000, but would be willing to sell it to the city for its tax valuation of $125,000 and await payment until the state revised the park law to permit an adequate tax levy for park development. The company would turn the park over to the Board and, pending payment of the principal, accept four percent interest on the balance and the payment of property taxes as a rental fee. Declaring the property worth no more than a thousand dollars an acre, or a total of $72,000, Major Lewis admitted the Board was so anxious to preserve the "great city park" that it would offer as much as $100,000.

Negotiations abruptly ended at that point, but Major James Head pursued another avenue toward securing control of the park for the city.[12]

Through his wide reading about municipal parks, Mayor Head had learned that Indianapolis had acquired its park funding by a settlement with its streetcar companies, charging the companies as the price of their franchises a percentage of their fare receipts and also requiring them to give the city their trolley parks. Mayor Head thought Nashville should secure its parks in a similar manner, for the city at the time was engaged in litigation against its own streetcar companies.[13]

In 1899 an investment syndicate of Baltimore, Maryland, had acquired control of the three streetcar companies in Nashville and sought to consolidate them into a single Nashville Railway Company. Believing the city should extract a price from the new company for the franchise, Head had made it an issue in his 1899 mayoral campaign. When the company in January 1900 proceeded with consolidation and issued $6.5 million in bonds, the Mayor brought suit, claiming the franchises held by the three older companies had been forfeited when they merged into the new company. The Mayor's law partners, Samuel Champion and James Brown, represented the city in the case, while two redoubtable attorneys named J. C. Bradford and J. J. Vertrees represented the streetcar company. It proved a spectacular case, lasting more than a year and ending in the Tennessee Supreme Court.[14]

Nashville's civic leaders resented control of the city's principal means of local transport by out-of-town investors. They claimed Nashville's interests were neglected by people who did not ride the streetcars, who were interested in profit and not in good service. They no doubt welcomed the company's bankruptcy in 1901, for the court appointed respected Nashvillians Percy Warner and E. C. Lewis as receivers to manage the streetcar line pending company reorganization. Warner and Lewis swiftly improved the city's streetcar service, building a new central transfer station and purchasing twenty new streetcars, which even had the luxury of heated interiors.[15]

While the litigation was in progress, Mayor Head applied the screws to the company in another fashion. Knowing that Percy Warner wished to acquire, for the streetcar company, control of the

Cumberland Electric Light and Power Company which supplied power for streetcar operation and for the city, the Mayor, claiming the rates charged by the power company were excessive, initiated construction of a city-owned power plant. With that ace in his hands, he reopened negotiations with Mr. Warner. At their meeting in May 1901, Mr. Warner proposed that his company buy the Cumberland Electric Company, entirely reconstruct the streetcar lines, and pay two percent of the gross annual receipts from streetcar fares to the Park Board for its exclusive use in park improvements. In return, he asked that the city suspend construction of its power plant, grant the company free right-of-way for its tracks on city streets, and waive the collection of privilege taxes from the company. Mayor Head responded that he was unwilling to stop construction of the power plant and wanted five percent of streetcar fares for city parks. Mr. Warner would not agree to those terms, though he offered to throw in Glendale Park as a gift to the city. They agreed to disagree, broke off negotiations for the time being, and the litigation went forward.[16]

After the owners of Centennial Park announced their plans to subdivide and sell it, Mayor Head resumed negotiations with Mr. Warner, and they eventually reached an amicable settlement which was entered as a consent decree by the Supreme Court on October 3, 1902, ending the litigation. Mr. Warner essentially received what he wanted in exchange for two concessions: Nashville Railway and Light Company would purchase Centennial Park and give it to the city and would pay to the Park Board two percent on gross streetcar receipts up to $1 million and three percent after the receipts exceeded $1 million. Mr. Warner, or rather his streetcar company, purchased Centennial Park for $125,000 and presented it to the Park Board in December 1902. At a single stroke, thanks to Mayor Head, the Board had acquired its first large park and the promise of funding sufficient to develop it and other parks in the system.[17]

While the Park Board in later years proudly and vigorously defended its political independence, it lacked that independence initially. All charter members were appointed by Mayor Head, he naturally chose those he thought his political friends, and the Board usually met in the Mayor's office, where his secretary kept the Board minutes. Harwood Wilson, the Board's first secretary left the city in 1901 for better paying work, and was succeeded in 1902 by Will Cherry, who was not only secretary to Mayor Head but also related to him by marriage. The motive for making the Park Board an independent commission which elected its own membership was to free its members from petty political considerations when setting park policies, but the original Board did not achieve a fully independent status until several years after its formation.[18]

The political harmony that had prevailed during the Board's early meetings disintegrated in 1902. During the streetcar litigation, Samuel Champion had represented the city and the Mayor as counsel for the plaintiff, while Major Lewis, as court-appointed receiver, supported Mr. Warner. And when Mayor Head in late 1902 lent his support to Jere Baxter's efforts to secure a city bond issue to finance the Tennessee Central Railroad, Major Lewis broke entirely with the Head administration.[19]

The Lewis-Baxter feud is a well-known episode in Nashville history. As engineer for the Louisville and Nashville Railway, Lewis opposed Baxter and his Tennessee Central Railroad for business reasons, and the dispute also became quite personal. City tradition says that when the Chamber of Commerce purchased a statue of Baxter after his death in 1904 and erected it on the triangle at Board and Sixteenth streets, Major Lewis installed a monument in Centennial Park, inscribed it with the name of infamous horsethief John A. Murrell, and said in essence: "The people of Nashville have seen fit to erect a memorial to a railroad thief, so I hereby dedicate this monument to a horsethief." Through records confirming the incident are lacking, Nashville historian Hugh Walker asserts that Major Lewis scratched Murrell's name on a sundial in the park, and older employees in the park even today point to a sundial base which still stands, albeit minus any trace of the name Murrell. The bitterness of the quarrel certainly was sufficient for the legend to be correct. The Baxter statue rankled Lewis even a decade after Baxter's death, and while lecturing in 1913 concerning Nashville's neglect of its historical resources, he wrote: "It builds statues to fakers while the fathers slumber unrequited. It proposes and plans memorials and monuments to swashbucklers of today, while the real heroes and benefactors sleep with Sevier and Robertson unhonored and unsung."[20]

Clearly, the political harmony of the Park Board was sundered when Mayor Head lent his support to Jere Baxter. As publisher of the *American*, Major Lewis during the election of 1902 opposed the Head administration of the city, and that no doubt explains an incident at the last meeting of the Park Board in 1902, at which time it was to elect its chairman for 1903. Major Lewis arrived late to the meeting, finding it in progress with vice-chairman McWhirter in charge. Samuel Champion resolved that the Board would elect its chairman without nominations and the secretary would call the roll of the members alphabetically, each member answering with the name of the member he preferred as chairman. The vote was four to one, and Ben Lindauer was elected.[21]

Mayor Head could not remove Major Lewis from the Board, for the law provided no means of accomplishing it, and the Major did not resign. Though never again serving as chairman, he remained on the Board and was the most active of its members in park development, devoting much of his time and some personal funds to their improvement. Working without pay, he actually served as unofficial chief design engineer and construction superintendent for city parks, and because of his impatient character left mysteries scattered about the parks. "It pains me to see things done wrong, so I preferred to do them myself rather than possibly," he said, "it might not be done quite so well by somebody else." That is, when he wanted something done, he dispensed with formalities and did it, perhaps with no more than the oral concurrence of the other Board members. Of the Shell Spring, tucked in a corner of Centennial Park, for instance, there is no mention in the records of the Park Board. All that is known is that Major Lewis picked up a beautiful seashell on a Florida beach, modeled the Shell Spring design after that shell, and built it sometime before 1912, apparently at his personal expense. The Major was a remarkable man indeed.[22]

4 MANAGING THE FIRST PARKS

Having acquired Centennial Park along with promised future funding from streetcar receipts at the end of 1902, Nashville's Park Commissioners prepared for their first efforts at managing public parks. None had any previous experience other than with the Centennial Exposition in park management, but they recognized the need to establish regulations for public use of parks, to hire administrators, patrolmen, and maintenance workers, and to plan group recreational programs. The crumbling plaster builders in Centennial Park required attention and considerable work was needed to convert the abandoned Exposition grounds into an attractive city park. While the Commissioners were to acquire no parks in addition to Centennial, Watkins, and Federal parks before 1908, managing those three would consume their time and establish numerous precedents.

The Commissioners moved their meetings from the Mayor's office into a building in Centennial park in early 1903 where they laid plans for the first active year of park management. They first ordered official stationery emblazoned with the Parthenon emblem as a letterhead and drew up their own bylaws. In the bylaws, they agreed to meet twice monthly with a majority of three constituting a quorum and to secure the services of two executive officers, a secretary and a treasurer. The Secretary would keep the records and accounts, write the correspondence and reports (the Board owned no typewriter), and write the checks, while the Treasurer would keep the park funds, submit monthly fiscal status reports, and pay the checks written by the Secretary and signed by the chairman of the Board. Will Cherry, the secretary to the mayor, became Secretary to the Board at $50 a month; having no office staff, he contracted part of his paper work to skilled stenographers. F. O. Watts, the president of First National Bank, agreed to serve as Treasurer without pay because the Board deposited its revenues in his bank.[1]

Commissioner Samuel Champion, the attorney who drew up the bylaws, also wrote the first regulations for public use of the parks. The rules forbade pasturing livestock in the parks, picking the flowers, discharging firearms or fireworks, drinking alcoholic intoxicants, indulging in disorderly conduct or sports that frightened horses, and driving a funeral procession through the parks. Traffic regulations provided that sleighs without warning bells on the horses would not be driven through the parks and that automobiles would not exceed a speed of six miles per hour, stopping moreover when necessary to avoid startling horses. Public meetings or demonstrations concerning religious, social, or political matters were forbidden without advance permission from the Board. At the "baths," or swimming pools, men and women were to be separated and were required to wear two-piece swim suits that were entirely modest. To enforce those and other park regulations, the Board agreed upon $50 fines or thirty-day sentences for violations and met with the city police chief, who assigned two mounted patrolmen to the Centennial Park beat. The Commissioners had authority under their state charter to employ park police and they employed a patrolman, or watchman, for Centennial and Watkins parks. J. C. Meadows, the watchman at Centennial Park, probably was the first park patrolman.[2]

In regulations drawn up to guide park patrolmen, the Board instructed them that their principal duties were to warn and guide visitors to the parks, not to make arrests except for flagrant violations, and to be indulgent toward children while still taking "discreet, yet firm and decisive action toward gangs of unruly boys." The Board did not clearly explain, however, how the patrolmen were to distinguish between minor and flagrant violations, nor between children and unruly boys. Those distinctions were left to the mature judgment of the officers, a trust generally well founded, but several incidents during the early years of park management furnished the Board with a practical education in law enforcement. The Board, for instance, instructed the patrolmen to shoot stray dogs and cats eating birds in the parks, but soon had to call patrolman John J. Borum to a Board meeting to explain why he had shot a dog belonging to a neighborhood lady. The Board in its wisdom publicly reprimanded Borum for his misjudgment in shooting the dog, thus satisfying the dog's owner, and at its next meeting it promoted Borum to be the first Chief of Park Police.[3]

At its February 1903 meeting, the Board adopted its first annual budget, proposing to expend $25,000 during 1903, and employed Robert Creighton as Superintendent of Parks and W. F. Josolyne as Chief Florist or horticulturist. Both men had held similar positions at the 1897 Centennial Exposition and were more familiar with the park grounds than other candidates. The first female employee of the park system apparently was Miss Alice Brown, appointed to be custodian of the History Building where the Board planned in 1903 to display the Civil War relic collection loaned them by President John W. Thomas of the Nashville, Chattanooga and St. Louis Railway.[4]

Hoping to open Centennial park to the public in May 1903, the Commissioners ordered Superintendent Creighton to purchase equipment, employ workmen, and rush the cleaning and mowing of the grounds. While the names of the first workmen were not recorded, the first power machine was a big mule named Dan who pulled a mower and hay rake. Old Dan took an entire month to mow Centennial Park the first time, and rake the resulting hay into stacks for his winter subsistence. The Board therefore was grateful when a public-spirited citizen donated two enormous Belgian draft horses, but it kept old Dan in service until 1908 when it swapped him for a faster mule. Creighton built in the park a stable for Dan and the horses and a fenced enclosure for the cattle and hogs the park police found entering the park. Centennial Park at the time was entirely fenced, and though the public wanted the fence removed the Board refused to do so "as long as cows are allowed to roam about the commons nearby."[5]

At the direction of the Board, Superintendent Creighton, James Dunbar, and Creighton's son Wilbur mapped Centennial Park and inspected the condition of the plaster and lath buildings left from the 1897 Exposition. The Auditorium was in such sad shape that Creighton demolished it, and the replica of the Parthenon also was crumbling but the Board instructed him to make emergency repairs. On the former site of the Mineral Building, Creighton began construction of a bathhouse and three "baths," or swimming pools, one for men, one for women, and one for children, completing the bathing facilities for $7,500. In order that children would not fish in vain, Creighton and the Board acquired some live bass from the United States Fish Commission without charge and stocked lake Watagua, also dumping into the lake two huge alligators that had been given to the Board; the alligators subsequently were removed when the flock of ducks, geese and other wildfowl at the lake began to disappear. Horticulturist W. F. Josolyne planted 850 trees and shrubs purchased for the park by the Board and also the dahlias, roses, and other flowers donated by florists George B. Moulder and Joy and Sons. For a hundred dollars, Josolyne acquired a small used greenhouse in order that the park would have the first flowers in the city to bloom in spring and the last to fade in autumn. Three-quarters of the $25,000 budget for 1903 went toward cleaning the grounds, restoring the roadways, and completing emergency repairs to the buildings, and the remainder for purchasing boats for rental on the lake, trees and shrubbery for the grounds, and salaries for the workmen. That budget was supplemented by gifts from citizens interested in park improvements: Foster & Creighton Company donated crushed stone for repair of the drives and walkways, and Cornelius A. Craig donated the lawn swings that were scattered about the park under the shade of the trees.[6]

Though the repairs to Centennial Park were incomplete, it opened on schedule in May 1903, and tired humanity turned out in force to enjoy the "beauties of nature's scenery." On Sundays and holidays throughout that and following summers, crowds crushed into the downtown transfer station, changing cars to reach Centennial Park and also Glendale Park and Mount Olivet Cemetery. For the refreshment of those crowds, Superintendent Creighton supplied free ice water and the Board awarded contracts to concessionaires for the sale of popcorn, peanuts, and soda from the pagoda in the park. During the first years of park management, several of the concessionaires failed to live up to the terms of their contracts, but about

1905 the Board contracted with the reliable Anthony Dentici who sold refreshments in Centennial Park for a quarter century.[7]

Superintendent Creighton opened the three adjoining public "baths" in Centennial Park on June 1, 1903, and they were the first public swimming pool in the city though they apparently resembled wading rather than swimming pools. Bathmaster Bradley Walker and his assistant Guy Denton managed the baths under contract with the Park Board, furnishing each patron a towel for the dime admission charge, making certain that swimmers observed safety rules, and assuring that all swimmers were decently clad, which then meant from ankle to neck. At a dime a head, the "baths" brought in $500 during the summer of 1903, a figure which in a few years had increased to $700 annually.[8]

As its first cultural recreation program, the Board contracted with Justin Thatcher and the Orpheus Opera Company to present summer opera in Centennial Park. Despite the lack of air-conditioning or even fans, many Nashvillians during the summer of 1903 attended the performances of *Pinafore*, *The Mikado*, and other Gilbert and Sullivan operettas. The opera company expected to profit from their performances by collecting a small admission charge, but the demolishment of the large Auditorium forced presentation of the operas in the smaller Mexican Building, apparently reducing the profits because the company did not renew its contract in 1904.[9]

Park Commissioner E. C. Lewis swarmed over Centennial Park during 1903. He negotiated an agreement with President John W. Thomas to straighten the northern boundary between the park and railroad property by which the park gained fourteen acres and lost four, or a net gain of ten acres. As a receiver of the Nashville Railway and Light Company, Lewis arranged with Percy Warner for streetcars traveling along Broad Street to run a loop into the park entrance. He also initiated negotiations with owners of the property and houses between the edge of the park and West End Avenue, aiming at acquiring those properties to extend the park to the south and to open a new entrance on West End.[10]

Having unofficial charge of monuments and statuary in the park, Major Lewis directed the placement of those memorials. He arranged an agreement between the Board and the ladies who formed the Centennial Club whereby the ladies took charge of the former site of the Women's Building, planted it with flowers, and paid for the erection of a memorial to the work of women, capped by a stone sphere and inscribed with the enigmatic epigram: "What is round cannot be made rounder." He helped the Nashville Red Cross Society acquire a marble tablet paying tribute to Colonel William C. Smith, the architect of the Parthenon replica who had died while leading Tennessee troops in the Philippines, which was mounted on the east front of the Parthenon originally and unveiled on July 5, 1903, in the presence of Smith's family and the troops he had commanded. Nashvillians watched with amazement as Major Lewis built a tripod of three giant oak logs and with block and tackle hoisted the 50-foot, 72,000-pound granite shaft sent to the Centennial by the State of Georgia into an upright position, then built a stone foundation under it and mounted plaques memorializing pioneer James Robertson and his wife on its sides. Thousands gathered at the shaft on October 12, 1903, to see the great-grandson of Robertson dressed in the Robertson tartan unveil the plaques and to hear Governor James Frazier and Tully Brown orate upon the illustrious career of Nashville's founder.[11]

The Park Board's first year of park management proved an eminent success, and the Board proudly proclaimed the results of its efforts at Centennial Park:[12]

> Here, picturesque and pleasing effects have been produced by combining art with nature. Dotted here and there, in cool, green grass plots, bounded by neatly trimmed borders and clean, white, well-kept drives and walkways were beds of the most gorgeous dahlias, cannas, roses, and geraniums that were ever grown anywhere. These, together with the quietude, the fresh country air, the magnificent maple trees, in whose shade many pretty swings were placed, have made this park the most desirable place in Nashville during the long afternoons and evenings of the summer season, and thousands of our citizens, regardless of station and conditions, availed themselves of this opportunity to get away from the din and bustle, to banish the worries of life and to commune with nature with all of its beauty and grandeur.

There was, however, a snake in the Board's new Eden. To get Centennial park open for the 1903 season, the Board had resorted to deficit financing, borrowing from the city's general fund in anticipation of streetcar fare receipts; and by the end of the year it had become apparent that those receipts were far from sufficient to support an annual $25,000 budget. By the end of 1903 in fact, the Board was again without a cent to its credit and was so far in debt that it had no funds for 1904. Superintendent Creighton laid off all employees, and he and Secretary Cherry, in view of the Board's financial emergency, resigned their positions, offering to continue as consultants when called upon. Only horticulturist W. F. Josolyne remained on the Board's payroll in early 1904, his task being to help the flowers get through the winter and prepare the flower beds for the 1904 season. Failing to obtain emergency funding from the city council, Mayor Albert S. Williams out of his own pocket paid the salary of a watchman at Centennial park, but none was supplied for Watkins park, where vandals that winter stole even the plumbing fixtures. To obtain funds for opening the parks in 1904, the Board appealed to Percy Warner, who agreed to advance money for parks in anticipation of future streetcar receipts.[13]

During the five years following 1903, the Board operated on severely restricted budgets averaging less than $10,000 annually, supplied by advances against streetcar receipts from Percy Warner and emergency appropriations from the city council totaling $6,000. The Board combined the offices of Secretary and Superintendent in 1904, employing at $50 a month William P. Wheeler, who had worked on the railroad previously for E. C. Lewis. When Wheeler left for better paying work in 1905, the Board made horticulturist Josolyn the Superintendent and hired Bradley Walker, the Bathmaster, as their Secretary, both of them at negligible salaries. Those two served until 1909, when Frank A. Butler, a local construction contractor, became Superintendent. The wages of maintenance workmen during those years also were quite low. The men at work repairing the Parthenon earned only a dollar a day at a time when a day meant from dawn to dusk, as long as fourteen hours. When those workmen struck for $1.50 in 1906, the Board fired the lot of them and discontinued the repairs.[14]

Ben Lindauer resigned at the end of 1903 as chairman of the Board after a year's service in that post. He traveled a great deal and evidently did not want the burdens of operating a park system with deficit financing. The other Board members then asked Major Lewis to again become their chairman, but he declined and they then elected Fountain McWhirter. McWhirter reluctantly accepted the chairmanship because, he said, no other member would take it, and he made a fine chairman, serving in that capacity until his death in

1914. All five charter members of the Board continued their service during the first decade of park management except Samuel Champion who died in 1906. The Board under its chartering law had authority to elect its own membership, if the individuals elected were confirmed by the city council: and never in the Board's history did the city council reject any Board members. Champion's successor elected in 1906 was Malachi Thomas Bryan, an Irish Catholic attorney who had served terms in the Tennessee legislature and as judge of the circuit and chancery courts. Widely known as the leader of the campaign which secured federal construction of locks and dams on the Cumberland River, Judge Bryan, like Champion before him, handled legal matters for the Board.[15]

Other than purchasing fireworks for public display at the Parthenon on the Fourth of July, during the five years following 1903 the constrained funding available to the Board prevented it from backing cultural recreation programs in the parks, but again the need was filled by public-spirited Nashvillians. The Tennessee Industrial School (now Tennessee Preparatory School) sent its fine school band to furnish without cost the concerts in the park during 1904, and in 1905 Percy Warner and the Nashville Railway and Light Company paid for concerts, employing the Bellstedt Band of Cincinnati, a German brass band which had become popular in the city during the 1897 Centennial. Playing popular and light classical tunes, the Bellstedt Band attracted crowds of up to 10,000 people to Centennial Park; the audiences could pay a dime for a reserved seat near the band or lounge on the lawn without charge. Musical concerts often were supplemented, for the entertainment of the crowds, by precision drills performed by the Nashville Grays, Porter Rifles, or other local militia units, who in return earned permission from the Board to hold their two-week summer camps in the park. Once, the militia even undertook a full-scale reenactment of Custer's Massacre, complete with a fireworks bombardment climax.[16]

As private contributions to the park system, two of Centennial Park's most prominent monuments were dedicated in 1907 and 1909. After forty-eight years of service with the Nashville, Chattanooga and St. Louis Railway, President John W. Thomas died in 1906, and his fellow railroaders funded an elaborate monument and heroic statue of Thomas placed near the Parthenon. The memorial plaque on its side noted that Thomas had also presided over the 1897

Centennial Exposition "which resulted in securing to Nashville this park." Near the Thomas monument, a unique memorial to Confederate private soldiers was funded by the Frank Cheatham Bivouac of Confederate Veterans and the Daughters of the Confederacy. In poignant ceremonies on June 19, 1909, uniformed Confederate veterans cheered both sculptor George Zolnay and the Tennessee Industrial School band's rendition of "Dixie," as a huge Stars and Bars draping the monument was removed to unveil it. The names of the men in gray were inscribed on the side of the monument.[17]

Centennial Park also became during those lean years the site of other interesting structures, which apparently resulted from the interest of Major E. C. Lewis in construction with reinforced concrete. The use of the reinforced concrete for construction then was novel, and the structures built in the park attracted nationwide attention among engineers. The first experiments with reinforced concrete came in 1906 and 1907, when Major Lewis and Robert Creighton's son Wilbur designed and built a bandstand and a bridge over Lake Watauga. The mushroom-shaped concrete bandstand became the subject of a feature article in *Engineering News*, and was much admired and copied at parks in other cities. The design of a concrete arch bridge over the lake became the subject of Wilbur Creighton's engineering thesis at Vanderbilt University, and when completed in 1908 it was the first reinforced-concrete arch bridge in Tennessee, if not in the South. Sometime during the same period, Major Lewis designed the unique concrete Shell Spring in a corner of the park and also the concrete replica of a ship's prow, on which the figurehead of the cruiser U.S. *Tennessee* was mounted in 1910. Because it was designed for use by a small brass band, the mushroom bandstand proved inadequate and subsequently was removed, but the other structures have remained for most of the 20th century.[18]

From 1901 through 1908, the city park system operated on a total of $131,000 in streetcar receipts and a $6,000 appropriation by the city council out of the general fund, an amoung inadequate even for proper improvement of the three parks then operating and certainly insufficient for major expansion of the system. The situation brightened in 1908, however, with the election as mayor of James S. Brown, the junior partner in the firm of Head, Champion and Brown, who supported the public park system as strongly as had his partners. Growing support had developed by 1908, moreover, for the opening of more parks in general and for the creation of neighborhood playgrounds in particular. The Park Commissioners, in their pleas to the city council for additional funding, may also have won support for their program through the good sense and passion of their appeals:[19]

> Nashville is growing rapidly, and no one will gainsay the fact that well located public parks will go far toward attracting to our gates those who are seeking a place in which to locate. For the entire civilized world has come to realize that the public park is no longer a luxury, but is indeed a necessity with growing cities in order that those who are unable to absent themselves during the warm months may have some place of recreation within their reach which will enable them to secure fresh air, shade and playgrounds for their children and themselves.

5 THE PLAYGROUND MOVEMENT

Nashville's Board of Park Commissioners soon after its organization was confronted by two seemingly opposed concepts of what constituted proper park management: whether parks should be places for quiet communion with nature, or whether they should, for purposes of social improvement, be the sites of active recreation. The older genteel concept defined parks as "breathing" places where people in high-collared Sunday suits and mutton-sleeved finery strolled or relaxed on benches, viewing flowers, manicured lawns, and stately monuments while communing with nature: parks were quiet retreats from urban life. A growing number of people at the turn of the century, however, defined parks as places for vigorous physical recreation, for children's playgrounds and team sports, for amusing exercise and interesting play that might draw young men out of saloons and children off the streets: parks were to provide instructive recreation to help combat juvenile delinquency and other moral afflictions of urban life. After lengthy consideration of these apparently conflicting park management concepts, the Commissioners determined that Nashville's park system could and should be made to serve both purposes, if only they had sufficient park space and funding to accomplish it. Thanks to Mayor James S. Brown, the

Park Commissioners in 1908–1909 acquired what they needed to initiate a playground program supplementing the parks serving the genteel set of Nashville's society.

As indicated by their developmental planning for Watkins, Federal and Centennial parks, Nashville's Park Commissioners initially subscribed to the older concept of what constituted a park: they aimed at creating quiet, restful, symmetrical environments of neat walkways, formal gardens, fountains, and statuary. That concept was challenged as early as 1902, however, by the city's ministry and social leadership, the same element of the citizenry which had fought in New York City and other urban areas on behalf of playgrounds. In New York City, for instance, the conflict between park management concepts had begun in 1891, at a time when that city had 6,000 acres of parks and not a single playground, and had been initiated by a group of New York's ministers and rabbis. There, the conflict had waxed bitter, and one advocate of playgrounds wrote with acid-tipped pen: "The present attitude of our park officials is that it is better for grass to grow green over children's graves than yellow under their feet. This must change, and a portion of every existing park must be devoted exclusively to the little ones."[1]

In Nashville the conflict was far less bitter, perhaps because it was a smaller city and the leaders of the playground movement included the Park Commissioner's pastors, wives, and daughters. How the playground movement reached Nashville is not a matter of record, though certainly Nashvillians had read of the movement at Boston, New York, and Chicago in the literary magazines of the day, but it first came to the notice of the Park Commissioners on February 4, 1902, when they were honored by the presence at one of their meetings of the Reverend David C. Kelley. "Honored" is the proper word, for the city contained no more distinguished and respected minister at the time. A missionary to China before the Civil War, Kelley was known as the "Fighting Parson," having served not only as chaplain to General Nathan B. Forrest's cavalry but as a colonel in that command; after the war, he became pastor of McKendree Methodist Church and by 1902 he was Presiding Elder over the Nashville District of Methodist Churches. He told the Park Commissioners they were neglecting the city's poor in their planning for city parks and prayed that they should open parks and playgrounds in the city's slum districts. The Commissioners perceived the wisdom of the

Reverend's remarks, for tiny Federal Park at the corner of Eighth and Board—the only public park in the central city—was attracting great crowds of children; and they were willing to accept the minister's advice, but had not a cent for the purpose. Revenue derived from streetcar fare receipts could be used for park improvement and maintenance, but not park or playground acquisition. They did send a message to the city council requesting its assistance in acquiring parks to "materially aid the healthfulness of all our citizens, especially those of the poorer classes."[2]

When it became apparent the Commissioners lacked the funding to acquire playgrounds, the ladies of the Centennial Club, the wealthiest and most socially prominent women of the city, initiated the playground movement in Nashville on their own. No doubt they were inspired by the work of the famous Jane Addams at Hulls House in Chicago, for Miss Addams had visited the Centennial Exposition in 1897 and had spoken to them of her work.

Though "sand gardens"—sand piles on vacant lots for children's play—had been established in Boston in 1885, Jane Addams in 1892 at the Chicago settlement house known as Hull House had created on a donated lot a model playground, complete with equipment and adult supervision. The three-quarter-acre lot had swings, sand piles, a handball court, and a ball diamond along with all the children it could contain under the supervision of a kindergarten teacher assisted by a policeman who also umpired the ball games. Following that model, socially minded women of the "Windy City" established playgrounds at other settlement houses and school yards in the tenement districts, and in 1901 Chicago's municipal government opened playgrounds throughout the city. With prominent women taking the lead and city governments following, that pattern was repeated in many other cities during the 1890s: Pittsburgh, Louisville, and St. Louis established their municipal playgrounds in 1900 and 1901. By 1910, of the 950 American cities with populations exceeding 5,000, 336 had publicly owned playground systems.[3]

The playground movement nationally grew out of growing public concern about the living and moral conditions in city slums. A leader of New York City's playground movement, for instance, was Jacob Riis, author of *How the Other Half Lives*, an expose of city slum life; Riis argued that parks furnishing "breathing space" became places where "one could do little else." When the Playground and

Recreation Association of America was formed in 1906, Riis and Theodore Roosevelt became its honorary leaders. "Playgrounds," said President Roosevelt at the formation of the Association, "are a necessary means for the development of wholesome citizenship in modern cities." The professional leadership of the new Association was supplied by Joseph Lee, Luther Gulick, and Henry Curtis, who earned enduring fame as the principal advocates of supervised recreation as a means of achieving individual character development and social progress.[4]

The feminine leadership of Nashville's Centennial Exposition had continued meeting after 1897, and in 1905 they formally organized the Centennial Club with Mrs. Samuel Champion as temporary chairman and Mrs. John Hill Eakin as acting president. Among the membership of the organization were Mrs. Van Leer Kirkman, Mrs. John Thomas, and Major E. C. Lewis's daughter. As part of a broad program aimed at improving urban life, they decided to emulate Jane Addams and establish a model playground in a working class neighborhood. Meeting with the Park Board in late 1905, they requested that it place Watkins Park under their management, and the Commissioners voted four to one to cooperate with them. Commissioner Fountain McWhirter voted in opposition, but his reasoning was not made part of the record.[5]

With funding largely supplied by Mrs. John Hill Eakin, the wealthiest person in Nashville, the Centennial Club fenced the park, finished a covered pavilion to shelter children from rain and provide a place other than the streets for roller skating, installed a complete outfit of playground equipment consisting of swings and a "merry-go-round," and laid out a ball diamond. Equally important, they provided supervision for the play of neighborhood children and maintained the park in clean condition.[6]

After the Watkins Park playground opened on June 1, 1906, it attracted not only children from the neighborhood but from other parts of the city, proving a huge success; and the Club opened two more playgrounds on vacant lots on Woodland Street in East Nashville and at the corner of Union Street and Seventh Avenue in the downtown district. Commissioner Fountain McWhirter rescinded his earlier opposition, congratulating the women on their work; and in 1908 when Jane Addams returned to Nashville for a visit the Centennial Club proudly escorted her to see Watkins Park.

According to the Park Commissioners, the efforts of the Centennial Club at Watkins Park proved to them and to Nashvillians in general that playgrounds were valuable municipal assets, "not only healthful and educational, but as economic and financial aids to the growth and wealth of a city."[7]

Before the Park Board could create municipal playgrounds, however, it had to acquire increased authority and funding. From 1901 through 1908, the city park system had subsisted on the $131,000 paid from streetcar receipts and a $6,000 emergency appropriation by the city council, all of which had been expended on routine operations and maintenance and extensive repairs to the buildings in Centennial Park. During the same period, the City of Memphis had collected $673,000 in taxes for parks and had issued $1.25 million in bonds for the purchase of new parks, therefore expending $2 million on its park system as compared to $137,000 in Nashville. The successors to James Head as mayor, Albert S. Williams and Thomas O. Morris who each served a two-year term, had supported parks but had not secured a revision of the 1901 law creating municipal parks to allow the collection of an adequate tax for the system and the issuing of bonds to purchase more parks. Mayor James S. Brown, elected in 1907, achieved that goal.[8]

Junior partner of the politically powerful law firm of Head, Champion, and Brown, James S. Brown was the son of the Paris, Tennessee, judge in whose office Samuel Champion had studied law. Brown was an 1880 graduate of the U.S. Naval Academy, had begun practicing law after ending his service with the Navy in 1895, and had served as the city's Director of Public Works during the Head administration. By the time of his election as Mayor, he was the last of the triumvirate in Nashville: Samuel Champion died in 1906 and James Head left the city after serving as mayor, moving to Boston as an attorney for a paving contractor.[9]

Like his former law partners, Brown avidly supported the public park system, and he took personal interest in the activities of the Park Board, attending most of its meetings. In fact, he apparently considered himself a member of the Board, participating in its deliberations, making motions, and casting votes. Yet, he did not dominate the Board, and sometimes found himself on the losing end of five to one votes. His first major contribution to the park system came in 1908 when he turned over to his fellow Board members the responsibility for three new parks acquired by city government when it annexed West Nashville into the corporate limits.10

Built on the plantation of Mark Cockrill, who raised prize-winning sheep on the land, West Nashville was a complete industrial community governed by the Nashville Land Improvement Company. In addition to installing water, sewer, and lighting systems, the land development company in its 1887 plat of West Nashville had reserved Cherokee, Richland, and Clifton parks for use of the community. Cherokee Park at eighty-three acres had once been the largest of the three and had been the site of an amusement park similar to Glendale Park, but the land developers had subdivided and sold all except two acres of the park in 1903. When the Park Commissioners inspected those two acres in 1908, they found the land too swampy for development, though the little plot did include the "Treaty Oak," a tree under which pioneer James Robertson had once negotiated a treaty with Chickasaw Chief Piomingo. They had the park fenced to keep out livestock and requested local contractors to dump material excavated from nearby building sites onto the park, hoping eventually to raise the elevation of the land and make it suitable for park service. Richland and Clifton parks, both containing about ten acres of land, were merely two blocks apart, and the Park Board therefore deferred development of Clifton Park and initiated work at Richland Park as funds became available, planting flowerbeds and building a playground. Being located several miles from the heavily populated sections of Nashville, the three new parks contributed little toward meeting the needs of the inner city population for parks and playgrounds.11

The sector of the city most in need of park space was South Nashville, which had not a single public park in its vicinity except ttiny Federal Park at Eighth and Broad streets. The only other city-owned property in that area was the 27-acre City Cemetery which had long served as a park of sorts, where people enjoyed shade, looked at the interesting monuments, and visited the graves of their forebears. Established in 1822, the cemetery contained about 23,000 graves, including those of many pioneer Nashvillians, of several Confederate generals, of two of the original Fisk Jubilee Singers, and of other notables such as Captain William Driver who had named the American flag "Old Glory." Other cemeteries had opened in the late 19th century, however, and the City Cemetery had fallen into disrepair. When a committee of South Nashville women, headed by Mrs. Stephen Driver, requested Mayor Brown in 1908 to restore the City Cemetery, he met their request by adding the cemetery to the park system, also providing through the city council some funding for repair work. The Park Board began the cemetery rehabilitation by hauling in thirty-two railcar loads of stone to resurface eroded drives and walkways and by righting the monuments and cleaning the grounds. It contracted with Wilbur Foster, the Confederate Army engineer who had served as Director of Works at the Centennial Exposition, to build a stone fence around the cemetery, and he designed and built it in memorable fortress style, with rifle embrasures along its crest. The Women's Federation of South Nashville had Major E. C. Lewis design an imposing entrance gate to the cemetery, and they paid for its construction.[12]

Major Brown also added an abandoned one-acre plot north of Capitol Hill to the park system in early 1909. The city had acquired it when it annexed the area north of the Capitol platted in 1887 by Frank McGavock. When subdividing his farm, Frank McGavock had left open a narrow triangle of land between Arthur Street and Eleventh Avenue, naming it Elizabeth Park, no doubt in honor of a member of his family. The land had never been developed as a park, however, and when the Park Board acquired it in 1909 it was covered with rock piles dumped there from nearby excavations. Its small size and shape limited its usefulness as a public park, but the board eventually established a neighborhood playground on the site.[13]

Mayor Brown thus added four parks and the City Cemetery to the municipal park system, and in 1908 he initiated efforts to increase funding for park acquisition and management. He invited State Senator Hilary Howse to meetings of the Park Board, and they and Major E. C. Lewis drafted a bill revising the 1901 state law chartering the Board. Senator Howse and the Davidson County delegation in the state legislature obtained enactment of the bill in the General Assembly in early 1909, which permitted the city to levy taxes for parks and issue bonds for the purchase of park lands. Under that authority, the city council in April 1909 approved a property tax of five cents per $1,000 valuation and directed the Park Board to establish with that increased funding new parks and playgrounds throughout the city.[14]

The Park Board in the summer of 1909 developed playgrounds at Centennial and Richland parks in West Nashville, took responsibility for the Watkins Park playground from the Centennial Club, and toured all sectors of the city, searching for sites suitable for playgrounds and parks. In October, the Commissioners purchased their first park—all previous parks had been given to the Board by city government. It was a three-acre German "beer garden" owned by Frederick Laitenburger at Hume Street and Fifth Avenue in North Nashville and in the midst of the crowded working-class neighborhood surrounding the Morgan-Hamilton Bag Company and Warioto Cotton Mill (subsequently the Werthan Mills). At the request of Major E. C. Lewis, the Board named it Morgan Park in honor of Samuel D. Morgan, the "Merchant Prince of Nashville" who owned the nearby mills and who had directed the construction of the state capitol building. The Board opened a playground in 1910 at Morgan Park, and in 1914 Robert Creighton arranged for the laying of a three-inch pipe to make available a public supply of mineral water in the park, a feature that made the park memorable. In 1889, the owners of the mills near the park had driven a 2,933-foot deep well which produced an abundant flow of sulphur water, and that water piped to the park was offered to the public without charge. Some Nashvillians would drink no other water, making daily visits to Morgan Park to fill containers for home use.[15]

From 1909 through 1913, the Park Board at the direction of Mayor Hilary Howse purchased several small parks and vacant lots scattered throughout the inner city for use as playgrounds. In South Nashville, it purchased the Fillmore Street, Gunfactory, and Chestnut Street playgrounds. The Fillmore Street playground, at the intersection of Fillmore and Decatur streets, was a 150-foot vacant lot near Mt. Olivet Cemetery; it served the neighborhood merely a few years, however, before being replaced by the larger South and Morton B. Howell parks. Gunfactory Playground, a 130-foot lot at the corner of Third Avenue and Mulberry Street, was intended to serve the needy neighborhood at the edge of Black Bottom, but the Board closed it after two years as a result of continued "ruffianism" at the site. The only playground of the three to survive was the one acquired in 1913 at the corner of Third and Chestnut streets. Larger at six-acres than the two other playgrounds in South Nashville, it was named Dudley Park in honor of Louise and Rebecca Dudley, after those two little daughters of Park Commissioner Robert Dudley who died in a 1913 automobile accident.[16]

The Board also purchased three playgrounds in East Nashville. The Fatherland Playground at Tenth and Fatherland streets and the Main Street Playground at Seventh and Main streets were 150-foot lots opened in 1910 as playgrounds and abandoned after the 1916 fire in East Nashville and subsequent creation of East Park. The Meridian Street playground, a similar lot, eventually was moved across the street from its original site to a four-acre plot and renamed McFerrin Park in memory of John B. McFerrin whose old home in the park served as the first community center in that neighborhood.[17]

Because playgrounds were opened at Watkins, Morgan, and Elizabeth parks in North Nashville, the Board purchased only one playground in that section. The Gay Street Playground, located on that street on a tiny lot, attracted large crowds of children, and in 1919 it was moved to a slightly larger lot at Jo Johnston and Fifth Avenue near the Fenterwald settlement house operated by the Council of Jewish Women, serving essentially as a playground for the children at the settlement house. It was renamed Ben Lindauer Park in honor of the Park Commissioner who headed the Board's playground committee and was the most active of the Commissioners in planning the playground program.[18]

With the opening of those playgrounds, most children in the city had access to at least one area for excerise and play, and the Park Board recognized that some adult supervision should be furnished. During the summers, children came to the playgrounds in the morning, and there they often remained until dark, the playgrounds in a sense serving as "day-care" centers for working-class parents. The Board employed its first playground supervisor, Mrs. W. M. Stephens, in 1911 to direct the play of children in Centennial Park; Mrs. Stephens thereby became the first recreation leader employed by the Board.[19]

Joseph Lee, Henry Curtis, and Luther Gulick, the professionals leading the Playground and Recreation Association of America, had launched a national campaign urging city park systems to employ trained recreation leaders after the formation of their association in 1906, and by 1912 the Nashville Park Board had become aware of the need for such personnel. The Commissioners therefore were receptive to the ideas of Dr. William Morrison, a dentist and city councilman, who met with the Commissioners in early 1912 to urge them to employ adult supervisors to instruct the children in play activities.

For the summer of 1912, the Board hired Miss Pauline Lewis, Mrs. Nellie R. Cannon, and Miss Martha Woolwine to supervise various playgrounds. The number of playground supervisors grew during following summers, and in 1914 the board appointed Miss Pauline Lewis as general supervisor of all playgrounds at $50 a month, she thereby becoming the first "Superintendent of Recreation" for the Nashville park system.[20]

Work as playground supervisors or recreation leaders initially was merely a summer job, but increased professionalism developed through the influence of Guy T. Denton, as assistant coach at Vanderbilt University, who also was a leader of the Boy Scout movement and Young Men's Christian Association in Nashville. In 1914, he requested the Board to extend him permission to take his YMCA recreation management classes into the parks for six weeks of field training, and the Board heartily concurred. Denton continued that work during several summers, and in 1919 he was named General Supervisor of Playgrounds for the city park system.[21]

Mayor James Brown's administration of 1908 and 1909 thus marked both the victory of the playground movement in Nashville and the beginning of a tax-funded program of park development throughout the city. Portraying the adoption of the playground program in the city as a victory overstates the case, however, for a major conflict between opposing park management concepts did not occur in Nashville as it did elsewhere, probably because the leaders of the playground movement were the pastors and wives of the Park Commissioners. By adopting the playground program, the Park Board expanded the park system to all areas of the city, providing recreation not only for the urban middle class but also for citizens living in the working class and poorer neighborhoods, and expansion which no doubt influenced the city council in 1909 when it approved a municipal tax for parks. Mayor Brown's administration therefore was pivotal in the history of Nashville's park system, as the changes continued to receive the support of Hilary Howse, his successor as Mayor. Brown, personally, never had an opportunity to enjoy the parks he had established, for he moved to Memphis after his service as Mayor, but many thousands of Nashvillians enjoy them every year.

6 PARK EXPANSION, 1910-1916

With additional funding accruing from the municipal parks tax of 1909 and increasing revenue from streetcar fare receipts, the Park Commissioners increased their annual budget from $75,000 in 1910 to $125,000 in 1916 and carried out their program announced in 1901 to acquire small parks scattered throughout the city and larger parks in each of the city's four sectors. They continued the development and expansion of Centennial Park in the city's western sector and initiated partially successful efforts to secure large parks in East, North, and South Nashville. They also purchased the first city park for Nashville's black community, which may very well have been the first such park in the South if not the nation. Expanding the public park system to all sectors of the city earned the Board additional support from Nashvillians and from the city council, which in 1913 doubled the park system's share of city tax collections, increasing the prorata figure from a nickel to a dime for each $1,000 property valuation. The Commissioners therefore were enabled during the years just prior to the First World War to carry out one of the major park expansion efforts in Nashville's history.

Looking first at the southern sector of the city, the Commissioners found no ideal location for a large public park, but considered creating one in the tenement district extending from Broad Street south between Second and Fifth Avenues. Lying in an area subject to flooding, the district was known as "Black Bottom" and contained unsanitary housing and crime-ridden dives, the most notorious being the Bucket of Blood saloon. Major E. C. Lewis first proposed in 1905 that the city purchase Black Bottom and convert it into a public park for South Nashvillians, and the ladies of the Centennial Club, as part of their broad campaign on behalf of civic improvements, joined the Major in calling for the creation of Black Bottom park. When Mayor Hilary Howse lent his influential support to the idea, the Park Commissioners proposed issuing bonds to purchase the land. That first proposed bond issue for parks was defeated by voter referendum in 1910, however, forcing Commissioners to reconsider their planning for South Nashville.[1]

Opposition to the proposed Black Bottom park emanated from Charles A. Marlin, the councilman for South Nashville who wanted Black Bottom converted into an industrial area and the proposed park located farther to the south on higher ground. In Marlin's opinion, it was not the Board's prerogative to undertake urban renewal projects in the name of parks, and in a letter to a Nashville newspaper he explained:[2]

> I respectfully submit it is not the function of the commission to wipe out the red light and tough residence districts. This properly is a power and duty attendant upon another arm of the city government. The park commission was established and funds placed at its disposal not to eradicate evil resorts and clean out undesirable neighborhoods, but to provide public parks for the recreation of its citizens and playgrounds for the amusement and improvement of its little children. I would ask, if the commission defers to these gentlemen and by selecting Black Bottom as a park site, wipe out the denizens of that section, where is the work to cease. They will be called upon to establish a park in the slum section of the city north of Linck's depot, to convert Jo Johnston avenue into a pleasure ground, and even make of Hell's Half Acre a modern garden of Eden.

Having difficulty finding alternate sites in South Nashville for a large park, the Park Commissioners in early 1913 invited Mayor Howse, Councilman Marlin, the leaders of the South Nashville community to meet with them to discuss the subject. The Mayor still insisted that Black Bottom should become a park, and he offered to arrange for the city council to supply half the costs of land acquisition there, if the Park Board would furnish the remainder; the land could thereby be acquired without the need for a voter referendum on a bond issue. He took Charles Marlin at his word and also proposed that the Park Board purchase Hell's Half Acre (located in the vicinity of the present site of the downtown branch of Tennessee State University), demolish everything on it, and open a park there. South Nashvillians attending the meeting, however, requested the Commissioners to investigate purchasing the state fair grounds, at old Cumberland Park on Nolensville Road, and convert that space into a public park. The Park Commissioners were more inclined to listen to people of South Nashville than the Mayor, and after the meeting they investigated the purchase of the fair grounds which proved too expensive for them to acquire without a large bond issue.[3]

The immediate need of South Nashville for parks was met in May 1913 when trustees of the defunct University of Nashville, which had moved west to become George Peabody College, offered to sell the Board the grounds of the University's medical school and of Montgomery Bell Academy. For $32,000, the Board snapped up the four-acre academy grounds and two-acre medical school lot and converted them into two city parks. Since both areas were already used unofficially by South Nashvillians for park purposes, the Board merely installed playground equipment and gave the areas new names. The old academy grounds became South Park and the medical school lot became Morton B. Howell Park, after a widely known Nashville Mayor and businessman of the 19th century.[4]

As a further contribution toward the park needs of South Nashville, the Board in 1914 opened a park on fifteen acres of city property surrounding the reservoir built in 1889 at Argyle and Eighth Avenue atop a hill once occupied by a Union Army fortification. The grounds were eroded as a result of the spectacular reservoir break that had occurred in 1912, but Mayor Howse promised to have the grounds graded for park use. There, the Board in 1914 built a playground, naming it Reservoir Park.[5]

The opposition of South Nashvillians to converting Black Bottom into a public park, and the lack of other suitable space for a large park on the south side, thwarted the Board's plans to create large public parks in all four quarters of the city. The Board therefore met South Nashville's need for park space through acquisition of a number of what then were considered medium-sized parks, starting with South, Howell, Reservoir, and Dudley parks to which Fort Negley, Coleman, and Sevier parks subsequently were added. The Board's plans for large parks met with better success, however, in East and North Nashville.

Interest in acquiring Shelby Park for East Nashville aroused in 1903 when the owners of the land offered to sell it and Percy Warner took the Park Commissioners out to inspect it aboard his personal executive streetcar. David Shelby had purchased the land now in Shelby Park in 1818 from James Shaw, who had received it as a Revolutionary War grant, and it had passed into the hands of John Shelby, the builder of the once famous Fatherland and Boscobel mansions in East Nashville. A land development company purchased the park about 1890 and for a few years operated an amusement park on the grounds, complete with roller coaster, shooting galleries, and other attractions. When the real estate company bankrupted, its creditors in 1903 had become eager to sell the land. After inspecting Shelby Park and East Nashville, however, the Park Commissioners declined in 1906 to purchase the park, declaring that "East Nashville is so much a sylvan city of itself where each one has his individual park that no park is essential to that section of the city at present." That was their public reason; in fact, they had learned that East Nashvillians did not then want a public park near their homes.[6]

The rapid growth of the Edgefield and Lockeland areas apparently changed public opinion about parks there by 1909, for in that year a delegation of East Nashvillians asked the Park Commissioners to reconsider their earlier decision. Commissioner M. T. Bryan thereon visited the park, met with the land owners, and reported the 151 acres of woodland would make an excellent park, though subject to flooding in the bottom near the Cumberland River, and that the 60 adjoining acres owned by J. P. Meredith should also be acquired. The Commissioners voted on July 27, 1909, to buy the 151 acres for $40,000 and to negotiate with Meredith the purchase of the additional 60 acres, and both purchases were completed by 1911 when development of Shelby Park began.[7]

From the Cumberland River back to the hills, Shelby Park was largely a forest-covered wilderness area when it was acquired, and the Commissioners decided to preserve most of the trees, limiting their initial development of the park to providing access by road, shelters for picnics and boats for public use on Lake Sevier. They opened a limestone quarry, purchased a rock crusher, and began production of macadam stone to surface some five miles of drives in the park. Serving as unofficial chief engineer for the park, Major E. C. Lewis enjoyed himself immensely while designing log cabin shelters at the mineral springs, a Spanish-style mission house for social activities, and the Sycamore Lodge, built of cedar logs with an attached shelter for automobiles. He again experimented with reinforced-concrete construction in the design of a decorative Dutch windmill and of a boathouse resembling a steamboat sitting on little Lake Sevier. Construction of the roadways and structures was still in progress on July 4, 1912, when Mayor Hilary Howse and the Board dedicated to public use the "most beautiful natural park in the southland." Subsequently the Board purchased adjoining properties as need and opportunities arose, gradually expanding the park to about 361 acres with more than a mile of frontage along the Cumberland River. Shelby park became the city's center for aquatic sports and nature study, serving as such until the Board acquired the Warner parks and public-use areas on Old Hickory and Percy Priest lakes.[8]

East Nashville received another park in the aftermath of the devastating fire of 1916 as part of what must have been the city's first experiment with urban renewal. According to city tradition, on the morning of March 22, 1916, a boy playing with a ball of yarn in a cabin at Second and Oldham streets rolled it into a fireplace, and when it caught fire tossed it out of the cabin. The grass in the yard then caught fire and a high wind drove the flames into sawmills along the riverfront and across East Nashville; by nightfall, 648 buildings and one life had been consumed by the wind-driven flames. Warner School, several churches, and homes along Woodland, Fatherland, Russell, Boscobel, and Shelby streets along with cross streets were laid waste in Nashville's greatest disaster.[9]

A week after the fire, the Park Board called a public meeting of East Nashvillians at a church near the burned-over district to ask if they wished to establish a public park in part of the fire-blackened area. Citizens at the meeting declared they wanted Warner School rebuilt and a public park opened in its vicinity, and the Board therefore purchased a three-block area between Sixth and Seventh streets and Woodland and Russell streets adjoining Warner School.

By September 1913, Commissioner Robert Creighton had completed plans for East Park, with a central bandstand, fountain, walks, flowerbeds, and trees, and the development of East Park began. East Park became the first city park conceived as part of an urban renewal effort and also the first opened in conjunction with public school construction.[10]

In North Nashville in 1912, the Park Board opened its third large public park and its first park serving Nashville's black community, but that park was not the first in Nashville used by black citizens: that honor went to Greenwood Park in South Nashville founded by the remarkable Reverend Preston Taylor in 1905. Taylor, a Union Army soldier, made a fortune after the Civil War as construction contractor and moved to Nashville, where he married one of the original Fisk Jubilee Singers, became a minister and undertaker, directed the black exhibits at the 1897 Centennial, opened Greenwood Cemetery, and in 1905 established Greenwood Park between Elm Hill Pike and Lebanon Road. The park became the site of a state fair conducted for blacks and of a summer camp for the first black Boy Scouts in the city. It had amusement and public picnic areas which were enjoyed, mostly on Sundays, by black families who rode the Fairfield streetcar line to the park for shade and recreation.[11]

Nashville's black community, probably because of segregation and perhaps because many were too busy securing a subsistence for their families, had not shown much initial interest in the city park system. That changed in 1911 when state government purchased the John L. Hadley plantation in North Nashville as the site of the agricultural and industrial college (now Tennessee State University). On receipt of that news, President George A. Gates of Fisk University approached the Park Board to advise them he wanted a park for the black community opened near his school and the new state university. Together with President Gates, Mayor Howse, and a delegation of black leaders, the Board in April 1912 inspected a 34-acre tract known as the Harding property between Albion Street and Centennial (John A. Merritt) Boulevard. When the owners offered to sell the land for $20,000 and Mayor Howse promised city government would pay half the cost to relieve the Park Board of the obligation to purchase the land on the installment plan as it had at Shelby and other parks, the Board bought the land. At the request of Major E. C. Lewis, the Board named it Hadley Park, perhaps in honor of

John L. Hadley whose plantation home stood in the park. A slaveholder before the Civil War, Hadley and his family after the war had assisted with the postwar readjustment of the slaves as freemen, in 1872 inviting the famous black statesman Frederick A. Douglass to addres the community from the front porch of their home. According to Isaiah T. Creswell who has lived in Nashville since 1902 and who served on the Park Board during the 1970s, however, the oral tradition of Nashville's black community states that the park's name honors Dr. W. A. Hadley, a pioneer black physician.[12]

On the Fourth of July in 1912, the day on which Shelby Park also opened, the Park Board and the black community dedicated Hadley Park with memorable ceremonies. The Fisk Jubilee Singers performed and the principal orations of the day were delivered by Benjamin Carr, the politically influential manager of the new state college, by Dr. Robert F. Boyd, the president of Nashville's black Board of Trade, and by Dr. Richard H. Boyd, head of the National Baptist Publishing House and publisher of the city's black newspaper. Mayor Hilary Howse proclaimed that Hadley Park was the "first and only public park purchased by any municipality in the world for the exclusive use of the colored citizens." He may well have been correct, and certainly so in relation to Tennessee. Memphis established Douglass Park, its first public park for blacks, in 1913.[13]

The Park Commissioners launched develpment of Hadley Park in 1912, authorizing construction of a public library on the grounds, installing playground equipment, and converting the plantation house into a community center under the direction of Benjamin Carr, Jr. Carr, who was paid $10 a week and lived in the plantation house, became the first black employee of the Park Board with a status higher than maintenance worker. Black recreation leaders were employed soon thereafter, Lucille Lacour for Hadley Park and Maple Hemphill at Napier Park.[14]

Credit for the creation of Napier Park in South Nashville properly belongs to the man for whom it was named. Black banker and attorney James C. Napier, who became Register of the Treasury during the administration of President William H. Taft, was an early advocate of children's playgrounds for Nashville's black community, and at his request in 1913 the Park Board examined various sites for a playground in South Nashville. It first proposed establishing a playground for black children on the grounds of Napier Public School on

Fairfield Avenue, but school board policy at the time frowned on the use of schoolyards at times when the schools were closed (a policy probably aimed at reducing opportunities for vandalism). The Board therefore purchased for $1,500 a large vacant lot adjoining the Napier schoolground, installed play equipment, and named it Napier Park, subsequently purchasing more land to expand it to 2.5 acres. Nashville as a result may have had not only the first but also the second public park for black citizens in Tennessee.[15]

During this period of rapid expansion of the system, when the Park Board acquired Napier, Hadley, East, Shelby, South, Howell, and Reservoir parks along with many small playgrounds, the membership of the Board changed as result of the retirement and death of its charter members. Major E. C. Lewis, his health failing, resigned from the Board in 1912 and died in 1917; even at death, he could not resist practicing his engineering skills, for he designed his own unique mausoleum at Mount Olivet in an Egyptian style. The Board elected Robert Creighton, the first Superintendent of Parks, as his successor. Fountain P. McWhirter died in 1914 and Ben Lindauer in 1916, leaving Robert Dudley as the sole remaining charter member, and Dudley became the chairman of the Board. McWhirter's successor was Whitefoord Cole, the son of W. W. "King" Cole, who, like his father, became president of the Nashville, Chattanooga and St. Louis Railway; Cole served on the Board only a few years before becoming president of the entire Louisville and Nashville Railway system and moving to Louisville. Ben Lindauer's successor was Lee J. Loventhal who like Lindauer was a leader of Nashville's Jewish Community. An athlete of no mean ability, Loventhal was a leader of the Young Men's Hebrew Association and also of many civic improvement organizations. He became the social conscience of the Park Board, always representing the interests of the city's poor and disadvantaged citizens in the Board's deliberations and planning. Even forty years after his death, Nashvillians remembered Loventhal's tenacious defense of minority rights. A story about Loventhal still told in 1985 concerned a person who in 1930 asked Dr. James I. Vance, the famous Presbyterian divine, if the Lord intended to consign all members of the Jewish faith to the nether world. Dr. Vance replied: "If He does, He will have considerable trouble from Lee Loventhal."[16]

Numerous changes also occurred in the Park Board's executive staff during the period of park system expansion just before the First World War. The Board employed John S. Lewis, the brother of Major E. C. Lewis, as its Secretary in 1911. A graduate of Washington and Lee College, John Lewis had worked as a cotton broker before becoming secretary-treasurer of Sycamore Powder Mills and the *Nashville American* in 1895; and he became Secretary to the Board just after his brother sold the *American*. An emphatic, precise, devoutly religious gentleman, he kept the financial and executive records of the park system in excellent condition during the score of years following his appointment. J. H. McBride succeeded W. F. Josolyne as park horticulturist about 1909 and served until 1917 when the Board hired George B. Moulder. Perhaps the world's foremost authority on water lily biology, Moulder had contributed the aquatic plant displays in Lily Lake to the 1897 Centennial. He was placed in charge of landscaping and planting the grounds around the stations of the Illinois Central Railroad, but when the government nationalized the railroads at the outset of the First World War he came to Nashville as park horticulturist. When Park Superintendent Frank Butler resigned in 1918, Moulder became acting superintendent.[17]

The park patrol also had several personnel changes from 1910 to 1916. The first Chief of Park Police, John J. Borum, became the park system's chief electrician in 1912 and was succeeded as chief of the patrol by J. H. Matthews. It was during Matthews' brief stint as chief that the first serious injury to a patrolman on duty occurred. According to the first report of the incident, a patrolman had his jaw broken when hit with a slingshot by two drunks in Centennial park. With red face, Chief Matthews later explained to the Board the incident had not occurred in the park but in a saloon on 25th Avenue, ending that patrolman's services with the park system. Ben F. O'Barr succeeded Matthews as chief of the patrol in 1914, and for better supervision of the thirteen-man patrol the Board purchased him an automobile for frequent inspection of all the parks.[18]

With increased funding for parks made available through the municipal tax of 1909 and tax increase of 1913, the Board began motorization of the system's equipment, starting with the purchase of a steam-powered road roller to compact macadam stone on the drives and roadways—the use of asphalt road surfaces began in 1914. The Board purchased its first automobile, a Stoddard-Dayton, in 1912 for the use of all staff members when needed, and it also purchased a used Buick car which was converted into a truck for use by the horticulturist. That auto-truck was replaced with a Ford truck in 1917, after it was damaged in a collision with an automobile. Mules remained the principal motive power in the parks, however, throughout the decade, with barns and stables housing them located in Centennial and Shelby parks. Mowing the parks was accomplished with hand-propelled and mule-drawn mowers until 1918, when the Board purchased its first gasoline-powered lawn mower.[19]

While the acquisition of large parks in South, East, and North Nashville occupied a considerable portion of the Board's attention from 1910 to 1916, Centennial Park was not neglected. A drive up Spiral Hill, now called Flagpole Hill, on the west side of the park was finished by 1912, complete with concrete curbing and steps designed by Major E. C. Lewis and decorated with mortars donated by the War Department at the request of Congressman Joseph Bryns. Two greenhouses together with a heating plant and smokestack were also completed in 1912; and in August of that year the Board granted permission to the Daughters of the American Revolution to place a granite boulder in the park and mount thereon a plaque commemorating the site of Cockrill Spring, from whence General Andrew Jackson and Tennessee troops had once commenced a march south along the Natchez Trace. Construction of a community center in the park, with a public shelter downstairs and kindergarten upstairs, began in 1916. Miss Lille Frankland taught a kindergarten in the upstairs room during the mornings, while Martha Woolwine, the playground supervisor, used the room on winter afternoons for community recreational activities.[20]

The Parthenon was in such sad repair by 1915 that it became necessary to rope it off to prevent falling plaster from injuring passersby, and plans to restore it were initiated. Representing the Engineering Association of Nashville, Wilbur F. Creighton appeared before the Board to recommend that it reconstruct the Parthenon in more permanent materials and employ Russell E. Hart of the firm of Hart, Freeland and Roberts as architect. Hart accepted the work, employed sculptor George Zolnay and scholar William Dinsmoor as consultants, and began extensive studies of the original Parthenon in Athens to assure that Nashville's permanent replica would closely resemble the original. Those detailed studies required several years, and the permanent restoration work did not begin until 1921.[21]

By 1916 and the onset of the First World War, the Park Board had largely achieved the goals it had established at its formation in 1901. It had proposed establishing at least one large park in all four quarters of the city—fifty acres then being considered a large park—and by 1916 it had Centennial Park in the western sector, Shelby park in the east, and Hadley Park in the north. It had failed to create a large park in South Nashville, chiefly as a result of political resistance from people living in that area, but as substitute it had acquired a large number of smaller parks scattered throughout South Nashville. It had aimed at creating small parks ranging in size from vacant lots to several city blocks in area throughout the city for the convenience of neighborhood communities, and by 1916 it essentially had accomplished that goal. The city's park development was considered so successful by civic leaders that, starting in 1912, the Park Board's annual report, previously merely an appendum to the Mayor's annual report to the city council, was printed as a separate and fully illustrated pamphlet and widely distributed by the city's Industrial Bureau and civic booster organizations in efforts to attract new industry to Nashville.

7 RECREATIONAL AND CULTURAL EMPHASIS

The first Park Board encountered opposition to its efforts to establish recreation programs in the parks from various Calvinist denominations of the city which thought recreation wasteful of time if not sacrilegious. Although John Calvin had enjoyed bowling, even on Sunday afternoons, his religious heirs subscribed to a "work ethic," and eschewed recreation unless it had some practical application. Some of the charter members of the Park Board were members of Calvinist denominations but personally considered recreation healthful and perhaps even morally virtuous, and from the first the Board sponsored cultural and recreational programs in the parks. Out of deference to Nashville's Calvinist community, however, the Board did not approve organized recreation in the parks on Sundays until after the First World War.

Historian Thomas Macaulay wrote that the Puritans of England in the 17th century suppressed the cruel sport of bear-baiting, "not because it gave pain to the bear, but because it gave pleasure to the spectators." Because that disapproval of recreation was carried to Nashville by its Calvinist pioneers, early recreation in the city generally was associated with practical activities. Hunting and fishing were acceptable forms of recreation because they put meat on the table. Wrestling, fighting, and physical competitions were accepted because they provided combat training for the Indian wars and allowed the settlement of arguments without a resulting death to one of the participants. Presbyterian Elder George Martin wrote, with apparent approval, that Nashvillians in 1799 often settled disputes with physical contests: "At that time personal difficulties were not settled by Pistols & Dirks. When any two persons had a quarrel to settle they chose their seconds, made a <u>Ring</u>, took off all their clothing but <u>Pantaloons</u>, tied a handkerchief around their heads, entered the ring, & settled the dispute by what was called <u>Fist & Scull</u>, and when one hollowed enough, the contest ended, shook hands, put on their clothes, & so ended the matter."[1]

Because horses provided the principal means of cross-country transport before the advent of railroads, fast horses were important to the everyday work of the pioneers; and horse-racing therefore was an acceptable recreation, in fact becoming the most popular spectator sport of the 19th century. The most rigid Calvinists disapproved of the gambling which accompanied the races, however, and with good reason, for gambling sometimes culminated with duels, canings, and other violence disruptive to the community. Horse-racing, nevertheless, remained quite popular in the community until 1906, when a state law prohibiting gambling ended organized racing as a professional sport throughout Tennessee.[2]

Nashville pioneers also indulged in jumping contests, games of quoits and horseshoes, and in cockfighting on an informal basis, and the youth played ball games of some sort. When a group of Nashville Calvinists in 1850 observed that an open field on Franklin Road had become a "common ground for Ball Plays & riotous assemblies on each Sabbath day," they immediately opened a Sunday School mission on the spot to combat such youthful delinquencies. That attitude toward organized sports continued well into the 20th century in Nashville, and as late as 1910 the Davidson County Sheriff arrested the entire Vols baseball team at Sulphur Dell when they attempted to conduct a game on a Sunday afternoon.[3]

Nashvillians with sufficient money and time increasingly took interest in sports and recreation during the late 19th century. They attended baseball games at the Dell and purchased croquet sets, roller skates, and bicycles for their children if not for themselves. Croquet became so popular that people even purchased game sets with candle holders on the wickets for night games. Roller skating required paved or flat surfaces, and rinks were built for the sport; the pavilions and bandstands in Nashville's first parks were often used for roller skating as much as any other purpose. Bicycling became as popular in Nashville during the 1890s as it was elsewhere in the nation, and Frederick Herrick, who operated bicycle repair shops in the city for a half century, established the world record in 1893 for speed in a twenty-five-mile bicycle race.[4]

Football, basketball, and other organized sports in Nashville originated in the athletic programs of the city's colleges and Young Men's Christian Association as outgrowths of their physical education curriculums. The physical education classes initially conducted at colleges and at the "Y" sought to apply physiology and kinesiology to exercise, aiming at precise control of movements. Had that medically oriented curriculum prevailed, American recreation today might resemble the drill exercises of the youth in Communist China and Russia, but Recreation course instructors in America learned that students preferred competitive games to formal exercises. College teams introduced football to Nashville in 1890, on November 27 to be precise at the Sulphur Dell where Vanderbilt defeated Peabody by a score of 40 to 0. YMCA leaders concocted the games of basketball and volleyball as alternatives to formal exercises; James Naismith invented basketball in 1891 and William Morgan devised volleyball in 1895. It appears that basketball arrived in Nashville within a year after its invention, and it had become quite popular by 1895. Records do not indicate when tennis was first played in Nashville, but by 1901 when the public park system was established the Nashville Tennis Club was already in existence.[5]

Though Nashville's first Park Commissioners sought to create parks that would be quiet resting places, they also recognized that space for organized recreation was needed. In 1903 they leased the thirty-acre Elliston tract across 25th Avenue from Centennial Park and entered into cooperative arrangements for the use of the tract. When the Nashville Tennis Club asked to build its courts on the tract, the Commissioners approved, provided the club built extra courts that could be used by the public. When Professor C. B. Wallace requested permission to build a football field for the use of his preparatory school located near the Elliston tract, the Commissioners also granted their approval, provided that the public could use the field when it was not being used by the school. The entire arrangement collapsed in 1906, however, when the Commissioners agreed to permit the Nashville Baseball Club to build a diamond on the tract for semi-professional baseball and the owners of the property objected. Through litigation, the property owners broke the lease on grounds that the Park Board lacked authority under its charter to enter into leases.[6]

Having lost their lease and having no other suitable land for the purpose, the Park Commissioners were unable to resume a recreational sports program until 1914, after they had purchased the Elliston tract and Shelby, South, and other parks. Renamed the Centennial Athletic Field, the Elliston tract eventually was expanded in area as space for active recreation; in 1915 it also became the site of the annual Barnum and Bailey Circus. On that tract and also at Shelby, South, and Richland parks, the commissioners in 1914 built the first baseball, tennis, and basketball facilities owned by the park system. Though the park system then had no gymnasiums, outdoor basketball courts were constructed and in 1915 Dr. A. S. Keim of the Nashville YMCA organized the park system's first basketball league consisting of eight teams which played on Saturday afternoons in Shelby Park.[7]

The Park Board in its first active year of park operations in 1903 had sponsored Gilbert and Sullivan operettas in Centennial Park, but the Board's funding difficulties limited its ability to sponsor cultural recreation for several years thereafter. Summer concerts in the park, consisting of music by a German brass band, continued from 1904 to 1910 only through the generosity of Percy Warner and the Nashville Railway and Light Company who paid the musicians. Mayor Hilary Howse in 1911 arranged a $2,000 appropriation by the city council to supplement the funds given by Mr. Warner to support concerts at Morgan, Watkins, Richland, and Meridian Street parks in addition to Centennial Park. By 1911 the brass band from Cincinnati had been supplanted by the first Tennessee Regiment band, organized by Herbert Kilbourne and E. Pellettieri, which performed concerts in conjunction with drills by local militia units. As indicated by an account of the Fourth of July concert of 1911, the cultural programs had become increasingly elaborate:[8]

> Centennial Park proved a popular place yesterday and thousands spent the day, afternoon or evening there. Two concerts were given by

the First Regiment Band and the Custer massacre on the Little Big Horn was reproduced by Company K. Some of the features were: the war dance of the Sioux Indians the night before the battle; bugle calls in Custer's camp before forming line of march; Custer's Cavalry on march to the Sioux camp; war dance music by the Indians; Indians rejoicing and scalp dance music; arrival of reinforcements, Gen. Buntline and cavalry; burial of Gen. Custer's body; volley of shots, muffled drums and bugles; sounding last call over grave, and finale, "Nearer My God to Thee."

Participation of the Park Board in art as cultural recreation initially consisted of granting permission for local art associations to display their work in the Parthenon, but in 1910 the Board purchased its first work of art at the suggestion of Commissioner Ben Lindauer, the Board's expert on matters cultural, who proposed that it buy a panorama of Palestine. At the request of the Board, Professor Gordon White and General Gates Thurston examined the huge painting, reporting it had no artistic merit but presented historical and religious scenes that would interest the public, and the board thereon bought it and placed it on display in the Parthenon. Painted by an unidentified artist after several years work in Palestine (Israel), the 124-foot long and 8-foot high panorama pictured the geographic features, such as the River Jordan, Sea of Galilee, and Mount Olivet, of a 127-mile section of Palestine. Guided by a Vanderbilt University divinity student, groups from the city's temples and Sunday schools circled through the Parthenon past the panorama in large numbers, and according to a reporter from the *Nashville Banner* the painting proved the greatest artistic triumph owned by the park system other than the Parthenon itself.[9]

At the request of Mayor Howse, the Park Board in 1911 began contributing $2,000 a year, matching an appropriation by the city council, to support the Nashville Art Association headed by Sarah (Mrs. J. C.) Bradford who directed most art exhibits in the Parthenon. Mrs. Bradford also organized the elaborate pageants presented in Centennial Park just prior to the First World War, the most memorable being "The Fire Regained" written by Sidney Hirsch of the Vanderbilt University "Fugitives" group. For that pageant, Mrs. Bradford, Leland Hume, and James M. Frank, with funding from the Nashville Merchants Association, built a grandstand seating 5,000 on the south side of the Parthenon, using the Parthenon itself as the stage for the production. Running four days in May 1913, no more spectacular event ever graced the city; it had a cast of several hundred sheep, a thousand doves, and nearly a thousand actors and actresses in Greek costume, including the wife of Governor Benton McMillin dressed in white robe and shining helmet as Athena. Featuring actual chariot races, a maiden carried off by a live bull, and an actor dressed as Hermes appearing atop the Parthenon at a tense moment in the drama, the pageant was filmed by a New York movie company for theaters throughout the country. The play subsequently was performed in the District of Columbia, and it was named one of the twelve best pageants ever produced in America. Sidney Hirsch penned "The Mysteries of Thantos" for presentation at the Parthenon in 1914, but interest in dramatic extravaganzas dwindled with the outbreak of war in Europe and with the advent of motion pictures.[10]

Tony Sudekum had opened the first motion picture theater in Nashville in 1907, and in 1914 the Park Board entered into contract with his company for the presentation of free movies in the parks at no cost to the Board except that of providing seating for the audiences. The contract provided that only educational and scenic films would be shown, the company's compensation for the service being an opportunity to run advertising previews of the movies showing at its theaters. That arrangement continued several years, until the novelty of movies had worn off, at which time the Board purchased its own projectors and rented films, expanding the film subject matter to suit the tastes of the audiences. It could not show the latest films, because of the costs and because they would have competed with the theater business in the city, but the audiences were not disappointed. "On some summer Saturdays I can remember sitting with hundreds of other kids at the creaking wooden bandstand waiting for the start of a free outdoor movie," recalled publisher John Siegenthaler, "a bad 'B' western and a Flash Gordon serial. We cheered the heroes, booed the villains and laughed at bad jokes that then seemed hilarious."[11]

Other than free movies in the parks, the park system's cultural recreation activities continued under the direction of Mrs. Sarah Bradford until 1928. The state legislature amended the city charter in 1917 to provide that the Park Board would "provide and maintain art exhibits and promote the interests of Art in the City of Nashville," and to accomplish that end the Park Board appointed Mrs. Bradford, Dr. George Hale, and Edward Thompson as the Nashville Art Commission, allocating $2,500 of the park budget each year toward the Art Commission's budget. Mrs. Bradford used that funding to purchase paintings for permanent display in the Parthenon, for the administration of the art exhibits, and for placing a memorial plaque in memory of Major E. C. Lewis in the Parthenon. That cooperative supervision of the city's cultural recreation program continued until 1928 when the board and the Art Commission had a disagreement concerning the interior design of the reconstructed Parthenon building.[12]

The first public golf course in Nashville opened in 1924, reflecting the growing popularity of that sport. The first golf links in the city had opened during the 1890s at the homes of James C. Warner and Overton Lea who had become interested in the sport during trips to Scotland. Edwin Warner headed the group which organized Nashville's first golf club in 1901 and opened a course at West Nashville's Cherokee Park, subsequently moving to the Richland course on West End Avenue at Elmington Park and in 1914 to land donated by Senator Luke Lea, where the course became part of the Belle Meade Country Club. Interest in opening a municipal golf course first surfaced in 1919 when H. G. Hill, Will Manier, Green Benton, and Charles Brown representing the Nashville Chamber of Commerce asked the Park Board to consider building links in Shelby Park. The estimated cost of building the course exceeded the Park Board's resources in 1919, but in 1923 when the Chamber of Commerce renewed its request the Board decided to undertake the project. After purchasing a 45-acre addition to Shelby Park for the course, hiring Tom Bendelow to revise the course plans made in 1919 by Walter Hatch and Donald Ross, and expending $12,000 on construction, the Board opened the Shelby Park golf course on July 21, 1924. Those first nine-holes became the back nine at Shelby when the front nine was completed in 1930.[13]

The Board employed Robert J. Brown as its first "professor of golf," or "gold pro," at the Shelby links, but within a year Brown was succeeded by Cletus E. Danis, who received not only a small salary but also the concession for the sale of golf clubs and other equipment. Danis remained as golf pro with the park system for more than a quarter century and trained other professionals, such as Herschel

Eaton and Luther Hickman, who supervised public golf courses until well into the 1980s. The Shelby course in 1925 became the site of the annual Schoolboy Golf tournament, the oldest golf tournament in the city. Sponsored by the Nashville *Tennessean,* the Schoolboy tourney produced many winners who took the Blinkey Horn prize and went on to professional golfing fame.[14]

Another major contribution to the park system's cultural attractions during the 1920s was the reconstruction of the Parthenon in permanent materials. The crumbling plaster of the 1897 replica forced the Park Board in 1921 to initiate reconstruction of the building in concrete on plans drawn up by Russell Hart aimed at making Nashville's replica resemble the original to the extent possible. Because the cost of building with marble, like the original, exceeded the Board's financial resources, concrete was selected for the permanent replica. Commissioners Robert Creighton and M. T. Bryan agreed to administer the reconstruction without charge, and in 1921 they employed workmen, purchased a concrete mixer, erected scaffolding around the building, and started work with Park Superintendent Clarence Connell as construction foreman. Sculptor George Zolnay modelled the figures to decorate the Doric frieze, Leopold and Belle Kinney Scholz prepared the figures for the pediments, and John J. Earley came to Nashville to apply his patented process for tinting concrete to reproduce the colors of the Pentelic marbles used in the original Parthenon.[15]

Removing the exterior plaster and wooden lath framing, the workmen installed metal lathing and wire mesh and hoisted concrete to the roof for pouring into the forms for the walls and columns. Earley's colored finish, composed of a mixture of cement, quartz, and Potomac River gravel, when applied to the concrete recreated the golden burnish of the ancient Parthenon. The exterior reconstruction was nearly completed by 1923 when a tornado tore off part of the building's roof and the repairs exhausted the funds then available for the work. The Board therefore suspended the reconstruction while seeking additional funding and considering various plans for the design of the building's interior.[16]

During study of the interior design, a disagreement between the Park Board and Mrs. Sarah Bradford and the Art Commission arose. Mrs. Bradford insisted that the interior should be converted into an art gallery, with a design and mezzanine similar to that of the Hall of

Sculpture at Pittsburgh's Carnegie Museum of Art, and she contacted Auguste Saint-Gaudens of the Carnegie Museum, securing permission to reproduce the Hall of Sculpture inside the Parthenon. The Park Board, on the other hand, wished the interior to be as nearly as possible a reproduction of the interior of the original Parthenon, relying upon studies by classical historian William Dinsmoor of Columbia University to supply the design details, and to use the basement built under the replica in 1897 for the display of art. The dispute became so acrimonious that in 1927 the Park Board withdrew its support from the Nashville Art Commission.[17]

Borrowing funds from the Fourth and First National Bank in 1928, the Park Board resumed the Parthenon's construction, awarding a contract for fabrication of the great cast-bronze doors, each pair weighing fifteen tons, for the east and west entrances to the building. After competitive bidding, the contract for completing the exterior repairs and rebuilding the interior went to Foster & Creighton Company, the low bidder. Wilbur Creighton and his firm went speedily to work and finished the job within two years, allowing the Board to reopen the Parthenon to the public on May 21, 1931, in a condition very much as it now stands. Benjamin Wilson, a retired mining engineer who became the first Director of the Parthenon, reported that the reconstructed building attracted many visitors; in a single month, he counted 10,757 tourists, about three-fourths of them from Tennessee and the remainder from 45 other states and 12 foreign countries.[18]

The interest of Nashvillians in recreation and organized sports so increased during the early 1920s that the Park Board concluded professional leadership of the recreation program was needed, and in 1924 it employed Philip LeBoutillier of New Orleans at $200 a month as its first fulltime Superintendent of Recreation. LeBoutillier organized recreation programs throughout the park system and directed the conversion of old homes at McFerrin, Morgan, Elizabeth and other parks into "recreation centers" for indoor cultural activities, mostly arts and crafts. He won local fame by organizing an annual Recreation Week starting in May 1925 to kick off the summer season with a celebration highlighting the benefits of outdoor recreation. Monday was Tennis, Swimming, and Playground day, with tennis tournaments, playground activities, and swimming and diving competitions. Neighborhood Day on Tuesday was celebrated with community singing and pageants at the playgrounds and roller skate races on four city streets the Mayor had closed for the purpose. More than 10,000 boys and girls took part in flower parades and doll shows for the little ones and track and field competition for older children on Wednesday. Thursday was Church Recreation Day, Friday was marked with gymnastic skill demonstrations on the playgrounds and at the Ryman Auditorium, and Saturday became a civic holiday. Mayor Howse led a parade of city employees to Shelby Park for a full day of recreation, followed by an address from Dr. C. F. Stimson, the executive secretary of the Playground and Recreation Association of America. According to reporter Mary Stahlman Douglas, Recreation Week was the biggest event of its kind ever conducted in Nashville and the South.[19]

Opposition from Calvinist religious denominations in Nashville to recreation in general and to games on Sundays in particular was fading by the late 1920s, and that was reflected in a change of its position on the subject by the Park Board. When the Board in 1915 took a vote on permitting Sunday baseball games and other organized sports in the parks, the Commissioners had voted four to one against it, with Ben Lindauer casting the sole favorable vote. By 1927 the membership and opinions of the Board had changed substantially, however, and when one staunch Calvinist complained about Sunday ball games in the parks, Commissioner Charles McCabe pointedly replied:[20]

> I would rather see 10,000 young men at a ball game, yelling in sheer delight, than not to know where they are. I would rather see two ball teams, with muscles tense and brains alert, out in the open with God's sunshine making the sweat pop out on their healthy bodies, than to see then squatting about on the ground, begging the ivories to "come seven" and learning the pernicious vice of gambling.

8 MANAGEMENT AND EXPANSION, 1917–1930

After the major park expansion of 1909 to 1916, park acquisition essentially ceased for a decade, and from 1917 to 1927 no parks were added to the system except when they came as outright gifts from other agencies or from citizens. The Park Board was burdened with heavy annual installments due on the park lands purchased before 1917 and by the cost of building diamonds, courts, and a golf course at the existing parks along with expenditures necessary to reconstruct the Parthenon. During that decade, however, a number of park system improvements were completed, several interesting changes in park management occurred, and the era was marked by a complete turnover in the membership of the Park Board which by 1926 was prepared to embark on a new park expansion effort. Under the leadership of Percy Warner, the Park Board during the late 1920s added several new parks to the system, including the largest public park in Tennessee.

The entry of the United States into the First World War in April 1917 had several effects upon Nashville's park system. That spring the Tennessee Home Guard trained its recruits at several city parks, and Colonel Harry Berry assembled troops of the First Tennessee Infantry for initial training before leaving for France at "Camp

Andrew Jackson," located on the site which was to become the Percy Warner golf course. The following winter, the Army commandeered the old Montgomery Bell Academy building in South Park as a military hospital, and park horticulturist George Moulder lost all his shrubs and plants because the U.S. Fuel Administration cut off shipments of coal needed to heat the greenhouses. The U.S. Food Administration requested assistance with food supply problems in 1918, and the plots in the parks formerly planted with flowers were used by many citizens to plant "Victory Gardens." Tony Dentici, the Centennial Park concessionaire, also suffered losses in 1918 when the U.S. Food Administration forbade the sale of ice cream and soft drinks in the parks. Those impacts were ephemeral, however, for the First World War ended twenty months after it had begun.[1]

The city park system gained one small park in the aftermath of the war. When state government in 1919 proposed building a war memorial building, the Park Board tendered the Parthenon, then in need of complete restoration, for the purpose, but the Tennessee legislature declined that offer, choosing instead to build a War Memorial Building downtown near Capitol Hill. The legislature provided for the construction of Victory Square Park adjacent to the new building, promising to give the title to the square to the Park Board, and the Board excavated the rock from the square and placed a few inches of soil atop the rock, planting it with shrubbery and flowers. Better known to the public as Memorial Square or Memorial Park, Victory Square never really worked as a public park except as a spot for a brown-bag lunch for office workers and a bus transfer point. The state fund for park development soon was exhausted and state government thereafter expected the Park Board to pay for maintaining Victory Square; yet, state authorities were also reluctant to part with the title to the square and did not give it to the Board until 1953. The Board was equally reluctant to expend city park taxes on state property, and thus Victory Square languished until the state government again took control of the property in 1969 and built a subterranean office beneath it.[2]

Four monuments to soliders of the First World War eventually were placed in Nashville's parks. The Catholic children of Nashville in 1919 planted a tree and placed a marker in Centennial Park in memory of Lieutenant James S. Timothy; and the Nashville Kiwanis Club in 1921 funded a monument to Davidson County Gold Star heroes also placed in Centennial Park. Colonel Harry Berry, with federal funding in 1936, placed a monument to the dead of his 115th Field Artillery on the spot in Percy Warner Park where they had assembled in 1917. And the H. A. Cameron Post 6, American Legion, in 1937 placed plaques listing the black soldiers who died in the service during the First World War on the gates to Hadley Park.[3]

During the five years following the war, Clarence Connell served the Board as Superintendent of Parks, spending much of his time directing the reconstruction of the Parthenon's exterior. Connell is best remembered in Nashville as a founder of the American Iris Society and developer of the "Dauntless," the first red iris. After leaving the park system in 1924, he became an administrator at Vanderbilt Hospital and, with proceeds from the sale of his patented red iris, built a unique home he named Dauntless Hill where the national iris society sometimes met. He and other iris fanciers appeared before the Park Board several times, seeking to make the iris the official Nashville flower, hoping it would become what roses are to Portland, Oregon, and azaleas to Mobile, Alabama.[4]

The Board made George Moulder the Superintendent of Parks in addition to his duties as chief horticulturist when Connell left the system, thereby saving enough payroll to permit hiring Philip LeBoutillier as fulltime Superintendent of Recreation. Moulder, an aquatic plant specialist, was chiefly responsible for the creation in 1922 at Centennial Park of a Japanese water garden featuring white and pink lotus and water lilies in the pond and cattails, irises, and wildflowers around its perimeter. Grottoes of stone, Japanese lanterns of concrete, and a statue of Buddha sculpted by Nashvillian Paul E. Schwab adorned the banks of the garden, which attracted national attention in gardening magazines. A mystery concerning the Buddha developed in 1935 when park patrolman A. W. Vester discovered that someone regularly placed coins in the uplifted palms of the idol; if the coins were removed, more appeared within a week. Vandals destroyed the Buddha during the 1940s, maintenance of the garden ended during the Second World War, and after Moulder retired, Frank Pickens and Z. N. Dobbs converted the water garden into a carefully manicured and planted sunken garden where weddings and other parties often were held, though the remains of the stone grottoes and concrete lanterns that once decorated the Japanese water garden could still be seen at the site.[5]

Though the Park Board acquired no new parks worthy of the name from 1917 to 1927, it did obtain two small playgrounds, one as a gift and the other by purchase. East Nashvillians in 1921 purchased a lot next to the fire hall at Holly and Sixteenth streets and gave it to the Board which named it Bass Park to honor Herman Bass, the first captain of Engine Company No. 14 who had arranged for the purchase. In 1926, the board paid $3,565 for a vacant lot at Eleventh Avenue and Vernon Street as the Edgehill playground for the use of black children in that community. Those two playgrounds, together with Victory Square, comprised the sole additions to the park system during the decade following the First World War.[6]

A nearly complete turnover in the board membership occurred during the early 1920s. Judge M. T. Bryan died in 1923, Robert Dudley in 1925, and Robert Creighton in 1926. In memory of Dudley, the last surviving charter member, and Creighton, the first Superintendent of Parks, the Nashville Kiwanis Club in 1927 built a wading pool in Morgan Park and a flagpole with an inscription on its base honoring those two members who had devoted a quarter century of their lives toward achieving a better city park system. Whitefoord Cole became president of the entire Louisville and Nashville Railway system in 1926, and he resigned from the Board to move to Louisville where the railroad was headquartered. Between 1923 and 1926, therefore, Lee Loventhal was joined by four new Board members: Charles McCabe, Percy Warner, J. P. W. Brown, and Rogers Caldwell.[7]

Subtle differences between the character of the men who had directed the system during its first quarter century and that of the new members of 1926 were to alter the system's direction and management. The early Board members had been distinguished local civic leaders but were not well known outside Nashville; the new members were known throughout Tennessee and had regional and even national reputations. The first Board members had been the "hands on" type of businessmen, who devoted personal attention to the details of their concerns and who enjoyed designing a shell spring, supervising the construction of structure, or planning a neighborhood playground. The new members of 1926 were urbane men of large affairs, accustomed to managing far-flung enterprises—in brief, empire builders—and their achievements earned them widespread public recognition.

Percy Warner, who became chairman of the Park Board at the

death of Robert Dudley, had managed the Nashville Railway and Light Company until 1914, providing continuing support to the municipal park system through advancing loans to the Board against streetcar receipts and sponsoring concerts in the parks. After 1914, Warner served as director of a half dozen Nashville banks and businesses and invested in utility companies at Memphis, Birmingham, Houston, New Orleans, Little Rock, and New York City, becoming known in financial circles throughout the nation.[8]

The first job held by John Preston Watts Brown, an electrical engineering graduate of Vanderbilt University, was as electrical inspector at the 1897 Centennial. He joined Nashville's electric utility service and became its general manager by the time he was elected to the Park Board; he subsequently became president of the Tennessee Electric Power Company, which built hydroelectric dams on the Caney Fork and Tennessee rivers and which supplied electric power to several states of the Upper South. He was one of the "Four Horsemen"—Lee Loventhal, Vernon Tupper, and W. H. Lambeth being the others—who were so named because they enlisted against flood, fire, famine, and pestilence and in 1922 were the leading organizers of the Nashville Community Chest (now called the United Way).[9]

Like Judge M. T. Bryan whom he succeeded, Charles McCabe was Roman Catholic and a power in the Democratic Party. He had been the city treasurer under Mayor James Head, worked for the U.S. Senate's committee on foreign relations, and served as postmaster at both Memphis and Nashville by appointment of President Woodrow Wilson. As the Tennessee Commissioner of Finance, he reorganized the State Police, and during the last decade of his life he worked as chief collector for the Internal Revenue Service in Tennessee.[10]

Most Nashvillians need no introduction to the financial wizard of the 1920s, Rogers Caldwell. The son of Nashville banker James Caldwell, Rogers plunged into the insurance and banking business with unmatched vim, flashing like a comet to the control of a vast financial empire covering the South. By the time he was elected to the Park Board, he was at his zenith as an economic, social, and political giant with nationwide fame.[11]

The five men constituting the Park Board in 1926 were, in sum, the most powerful quintet in Tennessee, perhaps in the South. It was said that they had clout sufficient to select the Governor of Tennessee; in fact, some have said that they did. They were elected to the Park Board by their predecessors, however, and their membership apparently had no political connotation, merely indicating that membership on the Board had become prestigious.

With those distinguished and financially knowledgeable leaders at the helm, the expansion of the municipal park system, quiescent since 1917, resumed in 1926, originating with the first professional plans for comprehensive park system development. No professional, comprehensive park planning had been undertaken before 1926: the Park Board merely announced in 1901 that it wished to acquire large parks in each of the four sectors of the city and smaller parks and playgrounds scattered throughout the urban area, and it had largely achieved those goals by 1916. Chairman Percy Warner and his colleagues in 1926 decided it was time to reassess the municipal park program and to lay plans for its future development. That spring, the Board contracted with Harland Bartholomew & Associates, landscape engineers of St. Louis, to become "consultants in park planning" at $2,500 a year for three years. A team from that firm headed by L. D. Tilton studied the park system during the summer, assessing existing facilities and forecasting the future park needs of the Nashville urban area.[12]

The park planning firm immediately observed the park system was not expanding to keep apace of the city's growing and increasingly mobile population. From about 100,000 in 1901, the city's population had increased by more than a third, reaching 136,000 in 1926. Nashvillians that year owned 32,500 automobiles, and the number of vehicles was multiplying faster than the population, producing a population no longer totally dependent on streetcars for transportation and which enjoyed using their new cars for Sunday drives and other recreation. Other than Glendale Park, there were no recreational areas to which they could drive; in 1926 there were neither federal nor state parks in Tennessee. Perceiving that the automobile would eventually become the personal and family transport mode of choice, the planning firm recommended that roads in Centennial and other existing parks be realigned, improved, and made into one-way thoroughfares, and the board immediately adopted that proposal.[13]

When the planning firm presented its preliminary assessment of

Nashville's future park needs to Percy Warner in August 1926, the Chairman convened a special meeting of the Board on the last day of the month to present the report. It recommended major expansion of the system by acquiring a series of large natural parks in Davidson County ringing the central urban area, all to be connected with a magnificent boulevard around the city with linking boulevards like the spokes of a wheel leading from the central hub out to the parks. Chairman Warner enthusiastically endorsed the plan, proposing that the Board issue bonds to purchase the park lands. His colleagues concurred, directing Secretary John Lewis and his assistant J. Glenn Skinner to prepare a full financial statement listing the assets and liabilities of the park system and appointing a special committee composed of Warner, J. P. W. Brown, and Rogers Caldwell to "look around for additional park area."[14]

A revision of the city charter in 1923 had given the Board the authority to issue bonds and borrow funds for the purchase of park lands on its own credit, not relying upon the financial status of city government, which sometimes was nearly insolvent and which in fact had once been in the hands of a receiver. John Lewis and Glenn Skinner prepared the financial report needed to market park bonds. They found the park system included real estate worth $1,186,437, structures worth $665, 225, equipment valued at $60,758, and total assets, including roads and utility lines, amounting to $2,097,420.70. Liabilities totaled only $102,024.50, chiefly comprised of debt remaining from the purchase of park land before 1916.[15]

With that excellent financial statement in hand, the Board decided to issue park bonds for $725,000, paying 4.5 percent interest over a thirty-year period—to 1957—with park tax receipts pledged for retirement of the bonds. After receiving four competitive bids for the purchase of the bonds, the Board in 1927 sold the bonds to the J. C. Bradford Company. The proceeds of this first bond issue for the park system went toward the completion of the Parthenon reconstruction and toward the purchase of more park land.[16]

Commissioners Warner, Brown, and Caldwell apparently discussed their search for additional park area with Senator Luke Lea, the son-in-law of Commissioner Warner, or at least Percy Warner did, for on September 26, less than a month after the search had begun, the Board met in special session to consider an offer made by the Senator. Senator Lea, who had earned fame as commander of the

114th Artillery in France and for his attempt to capture the German Kaiser in 1918, founded the Nashville *Tennessean* in 1907 and was the owner of the Belle Meade Park Company, a real estate firm developing a community at Nashville's western fringe. Lea offered to donate to the park system 868 acres owned by his real estate firm under the conditions that the land would always be used as a park, that it would not be used for a zoo or for athletics other than golf, that the firm would retain title to a reservoir essential to community water supply on the property, and that a year be allowed to get the livestock and crops off the land. At the September 26 meeting, Rogers Caldwell moved that Lea's generous offer be accepted and that the Board initiate the acquisition of more land adjacent to Lea's donation, a motion which the membership heartily endorsed, complimenting Senator Lea for his gift to the people.[17]

Senator Lea had seen Rock Creek Park in the District of Columbia and Swope Park in Kansas City, and his personal observations confirmed what the park planning firm and his father-in-law said concerning the benefits of large natural parks near urban areas. Critics of the Senator subsequently impugned his motives for the gift, implying that he aimed at some private gain. While the roads leading to the park and the Belle Meade area subsequently were improved, the Senator clearly had sufficient political influence to obtain those improvements or any other urban services needed in the community without giving away his land. He doubtless recognized that the creation of the park would enhance the value of his real estate near it, but he could have kept the park, as the Nashville Railway and Light Company had done at Glendale Park, and, after the surrounding properties had sold, subdivided it for sale at immense profit. If the Senator gained anything other than acclamation for his gift, it is not evident in the records.[18]

In November the Park Commissioners planned development of the new park, deciding that most of the land would remain in its natural condition, that scenic drives would be opened for public access, and that a golf course would be constructed. Estimating the park could be expanded to more than 2,000 acres at a cost of about $245,000, they initiated a major acquisition effort, employing the Stutson Smith and Caldwell and Chapman realty firms to negotiate the purchase of adjoining properties. When farm owners refused to negotiate fair prices, the Board obtained authority from the state legislature to condemn the properties in courts, which would establish the fair prices. For the fifteen families thus uprooted, the creation of the park was a heart-breaking experience; members of those families still lamented their loss a half century later, referring to the condemnation as a "conniving deed with a veneer of legality." That grief, common wherever any agency of government exercises eminent domain, can be assuaged only by the knowledge that those lands have contributed to the recreation and health of several generations of Nashvillians and, unlike other nearby farms which were or are becoming buried under housing developments, the farms included in the park will remain for the enjoyment of all citizens for generations to come.[19]

Four days after Percy Warner died suddenly on June 18, 1927, the Park Board named its new park in his memory, and a few months later it named the highest point in the park "Luke Lea Heights," a point now referred to as Lea Summit. The purchase of adjoining properties proceeded swiftly; another 995 acres were acquired by March 1928 and purchases continued until the park reached 2,058 acres in area. "We first planned on a 1,000 acre tract," explained Commissioner Charles McCabe, "but as it began to develop we realized that within some 30 years time 1,000 acres would be entirely too small; and so as it became possible we began adding adjoining tracts to the park we had begun and named it Percy Warner in honor of the man who did so much to make it a reality."[20]

There being no federal or state parks in Tennessee until the late 1930s, Percy Warner Park was for a time the largest park in the state and it remained one of the largest municipal parks in the nation. From the first, the Board sought to preserve most of the park in its pristine natural condition, and that goal was largely achieved, making it a veritable living laboratory for environmental and ecological research for university classes and nature enthusiasts such as Amelia Lasky, author of classic ornithological studies of Chimney Swifts and Eastern Bluebirds. "We tried to keep the atmosphere of the place," said Edwin Warner: "We wanted everything to be rustic—the cabins, the shelters, even the rails along the drives."[21]

Edwin Warner, who succeeded his brother on the Park Board, devoted much of the last twenty years of his life toward the development of Warner and other parks. He customarily spent half of each working day in the parks, and Ewell Costello recalled that near lunch time each day the phone in the park office would ring as Mr. Warner requested that they meet to attend to a park project. Often they drove to Warner Park, where with string, stakes, and some rough engineering they laid out the route of a scenic drive through the park. Edwin Warner became what Major E. C. Lewis had once been, an unofficial superintendent of park development, and in fact once served as Superintendent of Parks briefly during an interim while the Board recruited a new employee for the position. "Edwin Warner is worth the rest of us together," remarked Commissioner Charles McCabe, adding: "I don't believe a $25,000 a year man working full time could do as good a job as he does, and he does his work and makes his contributions without a thought of getting anything out of it."[22]

Construction of the scenic drives in Warner Park began in 1927, and in 1930 Mrs. Percy Warner donated $20,000 to fund the building of stone entrance gates to the park designed by Edward Doughery, and the stone steps and lane leading up the hill behind the gates designed by Bryant Fleming. Veterans who had served in the First World War under the command of Luke Lea eventually placed a monument near the park entrance commemorating Lea's gift of land to initiate park development. Edwin Warner also gave money in addition to his time to the park system, contributing $20,000 in 1930, which the Board used to purchase a 267-acre farm across Old Hickory Boulevard from Percy Warner Park. The board subsequently purchased more land to bring the park on that side of the highway to a total of 606 acres, which it named Edwin Warner Park, although the public commonly lumped both of the parks together as the Warner Park.[23]

In 1927 and 1928, the Board used the proceeds of its bond issues to purchase two additional parks, starting with fourteen-acre Elmington Park at the corner of West End and Bowling avenues. Edwin Warner's "Elmington" estate had occupied the site before he sold it to the Richland Golf Club and the Harding Realty Company. When the realty company asked $117,000 for the fourteen acres, the board countered with an offer of $55,000 and the transaction was settled at $65,000. Commissioner Lee Loventhal opposed the purchase, arguing that the site was too small for a park, that it was merely nine blocks from Centennial Park, that the money would be better invested in more playgrounds in the central city, and that the site was outside the city limits, which it was in 1927. Loventhal was correct on all counts, but a few years later the Board of Education built West High School adjacent to the park and the park became an excellent playfield for the school.[24]

The Board in 1928 purchased Fort Negley, an elaborate Union Army fortification crowning St. Cloud Hill in South Nashville off Chestnut Street, for $20,000. Absentee owners had abandoned the property at the time of the Civil War, the hill had long been a prominent eyesore on the city's horizon, and the stone used in the original fort had been removed in 1889 for use in construction of the city reservoir atop a nearby hill. Banker James Caldwell, the father of Rogers Caldwell, as head of the Nashville Battlefield Association had initiated efforts to acquire the site of the fort in 1913, recommending that Capitol Boulevard be extended from downtown to the fort to create an avenue similar to Pennsylvania Avenue in Washington and urging that the old fort be restored as a tourist attraction. Senator Luke Lea and Congressman Joe Byrns sponsored bills in Congress to designate Fort Negley as a national park and to fund its restoration, but when their efforts failed James Caldwell renewed his campaign in 1926 by asking the Park Board to purchase the forty-seven-acre St. Cloud Hill. No doubt Rogers Caldwell's membership on the Board had a great deal to do with its decision to accede to James Caldwell's request. But the Board lacked the funds needed to undertake restoration of the old fort, and in addition there were members of the Nashville community with Confederate ancestry who preferred that the bastions be leveled, the trenches filled, and all signs of Yankee occupation obliterated.[25]

Several events and legends concerning the history of Fort Negley deserve mention. Captain James St. Clair Morton, the author of a Union Army manual on fortification construction, designed the fort in 1862 and built it by conscripting every black man, slave or free, in the city for the task; he named it in honor of James S. Negley, a Union Army general who became the Congressman from Pittsburgh, Pennsylvania, after the Civil War. The guns of the fort were fired twice, once when General Nathan B. Forrest's Confederate cavalry entered the outskirts of the city in 1862 and again during the Battle of Nashville in December 1864, on neither occasion with much effect. It had a deep cistern, a subterranean powder magazine, and underground passages for safe movement of the garrison from one part of the fort to another, and those features apparently inspired the legend that a tunnel led from the fort downhill to a vault in the City Cemetery, a legend which has been seriously investigated and disproven. Legend says the fort was the site of conclaves of the Ku Klux Klan during the postwar years, but since that was a secret organization to confirm or disprove the legend appears impossible.[26]

Through acquisition of Fort Negley, Elmington, and Warner parks, the most powerful Park Board of history more than doubled the size of the municipal park system. The growth resulted from their recourse to professional park planning, from their legal and business acumen, and from the gifts they and their families made to the system. The Warner parks will serve always as a reminder of their efforts and achievements, but Elmington Park was less well conceived as a park and Fort Negley, despite major federal investment in its development, for several reasons never really succeeded as a public park. With the death of Percy Warner in 1927, the elaborate plan prepared by professionals for ringing the city core with large parks connected by boulevards was forgotten. Perhaps if the economic prosperity of the 1920s had continued uninterrupted, the plans made in 1926 would have been implemented over a period of years, but the Depression of the 1930s prostrated the park system's budget, as it did most others, and not until the formation of Metropolitan government in 1963 was a renewed effort made to devise comprehensive plans for proper development of an adequate park system.

9 BOOM TO BUST IN THE PARKS

Rising park revenues accompanying the general prosperity of the Golden 'Twenties allowed the Park Board to expand its cultural recreation and sports programs in the parks, employ a larger staff and increase their pay, purchase more motorized equipment, and improve park services to the public in general. Those were the golden years of baseball and the automobile, reflected by construction of scenic drives through the parks and by expansion of facilities for amateur baseball. That prosperous boom peaked in 1929, then began a precipitous decline, accompanied by curtailments in park programs, budget slashes, pay cuts, and various other expedient measures required to reduce expenditures in the face of dwindling revenues. Public use of the municipal park system did not diminish as a result of the Great Depression however, for Nashvillians flocked into the parks in even greater numbers than they had during the 1920s in search of low-cost recreation.

As a result of increasing tax and streetcar revenues, which permitted the Board to more than double its operating budget from about $100,000 in 1920 to about $250,000 in 1929, the salaries of the park system's employees increased and effort was made to motorize some of the work. Salaries of the playground supervisors nearly doubled during the 1920s, reaching $130 a month in 1929, and Secretary John Lewis, the employee with the top salary, was paid as much as $3900 a year. The Board purchased Dodge coupes for use of its superintendents and three new Model-T trucks, one for maintenance at Centennial Park, another for Shelby Park, and the third for work at the scattered playgrounds. The park patrolmen also received a badly needed raise after the Board learned they were leaving to join the better paid echelon of the city police department. One who left was patrol chief Ben O'Barr, who was succeeded in 1925 by William C. Scott. Scott was the sole patrolman with an assigned car, but after the acquisition of Warner Park the Board put patrolman Joe Hitt astride a motocycle to regulate traffic in that comparatively vast park area.[1]

Recreation in the parks was directed during the late 1920s and for years thereafter by Ewell "Cos" Costello, employed in 1926 as successor to Philip LeBoutillier as Superintendent of Recreation. Costello had achieved local renown as center for the Hume-Fogg High basketball quintet, including Boos and Lallie Richter, Bowser Chest, and Jack Diamond, which had originated the "fast-break" and won the state championship several times, also participating in the national basketball championship then conducted at Chicago by Alonzo Stagg. Costello recalls he was working in the Tampa, Florida, park system when he received a telegram from Percy Warner telling him to report to Nashville in three days to become the new Superintendent; he was neither interviewed, nor asked if he wanted the job, merely told to report. He did, and remained with the system thirty years. To better prepare him for the job, the Board sent him to meetings of the Playground and Recreation Association of America, and on his own he enrolled in courses at Vanderbilt University to learn sufficient engineering to lay out baseball diamonds and recreational facilities.[2]

Costello's new-found skills proved useful, for interest in both professional and amateur baseball blossomed during the 1920s, and by 1929 he had laid out eighteen new baseball diamonds to serve a growing number of teams and leagues. Thousands of Nashvillians attended and members of the Park Board took personal interest in the games. At that time, each large park in the system formed a team from the best players at each park and a park championship tournament was conducted at the end of the season. During the 1929 championship game at Dudley Park in South Nashville, a player for the Richland Park team hit the ball out of the park—literally. It landed on the head of a lady sitting on her porch across the street from the park. The Board members present naturally were concerned about liability, and they measured the distance, finding it to be 342 feet from homeplate to the edge of the porch. Rogers Caldwell then owned the Nashville Vols and took the hitter under his wing.[3]

Free movies and concerts at Centennial Park continued as they had since 1903 and expanded to include other parks in the system during the 1920s. Costello purchased projectors, rented films, and trucked the equipment from park to park each week; by 1932 movies were shown in fourteen city parks each week, and some were the new "talkies" with sound and music. Summer concerts in the parks were provided by S. S. Hughes and his Knights of Pythias Band at Hadley Park and by several bands at Centennial and Shelby parks. The Board then conducted summer concerts under competitive contracts, specifying that bands would present no less than two concerts weekly with no less than twenty-five musicians; and competition between bands directed by James Able, Gabriel Valdes, and Sydney Grooms was so fierce that rarely did the parks have concerts by the same band two summers in a row.[4]

At seven parks, the Board had indoor recreation centers in operation. The old houses and structures at Centennial, South, McFerrin, Morgan, Hadley, Lindauer, and Elizabeth parks had no gymnasiums or space suitable for active sports, but they served multiple purposes. Several had library rooms operated either as a branch of the public library or by a civic club; most were used for sewing classes or other sedentary adult recreation; and all furnished space for meetings by local community clubs. The fulltime playground supervisors—Martha Woolwine, Mignon Garfinkle, Lillian Hood, Myrtle Smith, Lillian McDowell, Mary Decker, and others—moved the children inside the houses during the winters, providing instruction in folklore and arts and crafts for the little ones. The Board in 1919 had employed Marie Ready as its first folk-dancing instructor and Anna Kennedy in 1922 as its instructor of community singing. At the request of people unable to afford them, the Board in 1923 purchased radios for use at community centers, and people in the communities gathered each evening to listen to the radio programs until the novelty faded or they bought their own receiver.[5]

The major addition to the park system's cultural arts program of the 1920s came as a result of Percy Warner's efforts. During frequent visits to New York city on business, he became acquainted with Walter Clark of the Grand Central Art Gallery and with a wealthy Tennessean who had collected paintings for many years. That Tennessean through Mr. Clark in 1927 offered to Mr. Warner to donate to Nashville's parks a collection of fine paintings then valued at $100,000 under two restrictions: the collection would be displayed in properly designed space in the Parthenon and would be named in honor of its donor, whose identity would not be revealed until after his death. Warner promptly accepted the gift, and the Board thereon awarded a contract to Foster & Creighton Company to renovate the Parthenon's basement to receive the collection. The collection of sixty-eight paintings was first displayed at Peabody College, then moved into the Parthenon in 1931, and it was a nearly priceless set of American art including works by George Innes.[6]

Nashville buzzed with speculation about the identity of the donor for several years, but the Board kept its promise and did not reveal his name until after his death in 1930. James M. Cowan, a Tullahoma native who entered the insurance business and retired as manager of the Northwest Mutual Company, had devoted much of his life to art, collecting thousands of paintings and founding several art museums in the Midwest. He told a member of his family he had given the collection to the Nashville park system because of the cordial reception given him when he visited the Parthenon during the 1897 Centennial celebration. Cowan was perhaps wiser than many others who have contributed their property to the park system, for he also left a $10,000 bequest in his will as a trust fund providing for permanent care of the James M. Cowan Memorial Art Collection.[7]

In 1929 the Park Board had an annual operating budget of $257,560 and also managed to retire $332,376 of the bonds and debts it had incurred for park acquisition and restoration of the Parthenon. Those figures were not again reached until 1941. Park tax and streetcar revenues declined in 1930 and fell precipitously in subsequent years, reflecting the onset of the Depression. Businesses closed their doors, banks failed, and the financial empire controlled by Board members Rogers Caldwell went down with the rest in 1930. The Park Board lost no funds in the collapse, for it had invested the proceeds of its bonds in land and park improvements, nor did the purchasers of the bonds suffer loss because their repayment was pledged against future park tax receipts which went on as scheduled until 1957. While it had funds on deposit in Caldwell's Fourth and First National Bank, it eventually recovered those funds and suffered no loss other than inconvenience while a bank reorganization was completed.[8]

Many Tennesseans blamed Rogers Caldwell personally for the financial hardships they suffered after 1930, and Caldwell retired from business and public life, resigning from amny organizations and from the Park Board on March 3, 1931. The Board elected Cornelius A. Craig, the insurance executive who had donated lawn swings to the park system in 1903, as Caldwell's successor. After many years of litigation, Tennessee state government, which had lost funds in the financial debacle of 1930, took Caldwell's assets and converted his Brentwood Hall estate into the Ellington Agricultural Center. A half century later, the Park Board opened the William Whitfield Park on the old Caldwell estate near the Ellington Agricultural Center. Had he known of it, Park Commissioner Caldwell would have been pleased.[9]

Because business failures reduced tax revenues, the park system received thousands less in taxes during the early 1930s, and because the unemployed no longer rode streetcars to work, revenue from that source declined from $63,587 in 1929 to $44,480 in 1932. The Park Board was forced to slash its operating budget by a third, and it was unable to accept an offer made by Commissioner Brown in 1932. As manager of the Tennessee Electric Power Company, J. P. W. Brown had acquired control of the Glendale Park and Zoo. Streetcar fares had financed that park, and when they declined the park had become unprofitable. Such public distress greeted his announcement that the park would close that Brown offered to donate the zoo to the city and lease the park to the Board for a dollar a year, but at a Board meeting, from which Brown recused himself, it rejected the offer. The Commissioners explained that operating the park would create a new fiscal obligation at a time when revenues were declining, and they did not wish to burden citizens with an additional tax to finance it. Zookeeper Clare Lovett sadly said goodbye to the pets, the famous Glendale Park closed at the end of 1932, and the land was subdivided and sold.[10]

To balance the budget, the Board in 1932 mandated a ten percent across-the-board pay cut for all employees from Superintendent down to summer help, and it followed that reduction with an even more painful twenty-five-percent wage reduction in 1933. Summer concerts in the parks ceased in 1932, over the objection of the city council, which resolved that musicians needed the work and that "good music played by trained and competent musicians, such as have always constituted our municipal bands, is not only excellent entertainment, but of fine cultural value and comports with the aesthetic values which the parks are supposed to contribute to the lives of our citizens." The Park Commissioners replied to that eloquent appeal by stating that it was in no position to fund concerts unless the city council were willing to appropriate money for the purpose. That ended the matter. Concerts in the parks did not resume until 1937, when the Nashville *Tennessean* began its sponsorship of organ concerts by Leon Cole.[11]

While the Park Board had few funds, neither did anyone else, and Nashvillians flocked into public parks in search of low-cost and free recreation wherever they could find it in the thirty-three parks and playgrounds open in 1933. In Centennial Park they enjoyed the Parthenon, Cowan collection, Japanese water garden, flowers, and fish and fowl at Lake Watauga. For small charges, they swam in the pools at Centennial and Shelby parks, or they splashed about for free at ten small wading pools at other parks. At little or no cost, they played on 31 tennis courts, 25 croquet courts, 34 horseshoe lanes, an archery range, 18 outdoor basketball courts, 15 baseball diamonds, 23 softball diamonds, 9 football fields, and 1 eighteen-hole and 2 nine-hole golf courses. Those attractions and others brought crowds of up to 30,000 people to the parks on Sundays during the early 1930s, meaning about one out of five Nashvillians were in the parks on those days. It was estimated that about two million Nashvillians visited the parks during 1934; there being only about 150,000 people in the city at the time, the figure meant that many returned for visits in the parks several times a year.[12]

Softball was the booming sport in the parks during the bust of the Depression, surpassing the popularity of baseball as amateur recreation. Devised as a modified form of baseball and at first given variant names such as recreation ball or mush ball, the game took on its official name with the organization of the Amateur Softball Association of America in 1933 which sponsored state, regional, and national softball tournaments to promote the sport. Softball swept

Nashville and the nation during the Depression, and by 1938 the national softball association claimed more members than any other amateur sports organization in the country. America by 1938 had about 8,000 formal softball diamonds in 800 towns with some 10 million players, and Nashville alone had 88 teams in the park leagues that year, not including school teams and informal teams playing wherever they could find an open space. Crowds of 6,000 spectators attended the Tennessee state softball championships conducted in Shelby Park in 1937 and 1938.[13]

Operating with restricted budget and personnel, the Park Board found it difficult to properly manage the mushrooming recreation program, and it was grateful when volunteer assistance was offered. It employed only twelve fulltime recreation leaders—the ten playground supervisors plus Superintendent Costello and golf pro C. E. Danis—and it therefore welcomed the formation of the Municipal Baseball Association in 1935 to manage baseball and softball programs. Association chairman W. McKinney Lynn and directors Will Cheek, Raymond Johnson, E. C. Faircloth, Vernon Sharp, Earl Wagner, Dick Lindsey, George Holloway, and Charles Knight met with Ewell Costello and the Park Board in February 1935 to explain they planned to organize twenty-four baseball and sixty softball teams on a budget of $4,000. They expected to collect $2,000 in membership fees and asked the Board to give $2,000 to make up the deficit. The Board not only approved the request, it also voted to install lights at diamonds in Centennial, Shelby, and Hadley parks for night games. Raymond Johnson and subsequently Johnny Boguskie served as the Association's executives, coordinating the sports program and conducting the umpire schools, and the program exceeded their expectatiuons, fielding 194 softball and baseball teams with 5,000 players during the first season. When James Shane organized a similar softball association for black teams at Hadley Park and elsewhere, the Board also contributed funding toward the expenses of that association.[14]

The game of softball became a summer obsession in the city during the Depression, and it was to continue as such during the following half century; local radio stations even broadcast play-by-play accounts of the Saturday games during the late 1930s. The municipal softball league initially included eight loops or circuits: the Capitol Loop which was the strongest; the Closed Industrial Circuit in which the players worked for the sponsoring companies; the Open Industrial Loop which permitted players from outside the sponsoring companies; the Civic Club circuit sponsored by Kiwanis, Rotary, and other clubs; the Girls Loop; the Junior Boys Circuit; the Church Circuit; and the Slow Pitch league. Some remarkable teams played in those circuits, notably the Hoover Motor Truck team which won state championships in 1943 and 1944. Johnny Hunter, the blazing pitcher for Hoover who once pitched four shut-outs in a single day of a state tournament, has been called the greatest softball player Nashville ever produced, but that was in 1943 and the city has since produced many other players with talent, not to mention blinding speed on the mound.[15]

Changes in several other sports during the 1930s deserve mention. As automobiles replaced horses for local transport, the popularity of one of Nashville's pioneer sports—horseshoe pitching—began to dwindle; the time was coming when one could no longer pick up the principal apparatus of the game from the streets and had to buy them, and eventually the game was to entirely disappear from the park system. The popularity of croquet also diminished; it was increasingly considered a game for senior citizens and in the park system tended to focus upon the courts in Centennial Park where an active croquet club sponsored the games. The interest in archery, practiced informally in the parks since 1903, retained its historic level, and in 1932 the Board granted permission to Professor A. C. Webb of Duncan School to open an archery range in Percy Warner Park, which was done without cost to the park system. Every autumn, boys and young men gathered in open spaces in the parks for friendly and otherwise games of football, and by 1934 the system had nine fields specifically set aside for the game. That autumn, the Board appropriated $400 to purchase footballs, lime the fields, erect goal posts, and pay referees of a new municipal football league. Baseball, which had been the most popular team sport during the early part of the century, declined in the face of the growing interest in softball.[16]

Frank Pickens, who became the park horticulturist during the Depression, recalled that during the winters of the 1930s the park maintenance force spent the winters sawing up fallen trees, which were loaded on city trucks for distribution as firewood to people unable to afford heat. Budget restrictions meant the system was unable to replace worn out maintenance equipment, and when Pickens began work in 1932 the sole equipment owned by the Board consisted of one truck, two Model-T cars, and eighteen mule teams, which proved totally inadequate to handle the disasters which struck the system in 1933. The Shelby Park barn and mule stable burned that year, and on March 14 a tornado swept through East Nashville, killing seven, injuring twenty-five, ripping the roofs off the community centers in the parks and covering the parks with fallen trees. It was more than a year before the park system budget permitted the maintenance force to clean up after the twister.[17]

In 1936 the Board sought to further reduce operating expenditures by reorganizing the park patrol. It then had seventeen patrolmen, eight of whom were permanently stationed at smaller parks where they performed routine maintenance in addition to their policing functions. Suprintendents George Moulder and Ewell Costello recommended, over the strenuous objection of Chief William C. Scott, that patrolmen serve only at Centennial, Shelby, Warner, and Richland parks, dispensing with patrolmen at the smaller parks; the city police department had acquired radio-equipped automobiles and the superintendents reasoned that city police could reach the small parks within five minutes after a call for help from a playground supervisor. The Board tried that as an experiment, laying off or transferring the patrolmen to maintenance, but soon abandoned the idea and recalled the patrolmen to duty. Play supervisors could not be armed, and they encountered several desperate situations; it became evident, moreover, that the mere presence of the patrolmen deterred vandalism in which children of even the best families of the community sometimes indulged as a prank. Many years later, publisher John Siegenthaler admitted that as a child he had frequently climbed the statue of John Thomas near the Parthenon to decorate it in some ludicrous fashion.[18]

Under financially straitened circumstances, the Board dropped all plans for acquiring large parks ringing the city as recommended in 1926 by the professional planning consultants and by Percy Warner, and in fact it acquired no new parks at all from 1930 through 1933. When a committee composed of James Napier, Henry Boyd, W. J. Hale, Calvin McKissack, James Roberson, L. S. Headen, and D. W. Crutcher asked the Board in 1932 to purchase a new park for the black community in East Nashville, the Board replied it could not afford to do so. It gave the same response to a delegation of white citizens headed by Judge John H. DeWitt and Howard Ansley who requested the purchase of a new park in the Waverly-Belmont community as replacement for the defunct Glendale Park.[19]

When the funding situation improved in 1934, however, the Board purchased two new parks for black communities in East and North Nashville. On Fite Avenue in East Nashville, it purchased seven acres, naming it the Fred Douglas Park. Available records do not identify the Fred Douglas for whom the park was named, and it is probable that the Board intended to honor black statesman Frederick A. Douglass, for many other black parks and schools throughout the nation were given his name. In 1934 the Board also purchased the first tract of Buena Vista Park at the intersection of McKinney Avenue and Buena Vista Pike in North Nashville. The park took its name from the pike and Buena Vista Springs, one of the early mineral spas in that vicinity; the name, which loosely translates as "good view," may originally have been a tribute to the American victory at the Battle of Buena Vista during the Mexican War.[20]

Two older North Nashville parks were converted to black parks during the mid-1930s, reflecting the changing character of the neighborhood. Because the Board of Education changed Head School at the corner of Watkins Park into a black school and planned the construction of Pearl High School, the Park Board designated Watkins Park as a black park. When the Fensterwald Settlement House adjacent to Ben Lindauer Park was transferred to leaders of the black community in 1937, at the recommendation of Commissioner Loventhal the Lindauer park was turned over to the settlement house leaders for use of the children at that house. Isaiah T. Creswell recalls that, because black citizens were forbidden to use "white parks," the transfer of Watkins and Lindauer parks along with the acquisition of Douglas and Buena Vista parks were "godsends" to the black communities around them.[21]

Two additional parks came into the system as gifts during the Depression. Mrs. William (Laura) Coleman in April 1935 gave in memory of her husband the ten-acre park at the intersection of Thompson Lane and Nolensville Road in South Nashville. Naming it William Coleman Park, the Board with federal funding assistance built a playground and ball diamond on the land and opened it to the public on June 11, 1939. The second gift came from Mayor Thomas

Cummings, who transferred an airfield to the Park Board in 1938 which the Board named McCabe Park in tribute to commissioner Charles McCabe who died in March 1939.[22]

The city in 1927 had purchased 131 acres of land now in McCabe Park to build the first municipal airport, called McConnell field in honor of Brower McConnell who died in the crash of a Tennessee Air National Guard plane that year; the airfield runways were to become the site of the McCabe golf course. With Works Progress Administration labor and federal funding, the city in 1938 was building Berry Field, a larger municipal airport near Donelson, and Mayor Thomas Cummings met with the Board to propose the exchange of the McConnell airfield for Clifton Park in West Nashville where the city wished to build a new school and for part of South Park where city government administrative offices eventually would be located. The Board made the trade with Mayor, giving up 26 acres at Clifton and South parks in exchange for the 131 acres of McCabe Park. Mayor Cummings subsequently transferred an additional 57 acres once occupied by the Municipal Children's Home to McCabe Park, and through purchase the Board expanded the McCabe Park area to 209 acres.[23]

The loss of park revenues during the Depression years disrupted and hampered park programs, but did not bring them to a halt. Through operational and wage reductions, the Park Board managed to maintain a balanced budget and even to expand its recreational services at minimum costs to serve the growing number of Nashvillians flocking into the parks as the alternative to more expensive recreation activities. Service expansion generally was accomplished through cooperative efforts between the Board and groups of volunteer citizens, who organized softball and baseball leagues, football leagues, golf tournaments, and other sports activities. The acquisition of additional park land ceased during the financial crisis of the early 1930s, then resumed in 1934 and by the end of the Depression the system had four new parks—Douglas, Buena Vista, Coleman, and McCabe parks. Except indirectly in the case of McCabe Park, none of the new parks were acquired with federal funding assistance, but beginning in 1933 federal funding was pumped into structural and physical improvements at practically all parks in the system.

10 FEDERAL ASSISTANCE BEGINS

Every May up to forty thousand Nashvillians crowd Percy Warner Park to enjoy the most spectacular sporting and social event of the year, the running of the Iroquois Memorial Steeplechase. The rolling green Harpeth Hills surrounding the course become literally hills of humanity gathered to watch superb horses and skilled amateur riders in colorful silks risk their necks at eighteen hazardous jumps along the three-mile steeplechase run. Some spectators perhaps take more interest in fashions worn by the people in the box seats than in the races, for the race also is a gala social occasion, a day-long party marking the azimuth of Nashville's green spring season and raising substantial amounts of money for charitable purposes. Nearly a half century of time and the beauty and excitement of the race have obscured its controversial origin during the depths of the Depression when the man who approved the course construction and the agency which built it were roundly condemned by Congress for undertaking the project. The steeplechase course and related facilities were initially constructed by the Works Progress Administration with federal work-relief funds, and it became the first and only racetrack ever built by the federal government. The steeplechase course and race remains one of the most visible results of the first federal assistance granted to Nashville's park system in an effort to get Nashvillians off welfare rolls and back to work.

During the first thirty years of municipal park operations in Nashville, the city's taxpayers, streetcar riders, and public-spirited citizens funded and developed the park system largely without state or federal assistance of any sort. Postmaster Andrew W. Wills in 1901 had permitted the Park Board to use the lawn at the Federal Customs House as tiny Federal Park, but that park had disappeared when wings were added to the Customs House in 1917 and the park system had enjoyed no further federal aid until President Franklin D. Roosevelt took office in 1933. Elected on a pledge to put the unemployed back to work, President Roosevelt acted to fulfill that promise as soon as he took office in March 1933. By April, Davidson County like local governments throughout the nation had received funds from the Reconstruction Finance Corporation to employ destitute men on road and public works projects. A portion of those funds were allotted to park improvement tasks, using labor supplied by the Tennessee Transient Bureau headed by Lewis P. Lindsay. Nashville at the time was overrun with hobos and vagrants who were riding the rails or walking from town to town in search of handouts or jobs of any sort, and it became the task of the Transient Bureau to get them off the streets. Through cooperation between that Bureau and the Park Board, two camps opened in the parks to temporarily house homeless men. The two hundred men camping in Buena Vista Park were put to work building playgrounds and athletic fields in that park and at Elmington Park on West End Avenue. Another transient camp at Morton B. Howell Park in South Nashville completely reconditioned that park—part of the old University of Nashville campus—and it was rededicated to the public on June 7, 1935, with ceremonies conducted by Chancellor R. B. C. Howell, a son of the man for whom the park was named.[1]

The following December the Federal Emergency Relief Administration (FERA), headed locally by J. A. Cayce and D. W. Eagan, took men out of the souplines at Nashville's churches and charities to put them to work in the parks. During 1934, the FERA built additional golf links in Shelby Park, started grading—mostly with pick and shovel—new scenic drives through Warner Park, and initiated planning for the restoration of Fort Negley, the Union Army fort atop St. Cloud Hill which the Park Board had purchased in 1928. Records of the Union Army were scoured for plans and photographs of the fort as it had existed during the Civil War, new plans for its reconstruction were drafted, and stone quarries were opened to obtain materials for its building. Though President Roosevelt's advisor Harry Hopkins continued to head the agency, in July 1935 it was renamed the Works Progress Administration and its work-relief efforts expanded.[2]

The acronym of the Works Progress Administration, WPA, was loosely translated by those who opposed federal work-relief programs to mean "We Piddle Around." That caustic sobriquet had justification, for the men thus employed were unskilled, or rather they were skilled but had lost their jobs as accountants, actors, coopers, teachers, and bankers and those skills did not prepare them for construction work. "The men would line up by the hundreds in the cold, before daylight, to work," observed the head of the WPA in Nashville, adding: "A lot of them were bookkeepers and the like and the blisters on their hands would break and bleed."[3]

The work-relief program involved federal reimbursement of the wages of labor, while local agencies such as the Park Board furnished the necessary tools and materials; and the local agencies often had scant funds to carry out their end of the bargain. Superintendent Ewell Costello recalls that when the work-relief program began the Park Board lacked the funds to furnish all the tools needed. He thus found himself with two complete working crews on some jobs but only a single set of tools, and he worked one crew for an hour then sat them aside while the second crew put in its hour on the end of the shovels. That necessarily involved considerable "piddling around," but more tools soon were acquired and the WPA undertook many park improvements of both ephemeral and enduring value.[4]

In July 1935 the FERA projects were rewritten as WPA projects and placed under the direction of Colonel Harry Berry, who served both as administrator of all WPA projects in Tennessee and as immediate director of the projects in Davidson County. Colonel Berry had headed the First Tennessee Infantry which went to France in 1917 and the 115th Field Artillery and had been appointed State Highway Commissioner by Governor Henry Horton during 1928 and 1929. He made H. E. Richardson the WPA Engineer for Davidson County and E. P. Scales director of WPA work in the city park system.[5]

Two other alphabet agencies in addition to the WPA performed work in Nashville's parks though on a much smaller scale. the National Youth Administration (NYA), which provided work for young men and for students on summer vacation, served in urban areas the same purposes served in rural areas by the Civilian Conservation Corps; its principal accomplishment in the park system was the building of a playground and ball diamonds in Fort Negley Park at a cost of $12,769, of which the Park Board's share amounted to only $620. The Public Works Administration headed by Harold Ickes was a bureaucratic competitor of the WPA, and the Park Board applied to Ickes for funding to construct swimming pools and recreation centers. Though the Park Commissioners went to Senator Kenneth McKellar in efforts to shake the funding loose from Ickes, their applications never were approved, and the principal PWA project of benefit to the park system apparently was the rock revetment placed along the bank of the Cumberland under direction of the U.S. Army Corps of Engineers to prevent portions of Shelby Park from caving into the river.[6]

At the outset of the work-relief program the overlapping authorities and responsibilities of the alphabet agencies created considerable confusion. Board Secretary J. Glenn Skinner, who succeeded John Lewis in 1931, and superintendents George Moulder and Ewell Costello often worked long into the nights preparing applications in triplicate for work-relief projects to submit to one or more of the federal agencies. After the initial shakedown phase, however, they ceased their efforts to secure assistance from agencies other than Colonel Berry's WPA because of that agency's more flexible requirements. WPA guidelines, for instance, allowed Ewell Costello to employ summer recreation leaders for the playgrounds with federal funding, on the sort of jobs that were not permitted by guidelines of the other agencies. He first secured WPA funding for his recreation program in 1936, hiring nineteen recreation leaders under the direction of Mrs. Marian W. Jones who supervised playground activities. The WPA recreation program continued at about that level until 1941, with the federal contribution toward playground supervision wages amounting to about $4,000 annually.[7]

Putting people to work for a basic wage of $21 a month, the WPA undertook throughout Davidson County and Tennessee a wide array of projects—armories, schools, roads, utility systems and similar public works predominantly. Renting equipment from construction contractor R. E. "Dick" Martin, the WPA began an immense earthmoving project near Donelson to create a new city airport. Completed in 1937 and named Berry Field in honor of the WPA administrator, it replaced McConnell Field in West Nashville, which Mayor Cummings transferred to the Park Board to become McCabe Park. At the peak of the work-relief effort in 1938, the WPA employed 40,000 Tennesseans, including 4,375 living in Davidson County and 790 employed on park improvement projects.[8]

Because WPA funds covered only labor costs, the Park Board, like other local sponsoring agencies, selected projects that were labor intensive, where the principal tools and materials it had to supply were shovels and dirt, holding local costs thereby to the minimum. Golf courses were ideal for the purpose, and WPA labor built golf courses at Shelby, Warner, and McCabe parks. A list of WPA projects in the park system would run several pages in length, but the work accomplished in 1936 alone will suffice as an illustration. At a total cost of $273,345, work was done that year in eighteen city parks. WPA labor installed playgrounds and outdoor basketball courts at Elizabeth, Watkins, Morgan, and Buena Vista parks, playgrounds and tennis courts in Shelby, Centennial, Hadley, and Richland parks, croquet and tennis courts at Napier, Dudley, Coleman, Edgehill, and Howell parks. Of the nearly $1 million expended on city park improvements from 1935 through 1938, the WPA supplied $729,590 as the wages for an average 600 workers annually while the Park Board spent only $190,344 for tools and materials.[9]

Because the new Warner parks surpassed the area of all other city parks combined, a major portion of the WPA work was done in those parks under the eye and indeed personal supervision of Edwin Warner. A list compiled by WPA Engineer E. P. Scales of the tasks accomplished in Warner parks included: 100 acres of picnic area cleared and graded; 12 wells dug and well houses constructed; 6 miles of macadam road built; 6 miles of hiking trails marked; 45 metal culverts installed; 15 rustic shelters, 36 picnic tables, and 18 privies built; playground equipment, a recreation building, a riding stable, 14 cottages and 3 stone entrances erected; 28,257 feet of stone retaining wall and 21,033 feet of guard rails placed; 15 acres of soil erosion control measures completed; and 1 monument, 1 golf course and clubhouse, and 1 steeplechase constructed. The Park Board for a brief moment thought all its financial difficulties had been solved when the WPA workers digging the wells struck natural gas which burned for a month; the Board ordered the wells dug deeper in the hope of striking oil but the effort failed.[10]

The WPA program provided the park system with its first facilities for boxing and indoor sports. While restoration of the elaborate Union Army fortification at Fort Negley was in progress, WPA workers also built the bleachers and six boxing rings where the Golden Gloves tournament was first conducted in Nashville. Blinkey Horn and Raymond Johnson of the Nashville *Tennessean* and wrestling promoter Jack Price Jones organized Nashville's Golden Gloves boxing competition—started by the *Chicago Tribune* in 1927—in 1937, providing boxing instruction at several city playgrounds and Saturday night bouts at the Fort Negley rings, culminating with the annual Golden Gloves tournament. The WPA also funded construction of the first gymnasiums for indoor recreation, using materials salvaged from the wreckage of old public buildings in the city. The first gymnasium in the park system, opened at Elizabeth Park on January 12, 1940, cost the Park Board only $7,736 for the tools used in its construction. The second gym opened in Dudley Park not long thereafter, and in those gyms Ewell Costello organized the first winter basketball recreation program in 1940.[11]

The WPA erected two monuments in the park system, one of which became politically controversial. At the request of the H. A. Cameron Post of the American Legion commanded by H. H. Walker, the Park Board approved a WPA project for the construction of entrance gates to Hadley Park as a memorial to black soldiers who had died in service to their country during the First World War. Designed by architects McKissack and McKissack, the Hadley Park stone entrance gates were completed by the WPA in 1938 and had on them lists of the names of black soldiers. Colonel Harry Berry in 1936 secured approval from the Board to build, entirely at WPA expense, a monument in Percy Warner Park at the site of "Camp Andrew Jackson" where the 115th Field Artillery (First Tennessee Regiment) had assembled in 1917 to prepare for service in France. Completed at a cost of $2,497, the monument consisting of a huge boulder mounting memorial plaques drew the attention of a committee of Congress. The committee objected to full federal funding for the monument and ridiculed it as a monument built to himself by Colonel Berry, who had commanded the 115th. The monument was described as a "crowning case of boondoggling" by the WPA, but the investigation was made after the fact and the monument still stands.[12]

As the sole racetrack ever constructed by the federal government, the Warner Park steeplechase also attracted Congress's attention. After the WPA built a stable in 1936 to shelter horses rented for riding in the park, Marcellus Frost, a riding enthusiast, suggested to Edwin Warner that a steeplechase course could be an excellent addition to the park's recreational attractions. Colonel Berry first rejected the idea as an inappropriate use of federal tax money, but Frost, Mason Houghland, John Sloan, and Henry Hines formed the Volunteer State Horseman's Association, offering to manage steeplechase races if the track were constructed and winning support for their idea from publishers Silliman Evans of the *Tennessean* and James Stahlman of the *Banner*. The group brought noted racing enthusiast William DuPont of Delaware, who had designed several steeplechase tracks, to Nashville, and he pronounced the natural amphitheatre site of the proposed track at Warner Park the best of its sort in the nation. By 1938, the WPA workers in the park system were running out of earth-moving projects of the sort suited to their abilities, and Colonel Berry reversed his earlier decision. At a meeting with Edwin Warner, he offered to furnish not only the labor needed to build the track but also the necessary drainage pipe, cement, and explosives, thereby reducing the cost to the Park Board. Under those conditions, the board voted on August 11, 1938, to proceed with the steeplechase course.[13]

WPA workers cleared and graded the course, building a 1.5 mile track with nine hazardous jumps, together with related structures including 156 box seats capable of seating 936 people. By the time the committee of Congress investigated the project, it had been completed at a cost of about $42,000, and the committee could do nothing other than ridicule the project as welfare for the rich and protest that it should have been built for half the cost. Criticism of the steeplechase and of WPA work in general did not perplex Colonel Berry, who frankly admitted: "Sure you can say WPA was inefficient. We spent hundreds of thousands of dollars on jobs that didn't really need doing very badly. And the way we did a lot of jobs would make an efficiency expert pull his hair. But we put hungry Americans on the payroll. We helped save democracy for America. The WPA was 100 per cent efficient that way!"[14]

The Park Board subsequently constructed a practice steeplechase course nearby, expanded the box-seating, and leased the stables as a riding academy to concessionaries, starting with Roy Branham, succeeded by Osa English, Elizabeth Kittell, John Fowlkes and others during the following forty years. The Volunteer State Horseman's Association assumed management of the annual steeplechase races, using proceeds from the rental of box seats and from concessions to furnish prizes for the race winners and the balance as a contribution to charity. Until 1985, spectators outside the box-seating area enjoyed the races without charge.[15]

Although steeplechase races grew out of the English, rather than the Tennessee, sport of fox hunting, in which riders followed the hounds, jumping any fences or obstructions encountered during the chase, the steeplechase was traditional in Tennessee years before the Warner track was constructed. The Harpeth Hills Hunt Club ran steeplechases on a field near Old Hickory Boulevard and Granny White Pike during the 1920s; Rogers Caldwell and John Branham organized the Southern Grasslands steeplechase on a preserve near Gallatin in 1930 and 1931, and in 1937 Mason Houghland ran steeplechase near Brentwood. Many skilled amateurs therefore were anxious to participate when the first race was conducted at Warner Park in 1941.[16]

Naming the main event the Iroquois Memorial race after a Belle Meade plantation horse which won the English Derby in 1881, the Volunteer State Horseman's Association held the first formal steeplechase races at Warner Park on May 10, 1941. Some 40,000 Nashvillians gathered at track side to watch a children's pony race, a mule race, a flat race, a short steeplechase race, and the Iroquois Memorial Steeplechase of three miles and eighteen jumps, the prizes being silver cups at first, to which cash awards later were added. When word came that Barbara Bullit of Louisville astride Rockmayne had won the first Iroquois Memorial in 5 minutes, 41 and $\frac{2}{5}$ seconds, Colonel Harry Berry gleefully declared: "Considering the fact that the Iroquois course was condemned by a minority report in Congress, it had a big day today, Tally Ho!"[17]

As the national Depression ended, funding for WPA work-relief projects declined, and the employees of the WPA searched for other work, one of them serving briefly as Superintendent of Parks. When park personnel were added to the municipal civil service program, qualifying them for pensions, Superintendent George Moulder retired at the end of 1938. The Park Board employed M. U. Snoderly, a WPA engineer with whom they had worked closely, as Moulder's successor, but Snoderly returned to federal service in April 1939 and Commissioner Edwin Warner then became Superintendent of Parks, serving without pay until the Board selected Ewell Costello to be its General Manager.[18]

Deaths and threats of revenue reductions seriously disrupted the park system's management from 1939 to 1941. When Charles McCabe died in 1939, the Board elected James G. Stahlman as his successor and Edwin Warner as its new chairman. That loss was followed in 1940 by the deaths of Commissioners Lee Loventhal and J. P. W. Brown. Loventhal had been the spokesman on the Board for minority rights since 1916, and the Board paid tribute to him by installing a memorial fountain in Hadley Park with funds given for the purpose by Mrs. Loventhal. Brown was sorely missed because he headed the Tennessee Electric Power Company from which the Board received considerable revenue, a funding source threatened at the time of his death by the Tennessee Valley Authority's purchase of the utility system and by the change from streetcars to buses for public transport. Vernon Tupper, president of the Nashville Rolling Mills, and Bascom Jones, head of the Tennessee Railroad Association, were elected as the successors to Loventhal and Brown.[19]

The Tennessee Valley Authority's purchase of the Tennessee Electric Power Company menaced park system revenues for several reasons. Because TVA was a tax-free government agency, the Board estimated it would lose about $9,000 of its prorata share of property taxes formerly paid by the private utility company. The company in addition had supplied electric power to the park system without charge, and the Board estimated it would be required to pay TVA about $6,000 annually for lighting the ball diamonds and other electric services. TVA, moreover, had purchased only the electric utility system, and the streetcar and public transport system had gone to another firm, which immediately reduced streetcar fares to regain riders lost to automobiles and which planned to convert from streetcars to buses. Reduced streetcar fares cost the Board $5,000 of its revenue in 1939, and the board was not certain it would be legally entitled to collect a percentage of the fares collected from buses as it had from the streetcars.[20]

In view of those financial troubles and declining funding for WPA projects, the Board slashed its budgets for 1939 and 1940 by $17,000, placing Manager Ewell Costello in a difficult bind, for with the addition of park personnel to the municipal civil service an increase in their wages had also been mandated to contribute to the city pension plan. Costello undertook a reorganization of park system personnel to reduce expenditures. When carpenter foreman A. C. Mitchell died, as an example, Costello made plumber foreman John Fuller also the foreman of the carpenters. He ordered the park patrolmen keeping order at the free movies to also run the projectors, and when they refused he, with full approval of the Board, laid off five patrolmen with the least seniority and abolished the position of patrol chief, transferring chief W. C. Scott to Shelby Park as superintendent of maintenance there. He also made J. H. Allen maintenance superintendent at the Warner parks and Frank Pickens the superintendent of maintenance at other parks in the system.[21]

Through conferences with Mayor Thomas Cummings, Park Commissioner C. A. Craig ended the Board's fiscal crisis of 1940. While TVA was not subject to municipal taxes, the Nashville Electric Service formed to manage the municipal power distribution system was, and Mayor Cummings agreed to give to the park system its share of those taxes, accomplishing it by amending the state law governing the parks. Legal interpretations subsequently granted to the Park Board the same percentage of bus fare receipts that it had collected from the streetcar company. With those favorable decisions, the fiscal difficulties ended in 1941, when park system revenues climbed to $287,606, surpassing the previous record set in 1929 and marking the end of the Depression.[22]

The WPA of the Depression often merited the criticisms it received, but the federal assistance it provided to the park system of Nashville and of other cities throughout the nation proved vital to continued park improvement and recreation programs at a time when those cities lacked revenues for the purpose. Nationally, the WPA and other federal work-relief agencies completed 12,348 park and recreation projects, built 3,267 social and recreational buildings, and employed about 49,000 people in park recreation programs. In Nashville, WPA efforts created golf courses at Shelby, Warner, and McCabe parks, gymnasiums at Elizabeth and Dudley parks, and ball diamonds, tennis courts, playgrounds, and other facilities in the majority of the city parks, plus a reconstructed Union fort, several monuments, and a steeplechase course that was to become a lasting city tradition. The WPA accomplished its fundamental purpose of putting people back to work and it left a legacy that remains visible in the Nashville park system today.[23]

11 THE PARKS DURING WARTIME

As it had been eighty years earlier, Nashville during the Second World War was occupied by American troops, but most of the troops thronging through the city during the 1940s were considered friendly. When Congress approved the first peacetime military draft in 1940 and mobilization began at Camp Forrest near Tullahoma as elsewhere throughout the nation, troop trains began rolling through Union Station and all passengers trains carried soldiers on the move from one post to another. What initially was a trickle of uniformed men in 1940 and 1941 became a gusher in 1942 and 1943 with the construction of Camp Campbell and other military installations in Tennessee and the army maneuvers preparatory to overseas embarkation. During stopovers and on weekend passes, those soldiers crowded into the city parks, even sleeping under the trees, and by 1943 it seemed the parks had been commandeered by the military, not only providing recreation for the troops but also being pressed into service for combat training and food production.

At the outset of the war in Europe, the Park Board made several decisions indicating its full support for national defense. When James G. Stahlman resigned from the Board to become a navy commander, his colleagues refused to accept his resignation, deciding to leave his chair vacant until he returned, and they extended that policy to all park personnel, advising them that if they volunteered for service in the armed forces their jobs would be awaiting their return. With the approval of the Board, community sewing clubs at the park recreation centers worked to produce "Bundles for Britain," clothing for Britons who had lost everything in the Nazi bombing raids. They also decided to prepare for war in accordance with advice they received from Secretary J. Glenn Skinner. Skinner in 1941 while writing the fortieth anniversary history of the park system learned that in 1918 the system had lost shrubs, flowers, and plants worth thousands because a war-related coal shortage had prevented heating the greenhouses, and the Board therefore ordered that sufficient coal be purchased and stockpiled in 1941 to heat the greenhouses during 1942 and 1943.[1]

So many servicemen were passing through the city and using the parks by the summer of 1941 that the Army decided it needed a post in the city for their use and for military police detachment that would help city police and the park patrol maintain order; it requested the Board to lease for a dollar-a-year five acres of Centennial Park fronting on 23rd Avenue as a military camp. Secretary Skinner informed the Board that the courts in 1907 had decided it lacked authority under its state charter to lease park lands, but the Commissioners decided the national emergency required that they cooperate with military authorities. On those five acres, the Army Engineers installed electric and utility systems and quickly constructed several temporary mobilization-type buildings: two 100-foot long barracks, one eighteen-foot-square officer quarters, a recreation building, a large mess hall, an orderly building and two latrines. The camp was to serve as temporary resting area for troops passing through the city, as a "brig" for wayward soldiers, and as headquarters for the military police who would establish regular patrols of Centennial, Shelby, and smaller parks.[2]

Many servicemen on travel orders had stopovers in Nashville during which they explored the city, and on weekends soldiers by the busloads came in from Camp Forrest, Camp Campbell, and other installations. During the day they walked the city streets and enjoyed the parks, attending the free movies and concerts by Leon Cole and baritone John Lewis, but at night every lodging space in the city was filled to capacity. The troops slept wherever they could find a place to lie down, and that often was in the open air on park benches or under the trees. While the Army had places for them to clean up the following morning at Centennial Park, the Park Board constructed showers in Hadley Park for use by the black soldiers sleeping there.[3]

Groups of Nashvillians also organized to furnish at least minimum comforts for the servicemen. Downtown, where there were no parks, the First Presbyterian Church placed cots and blankets in its basement, and when the basement filled moved the overflow upstairs to sleep on the pews. Taking pity on the men sleeping in Centennial Park, businessman Joe Werthan opened a house to them on nearby Elliston Place, supplying them with showers, towels, razors, and coffee without charge. Some Saturday nights in 1943, he sheltered as many as 500 men in the house and its outbuildings, with the soldiers even sleeping atop the piano and ping-pong tables.[4]

In addition to the use of the parks by soldiers, the park programs and resources were affected in several other ways by the war. The Board dispensed with night ball games after Pearl Harbor, in part to conserve electric power but chiefly as cooperation with the civil defense "blackouts" then practiced as a precaution against potential enemy air raids. Because the armed services desperately needed walnut lumber for the manufacture of gunstocks, the Board approved the harvesting of walnut trees in the Warner parks. Commissioner C. A. Craig personally selected the trees for the purpose, which supplied thousands of board feet of walnut lumber for the defense effort.[5]

American efforts to feed the armies and the Allied nations resulted in food shortages by 1943, and the Board took several measures aimed at helping alleviate that shortage. To keep park concessionaire A. B. Catignani from going broke in the face of advancing prices, the Board permitted him to double the price of popcorn and peanuts from a nickel to a dime a bag. To increase the food supply, it allowed community organizations to plant "Victory Gardens" in several smaller parks and it returned the farm land in the Warner parks to production. Park maintenance workers and equipment during 1943 harvested at the Warner parks 5,000 bales of hay, 400 bushels of corn, and 11 tons of Irish and 7 tons of sweet potatoes. Farming in the Warner parks continued several years thereafter, the 1945 crops including 784 bushels of wheat, 1,843 bushels of barley, 238 bushels of corn, and 4,700 bales of hay. The crops provided more than enough fodder for the mules used for park maintenance and also contributed toward meeting the needs of hungry people in a war-torn world.[6]

When the army in late 1942 selected Middle Tennessee as the site for large-scale troop maneuvers to prepare them for the D-Day invasion and combat in France and Germany, it again called on the Park Board for some assistance. As a contribution to the success of those maneuvers, the Board leased to the army for a dollar a year honorarium the Buena Vista Park in North Nashville near the point where the army practiced crossing the Cumberland River as advance training for its future crossings of the Rhine and other European waterways. It also granted permission to the Army Ferry Command to use the Centennial and Shelby Park swimming pools at dawn each morning before the pools opened to the public to train soldiers in the proper inflation and handling of rubber assault boats.[7]

In addition to soldiers, defense workers and their families streamed into the city to construct military installations and to work in the industries producing such military supplies and equipment as the Vultee bomber, and the children of those families placed added burdens on the park system's recreation programs. Assistance from the WPA ceased in 1942, but the need was met by a 1943 act of the state legislature establishing the "whiskey and wine fund," providing that all fees collected from liquor licenses in the city would be placed in a separate account to be used exclusively as funding for the operation of playgrounds and recreation centers. With proceeds from that fund, the Board during the summer of 1943 employed more recreation leaders and opened thirteen new playgrounds on vacant lots throughout the city, including one at the Army Classification Center in Berryhill, where families of soldiers were temporarily lodged in barracks without a single playground for their children. Collected for many years after the war, the "whiskey and wine fund" continued to finance summer playground recreation and nudged the park system's budget in 1945 to $348,000, for the first time exceeding $300,000.[8]

In 1943 the Board granted permission to the U.S. Coast Guard and the Army Engineers to moor their fleets at landings along the Shelby Park riverfront. The Coast Guard was patrolling the Cumberland to prevent sabotage to navigation structures and to maintain aids to navigation, while the Nashville District of the Corps of Engineers was keeping the river's channel clear for use by commercial boats and by the military craft manufactured at Nashville Bridge Company. At the end of the war, the Board also granted permission for the Eighth Naval District to lease an acre of Meredith's Grove in Shelby Park for the construction of a U.S. Naval Training Center. Commander J. E. Ward of the Navy's Organized Surface Battalion No. 6-24 announced in 1949 that the reserve center, uniquely designed with concrete walls resembling the prow of a ship, was completed.[9]

Near the end of the war, the Park Board cooperated with the Thayer General Hospital and the Army Convalescent Center in organizing recreation programs for the returning wounded veterans. It granted the hospitals permission to use park swimming pools to supply the veterans with their morning exercise without charge. At the request of medical authorities, it also granted the veterans use of park golf courses without charge as contribution toward their health and early recovery. This cooperative program apparently originated the Board's custom, since continued, of granting free or reduced charge use of park recreation facilities to disabled veterans.[10]

Many park employees joined the armed services during the war and the Board was unable to find even temporary help to replace them because it could not afford to pay wages that would compete with those paid at defense plants and military construction jobs. For that reason, and because some of its personnel were needed to raise the crops in the Warner parks, park maintenance needs were neglected during the war years. Park superintendent Frank Pickens, a professional landscape gardener from Louisiana, and greenhouse foreman Z. N. Dobbs were the only two gardeners left in the system in 1945, and they faced the immense task of restoring the floral displays then occipied by the ruins of Victory cabbage patches. War-time neglect had also ruined the Japanese water garden in Centennial Park, so Pickens and Dobbs drained it and began filling and planting the site, initiating its conversion into the colorful Sunken Garden that now occupies the site. To speed the annual grass cutting job, Pickens replaced mule-drawn mowers with three gangmowers pulled by tractors, which permitted three tractor operators to mow all parks in the system every eight days, performing what had once been a fulltime job every summer for seventeen men behind thirty-four mules. That freed more personnel for assignment to the Centennial Park greenhouses, which supplied the entire system with bulbs, plants, and shrubs, and to maintaining the 169 flowerbeds then in the parks along with the benches, structural repairs, and thousand other tasks required for proper park maintenance.[11]

Pickens, Dobbs, and their maintenance personnel gradually restored the parks to their prewar condition during the late 1940s, but could not restore the Centennial Athletic Field entirely until the army ended its lease of its recreation camp and military police post. It required several years for the Board to reach a settlement with the army because it insisted that the army should restore the land to its original condition before abandoning the camp. Not until 1948 was a final agreement signed, whereby the Board undertook to restore the area of the camp as a part of the park in return for a payment of $593 for performing the work.[12]

Fully occupied by the exigencies of operating a park system under crowded wartime conditions, the Board had made no effort to further expand the number of parks during the emergency. It did acquire one small playground as part of a bargain struck with Robert Lawrence, Director of Public Works for the city. In return for permission to use Morgan Park as a polling place during elections, Lawrence turned over to the Board a lot at the corner of Division Street and Sixteenth Avenue. The Board named the lot Tony Rose Park in honor of a well-known musician and band leader, purchased an adjoining lot to increase the park area, and with proceeds from the Whiskey and Wine Fund opened a playground there in 1943.[13]

The Board purchased its first park in nearly a decade at the end of the war in 1945, acquiring for $50,328 the twenty-four-acre estate of Granville Sevier called Sunnyside at Kirkwood Avenue and Granny White Pike. State historian Stanley Horn took great interest in the park, because the mansion had been the home of Mrs. Jesse Benton, wife of a Nashville pioneer who had once fought a memorable brawl with General Andrew Jackson on the Public Square and also the sister-in-law of Thomas H. Benton who had represented both Tennessee and Missouri in Congress. During his study of the mansion, Horn observed bullet marks in the building as visible evidence that it had stood in the thick of the 1864 Battle of Nashville, along with log structures at the rear of the mansion which local tradition said had served as French trading posts with the Indians, which if true would have made them the oldest structures in the city.14

Colonel Granville Sevier, the last occupant of the mansion, was a retired army officer and world traveler who had furnished the mansion with antiques and curios collected during his travels, and Stanley Horn therefore asked the board to lease the house to the Tennessee Historical Society as its office. Legal complications prevented leasing the mansion to the Society, so the Board auctioned off the furnishings and moved maintenance foreman John Fuller and John "Jack" Spore, the new Superintendent of Recreation, into the mansion to protect it from vandalism. Naming the park in honor of Granville Sevier, the Board had playgrounds, tennis courts, and picnic shelters built and subsequently added a small swimming pool and other recreation facilities.15

General Manager Ewell Costello had supervised the park recreation program during the war years with part time and seasonal assistance, but at the end of the war the Board employed a new Superintendent of Recreation, the lively John "Jack" Spore, who held a degree in health and physical education from Peabody College. He also was a founder of the Tennessee Recreation Society, an Ohio Valley Conference referee, and an official with the American Amateur Softball Association. A Nashville native, he spent his childhood in Centennial Park, and when he first called the playground supervisors together in 1946 to plan a postwar recreation program, Martha Woolwine, supervisor at Centennial Park for many years, warned him: "I raised you on the playground; don't you tell me how to run one!" She and the other playground supervisors were fiercely independent people, who maintained order on the playgrounds chiefly through the force of their personalities, rarely needing the whistles they wore around their necks to call for help fro the patrolmen.16

Jack Spore moved his family into an apartment in the Sunnyside Mansion at Sevier Park, and in 1948, when the Board's Centennial Park administrative office—then merely an old house—became overcrowded, he moved the Recreation Department headquarters out to Sevier Park into the ground floor of Sunnyside. As an organizer of the statewide park and recreation association for professional park managers, Spore often traveled to the association meetings, and he recalls with amusement the first time he met with Park Commissioner James Stahlman to request advance approval for his travel expenses. After examining the expense voucher critically, Stahlman gruffly told him: "You will represent the City of Nashville at this meeting. Take this voucher back to the office and add more money to it so you can properly represent this great City!"[17]

As recreation superintendent, Spore faced quite a challenge during the postwar years. American workers during the Depression had been reduced to forty-hour work weeks and had received more paid holidays and vacations, providing them with more leisure time for recreation. During the war, average salaries and wages had advanced to the point that even workers at the lower end of the pay scale could afford some sports equipment and an automobile to take them and their families into the parks, which they did in ever increasing numbers. Spore reported in 1946 the children of the city had visited the playgrounds 611,677 times, that 214,300 people attended the 142 showings of free movies in the parks, 52,614 toured the Parthenon, 15,000 spectators watched the weekly boxing matches, and 45,000 listened to Leon Cole at the organ in Centennial Park. In addition, baseball, softball, tennis, golf, and croquet games and tournaments had attracted untold numbers of participants and spectators. The experiences of servicemen during the war had clearly demonstrated the value of the ability to take care of oneself in water, and in 1946 the Nashville Red Cross with sponsorship from the *Nashville Banner* initiated their annual "Learn to Swim" programs at pools in the park system and elsewhere. Including the learners, about 128,000 people swam in the park pools during 1946.[18]

Several features were added to the park recreation program during the immediate postwar years. The Miniature Air Meet Association began flying model planes in competitive contests on a field near the Warner Park steeplechase in 1946; model planes had been flown in the parks before 1941, but during the war the armed services had sponsored model plane design contests to better acquaint the young people of Nashville and elsewhere with aviation. At the request of fly and bait casting enthusiasts, the Board ordered the construction of a casting pier in Lake Watauga at Centennial Park in 1947, and Mid-South Casting Tournament was first conducted that September from the pier, using hookless bait, the object being not to catch fish but to land the bait inside hoops floating on the lake at various distances from the pier.[19]

Jack Spore in 1947, as a climax of the summer playground recreation program, initiated playground competition days and an intercity rivalry with the park systems of Columbia and Memphis. In late August, children who were the champions of their playgrounds gathered at Centennial and Hadley parks, where they competed in tennis, horseshoes, baseball, softball, and other playground activities. The Board sent the city champions aboard chartered buses to Memphis and Columbia to compete against the playground champions in those cities. The following year, champions from Memphis and Columbia came to Nashville, establishing a cooperative intercity competition that was to continue more than a decade until the state recreation association organized state championship tournaments.[20]

By the late 1940s, the park system had golf courses open in four parks: the eighteen-hole links at Shelby and McCabe parks, the little Riverview course at Shelby, a nine-hole course at Warner Park, with another nine-hole course at McCabe and an eighteen-hole course at Warner Park on the drawing boards. In 1947, 148,992 nine-hole rounds of golf were played in the parks at thirty cents a round. The system's first golf pro, C. E. Danis, moved from Shelby to McCabe Park, while Luther Hickman took over golf management at Shelby and A. J. Shively managed the Warner course. Hickman introduced golf carts to the game in Nashville in 1955, and he was one of the few people who knew the identity of the "Lone Golf Ranger," who rode from course to course, checking tickets and cards to assure that no players had slipped onto the courses without paying the small fees that were charged.[21]

Efforts to improve cooperation between the Park Board and other municipal agencies began during the postwar years, largely as a result of a change in Board membership. When Chairman Edwin Warner died in 1945, the Board elected theater magnate Tony Sudekum as his successor, and when Vernon Tupper died the following year the Board elected William Hume, who also was chairman of the city's Board of Education and therefore in a position to assure improved coordination between school and park programs. The Park Board at the time wished to open new swimming pools in Hadley and South parks, but lacked the funds, while the Board of Education and the new Children's Museum association were interested in a joint development at South Park along the lines proposed by architect Edward Keeble and urged by Charles Hawkins, the director of the city planning commission.[22]

Founded in 1945 by a volunteer association led by Vernon Sharp, Jr., and with the assistance of Army Air Corps Sergeant John R. Forbes who was stationed in Nashville, the Children's Museum moved into a University of Nashville building near Howard School and South Park with Harry Vaughn as its first director and Mrs. W. W. Brockner as its first curator of education. A quasi-official association, the museum operated with both private contributions and funding from municipal government. The Park Board in 1946 contributed $2,500 toward the museum's annual budget, a figure which substantially increased in later years, and the museum in return sponsored field trips and environmental-ecological studies in the parks. The museum used materials from the parks to create natural history displays, in 1947, for instance, exploring an archaeological site at the McCabe golf course and preserving the artifacts for display in the museum.[23]

Commissioner William Hume brought all agencies interested in the South Park situation together at a February 1947 meeting, where Mayor Thomas Cummings, Planner Charles Hawkins, School Superintendent W. A. Bass, museum leader Vernon Sharp, and the Park Board entered into a mutual understanding. City government would give a playground area to the Park Board and the site of an athletic field to the Board of Education which would develop it for the use of Howard School in the winters and as part of the park system in the summers. Land back of the Children's Museum would be made available for museum use. The Board of Education would build a swimming pool at South-Howard on land donated for the purpose by the Park Board, and would then turn the pool over to the park system for operation and maintenance. South Park thereby became a multi-agency complex.[24]

Because the park system's facilities for indoor sports were entirely inadequate, Park Manager Costello and School Superintendent Bass agreed to a jointly operated evening recreation program, with the school system furnishing the gyms, utilities, and janitorial services and the park system supplying recreation equipment and paying the play leaders. That cooperative effort began at Cameron and Cavert schools in 1948 as a demonstration project, but budgetary problems in both the park and the school system brought the project to an end in 1950. Superintendent W. A. Bass, however, in 1951 turned over to the Park Board the old Eastland School building and property on Douglas Avenue in East Nashville, which the Park Board named Eastland Park, converting the building into an additional community recreation center. To meet its immediate need for more indoor recreation space, the Park Board during the early 1950s acquired several war-surplus Quonset huts and installed them in various parks to serve as gymnasiums for basketball and other winter sports programs.[25]

Board Secretary J. Glenn Skinner reported that 1948 marked the full recovery of the park system from the neglect that had occurred during the defense emergency of the early 1940s; in 1948, for the first time, park system revenues had surpassed the $400,000 mark. The son of a minister, Skinner had begun work for the park system in 1919 as assistant to Secretary John Lewis and had succeeded Lewis as Secretary in 1931. A superb bookkeeper of the old school, who wore a green eyeshade while posting entries in the ledgers by hand, Skinner ran his life by the clock and by the Book and faithfully served the Board for many years without incident until 1949 when he was embarrassed by an event at Lake Watauga.[26]

The ducks, geese, and fowl at Lake Watauga multiplied endlessly each year, and park personnel thinned the flock at Christmas, selling the birds to local produce dealers who retailed them as Christmas dinners; and it had become Skinner's custom to purchase some birds each year for his own table and as gifts to friends. Just before Christmas in 1949, Skinner asked a maintenance worker to bring him three birds, which he planned to give to a park employee who had twenty children. After chasing the birds around the lake and failing to catch them, the worker took a rifle and shot them. As it happened, a reporter from the *Tennessean* was in Centennial Park at the time, and on Christmas Eve he published a moving article deploring the slaughter. Red-faced, Skinner apologized to the Board, which then voted to reduce the size of the flock and donate each year's surplus to the city welfare department for charitable distribution. Mr. Skinner retired shortly thereafter and was succeeded by Bert Elmore, who had been his assistant since 1941.[27]

The postwar demobilization and recovery of Nashville's park system was completed by 1950, leaving little trace of the contributions made by the system and its personnel to national defense efforts. The parks contained four monuments to the veterans of the First World War, but only one has been placed in the parks in memory of the veterans of the Second World War. Placed at the Morgan Park ballfield by the North Nashville Men's Club, the monument bears a strikingly vigorous inscription: "To those boys of North Nashville who in life's early afternoon left the red wine of athletic competition for the red blood of war—to get a job done, this field is reverently dedicated, April 10, 1949." Perhaps in the future more gifts to the park system will be made in tribute to the servicemen of the Second World War, and when that time arrives it should be remembered that the parks also were mobilized in 1941, contributing their forest and soil resources to the effort, providing space for military installations and maneuvers, and offering recreation to tired, lonely, and wounded American soldiers and sailors.

12 PARKS IN THE WEST ADMINISTRATION

When Ben West succeeded Thomas Cummings as Mayor in 1951, the Park Board was celebrating its golden anniversary of fifty years service to Nashville, and it took pride not only in its park management accomplishments but also in its independence from local politics, for not since 1901 had a Mayor appointed a member of the Board. With the election of Mayor West, however, the most troubled decade in the park system's history began, a decade marked by developing opposition within the black community to the segregated system, by sometimes vitriolic attacks upon the board by city councilmen who thought too much park funding was spent outside the city limits, and by a campaign led by Mayor West to curb the board's autonomy.

    The self-perpetuating feature of Board membership had long insulated the Board from petty politics, and the character of its unpaid membership had protected it from the fiscal scandals at times uncovered in other elements of municipal government. The board had become proud of its political independence, and under the leadership of chairmen James Stahlman and Edwin Crutcher during the postwar years it became positively intransigent toward its critics. When a councilman criticized the Board on the front page of the

Tennessean in 1947 for its spending on parks outside the city limits, the Board issued a demand that he attend its next meeting and on the morning of the meeting the Commissioners phoned him to extend personal invitations. The councilman caught a cold and could not attend. When, in another instance, a proposed city charter revision that would have reduced the Board's prerogatives was under consideration, the Commissioners unanimously revolved: "That this Board would consider any changes in the City Charter, dealing with the Park Board, or its authority, not only unnecessary, but undesirable and objectionable."[1]

While the Board sought to be responsive to all requests from city councilmen, a growing number of councilmen during the postwar years were disturbed by expenditures on parks located in Davidson County, whose residents contributed nothing toward park funding, because those outlays left less for park development within their districts. The most persistent critic of the Park Board was Councilman Charles Riley who represented South Nashville and who often attacked the Board for not properly attending to the park needs of his constituents. Members of the park staff learned that when Riley stood up at the council meetings and snapped his suspenders, the time had come for their weekly verbal chastisement. When Riley began one jeremiad by telling the council he was "going to give the park board hell," H. Sanders Anglea, presiding, told him it might be best if he said "remind" rather than "give 'em hell." Riley responded: "Why should I say I'm going to remind them when I'm going to give them hell?"[2]

In comparison with councilmen like Riley, the Park Board enjoyed a better relationship with leaders of Nashville's black community, though it too became increasingly tense. Isaiah T. Creswell, who subsequently became chairman of the Metropolitan Board of Education and served on the Park Board, recalls an especially acrimonious meeting with Board Chairman James Stahlman during the postwar years at which Stahlman essentially told the black delegation that they should be happy with the parks that they had. A philosophical division became apparent in Nashville's black community during the postwar years: one element of black leadership worked with the Board to secure more parks and facilities, while another element contended through litigation that segregated parks, no matter how plentiful and well tended, were inherently unequal and denigrating.[3]

Since 1932 the Board had met regularly with black delegations usually including J. T. Patton, I. T. Creswell, Rev. W. J. Faulkner, Dr. M. J. Bent, Dr. S. S. Morris, and D. W. Crutcher, with Crutcher normally serving as spokesman. Those leaders generally presented a list of park improvements needed in black parks and, though delays ensued while the Board sought funding, they often got what they requested. At a 1947 meeting with the Board, for instance, black leaders requested the Board to build a swimming pool and other improvements at Hadley Park, secure additional park space in North Nashville, and purchase Greenwood Park on Lebanon Road; and the Board honored all save one of those requests.[4]

Through cooperation with the Board of Education at Howard School, a swimming pool was opened in South Park, and the Park Board built in Hadley Park a swimming pool, a community center, and a bandshell. To add to North Nashville's park space, the city traded property in 1948 with Calvin McKissack, who was building the Preston Taylor Homes at the time. In exchange for other land, McKissack transferred to the Park Board land between the Preston Taylor Homes and the McKissack School, and at his request the Park Board named the new park in honor of R. H. Boyd, the head of the National Baptist Publishing House, the Citizens Savings Bank, and the *Nashville Globe*, then the city's black newspaper. The Reverend Preston Taylor had bequeathed the seventeen-acre Greenwood Park, complete with pool, picnic grounds, and ballpark, to his Disciples of Christ Church Convention, which planned to sell the land in 1949. At the requests of Nashville's black leadership, the Park Board considered purchasing the Greenwood Park, but found the cost exceeded its resources. Challenging black leadership, the Park Commissioners declared that if the black community could arrange the gift of Greenwood Park to the city system or negotiate a long-term lease, the park system would assume the costs of its continued operation, but suitable arrangements were not made and Greenwood Park closed permanently.[5]

Returning black veterans of the Second World War took greater interest in the game of golf, a game previously dominated by the white upper and middle classes, and efforts to secure public golfing facilities for black sportsmen during the postwar years highlighted the philosophical division in Nashville's black community, as represented by City Councilmen Robert Lilliard and Z. Alexander Looby.

Lilliard worked within the system to obtain a public golf course serving black golfers, and Looby worked without the system to obtain access for black players to all public links.

When black leaders requested a course be opened for the city's black golfers, the Board in 1950 asked the city council to transfer to the park system land in North Nashville near the Cumberland River that had been the site of a juvenile detention center and to appropriate the funds needed to build on it a golf course and clubhouse. Councilman Lilliard sponsored a bill in the council for the purpose and in 1953 secured more than a hundred acres of land and the $40,000 needed for its initial conversion into golf links. The conversion was rapidly accomplished and the golf course opened on July 10, 1954, with Joe Hampton as its first, and in 1985 still only, golf pro. Originally known as Cumberland Park, at the request of Councilman Lilliard it was renamed the Rhodes Golf Course in 1969, honoring Theodore "Ted" Rhodes, a truly great black golf pro from Nashville who twice won the United Golfers Association tournament.[6]

While planning for the black golf course was underway, Councilman Z. Alexander Looby initiated litigation in federal courts demanding that all Nashville parks and golf courses be opened to the public without regard to race. An attorney for the NAACP, Looby was spearheading the integration of public facilities in Nashville and throughout the South through legal action, with able assistance from Thurgood Marshall, who subsequently became a Supreme Court Justice, from Avon Williams, and from other civil rights leaders. Councilman Looby voted against funding for the segregated golf course on the Cumberland, and in 1951 filed suit on behalf of Herman Long and other black golfers who had been denied the use of municipal links. The case went to court while the Rhodes Golf Course was under development, and in 1952 a Federal District judge ruled in favor of separate but equal golf courses. Looby and Marshall thereupon appealed the case to the Supreme Court and in early 1956 won a reversal of the District Court's decision.[7]

Shortly after Looby's victory at the Supreme Court, the Park Board was slapped with a countersuit filed by a group of Nashvillians headed by Donald Davidson, a Vanderbilt University professor of English, contending that ending segregation on the golf courses would constitute a violation of state laws. Those plaintiffs failed to win an injunction against the Board, and the Board opened as directed by the federal courts all public golf courses to black golfers on February 14, 1956, without incident worthy of notice. A year later, the Board denied permits to segregationists who wished to conduct rallies in the city parks.[8]

While segregation and civil rights litigation garnered the headlines during the 1950s, the Park Board continued its usual park programs without much notice from the media. When James Stahlman resigned from the Board and William Hume died in 1950, Edwin Crutcher, an executive of local textile mills and of First American Bank, was elected board chairman, and he was to continue his service in the capacity until the formation of metropolitan government. The new Park Commissioners of the early 1950s were Charles Madison Sarratt, Newman Cheek, and Bascom Jones. Sarratt of Vanderbilt University and Cheek, a real estate developer, assumed responsibility for the park cultural recreation programs, taking such intense personal interest in art that in 1952 when a new exhibit area was needed in the Parthenon's basement Cheek funded it with a $13,400 cash gift for the purpose.[9]

Bascom Jones had served on the Board from 1946 to 1949 until his appointment to the Election Commission. He returned for his second term in 1951 when C. A. Craig retired. Once employed by the Nashville, Chattanooga and St. Louis Railway, he had become the executive of the Tennessee Railroad Association and he helped arrange the donation by the N.C.&St.L. of Locomotive 576 to the park system in 1953. While visiting Memphis, City Councilman Wrenne Phelps saw children enjoying an obsolete steam locomotive in a Memphis park, and at his suggestion Jones and the Park Board requested the donation of a locomotive from President W. S. Hackworth of the N.C.&St.L., which then was converting from steam to diesel. For the benefit of children who might not otherwise ever see a steam locomotive, President Hackworth donated the last Dixie Stripe J-3 locomotive, along with $6,000 needed to lay track from the nearby railroad shops into the park and to provide a place for the display, to the park system. Giant Locomotive 576 went on display during the summer of 1953 with James H. Fahey, who had been its first engineer, as its custodian, and the steam engine was for a time the most popular attraction in the park.[10]

Eight years later, Mayor Ben West and Councilman Charles Bramwell obtained the gift of a surplus F-86 jet fighter plane from the Tennessee Air National Guard, which the Board put on display in Centennial Park as a companion piece to the locomotive, contrasting the historic with modern transport technology. The two impressive machines subtly hinted at a change in outlook on the part of the Park Board and perhaps Nashvillians in general. Fifty years earlier, Major E. C. Lewis and Board members had been interested in preserving with bronze statuary the memories of heroic people who had been the pioneers of Nashville and leaders of the Confederacy, and even President John Thomas of Nashville's railroad had been immortalized in bronze. By the mid-20th century, the Board no longer erected bronze monuments to people, apparently preferring to preserve the artifacts of historic technology. Yet, that change may have been more a result of chance than a philosophical metamorphosis, for Board members still respected the old statuary. In 1954, for instance, when the City Beautiful Commission requested that the Board order the statues steam cleaned and painted, the Board refused, replying that they thought the green patina resulting from the exposure of the bronze to weather quite impressive.[11]

Another unique exhibit in Centennial Park went on display in 1953, donated at a cost of $20,000 by the flamboyant Fred Harvey, founder of the department store chain bearing his name. Inspired by a nativity scene he had seen in Germany, Harvey in September 1953 proposed a similar display at the side of the Parthenon, promising the Board he would pay all the costs and would not use it for advertising, which was prohibited in the parks. When the Board approved, he installed a display of forty-five human figures, seventy-eight animals, and ten angels sculpted by Rebbecini of Italy with a rubber-based material and including the holy family, three wise men, and shepherds with their flocks. The 280-foot long and 75-foot deep exhibition, brightly lighted by thousands of vari-colored lights at an annual cost of $6,000, was greeted with some caustic remarks from those who thought it odd to find a "pagan temple deep in the Bible Belt decorated with giant Nativity scenes and lighted in purple neon," but it drew an average of a million visitors annually from Nashville and throughout Middle Tennessee to the park every December. After fifteen years of popular acclaim, the figures in the display began to deteriorate and they were sold to a shopping mall at Cincinnati. Nothing with the appeal of Harvey's display has replaced it, although a crowd does gather each Christmas at the park for the annual tree-lighting ceremony.[12]

Musical concerts sponsored by the Board each year in the parks during the 1950s varied but little from year to year. Leon Cole continued his organ concerts at Centennial and Don Q. Pullen orchestrated concerts at Hadley Park. In May, local school bands in massed formations kicked off the summer recreation season with a park concert, and on six to eight Sunday afternoons each summer the *Tennessean* presented variety concerts with Fred Waller as master of ceremonies. Concerts by stars such as Eddy Arnold and Red Foley drew as many as 20,000 people to Centennial Park's bandshell some Sundays, and each of those concerts featured a future star, a "Discovery of the Week," one of whom was Nashville's Pat Boone. In those days before home air-conditioning was affordable to most Nashvillians, the shade of Centennial Park provided one of the cooler refuges on a steaming Sunday afternoon, lounging on the lawn or one of the park benches while enjoying the music and socializing. Many a Grand Ole Opry Saturday night hangover found its cure with soothing country music at Centennial Park on Sunday, and many a romance blossomed on the grass around the bandshell. Publisher John Siegenthaler fondly recalls that it was at one of those concerts that he met his future wife.[13]

After a half-century run in the parks, free movies came to an end in 1955, in part as the result of competition from television. The cost of showing the films had risen to $3,000 annually, the projectors were wearing out, the operators were demanding time-and-a-half pay, and attendance was dropping as more Nashvillians acquired television receivers. In addition, several fights had occurred at the movies after the park lights were dimmed. As substitute for free movies, the Board purchased television sets, placing them in the community centers where people who could not afford sets could view the regular programming and also watch the Centennial Park ball games or the running of the Iroquois Memorial Steeplechase, which John H. DeWitt, Jr., of WSM television had begun telecasting in 1953.[14]

At Warner Park, the spectacular steeplechase race continued as an annual extravaganza, the model plane enthusiasts conducted their annual competitions on the model aviation field, and in 1956 the Board opened a new archery range. Elizabeth Kittell succeeded by

John Fowlkes operated the riding academy concession with varying degrees of success, and Margaret Lindsley Warden, editor of "Horse Sense" column for the *Tennessean,* arranged annual horsemanship tournaments and other equestrian events, perhaps most notably the 1953 Olympic trials conducted by the U.S. Equestrian Team. The Army had once trained Olympic equestrians, but by 1950 it no longer had horse cavalry and a volunteer association directed the Olympic training, holding a three-day competition in 1953 at Warner Park.[15]

The Municipal Baseball Association, which had managed for the Board the softball and baseball leagues in the parks since 1935, ended that service in 1948, and the Park Board had its staff assume that responsibility, soon receiving a practical lesson in the difficulties involved. When the board in 1952 proposed to raise entrance fees for the softball and baseball teams to permit an increase in the pay of umpires, the players organized a mass protest meeting in the War Memorial Building. Mayor Ben West attended, personally promising that the fees would not be raised, and he fulfilled his promise. The City Council voted a $6,000 appropriation to pay the umpires, provided the Park Board left the entrance fees as they were, and it continued to make similar appropriations in later years. Seldom had the board encountered political clout the magnitude of that held by the baseball and softball fanatics of Nashville. That constituency after 1952 extended even to small boys, for in that year the *Tennessean* introduced Little League ball to the city, sponsoring the first city championship at the Fort Negley diamonds.[16]

Recreation Superintendent Jack Spore had more than he could handle after management of baseball and softball leagues was added to his duties, which included the usual summer playground program, plus the annual Playground Circus, Playday of Champions, and Junior Olympics. To obtain assistance, he recruited local coaches and sports officials as part-time and temporary help during the summer ball seasons. Joe Shapiro, coach at West High, became his chief assistant, along with Jimmy Huggins, Archie Grant, S. L. Hall, Louis Catignani, Edgar Allen, and Hale Harris among others. They supervised about 165 recreation leaders who in turn directed about 6,000 players in the annual competitive sports programs, which were normally marked by intense rivalries and often by considerable furor. So many protests arose concerning the type ball used in a game, or the wearing of spikes, or the decisions of umpires, that Spore established a $5 per complaint fee to squelch them, though without signal success.[17]

While park system funding nearly doubled from a half million dollars annually in 1952 to one million in 1959, the growing recreation program and increasing maintenance and operations costs consumed most of that increase; and very few new parks were added to the system during those years except when they came essentially as gifts. Lock Two Park was added to the system in 1956 as a gift from the Nashville District, U.S. Army Corps of Engineers. Located at the apex of Pennington Bend north of Donelson, it had been the reservation and home of the lockmen at one of the old locks and dams replaced by Cheatham and Old Hickory Locks and Dams; and with the addition of playground and picnic facilities it became a pleasant, albeit isolated, spot for riverside recreation. The twenty-six acre West Park on Morrow Road was given to the park system at the request of Mayor Ben West, for whom the park was named, in 1952 by city government in exchange for the two-acres of land in Cherokee Park which had never served as more than a neighborhood playground. At the larger West Park, the board was able to supply West Nashvillians with ball diamonds, picnic areas, and other recreational attractions.[18]

Neither the amount of park space, nor the amount of park funding, proved adequate to the needs of the Nashville urban area during the 1950s, when population was increasing and the use made by people of the parks growing at an even faster pace. The average expenditure in the city for parks actually was declining on a per capita basis. When Park Commissioner Alvin G. Beaman, the automobile dealer, visited Milwaukee in 1957, he was amazed at how that city, which had a population and park system similar in size to Nashville's, maintained much cleaner and better managed parks than Nashville. After investigation, he learned the simple reason: Milwaukee annually expended five times as much as Nashville on its park system.[19]

Mayor West and the council in 1953 granted the Park Board an increase in the park tax rate of eight-tenths of a mill, but in 1955 the Board lost its three percent of bus fares when the state legislature freed the Nashville Transit Company of that obligation, thereby reducing park system revenues by $110,000 annually. As compensation, the legislature also authorized the Park Board to retire all its bonded indebtedness out of the city's sinking fund, which was accomplished through a council ordinance of April 13, 1955. The amount of the bonded indebtedness was not large, for the bonds had been issued before 1931 and would have been retired by scheduled payments in 1960, and the Board therefore suffered a net revenue loss in the transaction, also losing the $110,000 annually from bus fare receipts that would otherwise have continued after 1960. When the city council in 1956 further reduced park revenues by rescinding the tax increase granted in 1953, Chairman Edwin Crutcher and the entire Board threatened to resign in protest. "We're getting tired," said Crutcher, "of trying to operate the parks without enough money to do the job."[20]

The Board's fiscal crisis of 1956 grew out of efforts by Mayor West and the council to force the Board to stop making capital improvements out of its current revenues and to force it to issue bonds to expand and improve the system; and it climaxed a running dispute between the mayor and the Board concerning a proposed park on Edgehill Avenue in South Nashville. James Stahlman in 1946 had recommended that the Board acquire the city-owned "Rockcrusher Hill," an abandoned rock quarry, on Edgehill Avenue and make it a park, but the quarry was fifty feet deep in places, the cost of filling it to create a park seemed exorbitant, and the Board began a search for an alternate site for a park in that vicinity. In early 1956, however, Mayor West and members of the Southwest Nashville Civic Club with Reverend E. S. Rose as their spokesman met with the Board to demand that it approve the construction of a park and community center at the quarry. The Board refused, declaring the loss of bus fare receipts prevented any park acquisition, and Mayor West rejoined that he would consider it a personal favor to him if the Board would issue bonds to finance the Edgehill park. He later told the Commissioners privately that he desired their help and also wanted to help them. He warned them that members of the council were upset because some of the Commissioners lived outside the city limits, and he requested them to begin conducting their regular Board meetings in public places instead of a bank.[21]

Board Chairman Edwin Crutcher also served as director of First American Bank, and as a convenience to his colleagues he had moved the Board meetings into a conference room at the downtown bank. Most of the Commissioners worked downtown and could attend the meetings merely by walking to the bank during their lunch hours. It was true that some Commissioners lived outside the city limits, for the limits had not expanded as fast as the city had grown; not even all of Shelby Park was within the city limits before 1954. Those were chimerical concerns, however, for the real issue at stake in the conflict between the Board and the Mayor was the future and funding of the park system. Several of the Commissioners had suffered financial losses during the economic collapse of 1930 and subsequent Depression, and having paid off the 1927–1930 bond issues in 1955, freeing the park system of a $70,000 annual drain on its budget, they were not eager to incur new bonded indebtedness. Commissioner Newman Cheek bluntly told reporters he would never support a new bond issue and that his position represented the consensus of opinion of the Board. Afters its 1956 meeting with Mayor West, the Board pointedly convened its next regular meeting back in the conference room at First American Bank.[22]

13 ENDING THE CITY SYSTEM

The conflict of 1956 between Mayor Ben West and the Park Board concerning the future of the municipal park system continued until 1959, with the Mayor urging the Board to issue capital improvement bonds to take advantage of federal matching funding for urban renewal and with the Board refusing on grounds that it did not wish to burden the system with debt. By applying the screws with every means at his disposal, the Mayor eventually achieved a victory. In time, it was also to prove a victory for the Board because the planning and funding initiatives of the Mayor placed the park system in a much improved position to meet the obligations thrust upon it at the formation in 1963 of the Metropolitan Nashville and Davidson County Government.

Meetings to publicly protest the Park Board's opposition to bond issues began in late 1956, apparently with the support of Mayor West. At the request of the Board, Jack Spore attended one of those meetings in October 1956 at the Carter-Lawrence School auditorium on Edgehill and 12th avenues. Spore afterward informed the Board that more than 150 citizens attended to hear speeches by Mayor West, Councilwoman Gertrude Bartlett, and Councilmen George Farris and Frank Melfi. Councilman Farris, representing the Edgehill community, termed it a disgrace that members of the Park Board lived outside the city limits and called for their immediate resignation. Mayor West complained he had no control over the Board, lamenting that it even refused to conduct its meetings where he asked and that it refused to issue the bonds needed to fund construction of the park on Rockcrusher Hill desired by the Edgehill community. He suggested that the citizens present request their representatives in the state legislature to seek the abolition of the Park Board, and in fact an amendment soon was introduced in the legislature giving the Mayor the power to appoint new Park Commissioners.[1]

Resorting to other means of increasing the pressure upon the Park Board, Mayor West ordered an audit of its accounts and arranged through contract for an independent planning consultant to undertake a study of the park system. City auditors combed the Board and park staff's financial and accounting procedures, but reported to the Mayor they could find nothing that was not both efficient and effective. "Their system of records and manner in which they follow through each procedure indicates," concluded the audit report, "that there is no lack of administrative control in this organization."[2]

Through the Board of Education, the Mayor in 1957 funded a wide-ranging scrutiny of the city park system and assessment of its future development by the National Recreation Association, which had unimpeachable credentials for the study. In its massive report, the Association chided the Park Board for neglecting comprehensive planning and capital improvements. It pointed out that the Board had made no effort at comprehensive planning since completion of Percy Warner's study in 1926 and had issued no bonds for capital improvements and system expansion since 1930. The population of Davidson County, including the city, had been 320,000 in 1950, and it was rapidly increasing, expected to reach 400,000 in 1960; moreover, by 1960 the population of the county outside the Nashville city limits would surpass that of the city. Because with the formation of the Warner parks the Board had ended significant efforts to reserve land for parks in the area ringing the central city, the fast-building county suburban areas were becoming even more deficient in park space than the city. The Park Board and the city and county governments should not view money expended on the park and recreation system as debt, but rather as "an investment that pays rich dividends in a more beautiful city, higher and more stable property values, and happier and better citizens."[3]

Predicting that Nashville and Davidson County would experience unprecedented growth with accelerating urbanization during the quarter century following 1960, the National Recreation Association recommended that the city and county governments establish a jointly funded and managed Board of Parks and Recreation. It urged that the new board be provided funding sufficient to permit purchase as quickly as possible of at least 4,160 acres of new park land including about 600 acres of small playgrounds adjoining elementary schools and neighborhood recreation centers, 600 acres of playfields adjacent to secondary schools and community centers, 1200 acres of larger natural parks, and additional acreage to be reserved for future use. In sum, the Association's planners considered the park situation in Nashville and Davidson County no less than an emergency demanding the combined efforts of both governments to obtain more parks through a major capital investment program; or, more briefly, Mayor West was right and the Park Board wrong in their dispute over bond issues.[4]

The National Recreation Association also recommended a complete reorganization of the park system staff, and that became the first of its recommendations to be implemented. The Association noted that the Park Board's Secretary, General Manager, and Superintendents of Parks and Recreation all worked more or less independently of each other without a clear chain of authority and responsibility, resulting in a lack of harmony of purpose, and it proposed that a single person be placed in charge of the entire system. When General Manager Ewell Costello retired in 1957, the Board selected Secretary Bert Elmore as its director in charge of the total park system and program. Frank Pickens continued in charge of park maintenance, Jack Spore responsible for recreation programs, and Bill Crouch supervising budget and accounting matters, but all reported to Bert Elmore. The Board even gave Elmore the authority to spend as much as $500 for repairs or supplies without requesting its advance approval.[5]

The Park Board did not adopt all recommendations made by the National Recreation Association, nor did it surrender to Mayor West on all counts. It continued meeting in fact at the downtown bank so long as it existed, but in 1958 it conceded that capital improvement bond issues were, as Mayor West maintained, vital to the future of the park system. It prepared a $2.3 million shopping list of capital improvements—new parks, community centers, and recreational facilities—the park system needed and submitted it to Mayor West. After review by the Mayor, the city planning commission, and city council, who added and mostly subtracted from the list of projects, a $1.6 million park improvement program emerged for which bonds were issued in 1959. The list included new community centers at Centennial, Shelby, and McCabe parks, the Centennial Croquet Clubhouse, community centers and gymnasiums at Edgehill, West, and Douglas parks, lighted tennis courts and ball diamonds at many parks, new filter systems for the park swimming pools, and a half dozen new playgrounds.[6]

Perhaps the most significant project included in the 1959 bond issues was the park at Rockcrusher Hill on Edgehill Avenue, where it was necessary to fill a fifty-foot deep and eight-acre broad hole in the ground to create a park. Fortunately, the cost of filling that hole proved far less than projected because the interstate highway construction through Nashville was starting at the time and the contractor was able to fill the hole with materials excavated to make way for the new interstates. By 1962, the quarry was filled and graded, a new community center and swimming pool were completed, and the park was opened in a strategic location between the Carter-Lawrence and Rose schools. The Board named the park in honor of the Reverend E. S. Rose, the pastor of Bethel African Methodist Episcopal Church and leader of the Southwest Nashville Civic Club who died in 1956, and named the Easley Memorial Community Center in tribute to the Reverend T. H. Easley, the pastor of the New Hope Baptist Church who died in 1954. When E. S. Rose Park opened in 1962, the Board turned its old Edgehill playground over to the Nashville Housing Authority.[7]

Headed initially by Gerald Gimre, the Nashville Housing Authority had been created in 1939, and after the Second World War it coordinated an urban renewal program which indelibly altered both the facade and character of the city. Gimre along with Charles Hawkins, the director for many years of the city planning commission, presided over a revolutionary reconstruction of the city during the postwar years, largely with federal funding for the always controversial urban renewal program. Starting with the conversion of army barracks at Berry Field and on Thompson Lane into family housing, Gimre and the Nashville Housing Authority coordinated a broad effort to provide improved and low-cost public housing for Nashvillians at the Andrew Jackson courts, J. C. Napier, Cheatham Place, James A. Cayce, Edgehill, Preston Taylor, John Henry Hale, and Tony Sudekum homes, usually called "the projects." According to Charles Hawkins, Nashville was the first city in the nation to take advantage of the 1949 urban renewal act providing federal funding for public housing and was the first city to complete a "project."[8]

The E. S. Rose Park became part of the Housing Authority's urban redevelopment effort in Southwest Nashville, and redevelopment programs in other city sectors also affected the park system. The Capitol Hill Redevelopment in 1954 took in the Ben Lindauer Park at Fifth and Jo Johnston Avenues, which the Park Board turned over to the Housing Authority. The Authority in 1958 advised the Board the East Nashville Urban Renewal Project would require the closing of several parks, would permit the expansion of others, and would create two new parks. Plans called for the expansion of East Park, the closing of Douglas and McFerrin parks and their relocation to areas with more space for recreation, and the creation of the Kirkpatrick and Cleveland parks. Two-thirds of the costs of the redevelopment would be reimbursed by the federal government, and the creation of new parks would count toward fulfilling the required local contribution to the city.[9]

Mayor Ben West in 1961 called the Park Board to his office to ask their cooperation in obtaining federal assistance under a new program authorized by the 1961 Federal Housing Act. The act, providing an initial $50 million in federal funds to assist local governments with the purchase of land for parks and recreation, creating the "Open Space" program with seventy percent grants matching thirty percent local contributions. On the spot, the Board voted to issue another $1 million in capital improvement bonds to take advantage of the Open Space program and appointed Bert Elmore to serve on a committee including Charles Hawkins of the planning commission and Councilman Charles Bramwell to select the sites of new parks to be acquired through the program.[10]

Mayor West by 1961 had, in sum, secured the full and indeed wholehearted cooperation of the Park Board in acquiring park land

and capital improvements in connection with overall city planning and urban renewal efforts. Funded by a series of capital improvement bond issues keyed to rapidly shifting federal programs and policies on a matching grant basis, the first major park expansion effort since 1930 began during the last years of the West administration and was to continue after the formation of metropolitan government.

With federal funding, Nashville in 1962 almost obtained a zoo and children's amusement park, which if successful would have ranked with the Warner Park steeplechase as a coup for local government. Having seen a kiddie zoo and amusement park in another city, Park Commissioner Newman Cheek recommended that the Board build such a "Land of Enchantment" in Centennial Park, including miniature train rides, artificial ponds, and walkways through a maze of statues of various cartoon and storyland characters. When the Board received offers from several businessmen to contribute the money needed to fabricate the characters, it added funds to build the "Land of Enchantment" to the 1962 bond issue, which was approved by the mayor and the council. When Fred Massey, owner of Fair Park at the state fair grounds, objected to the "Land of Enchantment" as unfair competition to his business, the Board quietly dropped its plans, however, and in 1964 the funds for the project were transferred to the construction of the Harpeth Hills Golf Course.[11]

Support for building a city zoo had existed in Nashville since 1932 when the Glendale Park zoo closed, and while the kiddie zoo was under construction a number of advocates of a full-scale city zoo headed by Joseph Hart met with the Board to request that it open such a zoo in one of the parks. In addition to initial construction costs, the annual zoo operating costs were estimated at $30,000, and the Board therefore responded that it was willing to permit the use of Fort Negley Park as a city zoo, but the proponents of the zoo would first need to obtain the necessary authority and funding from the mayor and city council. Fort Negley was the dead end for many interesting projects, and so it was for the zoo.[12]

When James E. and Rogers Caldwell arranged the purchase of Fort Negley Park in 1928, the purchase was predicated upon the restoration of the old fort, the construction of a boulevard from Capitol Hill to the fort, and the value of the fort as a tourist attraction. The WPA had reconstructed the fort at a cost of thousands, but the boulevard was never constructed, nor did the fort attract any tourists. Because the Park Board's budget scarcely sufficed to properly maintain the ball diamonds at the base of St. Cloud Hill, the fort had fallen into disrepair and become the resort of a rough crowd. When Tennessee Adjutant General Hugh Mott in 1955 requested permission to build a National Guard Armory at the former site of the army base in Centennial Park, the Board courteously offered the use of Fort Negley as an alternative site and officially declared it surplus property to make it available for the purpose. The Armory was built elsewhere, and in 1958 when the School Board considered building a new vocational school the Park Board tendered Fort Negley to School Superintendent William H. Oliver as the school site, even offering the ball diamonds to boot. The school also was built elsewhere, and as the Civil War Centennial of 1964 approached the Board welcomed a proposal by the "Confederate High Command" to erect a Civil War museum at Fort Negley, financed by public subscriptions, souvenir sales, and similar voluntary efforts. A Confederate organization occupying a Union Army fort would have been an interesting project, but it never materialized. The city Park Board could not properly maintain the old fort, nor could it give it away, and it left the problem for solution by Metropolitan Government.[13]

One of the last major park improvement efforts launched near the end of the West administration was the repair of the Parthenon, which had deteriorated during the three decades after it opened in 1931. The Board employed sculptor Puryear Mims to plan the repairs without major structural alterations, and with his estimates in hand it met with the mayor. Mayor West demanded that the Parthenon be repaired regardless of the cost, and the Board entered into contracts for the repairs with the people who had built it thirty years earlier. Wilbur Creighton, Jr., whose father had directed the 1931 reconstruction and whose grandfather had built the 1897 replica, became the general contractor for the 1962 repairs, under the direction of Architect John Charles Wheeler, while Ernest Ford of the Earley Studios and plasterer Hobart Spears returned to work on the temple as they had thirty years earlier. The building exterior had become so dirty that its colors were no longer visible and many of the gods and goddesses decorating the temple had lost portions of their anatomy. Ford, Mims, and Spears cleaned the building and moulded replacements for the parts lost as a result of weathering, while the General

Bronze Corporation repaired the huge doors at the entranceways, completing the job in 1963.[14]

The City Council in 1961 reduced the park system's prorata share of property taxes, forcing the Park Board to again curtail expenditures for operations; and because swimming pools had been operating at a loss the Board ordered them closed on July 20. They were to remain closed until the formation of Metropolitan Government. The lack of funding was the official explanation for the closing, and it is possible that the closing was city government's means of warning voters in the county that services would be reduced unless county tax support for the system were forthcoming. However, civil rights demonstrations were in progress at the time, and it is the opinion of some that Mayor West and the Park Board ordered the pools closed to avoid the sort of disturbances that had occurred in other cities when swimming pools were integrated. Segregation of all public facilities was coming to an end at the time in Nashville as throughout the nation, chiefly as a result of litigation and demonstrations organized by such leaders of the civil rights movement as Z. Alexander Looby and Avon Williams. In 1963 the U.S. Supreme Court ruled that segregated park systems were an unconstitutional violation of the rights of citizens.[15]

Because Davidson Countians used the city park system as often as Nashvillians, the Park Board had sought since 1950 to obtain funding support for the system from county government. Davidson County had essentially no public parks, and organized recreation was supplied there either by city government or by churches, schools, civic clubs, and community organizations. The sole recreation centers with year-round programs in the county were at Old Hickory and at the Boys Club in Woodbine. The Park Board brought Mayor Thomas Cummings and County Judge Beverly Briley together to discuss the situation in 1950, and they agreed to request the state legislature to authorize contributions by county government to the city park system. The legislature in March 1951 approved a jointly operated county-wide park and recreation program and an annual $150,000 contribution by Davidson County toward the park system's budget. But, while Judge Briley was supportive of the park program, convincing county voters that they should contribute to the city park system proved difficult, and in fact was never accomplished though Judge Briley in 1962 did arrange for William Lamb, the county engineer, to assume maintenance responsibility for roads in the Warner parks.16

The apparent need for a unified park system with combined city and county tax support and direction no doubt influenced the decision of certain city and county administrators, if not the voters, to support formation of one of the first metropolitan governments in the nation. Certainly, the difficulties of operating a park system serving the entire county without county voters participating in the management and funding of the system was not the sole or even the primary reason for the creation of metropolitan government, for the two separate governments also complicated urban planning, road and public works design and construction, police and fire protection, and other urban services. Yet, the promise that a metropolitan government would expand the park and recreation system throughout the county surely must have influenced the voters when, after a decade of political controversy and one defeat at the polls, they approved by referendum the formation of the Metropolitan Nashville and Davidson County Government.

Ben West decided not to enter the 1962 race to become mayor of the new metropolitan government; yet, his leadership as mayor of Nashville during the twelve years preceding the formation of "Metro" contributed substantially to subsequent development of the metropolitan park system. It was West who literally forced the Park Board to initiate a major park expansion and capital improvements program during the late 1950s, thereby taking advantage of federal funding offered for parks as part of urban redevelopment and for the creation of more open space in the greater Nashville urban area. The Park Board itself recognized the value of West's contributions and by 1963 had forgiven if not forgotten its disagreements with the mayor. At one of their last meetings, the city park commissioners voted to name the new eighteen-hole golf course at Warner Park in honor of Ben West, although the name did not stick because heirs of the men who had donated the land forming the nucleus of Warner Park objected naming features in that park after anyone other than members of the Warner or Lea families.17

Chairman Edwin Crutcher called the Nashville Board of Park Commissioners together for the last time on March 12, 1963—in the conference room of the downtown bank—after sixty-two years of service. When the Park Board had first met at the call of Mayor James

Head in 1901, it had no parks, no personnel, and no funding; when it closed its business in 1963, it had about 4,000 acres of park land, nearly one hundred full-time personnel, and an annual budget of more than $1 million. In addition, it had embarked by 1963 upon a major park acquisition and improvements program that would be inherited by the Metropolitan Board of Parks and Recreation.[18]

From the first, the Park Board had been composed of the city's most public-spirited leaders, willing to give not only their time but quiet liberally of their personal property and funds. After Samuel Champion and Mayors James Head and James Brown, the political triumvirate which had selected the charter Board members, departed the city, the Board had become an autonomous entity, always listening carefully to the opinions of Mayors Hilary Howse, Thomas Cummings, and Ben West, always consulting the city councilmen and people living in the neighborhoods near the parks, and always calling on people with ideas or complaints to present them publicly at Board meetings, but never supinely catering to anyone. And if any serious financial scandal ever tainted the operations of the Board itself, neither its records nor newspaper reports reveal it.

The principal difficulties resulting from direction of the park system by an independent board involved a lack of comprehensive planning coordinated with other elements of municipal government and a certain insensitivity to sociopolitical movements and changes within the community. Before the West administration, the Park Board made few efforts, and those largely unsuccessful, to coordinate its planning and programs with the city planning commission, city school board, or the other branches of municipal government. Except in 1901 and 1926, little effort was made to devise a comprehensive park development program until Mayor West forced the issue in 1957. From the first, Board membership was balanced to reflect the interests of the city's religious denominations, but no woman, black, or other minority was ever elected to the Board. While it established in 1912 the first park in the South and perhaps the nation for black citizens and worked closely with black leaders to provide recreational facilities for the city's black community, it was not noticeably responsive to the civil rights campaign to end segregation. Even conservative columnist Dick Battle of the *Nashville Banner* had concluded by 1957 that the autonomous Board should be eliminated. Battle admitted the Board members were citizens of unimpeachable integrity, devoted not only to the park system but also to the progress of the city as a whole, but he declared that its political and financial independence inherently contradicted the "principles of democratic government."[19]

14 THE METROPOLITAN PARK CHALLENGE

"If we can get out of our minds some of the old thinking about county and city governments, and recognize that Metro is a new concept, it will help us greatly to accomplish our mission," declared Mayor Beverly Briley when addressing the first meeting of departmental executives in the newly formed Metropolitan Nashville and Davidson County Government, a title commonly abbreviated to "Metro" as it will be herein. Metro was indeed a radically new concept of municipal government and was to produce as many revolutionary changes in the park system as it did in other elements of urban life in Nashville. Merger of the city and county increased the service area of the park system from 72.47 to 533 square miles and more than doubled the number of people served from 200,000 to 425,000; and when Metro was organized the county, except for the Warner parks, had essentially no public park space or services at all. And in Beverly Briley, Metro had a leader who was determined that the voters of the county would receive, as swiftly as possible, the urban services they had hoped to attain when they cast their votes for the government merger.[1]

Beverly Briley, an East Nashvillian who at eighteen had become the youngest practicing attorney in Tennessee, in 1950 had succeeded

Litton Hickman as Davidson County Judge. Where Hickman, the county judge for thirty-two years, had sought to hold tax rates near the level of Tennessee's rural counties by eschewing such "frills" as public parks, Briley had supported a reasonable tax base needed to secure improved government services, though he had been unable to obtain county taxpayer support for contributions to the city park systerm. Briley at the outset of Metro mandated a three-point program for the park system. First, recreation programs would be extended as rapidly as possible into the suburban areas of the county; second, a fully cooperative Park-School developmental plan would be adopted; and third, large urban parks would be acquired under the Federal Open Space program as a hedge against future urbanization.[2]

To implement that mandate, the Mayor in accordance with the Metro charter appointed the first Metropolitan Board of Parks and Recreation in early 1963, and on June 5, 1963, the Board conducted its first meeting in the conference room of the Centennial Park administrative building. Under the charter, the Board was to consist of seven members, five appointed by the Mayor and one each by the Metro Planning Commission and Board of Education. Like the old city board, members were to receive no compensation for their services to the park system, and on the new board was one familiar face: Bascom Jones was appointed by Briley to the new board. At its first meeting, the Metro Park Board elected Dr. George W. Reichardt as its chairman and Ernest K. Hardison, Jr., as its vice chairman. Dr. Reichardt, who was to continue as chairman more than twenty years, was a chiropractor who had become acquainted with Mayor Briley through Scouting. Holder of Scouting's Silver Beaver Award, Dr. Reichardt had become an assistant to Briley in volunteer Scouting work after Briley made him an offer he couldn't refuse: "Do you want to help me, or do you want your taxes raised?" Other new Park Commissioners present at that first Board meeting included Mose J. Davie, A. J. Roper, and Charles Mager. E. D. Chapell and Mrs. Irwin Eskind were subsequently appointed.[3]

Having organized, the Park Commissioners decided to meet the first Wednesday every month and adopted a format to be followed at each of their meetings. Their first action as a Board was to assume a cooperative attitude toward the public school system, authorizing the loan of park bleachers to schools in emergencies and specifically approving the loan of bleachers to Hillsboro High School while it was relocating its athletic field. By denying a request to use a park community center as the site of a church revival, they uphelp the policy established in 1903 by their predecessors of not permitting the use of park facilities for religious purposes. It should be noted, however, that the policy was not ironclad, for the old Board had sometimes permitted the use of a swimming pool for a baptism, of Fort Negley for an Easter service, or of a community center for temporary services of congregations whose churches had burned.[4]

The Commissioners approved a budget for the 1964 fiscal year of $2,244,806 to fund expansion of park services into the county and to allow the reopening of park swimming pools which had been closed since 1961. On inspection, however, it became apparent the Centennial and Shelby Park pools had suffered such weathering damages while closed that it was necessary to demolish both. Eleven of the twelve small pools in the system were found serviceable, repaired, and reopened to the public on June 24, 1963, with some 2,500 children enrolled in the Red Cross Society's "Learn to Swim" program.[5]

At their first meeting, the Metropolitan Board members acquired their first new park from the Madison Community Park Association headed by realtor J. R. Coarsey and James Pigue. Madison civic clubs in 1956 had campaigned for a park in that thriving community and, thanks in part to a large donation from Colonel Tom Parker, the promoter best known as manager of Elvis Presley, the park opened in 1959 in thirty acres at Delaware and Dupont streets. With contributions from Madison businessmen and proceeds from the Madison Hillbilly Day annual celebration, the Madison Community Park Association built ball diamonds and other recreation facilities. It proved quite a successful park under their management, although they encountered problems similar to those sometimes faced in other parks. When a parent pulled a knife on an umpire after a Kiddie League game at the park, for instance, the Madison Park Association bluntly warned in the local newspaper: "Such disgusting and rotten examples of adult behavior will not be tolerated, and repetition will result in the publishing of these folks' names and their banishment from the park." After negotiations, the Metro Board purchased Madison Park for $16,500, also promising to build a community center there.[6]

Within a month after its organization, the Metro Board was

made responsible for operating and maintaining the City Cemetery and Fort Nashborough. Although the old Park Board had operated the cemetery as a city park in 1908, after a city appropriation had been exhausted on construction of a fence and gates around it the City Cemetery Commission took charge of it. The Metro Park Board was to maintain the cemetery as part of the park system after 1963, and in 1981 turned its administration over to the Metro Historical Commission. Fort Nashborough, a representation of the log stockade and cabins built by pioneers in 1780, was erected under the sponsorship of the Daughters of the American Revolution during the 1930s on the bank of the Cumberland near the foot of Church Street. Though caretakers lived in the cabins, cooking in the fireplaces and practicing other folk crafts to reenact the pioneer heritage of Nashville, the fort for many years scarcely received the attention it deserved until Bicentennial and Riverfront parks were established on each side of the fort, making it a tourist attraction important to the city.[7]

The Metro Board made no radical changes in the park staff and organization inherited from the city Board. Bert Elmore continued as the Director of Parks and Recreation with Jack Spore and Frank Pickens as the superintendents of recreation and maintenance. Bill Crouch in charge of accounting and administrative matters became the Assistant Director without any significant change in duties except the additional responsibility for park planning, in which capacity he became the principal advocate of user fees to make the park system more self-supporting and less dependent upon fluctuating tax revenues.[8]

Bill Crouch and Charles Mager during visits to other municipal park systems during 1963 and 1964 learned of the "cost recovery" concept of park management, whereby the basic facilities were provided with tax-generated dollars and the costs of more elaborate facilities were recovered through user or admission fees. At federal parks during the 1960s, for instance, camping space was provided without charge but if campers wanted running water and electricity they paid a fee sufficient to recover the costs of those utilities. Under Crouch's leadership, the Metro Board began gradual increases in fees for the use of golf courses and other park facilities to more closely balance revenues with the costs of those facilities and started to phase out the contract concessions for boat rental, golf carts, and the like and to initiate their operation by park personnel, reserving revenues for reinvestment in the park system.⁹

Immediately challenging the new Board and its staff in 1963 was not cost recovery nor future planning, however, but opening parks and playgrounds throughout Davidson County in accordance with the wishes of the voters who had approved the change to Metro government. "A lot has been waiting a long time to get done," said Jack Spore in comment on the challenges of 1963. During that first summer, swimming pools reopened, the number of playgrounds increased from sixty to eighty-two, and thirty-one new ball diamonds opened, bringing a total of seventy diamonds serving 150 teams in nineteen leagues into service. Most of the new facilities were in the previously parkless county, with the playgrounds located on county school grounds. A temporary summer staff of 230 teachers and college students taught games, arts and crafts to children each day from nine to five, providing free swimming and tennis instruction where pools and courts were available. At the end of that first summer, Dr. Reichardt declared:[10]

> The first Metropolitan Board of Parks and Recreation considers the accomplishments of its obligations are being achieved in a twofold manner. First, a strong functional organization has been developed to effectively carry out the Park and Recreation Comprehensive Plan adapted for the expanded service to the total citizenry of Davidson County. Second, by joining with other government units to fully utilize available community facilities, we hope to influence an "education for leisure program through recreation."

The Metro Board expanded the park recreation program into new county areas during following years, the number of playgrounds rising to ninety-five and of ball diamonds to eighty-five in 1964. Jack Spore's summer recreation staff increased to 300, and to assist him with managing the burgeoning program the Board in 1965 made Mary Wherry the assistant superintendent of recreation in charge of community programs and James H. Fyke the first full-time sports supervisor. Thus, within twenty-four months of the formation of Metro government, the Park Board fulfilled Mayor Briley's mandate ordering that recreational programs be extended to the entire county.[11]

While the major expansion of recreation programs was in progress, the number and size of the parks in the system also grew as a result of massive urban renewal developments then underway. In the East Nashville Urban Renewal Project, East and McFerrin parks were expanded to more than ten acres each, while Douglas Park was relocated to a new twenty-four acre site adjoining Meigs School. Cleveland Park at the Cleveland Street Viaduct and Kirkpatrick Park next to Kirkpatrick School at Sevier and South Ninth streets opened to the public in 1964. Cleveland Park took its name from the street on which it fronted, which presumably was named for President Grover Cleveland, and Kirkpatrick Park took its name from the school, which in turn was named for C. T. Kirkpatrick, a teacher and principal from 1900 to 1940. At some of these parks, new community centers opened, replacing the Quonset huts used for the purpose since the Second World War.[12]

Urban renewal also resulted in the closing of two older parks. Tony Rose Park at Sixteenth and Division Street was engulfed by the "Music Row" commercial development and was closed at the end of the 1964 playground season. It became the site of the Country Music Hall of Fame, but musician Tony Rose's name was assigned by the Board to a new two-acre playground at Music Circle East and Hawkins Street. Victory Square, the little park downtown used as a transfer point for the city bus system, was returned to state government in 1969, and the state built an underground office complex on the site, making old Victory Square Park the new Legislative Plaza atop the roof of the office complex.[13]

Mayor Briley directed the Metro Board to initiate planning for the acquisition of more park land in the county ringing the city, but, because the Board had no professional planners until 1964 when it employed Frank Atchley and Lallie Richter to form a Planning Section under Bill Crouch's direction, the Board relied on the plans prepared by Irving Hand and Joe Williams of the Metro Planning Commission under Title VII of the 1961 Federal Housing Act. The 1961 Housing Act permitted the Federal Housing and Home Finance Administration—subsequently merged into the Department of Housing and Urban Development (HUD)—to grant seventy-percent matching funds to local governments for the purchase of "open space" or park lands; it therefore was known as the Open Space Land program. While Hand and Williams were preparing comprehensive plans for park development throughout the county, they became aware of an opportunity in 1963 to purchase one new park immediately; and it became the first park acquired under the Open Space Land program. Located on McGavock Pike near Berry Field, Seven Oaks Park was purchased in 1963 for $148,392 of which the Metro Park Board paid only thirty percent, the remainder being paid with federal matching funds.[14]

In December 1963 the Planning Commission completed its study of large park areas needed to serve the county and submitted its proposals and maps to the Park Board for approval. In addition to the seventy-six-acre Seven Oaks Park already purchased, the plans called for acquisition of large parks on Dickerson Road, Old Hickory Boulevard, McGavock Pike, Charlotte Pike, and in the Richland and Dupontonia sections of the county, aiming at providing adequate park area in the county until about 1980. "We have the time and the terrain to really do something," said Irving Hand when submitting the Planning Commission report: "We have a plan projected to 1980. Whether or not we accomplish what we want depends a lot on our desire and our ability to work together."[15]

Under the Open Space Land program, the Park Board in 1965 purchased 225 hilly and cedar-covered acres at the intersection of Old Hickory Boulevard and Dickerson Road near Goodlettsville, naming it Cedar Hill Park and reserving it for future development. When funding became available a decade later the park opened in 1976, becoming well known for the ingenious engineering of its softball complex. In 1965 the Board also purchased the 25-acre Charlotte Park on Eastboro Drive in West Nashville, and the following year it acquired the nineteen-acre Rock City Park adjoining Inglewood School in East Nashville. Charlotte Park took its name from the Charlotte Park subdivision around it, and Rock City Park, on the site of a rock quarry, was renamed South Inglewood Park in 1972 at the request of the East Nashville Civic League.[16]

To meet urgent needs for park space in the Bordeaux area northwest of the Cumberland River, the Metro Board acquired two parks by transfer from the city convalescent and tuberculosis hospitals in that area, thanks largely to the efforts of Metro Councilmen Arch Carney and James Bates. Twelve acres of land on Snell Road became the Bordeaux Garden Park with a playground and ball diamonds, and twenty-five acres on Tucker Road became the Richard W.

Hartman Park, the naming honoring a civic leader who had worked many years with the youth of Bordeaux.[17]

The third of Mayor Briley's three-point park development program involved achieving better cooperation between the park and school systems, and the relationship certainly needed improving. Efforts toward a cooperative Park-School program had begun in 1910 when Hume-Fogg High School was built at Eighth and Broad and the Park Board proposed to the School Board that they jointly purchase two entire city blocks at the site and place the school building in the center of a park; the $200,000 price tag had scuttled the plan and Hume-Fogg School was built on the corner without even a sizable lawn. A successful Park-School plan was completed in 1916 after the East Nashville fire when East Park and Warner School were jointly developed, but no continuing cooperation between the two systems developed until 1947 when William Hume, member of both the Park and School Board, arranged the joint development of South Park and Howard School. There remained, of course, no cooperation at all between the county school system and the city park system, and county school grounds stood vacant during the summers except where civic clubs organized a few recreation programs. The Metro Charter sought to improve cooperation between the systems by requiring that a member of the School Board also serve on the Park Board, and Mayor Briley was determined that a fully coordinated program would be implemented after 1963.[18]

The Metro Planning Commission in 1963 recommended that the planning of combination park and school complexes be initiated. "Schools will be designed so that the recreation part of it—the gym, pools and the like—can be conveniently used after the rest of the school is locked up," commented Joe Williams of the Planning Commission, adding: "It would be adjacent to enough acreage to provide room for sports and passive recreation—some trees and grass." Savings could be accomplished by locating new schools in public parks, or by choosing the sites of new parks near existing schools, permitting use of the recreation facilities by both the students at the schools and by the public when school was not in session.[19]

To coordinate the Park-School program, the Planning Commission, Board of Education, and Park Board organized a joint committee, with Bert Elmore, Bill Crouch, and Charles Mager representing the Park Board on the committee. A pilot program began in 1965 at Hillsboro, Maplewood, Overton, and Neeleys Bend schools, where the Park Board expended $95,000 building tennis courts and ball diamonds. At E. S. Rose Park on Edgehill Avenue, the committee arranged joint development, with the Board of Education using the park as a playground for the Carter-Lawrence and Rose schools and the Park Board building a community center and swimming pool in the center of the complex. Similar cooperative efforts were undertaken at the new Douglas Park serving Meigs School. Under a memorandum of understanding signed in 1965, the Park Board was permitted to use certain school facilities for public recreation purposes in the evenings and on weekends.[20]

By the end of the 1960s, the Metro Board of Parks and Recreation had largely achieved the three goals set for it by Mayor Briley in 1963. It had expanded the summer playground recreation program from the city limits throughout Davidson County's suburban areas, adding large numbers of ball diamonds, tennis courts, and other recreation attractions and using school grounds where park land was unavailable. It had initiated comprehensive planning for the acquisition of large public parks in the county around the city, and it had participated in a joint Park-School development program. Those program expansions were costly, but the Park Board received no substantial increase in its operating budget during the 1960s. It had begun in 1964 with a $2.25 million budget, but in 1968 when it asked a $3.5 million budget, the Mayor reduced it to $2.6 million and the Metro Council slashed it further to $2 million. That cut forced the Park Board to lay off 184 seasonal and 44 fulltime employees and curtail many programs, and Director Bert Elmore commented that in the future: "We will have to do one of three things. We can ask the city for more money to operate. Or we can cut back on our services. Or we can start charging for the use of facilities which have been free."[21]

To deal with that funding exigency, the Metro Park Board in 1969 reorganized its budget process and its staff. Instead of submitting a single annual budgetary request, starting in 1969 it submitted three, called the status quo, minimum service, and progressive budgets, to assist the Mayor and Metro Council in selecting the budget best suited to the city's fiscal condition. In practice, of course, the park system seldom received a budget allocation greater than its status quo budget, and sometimes not even that. During the preceding half century, the Board's staff had essentially functioned within three administrative divisions—recreation, park maintenance, and administration—but the 1969 reorganization increased the number of divisions to five, adding the Special Services Division and the Research and Planning Division. The formation of the Research and Planning Division with Lallie Richter as its chief marked the end of relatively haphazard park acquisition and development efforts of earlier years; that new division would become responsible for comprehensive park system planning, for individual park master planning, and for other research and planning responsibilities to assure a more orderly future for the system. Sports supervisor James H. Fyke became the chief of the new Special Services Division, which was to be responsible for the system's "cost recovery" or revenue enhancement efforts, including the golfing, tennis, riding, and other revenue-producing park programs which could help the system become less dependent upon the vagaries of tax-generated revenues.[22]

Several other noteworthy changes in the Board's executive staff occurred at about the time of the 1969 reorganization. Park maintenance superintendent Frank Pickens and park horticulturist Z. N. Dobbs, who had worked as a team during several decades retired in 1967 and 1968. By the time of their retirement, they were supervising the mowing of 80,000 acres annually, the yearly planting of 77,000 flowers plus shrubs and trees, building painting and maintenance, the painting and repairing each winter of 15,000 park benches and 5,000 picnic tables, the conditioning of hundreds of ball diamonds, tennis courts, and playing fields, and the disposal of tons of litter and repair of damages done by vandals. Those monumental tasks were passed on to the new horticulturist, James H. Pirtle, and Frank Atchley, the successor to Pickens. Both Director Bert Elmore and Assistant Director Bill Crouch resigned in 1970 to enter private business, Elmore joining Hardaway Construction and Crouch the General Transportation Services Corporation. With permission of his company, Crouch later returned as interim Director for eighteen months while the Park Board searched for a new Director, and then he was appointed to the Park Board. Crouch recalls visiting Frank Pickens in the hospital a few days before his death, and Pickens needling him: "So, now you are a Park Commissioner, eh? I can remember when you couldn't even spell commissioner."[23]

In reflection upon the changes in the park system he observed during the early years of Metro government, Bill Crouch credits Dr. Reichardt and several of the Board members with the leadership which imbued life into the system. Dr. Reichardt, an active golfer and boater, brought fresh and professional thinking to his duties as Board Chairman, instituting modern business practices in park management and gaining the Nashville park system recognition from the National Recreation and Parks Association. Mrs. Irwin Eskind was instrumental in the development of a strong cultural arts program in the system; A. J. "Joe" Roper performed yeoman service in the development of the Harpeth Hills and Rhodes golf courses; and B. R. Allison took special interest in improving the system's equestrian facilities. They and other Board members devoted "worlds of their time" toward the creation of a modern, viable parks and recreation program in the metropolitan city.[24]

15 PARKS FOR AN AFFLUENT SOCIETY

During its first decade of park management, the Metropolitan Board of Parks and Recreation learned it was expected not only to extend the park and recreation program throughout the 533 square miles of its service area but also to make those parks serve the increasingly complex needs of what was termed "Affluent Society" during the 1960s. The administration of President Lyndon Johnson called upon the park system to help alleviate unemployment and other social ills. Preservationists urged the Board to help save historic structures as part of Nashville's heritage by fitting them into planned park developments. Leaders of the national environmental movement wanted parks that would become wilderness preserves, without any development, recreational or otherwise, to mar their solitude. Citizens interested in the fine arts wanted a more active cultural recreation effort; and then there were the "hippies," and no one knew what they wanted. Through considerable manipulation of its resources, the Metro Board somehow found a place for all of those loud and sometimes conflicting public demands within the park system.

When the Board received a letter in 1964 from Senator Gaylord Nelson asking it to participate in President Johnson's "War on Poverty" by hiring unemployed youth for job training in the parks, it referred the letter to Mayor Briley, who formed the Metropolitan Action Commission to coordinate the city's participation in social programs under federal contracts. Under one of those contracts, a Neighborhood Youth Corps was established to enroll unemployed youth in a work-experience program somewhat reminiscent of the WPA of the 1930s and with ninety-percent federal funding under park staff supervision. Frank Atchley became the park director of that work-experience program, using maintenance foremen and other personnel as supervisors of the 345 young people put to work in 1965.[1]

Employed largely for park maintenance work at minimum wages, for many members of the Neighborhood Youth Corps it was the first paying job they had ever held. Like other social reform efforts of President Johnson's "Great Society" programs, the Neighborhood Youth Corps became the subject of political controversy; yet, the park system staff which supervised it believe the young people earned not only wages but also invaluable work experience and other benefits through their participation. Bill Crouch recites the names of young men whose lives were turned around by the program, of men who previously had lived chiefly through theft and who, through ttheir participation in the Corps, became contributing members of the Nashville community. Their work also permitted the accomplishment of tasks in the parks that otherwise would have gone undone because of the budgetary constraints and personnel restrictions under which the system operated.[2]

Funding provided for the work-experience program tapered downward soon after the program was initiated. In 1966 the number of young people hired dropped to 119 and the salaries of the park supervisory staff were no longer reimbursed with federal funding. During the following decade, a Youth Conservation Corps worked ten weeks each summer at a camp in Warner Park, their principal efforts being directed toward development of the Warner Park Nature Center and such environmental recreation features as hiking trails, while work at inner city parks was funded under the Comprehensive Employment and Training Act (CETA), providing assistance at community centers, playgrounds, and the "mini-parks."[3]

Under another "Great Society" program, the Demonstration Cities and Metropolitan Development Act of 1966 called the "Model Cities Act," Nashville's metropolitan government undertook a comprehensive city demonstration project, featuring recreation projects in the parks and community centers with full federal funding. Among the demonstration projects funded under the Model Cities Act were programs for senior citizens, park-school playgrounds, day camps, expanded athletic leagues, after-school recreation, and recreation for the handicapped. Those efforts were supplemented in 1968, at the recommendation of Mrs. Irwin Eskind, a Park Commissioner, with a "mini-park" project in the inner city funded by the U.S. Department of Labor at about $100,000 annually. On vacant lots and school playgrounds in the sweltering inner city, "mini-parks" were created on a scale reminiscent of the street-corner playgrounds opened in 1910 on 150-foot lots to provide summer recreation for children ages eight to thirteen.[4]

Most "Great Society" social programs were, to use Lallie Richter's computer metaphor, software rather than hardware; they were aimed at social benefits rather then the physical plant improvements, and they left few traces in the park system of their existence after President Ronald Reagan's administration ended the programs in 1981. Few of the fourteen "mini-parks" open in 1972 remained in operation during the 1980s, and only the Warner Park Nature Center remained as a monument to the work of the Youth Conservation Corps. The Model Cities program, however, funded two major physical improvements: the community center at R. H. Boyd Park and the elaborate Z. Alexander Looby Center. Both designed by McKissack and McKissack, the centers were completed in the early 1970s; and the North Nashville Cultural Center was renamed by Metro Council ordinance in tribute to the memory of councilman and civil rights leader Z. Alexander Looby who had spearheaded the integration of Nashville parks. The Looby Center included not only the usual community recreation facilities, but also a theater and a branch of the public library.[5]

Out of the "Great Society" programs came renewed interest in the old City Beautification Commission, stimulated in part by the personal interest taken by Ladybird Johnson, wife of the President, in creating more attractive cities. Nashville's Beautification Commission had been established at the turn of the century at the insistence of the Centennial Club, then serving a purpose not far from that served by the modern Planning Commission. With the formation of the Planning Commission in 1933, however, the Beautification Commission became responsible for city improvement projects that did not quite fall under the responsibilities of the Planning, Parks, or Public Works departments. After the Second World War, it was directed by Mrs. Mary Poag, a veritable dynamo who became the first chief of the Metropolitan Beautification Commission. She and eight employees patrolled the city to assure that trash and unsightly clutter were removed and also organized citywide cleanup campaigns, supervising the annual spring city-cleaning days; several times their efforts brought Nashville recognition as one of the nation's cleanest cities. After the 1963 formation of Metro, the commission became a department of government and then a division of the Department of Public Works. Rena Wright, secretary to Mayor Briley, became director of the Beautification Division in 1975, and six months later it was transferred to the park system. In every year after the transfer, Wright's Beautification Division earned the national "Keep America Beautiful" award for its efforts toward maintaining a clean and attractive city.[6]

Because the "Affluent Society" of the 1960s showed greater, or at least more widespread, interest in the fine arts than had previously been the case, the Metro Park Board initiated an extensive participatory arts program in the system to supplement the traditional fine arts displays long conducted at the Parthenon. Sarah Bradford, James Cowan, and Newman Cheek had contributed the initial art and facilities which made the Parthenon a city cultural center, and efforts by Benjamin Wilson, Malcolm Parker, Wesley Paine and other directors of the Parthenon had secured displays of Oriental art, archaeological artifacts, the silver set of the U.S.S. *Nashville*, and other additions which made the Parthenon a showcase of fine art. The Metro Park Board recognized at its formation in 1963, however, that the recreation program should include participatory arts and crafts classes, giving the supplies needed to children and charging adults small fees, and the Board capped that program in 1963 with sponsorship of an annual arts festival in Centennial Park which continued every year thereafter.[7]

While studying the park system's program and the city's cultural arts facilities, Commissioners B. R. Allison and Mrs. Irwin Eskind concluded in 1965 that an additional art gallery and workshop together with a sculpture and pottery garden could be an excellent addition to park sponsorship of creative arts. The other members of the Board concurred and construction of the new Centennial Art Center began at the site of the abandoned swimming pool in Centennial Park. When it was completed in 1972, the Board appointed a director. The Board also established a cultural recreation division to administer the park system's arts, crafts, dance and musical programs. Painting and pottery classes were conducted in the new art center on a year-round basis, with other art classes organized at various appropriate times. The art center building offered local artists opportunities to display their creations, the old swimming pool became a unique sculpture and pottery garden, and in front of the center the Nashville Herb Society maintained an herbal garden as a public education effort. The Cultural Recreation division also became responsible for coordination of the extensive annual round of concerts, lectures, drama, and festivals in the parks as part of its Family Outing Program.[8]

The traditional summer concerts in the parks underwent metamorphosis during the late 1960s. While Don Q. Pullen continued directing the lively musical concerts at Hadley Park, organist Leon Cole retired in 1967 after more than a quarter-century run during the summers in Centennial Park. Elmer Hinton, renowned forklore columnist for the *Tennessean*, assumed direction of country and gospel music concerts at Centennial Park, which continued into the 1970s when his newspaper ended its sponsorship of the series. The headline-making concerts of the 1960s were not the traditional Sunday concerts, however, but the rock-and-roll extravaganzas. Joe Sullivan of WMAK radio organized rock concerts at Centennial Park in 1968, drawing some 70,000 young people to a three-day event that August. A similar festival held in 1969 drew a rowdy crowd of 150,000, and as the size of the crowds mushroomed, so did criticisms from the more conservative members of the community. At the request of Commander George Currey of the Metropolitan Youth Guidance Division, who warned the size of the crowds prevented proper enforcement of laws against drug abuse, obscenity, and disturbances, the Metro Board in 1972 voted not to permit more rock concerts in the park for the time being.[9]

One attraction at the rock concerts of the late 1960s was the flower-children, or "hippies," whose eccentric behavior fascinated less avantgarde spectators. When not attending the concerts or a demonstration, the "hippies" gathered near the Parthenon in large numbers, "doing their thing." When other visitors complained, the park patrol investigated but generally found the "hippies" tossing frisbees, strumming guitars, and staring off into space without violating any specific park regulation. After attending a 1968 forum concerning the "generation gap," Dr. George Reichardt recommended that the park system initiate programs aimed at the disenchanted youth of the city; and during 1969 teen centers, sometimes called coffee houses or rap centers, opened at several community recreation centers. But the flower-child phenomenon soon faded as mysteriously as it had arisen, leaving no trace in the park system unless one counted the psychedelic serpent to be seen in Dees Park.[10]

The youthful revolution of the late 1960s apparently was one feature of a broader public reaction against the effects of proliferating technological change and urbanization, against environmental deterioration and in favor of preserving as much of the natural environment as possible. Culminating on Earth Day in April 1970, with nationwide demonstrations graphically portraying the perils of pollution, of overpopulation and unchecked urbanization, the environmental movement had ineluctable effect on Nashville's park system, generating a substantial, albeit unquantifiable, increased public support for more parks as a hedge against advancing pavements. The preservation of the environment and also of historic sites was a fundamental tenet of the environmental movement, and that concept left at least three landmarks in the city park system: the Warner Park Nature Center, the Two Rivers Mansion, and the Cumberland Museum and Science Center.[11]

At Two Rivers Park, the Metro Board embarked upon the park system's second major effort to preserve the city's historic heritage, the first having been the Sunnyside Mansion at Sevier Park. When 1300 Donelson residents petitioned the Metro Board for the purchase and preservation of the mansion and estate of the late Mrs. Spence (Louise Bransford) McGavock, the estate was purchased in 1966 with a fifty-percent matching grant under the Open Space Land program. Three government agencies took parts of the estate: public works took a strip for the construction of Briley Parkway, the Board of Education took thirty acres for the construcion of the McGavock comprehensive high school, and the remaining 384 acres became Two Rivers Park. In the new park was the McGavock home, an

Italianate manor built in 1859, along with an older home built in 1802, and the Board employed historian Hugh Walker to study the mansion and recommend measures for its preservation while Malcolm Parker, Mrs. Gladys Reichardt, and volunteers excavated archaeological sites on the estate to recover the artifacts for display. Under the direction of the Metro Historical Commission, restoration of the McGavock home—Two Rivers Mansion—began during the 1970s, with facilities for public convenience added and with period furnishings supplied largely through volunteer efforts by the Stone's River Women's Club, making it the most successful historic preservation project completed by the Park Board.[12]

Two Rivers Park and McGavock High School, it should be added, became one of four comprehensive Park-School developments undertaken by Metro government during the 1970s, the other three including Glencliff, Whites Creek, and John Trotwood Moore (Green Hills Park) school complexes. Facilities at each of the Park-School developments varied, with community recreation centers and indoor swimming pools at some for joint park and school use, while the facilities at Two Rivers-McGavock High School consisted of tennis courts, ball diamonds, picnic areas, and a golf course, all of which were more heavily used than initially expected because of the construction nearby of the immense Opryland tourist attractions.[13]

Efforts at the historic preservation of old Fort Negley were less successful, though the fort was placed upon the National Register of Historic Places in 1975. The park surrounding the fort was put to good use, however, starting in 1966 when Vernon Sharp, Joe Thompson, and Philbrick Crouch met with the Park Board to ask that it permit use of the park as the new home of the Children's Museum, then located in South Park. The initial plans included not only a new museum building but also restoration of the old fort and the connection of the fort via a footpath with the City Cemetery at the base of St. Cloud Hill. The Board agreed it would permit the construction of the museum in the park and also make a substantial contribution toward funding its construction. Renamed the Cumberland Museum and Science Center, the building was completed during the 1970s on the west side of St. Cloud Hill, and its staff instituted a broad program of environmental science studies and natural history educational endeavors, but Fort Negley was not restored.[14]

On the opposite side of the hill below Fort Negley, Greer Stadium was built during the 1970s as the new home of professional baseball in the city. The Nashville Vols had played their last Southern League game at Sulphur Dell on September 8, 1963, defeating Lynchburg in a double-header, and that stadium, long famous for the freakish home runs hit in and out of it, subsequently was demolished, concluding a century of baseball at the site. The Nashville Baseball Club headed by Larry Schmittou asked the Metro Board in 1976 for permission to construct and lease a professional baseball stadium at Fort Negley Park, choosing the site because of the available parking space and its convenient location near the interstate highways. Completed in 1977, the park was named Herschel L. Greer Stadium, honoring a Nashville businessman whose family made a large contribution in his memory toward stadium funding. It seemed appropriate that professional baseball, introduced to Nashville by Union Army soldiers, should be played at the site of a Union Army fortress, although the fort itself remained covered with vines and brush.[15]

Retaining all the vines, brush, and trees possible at the Warner parks in the face of increasing public use pressures became a fundamental goal at those parks as the result of a movement emphasizing their role as a sanctuary of historical and ecological significance. The Warner parks had served Nashvillians since 1927 as a living laboratory for field research in environmental and ecological sciences, and the Metro Board in 1973 took advantage of that tradition, and also of support for such programs generated by the environmental movement, by establishing a Nature Center in Edwin Warner Park. The programs featured guided tours of the parks, natural-science classes, and other environment-oriented activities. With labor largely supplied by the Youth Conservation Corps from 1974 through 1980, nature trails, vegetable and flower gardens, along with the C. E. Farrell Museum of Natural History were established in connection with the Nature Center.[16]

As intensive residential construction proceeded around the perimeter of the 2,665 acres in Warner parks, public use of the parks multiplied and various intrusions into the sanctity of their environment occurred, consisting of illegal dumping and encroachments and also of well-intended efforts by the Metro Board and staff to serve public recreation needs. A new ball diamond opened in Edwin Warner Park in 1967, largely through the efforts of Bob Heriges in whose honor the field was named. Margaret Warden and the *Tennessean* sponsored horse trials, dressage trials, pony shows, carriage horse shows, and other equestrian events in the park steeplechase area, all drawing large crowds; and as interest in equestrian sports grew in 1970, at the recommendation of Commissioner B. R. Allison the Metro Board approved the opening of a polo field near the Nature Center on Highway 100. Those facilities built to meet public recreation demands intruded on the park environment, no matter how sensitive the facilities were to environmental considerations, for they involved some construction and reordering of the natural environment and attracted even more people into the parks.[17]

The Board in 1979 initiated a master study to plan the future use of the Warner parks, which recommended that the larger Percy Warner Park should be reserved for passive recreation—riding, nature study, picnicking, scenic drives—while Edwin Warner Park should have both passive and active recreation programming, with environmental impacts becoming a primary consideration in determining the future of the parks. The parks in 1980 were placed on the Tennessee Register of Natural Areas under state environmental preservation legislation and in 1984 were added to the National Register of Historic Places. Over the years, the programs in the Warner parks received many contributions from the Audubon Society and other organizations; and in 1985, Peggy Joyce, president of the Garden Club of Nashville founded in 1928 by Mrs. Edwin Warner and others, announced the club would donate $10,000 for the construction of a library and other improvements at the Nature Center.[18]

Events at the April 1985 meeting of the Metro Board highlighted growing and sometimes conflicting public pressures for the use of Warner parks. Representatives of the Volunteer State Horseman's Association, which had managed the Iroquois steeplechase since 1941, announced they would fence off a portion of the hillside near the finish line and charge a small admission fee for improved crowd control and for larger racing prizes; and when Chairman Reichardt commented that "the day of view for pay has arrived," the Board approved the request. When representatives of the Nashville Charity Horse Show asked permission to use the Model Airplane field as the site of their benefit riding show and also to install the utility systems needed, members of the Model Airplane Club objected, declaring the model flying field the "oldest and best of its sort in the nation" and complaining of the disruption to model flying that the horse show would cause. Apparently no acceptable alternative site for the horse show existed, for the Board voted to permit it at the flying field for a one-year trial period.[19]

Meeting multiple public demands for park services necessitated continuing expansion of the park system in the old county area, in the hills, so to speak: Cedar Hill, Green Hills, and Trinity Hills. Cedar Hill Park on Dickerson Road, acquired during the 1960s for future use, was developed during the mid-1970s with a four diamond, back-to-back, softball complex centered about a modern concessions building. Described by the director of the American Amateur Softball Association as the "finest softball facility in the nation," Cedar Hill Park opened on August 28, 1977, with a softball game between Mayor Richard Fulton and his department heads versus a Metro Council team. In the central building of the complex, the Park Board in 1979 established what was called the "softball hall of fame" consisting of memorials honoring Fred Hazlewood, Rose Way, Stan Cioccia, Ellis Cook, and Paul Spears who had contributed substantially to the success of the sport in Nashville.[20]

At the end of the county opposite from Cedar Hill Park, plans of the 1960s had called for creating a large park in the Green Hills area with federal Open Space funding, but efforts to acquire the land for the park were delayed too long. By the time the land acquisition for the park began, the rapid urbanization of the Green Hills area had driven real estate prices skyward. Expecting to market their land to apartment and business developers for prices higher than appraised values, the land owners were reluctant to sell the properties for park use; and when Councilman Tandy Wilson, representing the Green Hills community, opposed the land acquisition, the Metro Park Board dropped its plans for a large park. The Board did, however, purchase sixteen acres on Lone Oak Road as the Green Hills Park, which served essentially as a playing field for the adjoining John Trotwood Moore school.[21]

Plans for a large park north of the Cumberland River and Trinity Lane in the Haynes Heights community also were scuttled by escalating land prices. When the Board proposed in 1968 to create a Trinity Hills Park, private owners objected that they would be unable to replace their properties at the appraised values, and the Metro Board in 1970 withdrew its application for federal Open Space funding of the proposed park. Builders of the Trinity Hills Village low-rent housing development left fifty acres of land adjacent to the village open to serve as Trinity Hills Park, but the Park Board's application to fund park development had not been approved in 1985.[22]

Quick action by the Board brought E. N. Peeler Park into the system under the Open Space Land program in 1963. Learning that Mr. Peeler was willing to sell his 259-acre farm on Neelys Bend Road near Madison for a relatively low price, the Board took an option to buy it in November 1963, then applied to the federal government for matching funds which was forthcoming in late 1964. Dr. Reichardt hoped to build a golf course there although that plan was deferred to avoid competing with a privately operated golf course which opened nearby. Through another fortunate circumstance in 1970, the Board acquired the Sun Valley Swim Club adjoining the Peeler farm because its owner, Homer Chance, sold it to the park system at about half its appraised value in order to keep it in public operation. The swim club increased the area of Peeler Park to about 274 acres and provided a pool, outdoor skating rink, and other facilities for the park.[23]

Gifts from and leasing arrangements with the Nashville District, U.S. Army Corps of Engineers, substantially increased the total park area during the 1960s. The Corps leased the system tiny Lock Two Park in Pennington Bend and Lock One Park in Bordeaux as surplus federal properties, and in 1964 leased the public beach on Old Hickory Lake to the Metro Board for operation. As the J. Percy Priest Dam and Lake neared completion in 1965 near Donelson, the Board also agreed to lease and operate a 790-acre area on the lake's east side, naming it Hamilton Creek Park. Through cooperative development with the Corps of Engineers, a beach and launching ramp, opened in Hamilton Creek Park, and in 1975 the Board took part on a cost-sharing basis in the construction of a sailboat marina which opened in 1980. In 1982 a bicycle motorcross Track was built. For an inland city, the sailboat marina was truly a unique recreational facility.[24]

The Metropolitan Board of Parks and Recreation somehow managed to meet all the demands placed upon the park system during the late 1960s and early 1970s. During its first decade of operation, it provided space in park programming for the social reform campaigns of the "War on Poverty," it initiated new cultural recreation programs and facilities, and it responded to the national environmental and historic preservation movements. It found space in the park system for softball complexes, museums, nature centers, art centers, historic mansions, and professional baseball, for flower children as well as polo enthusiasts. Recreational opportunities were made available to both Nashville's "Affluent Society" and those less affluent having a broad spectrum of lifestyles. Indeed, one of the attractive features of Nashville's park system was that no one was required to have a lifestyle in order to enjoy the parks.

16 PARK MANAGEMENT IN THE 70's

The Metropolitan Board of Parks and Recreation selected Charles R. Spears as its new Director of the park system in 1971, replacing interim Director Bill Crouch who returned to private business and was elected to the Park Board. An associate of Bill Crouch, Spears was a professional park manager from Louisville and had served as chief of Special Services for the Minneapolis parks before coming to Nashville. In Minneapolis, Spears had directed the "cost recovery" program aimed at making park facilities there more self-supporting, and he was to preside over a similar program in the Nashville system, planning the addition of such recreation-for-pay facilities as Ice Centennial and Wave Country. He also persevered with the major park expansion effort initiated by Dr. Reichardt and Directors Elmore and Crouch, adding to the system new parks purchased with federal funding, received as gifts from citizens, leased from state government, and created as a result of a policy adopted by the Metropolitan planning commission. Spears hoped to help make the Nashville park system one of the best in the nation, and by the time he left the system toward the end of the 1970s it was earning national awards as the tops among cities of comparable size.[1]

Although the Nashville park system seemed always in transition as a result of efforts to keep apace of advancing urbanization, changing municipal government, and recreation trends, continuity was provided by an executive management which essentially devoted their lives to system advancement; and although Spears was not a Nashville native and had not grown up within the park system he made practically no changes in the administrative staff. Frank Atchley continued as Park Administrator, Lallie Richter as Planning Administrator, James H. Fyke as Special Services Administrator, James R. Derseweh as Business Administrator, and Jack Spore as Recreation Administrator with assistance from Mary Wherry and sports supervisor Tom Andrews. Spears did place increasing emphasis upon advising the public about the park operations, and his principal staffing innovation was the formation of a public information office.[2]

At the time Spears arrived in Nashville, the park system was undergoing one of its perennial budget crises. When the Park Board had submitted its 1971 budget, Metro Finance Director Joe Torrence insisted it should be reduced by $700,000, to a figure $182,000 less than the 1970 parks budget. The Board therefore initiated severe personnel cutbacks and reductions in park and playground services to achieve the $700,000 budget severance, but the Metro Council restored a portion of that year's budget, setting it at slightly over $3 million. That essentially was the budgetary pattern through the Spears years: the Park Board submitted its budget request, the Mayor and the Finance Director slashed it, the Board announced service cutbacks, and the Metro Council restored part of the budget to avoid the more controversial closings of recreation programs and park facilities. On the face of it, the annual budget furor seemed the "elevator gambit," the ploy used by building managers when facing budget cuts of closing the services—the elevators—which would generate the greatest public outcry in opposition to the reductions. That was not the case in the park system, however, where every single park and playground in the city was considered an elevator by the neighborhood it served.[3]

During the seven years Spears served as Director, the annual park system budget grew from $3 million to $4.6 million, or an approximate fifty percent increase; yet, it never seemed adequate, and for good reason. Many new park facilities opened during the same period, and each new facility required additional personnel for its operation and funding for its maintenance; the 1970s, moreover, were marked by runaway monetary inflation. Each gallon of gasoline used to mow the parks more than doubled in price during the 1970s, and that pricing trend prevailed through practically the entire national economy. If reduced to constant dollar values, and taking into account the new park facilities opened during the period, the $4.6 million park budget of 1978 probably amounted to less than the $3 million of 1971.[4]

Runaway inflation and skyrocketing real estate values in Davidson County during the 1970s severely hampered the Metro Board's efforts to acquire additional park land and open spaces for future park development. The resulting failures to create large urban parks in the Green Hills and Haynes Heights communities have been described in a previous chapter, but some new parks were acquired during the 1970s through gifts from citizens, leasing arrangements with state government, and a newly enforced policy of the city planning commission.

The gift of tiny Cecil R. Crawford Park at Cane Ridge School in the southeastern sector of the county deserves special mention, for Mr. Crawford essentially gave the park system everything he owned. Crawford, an Oklahoma native who had moved to Nashville, taught music and often had his students perform for the Cane Ridge Community Club meeting in the abandoned Cane Ridge School at the intersection of Old Hickory Boulevard and Cane Ridge Road. In 1971, he modestly donated his property to the park system, requiring that his donation remain secret until after his death. The Metro Board complied with his request, and in 1982 added his 4 acres to the 3 acres known as Cane Ridge Park and renamed it Cecil Rhea Crawford Park, an approproate tribute to the donor who not only gave the land but also bequested a surprisingly large estate to assure tha future maintenance of the park. If his example were followed, the annual park budget furor could eventually be eliminated.[5]

Notable also is little Fannie Mae Dees Park at Blakemore and 24th avenues in the Vanderbilt University urban redevelopment area. Purchased outright by the Park Board because it was situated to serve the adjacent Cavert, Eakin, and Harris-Hillman schools, the park was named at the request of the Eakin Community Council for a civic leader who had vigorously defended the rights of area property owners during urban renewal planning. Development of the park began in 1977 and was uniquely marked by the sea serpent sculpture of Pedro Silva. Board member Ann Roos, who was impressed by Silva's art works in New York, invited him to Nashville to design the sculpture with an $8,000 grant from the Tennessee Arts Commission and to orchestrate the privately funded project. Vanderbilt University, local businesses, and residents in the vicinity contributed materials and labor toward creation of the serpent decorated with a mosaic of ceramic tiles. It was to serve not only as decorative art but also as a functional piece of playground equipment with seating along its tail and slithering coils. Among the many original mosaic designs covering the coiling beast was a portrait of Fannie Mae Dees by Chris Talbott.[6]

State government never lent much support to the development of Nashville's park system prior to the 1970s, but that relationship improved during the Spears years, in part because former Park Commissioner B. R. Allison became the state Commissioner of Conservation. Other than the state charter for the original Park Board and subsequent legislative amendments to facilitate Board functioning, Tennessee state government had contributed little to the city parks; even Victory Square Park near the War Memorial Building—the sole park given to the city by the state—eventually was returned to the state, which built its underground legislative plaza on the site. During the 1970s, however, considerable federal funding assistance was funneled through the office of the Tennessee Commissioner of Conservation into park system development, and the Park Board leased two new park sites from state government.

The Park Board in 1976 negotiated with state government for a park at the Ellington Agricultural Center and another near the Central State Hospital (DeBerry Correctional Institute). For a dollar a year honorarium, it leased from the Tennessee Department of Conservation eleven acres at the Ellington Agricultural Center, once the Brentwood Hall estate of Park Commissioner Rogers Caldwell; at the request of Metro Councilman Carney Patterson, the Board named the park in honor of William D. Whitfield, a leader of the Little League baseball organization in South Nashville. Sixty-five acres in the Mill Creek valley on Ezell Road near Central State became the Ezell Park and was subleased to the Junior Pro Football League, which built fields and facilities for amateur football on the site, expending thousands of contributed dollars and supervising an active recreation program.[7]

The Tennessee Commissioner of Conservation in 1967 became also the state administrator of the Land and Water Conservation Program of the Federal Bureau of Outdoor Recreation (BOR), which in 1978 was renamed the Heritage Conservation and Recreation Service (HCRS). While the older federal Open Space Land program administered by the Department of Housing and Urban Development (HUD) offered matching funding for the acquisiton of park lands, the HCRS program offered matching funding for lands and also for construction of the physical recreation facilities. The Metro Park Board during the early 1970s therefore submitted park project applications to both federal agencies, and if both approved an application it accepted the greater assistance supplied by HCRS. Another change in federal policies occurred in 1974, however, when President Gerald Ford signed the Community Development Act, consolidating the various assistance programs administered by HUD into a single "block grant" program. Urban areas received under the new program a specific lump sum grant to be allocated to the projects selected by municipal governments. Metro Nashville in 1974 received its first $54 million Community Development grant, from which the sum the Mayor and the Metro Council allocated about $2 million toward park expansion, notably the initial development of Riverfront Park. The park system's capital improvements budget after 1974 therefore often came through the Metro Council from Community Development block grant funding, with structural facilities often funded through the Tennessee Commissioner of Conservation from the HCRS Land and Water Conservation program. Federal assistance to the Nashville park system was in operation, frankly, about as complicated as it sounds in print.[8]

Through a policy adopted in connection with the rapid construction of multiple family housing developments throughout Davidson County, the Metro Planning Commission headed by Farris A. Deep added several small parks to the city system. The Planning Commission required real estate developers to provide a certain amount of land for each housing unit constructed and did not relax that requirement when the developers built multi-unit apartment complexes. Considerable open space therefore remained in the vicinity of each new large apartment or townhouse complex which the developers were encouraged to give to the park system to assure future preservation of the land as open space. That policy, plus certain tax benefits, resulted in the creation or expansion of several parks: Parkwood Park, Paragon Mills Park, Bordeaux-Timothy Drive Park, Willow Creek Park, and William A. Pitts Park of Tusculum Road. The latter park was named at the request of Mayor Briley and Farris Deep to honor a member of the Davidson County Planning Commission who also had served as the first Metro Director of Codes. Most of the parks thus acquired were ten to twenty acres in size, and where possible the Park Board expanded them by purchasing adjoining property, installing recreation facilities as funds became available. The Planning Commission policy promised that as multi-unit housing expanded ever farther toward the outer limits of the metropolitan area the park system also would follow.[9]

Coming from Minneapolis, which had been the first city in America to adopt a cost recovery program, euphemistically known as "revenue enhancement," for the better support of its park system, Charles Spears was well qualified to direct the implementation of such a program at Nashville. Though small admission fees had long been collected at golf courses and a few other facilities in Nashville's parks, during the Spears years those fees were increased to bear a more reasonable relationship to the cost of the facilities provided, and the park system assumed direct management of park concessions, formerly handled by contractors who paid fees for the privilege or by employees who thereby supplemented meager salaries. The revenue derived from those sources was to be reinvested in improvement of the facilities where it was generated.[10]

Cost-recovery efforts often encountered public opposition, for people who previously had used park facilities at little or no cost naturally were reluctant to pay more or to pay at all. Being the voters for whose use the parks were designed, they could cast a vote with their feet by refusing to patronize the facilities; and fee increases necessarily were imposed gradually and kept at relatively low rates in order not to lose the clientele. Voters could also appeal fee increases to the Mayor, Metro Council, and Park Board and sometimes defer or entirely defeat the proposed increases. Charging admission to the Parthenon, for instance, has been considered many times over the years, but while the resulting revenue would go far toward meeting the maintenance needs of the structure only "suggested donations" have been collected. And because the cost recovery program was implemented gradually, the resulting revenues scarcely kept apace of the inflationary trends of the 1970s.[11]

The cost-recovery program received a boost toward the end of the Spears years with the planned construction of Ice Centennial, an ice rink, and Wave Country, a swimming pool with a mechanism capable of producing a surf. The two facilities grew out of a joint study funded by the Park Board and the Metro Tourism Commission in 1977 to identify recreation facilities which could serve Nashvillians and assist in attracting more tourists to the city, thereby creating sources of additional revenue for the park system and also contributing to the prosperity of the local tourist-service industry, a major element of the city's economic base. Similar facilities had been successfully operated in other cities, and the Metro Council approved capital funding for the wave pool and ice rink in 1978. When completed during the 1980s, both were well patronized, and the wave pool proved such a success that a private investor sought to purchase it. Perhaps the most important aspect of their construction was the implicit recognition by the Metro Council that the park system has a significant role in the future economic prosperity of the city.[12]

Fee increases had little apparent dampening effects upon the enthusiasm of sportsmen using the park golf courses and softball diamonds. Nashvillians by the thousands limbered up every spring for a summer on the softball diamonds, and Nashville had a national softball championship team in the Dealers Supply nine behind the blazing fastball of Gary Martineau. The most significant trend in the sport during the 1970s was the growing popularity of softball among women, who began to rival men in their participation in park leagues. Increasing numbers of Nashvillians also enjoyed the public links, and the system's golf managers and professionals made both skilled players and duffers welcome. The system's golfing managers in 1970 included Herschel Eaton at Harpeth Hills, Luther Hickman at McCabe, Ronald Hickman at Shelby, Jerry Shively at Percy Warner, Joe Hampton at Rhodes, and Danny Gibson at Riverview. The long service of some of those managers provided a living testimonial to the healthfulness of the game. When Herschel Eaton retired in 1981, he had completed fifty-three years of service on the links; and in 1985 the Park Board honored Joe Hampton for thirty years and the remarkable Luther Hickman for fifty-five years of service to Nashville golfers. Hickman, who had begun work in 1929 for C. E. Danis at Shelby Park, then the only public golf course in the city, by 1985 had become the sole employee of Metro government with a service record of such length.[13]

Basketball, boxing, soccer, and other sports attracted fewer participants than softball and golf but were no less important to a well-rounded recreation program. With the formation of professional soccer teams in the United States, interest in amateur soccer increased, and in 1979 the United Football Club of Nashville renovated at its own expense an old soccer field at South Park. Winter basketball leagues attracted many youngsters to community center gymnasiums, and in 1979 the Tennessee Parks and Recreation Association initiated state championship tournaments, won the first year by teams from the Preston Taylor Homes and Looby Center and the second year by Cleveland and Napier Park teams. Organized boxing at the community centers, begun in 1939 at Fort Negley Park, had a rather checkered career because several different organizations sponsored boxing programs in the city. Sam Bernow and the Nashville Boxing Association used the East Park community center for Golden Gloves training, Chuck Chellman directed a boxing program at the West Park community center, and during the 1980s the Metropolitan Police Athletic League renovated the Eastland community center at its own expense for a supervised boxing program. The real "growth" sports of the 1970s, however, were individual rather than team sports: bicycling, jogging, running, and other "physical fitness" activities.[14]

The parks served as more than sports arenas during the Spears years, and during his last year as Director their use further expanded with the termination of a historic Board policy. When the Park Board in 1903 first adopted rules for public use of city parks, it had forbidden political and religious rallies and demonstrations in the parks and that policy had been adhered to for three-quarters of a century. While the Board sometimes relaxed its rules to permit a congregation whose church had burned the temporary use of a community center, it had rigorously enforced its ban against political activities. It had extended that ban to social demonstrations during the 1950s, denying permits to civil rights and segregationist organizations alike. The first crack in that policy occurred in 1978, when the Board approved a meeting of the National Association for the Advancement of Colored People (NAACP) at Centennial Park. When the NAACP first requested a permit for a rally at the park, the Board cited its prohibition against political demonstrations but referred the issue to Mayor Richard Fulton. After Benjamin Hooks of the NAACP assured that the rally would be orderly, Mayor Fulton determined that Board policy prohibited partisan political or religious activities while the NAACP rally concerned nonpartisan human rights. The Board thereupon granted the permit.[15]

The Metro Council shortly thereafter declared the Board's policy archaic and enacted an ordinance permitting political rallies in the parks, provided fees established by the Board were paid and its regulations for park use observed. The first political rally in a city park took place in July 1978—a rally for gubernatorial candidate Jake Butcher at Hadley Park. Another archaic Board policy fell in 1979 when Mayor Fulton initiated an annual watermelon feast in the parks: if the members of the Park Board and staff knew it, they did not bother to tell the mayor that after some now forgotten incident in 1914 the city Park Board had resolved: "No watermelons shall be eaten in the parks under any circumstances."[16]

Director Charles Spears resigned in late 1978 to return to Minneapolis as its chief park executive, and noted with pride as he left the progress made at Nashville during his seven years of service: the system had added what he considered the best softball facility in the nation at Cedar Hill Park, the best junior football fields at Ezell Park, fine cooperative park-school complexes at the McGavock, Glencliff, and Whites Creek comprehensive schools, along with a number of new parks and other facilities. He also pointed out the growth had not been accomplished solely with tax revenues but also with revenue produced at the park facilities and with substantial voluntary community support, for the system had received private contributions in land and money during his seven years valued at about $1.6 million. He declared that he had hoped when he came to Nashville to help make its park system the best in America, and since the system had earned its first National Gold Medal Award in 1976 as the best among comparably sized cities, he concluded that goal had been achieved.[17]

17 PARK MANAGEMENT IN THE GOLDEN AGE

The architecture of Pericles, the sculpture of Phidias, the drama of Sophocles, and the Olympic athletics of the Golden Age of Ancient Greece are echoed in Nashville today because both the people of Ancient Athens and of the Athens of the South used their leisure time to the fullest. But Ancient Athenians were able to enjoy art and athletics because slaves performed the work, while in Nashville of the 1980s there were no slaves and all citizens had an equal right to the pursuit of happiness through recreation. No richer or more diverse recreation opportunities were ever open to the citizens of any city in history than to Nashvillians during the 1980s, and still the Metropolitan Board of Parks and Recreation and its staff sought to expand and manage the park system in a manner that would allow Nashvillians to rival the achievemenhts of the Ancient Athenians.

In their efforts to provide park and recreation services sufficient to meet the needs of Nashvillians and to maintain the system's national ranking, Chairman George Reichardt and the park commissioners Ann Roos, Tom Keysaer, Fred Russell, A. D. Holloway, A. J. Keitner, Mrs. Ernest Buchi, Isaac Northern, and James Vance—dealt with new challenge at each of their monthly meetings at the Centennial Park office building. Like the first park board of 1901, their principal challenges involved park expansion and improvements, personnel and funding, or in sum the future of the system; yet, they also demonstrated a sensitivity to the park system's history. When, for instance, the Luke Lea Barracks of Veterans of the First World War requested waiver of the usual fee for a Centennial Park picnic, the Metro Board denied the request as a violation of policy, and the Board and staff members then reached into their pockets and personally paid the fee in tribute to the contributions made by Lea and the veterans to the park system.[1]

In coming to decisions concerning management of the park system, the Park Board relied upon its experienced executive staff, many of whom had years of service within the system. James H. Fyke, a native Nashvillian, had joined the system in 1964 as Sports Supervisor and served as Special Services Administrator before succeeding Charles Spears in 1978 as Director. His Assistant Directors heading the system's six major divisions during the 1980s were Lallie Richter for research and planning, Frank Atchley for park maintenance, Thomas Burns for administration, Rena Wright for community beautification, Thomas Lynch for special services, and Mary Wherry, who had succeeded Jack Spore in 1978 as chief of recreation programs. Most had known and used the parks since their childhood and felt a personal stake as well as executive responsibility for the success of the system.

Many problems encountered by those executives and by the Metro Board emanated from the level of funding available for system operations. While the annual budget for parks more than doubled under the administration of James Fyke, from $4.6 million in 1978 to $9.6 million in 1985, it remained inadequate to support a program fully responsive to all recreational needs of Nashvillians. Metropolitan government invested less than half the $30 per capita annual expenditure for urban parks recommended by federal agencies and less than other cities of comparable size. Memphis and Shelby County, for instance, in 1984 had about 6,000 acres of park land like Nashville and had a population of 800,000 as compared to nearly 500,000 in Nashville, but expended approximately $16 million on its park system as compared to $9 million at the Athens of the South. That should be ample explanation of why certain park facilities, even new community centers, could not be opened to the public in 1985. The difficulties of operating and maintaining all park facilities without increased tax revenues would continue to trouble the Board and its staff, along with the Mayor and Metro Council, throughout the 1980s, and they faced in addition the possibility that President Ronald Reagan's administration would severely curtail federal-funding support for parks in efforts to reduce the national deficit.[2]

Director James H. Fyke continued cost-recovery efforts to generate additional revenue from park facilities, and some of the facilities serving that purpose proved so successful that private investors indicated an interest in purchasing them as the nucleus of a profitable business. The most notable case involved "Wave Country," the swimming pool with a surf-producing mechanism at Two Rivers Park near the Opryland complex on Briley Parkway, which an investor sought to purchase as the proposed centerpiece of a larger acquatic recreation center. Because the private firm would keep the pool in service and the public investment therein could be recovered through sale for use elsewhere in the system, city leaders were willing to consider the sale, but Nashvillians protested that private operators would increase admission fees and thereby deny use of the pool to people with lower incomes. At a 1984 public hearing, nearly unanimous public opposition to the sale was expressed and the negotiations ended. Nashville citizens by 1984 evidently considered park recreation one of their inalienable rights and were prepared to vigorously defend that right.[3]

Other than the inadequate staffing of some park facilities as a result of budgetary constraints, the Metro Park Board was troubled by relatively few personnel problems during the early 1980s except the reorganization of the park patrol as the park rangers. Under Metro government, the park patrol had become mobile, using radio-equipped cars to respond to emergencies at parks scattered throughout the 533 square miles of the county. Cooperation between the patrol and the Metro police allowed each to call on the other for assistance, and several park patrolmen distinguished themselves by apprehending bank robbers and other felons, but differentiating between the duties of the park patrol and those of the police became problemmatic and a 1983 park management study recommended that Metro police assume the duties previously performed by the patrol. After consulting with Police Chief Joe Casey, Director James Fyke and the Park Board converted the park patrol into park rangers with resplendent ranger uniforms for enhanced public recognition, also freeing them of time-consuming arrest and booking procedures to provide more time to assist the public using the parks. After observing the value of rangers on horseback at the 1983 National League of Cities in New Orleans, Mayor Richard Fulton urged that some of Nashville's park rangers be mounted on horseback to further increase their visibility and accessibility to the public, and Director Fyke discussed it with Patsy (Mrs. Ed) Bruce, who raised horses. Mrs. Bruce contacted the Tennessee Walking Horse Breeders and Exhibitors Association which donated two handsome Tennessee walking horses to the park system, and in 1985 several park rangers began riding training at Warner Park, preparing for the first horseback patrols of city parks since early in the century.[4]

As the city population climbed toward a half million by 1990, the Metro Park Board and its managers vigorously pursued further park expansion, acquiring several parks worthy of note during the 1980s. Rena Wright and the Beautification Division took the lead in developing William Edmondson Park on a strip of land serving as a buffer between the John Henry Hale Homes and Charlotte Avenue on which a marker was placed in tribute to the memory of Edmondson, a noted stone carver who was the first black artist to have a one-man show at New York's Museum of Modern Art. The board also acquired a small park on Wedgewood Avenue in 1981 from the Metro Housing Agency, naming it in honor of druggist and community leader Dallas Neil; and in 1982 the Board began acquiring land for North Fisk Park, a playground at Osage and 25th avenues. North of the city, the Board acquired through a land exchange with a construction firm an area of about thirty-two acres scheduled to become Brick Church Park; and at the southwestern edge of the county, the Board of Education transferred to the park system the 7.58 acres on which the old Bellevue High School sat. This site became Bellevue Park and it along with the 10.5 acres of undeveloped land that became Harpeth Knoll Park in 1978 stood ready to be developed as rapidly as funding became available in order to serve the mushrooming communities located near them.[5]

To add to the ring of large urban parks encompassing the city, the board began planning Battle Road Park in 1983 in the southeastern corner of Davidson County, the last sector of the county without access to a large park. Known as Battle Road Park because that road bordered it, the land had been acquired with both federal and local funding in 1976 as a natural preserve consisting mostly of steep, forested hills; the opening of Hickory Hollow Mall and rapid urbanization of the surrounding area enhanced its significance as a natural park reserve. Yet, when Mayor Fulton announced in 1983 that park plans included not only environmental preservation but also the construction of such facilities as softball diamonds, tennis courts, soccer fields, and playgrounds, opposition to the park was expressed chiefly on grounds that it was located too far from the central city, noting that it bordered Rutherford County and might be used as much by residents of that county as by Davidson countians. That opposition was reminiscent of opinions expressed by Nashvillians during the 1950s when they opposed park development which would serve residents of Davidson County who did not then contribute to the tax support of city parks. The controversy concerning Battle Road Park therefore may presage conflicts to come in the 21st century, when the rapidly urbanizing counties ringing Davidson County will have become a part of the metropolitan area without sharing in the tax base supporting urban services.[6]

The most controversial new park of the 1980s was, however, the Riverfront Park in the center of the city. With the demise of steamboat traffic on the Cumberland during the 1920s, Nashville had turned outward, away from the river, leaving its riverfront to moulder. As part of the city's downtown revitalization efforts, renewed interest in the riverfront developed during the 1960s, receiving an additional boost in 1972 when the Park Board exchanged 45 acres of park land near Rhodes Golf Course for 104 acres owned by Robert C. H. Matthews, Jr., and the developers of the new Metro Center complex. Park planner Lallie Richter suggested the entire city waterfront should be redeveloped, with a bikeway and jogging path from a point on the riverbank opposite Shelby Park downstream along the crest of the bluff past Fort Nashborough and along the crown of the Metro Center levee to Rhodes Golf Course, Buena Vista Park, and the Z. Alexander Looby Community Center. That river walkway plan was not implemented, but through cooperation with the Metro Housing and Development Agency and the Horticultural Society of Davidson County the Park Board in 1979 opened Bicentennial Park immediately downstream of Fort Nashborough during the city's bicentennial celebration, moving the Puryear Mims statue of James Robertson and John Donelson from inside the stockade of Fort Nashborough to the center of Bicentennial Park. And in November

1980, Sandra (Mrs. Richard) Fulton, and Betty Brown co-chairman of a Century III Commission committee, presented the Park Board with plans for a park upstream of the fort at the foot of Broad Street as the cornerstone of the city's downtown restoration efforts, to become known as the Riverfront Park.[7]

With substantial federal funding assistance MOHA & Community Development funds, and with engineering and construction management supplied by the Nashville District, U.S. Army Corps of Engineers, the three-phrase construction of Riverfront Park began in 1981, accompanied by considerable ridicule from citizens who complained it would become merely a $4 million camp for drunks and transients. Mayor Fulton vigorously defended the park concept, urging that it was the key to attracting Nashvillians and tourists to the city core for recreation and also to the continuing prosperity of the shops and businesses opening in the historic Market Street area in buildings which had once warehoused goods delivered to the city by steamboats. Director James Fyke declared that the mayor's firm support of the Riverfront Park development in the face of major public criticism was the key to its successful implementation; it might not have been finished without the mayor's advocacy of it as the "catalyst of downtown development." Completion of its first-phase construction in 1983 was marked on July 10 with an entertainment extravaganza drawing some 40,000 celebrating Nashvillians to the new park, and Mayor Fulton afterwards remarked: "I've never seen the people so proud of anything."[8]

Concerts, dances, art festivals, and the annual Market Street festival continued to draw immense crowds of Nashvillians to Riverfront Park while construction of the final phases connecting the initial park area with Fort Nashborough was in progress. Fort Nashborough, a long neglected city tourist attraction, was improved to serve a growing number of visitors, while private investments in restoration of the surrounding historic district and other structural improvements near the park multiplied by millions of dollars, with accompanying increases in property tax revenues sufficient eventually to fully reimburse public investments in the park and related facilities. When critics complained of overcrowding and concrete-reflected heat at Riverfront Park, Director Fyke responded that future plans included a shelter for entertainers, a boat dock, and other measures to meet the needs, remarking that those problems verified the viability of the original concept. "It is a tremendous success," he said.⁹

Recognizing the historic trend in Nashville and Davidson County had been one of steady population growth accompanied by increased public demands for parks and recreation, Chairman George Reichardt and the Metro Board of Parks and Recreation had pursued an aggressive park area and services expansion effort since the formation of Metro government, not only to extend park services into the county but also to keep pace with population increases. From 1963 to 1985, the metropolitan population grew from about 400,000 to 500,000, or nearly a twenty-five percent increase, and as those people as a whole became more prosperous and acquired more leisure time their demands for park services grew at an even faster rate than their numbers. Since the formation of Metro government, the Park Board has increased the number of parks from 36 to 72 and their total area from 3,915 to 6,543 acres. The number of recreation centers went from 19 up to 30, tennis courts from 32 to 160, golf courses from 4 to 7. About 150 softball teams used park diamonds in 1963 compared to 780 in 1985, and the number of basketball teams rose from 58 to 240.[10]

But park system progress cannot be measured in terms of increasing numbers alone, but must be considered in light of the diversity of the recreation experiences offered. By that measure also the Nashville park system ranks high, for since 1963 the system has been diversified through the addition of such features as Wave Country, Ice Centennial, the Looby Center, the Warner Park Nature Center, the Hamilton Creek sailboat marina, the indoor swimming pools at the Whites Creek, Glencliff, and Napier Park school-park centers, to which could be added the Ezell Park junior football program, the Cedar Hill softball complex, the Dees Park serpent, and a variety of other innovative attractions. In addition, the Metro Board had established a stirring cultural recreation program featuring concerts, drama, and arts and crafts festivals in the parks, a broad spectrum of arts, crafts, dance, and other classes offered for those who wished to participate at the Centennial Art Center and community centers throughout the county, and special programs for senior citizens and the handicapped. There seemed a place for every conceivable athletic or cultural recreation activity within Athenian Nashville's parks.

Yet, the metropolitan park system was merely one element of a recreation renaissance altering the lives of Nashvillians during the late 20th century, for the city's churches, civic clubs, and businesses also sponsored recreation for pleasure, health, profit, or spiritual development. The city's Calvinist churches, which early in the century had viewed recreation as wasteful of time if not worse, by 1985 not only sponsored many teams in the park sports leagues but built or were building their own recreation centers, some with gymnasiums, pools, and elaborate physical fitness programming. Civic clubs sponsored sports teams, scouting, boys and girls clubs, and a broad array of recreation activities; and the number of businesses furnishing recreation facilities for their employees and engaging in recreation as a profitable venture burgeoned. Nashville had countless businesses operating game and video arcades and fitness spas. It had five private campgrounds, twelve bowling emporiums, two private tennis and racquet clubs, seventeen private golf, riding, and yachting clubs, five private skating rinks, five marinas, and six miniature golf courses and driving ranges. Those did not include the famous Opryland complex, professional baseball's Greer Stadium, Fair Park, the Fairgrounds Speedway, the 7,800 acres of state and federal park land in Davidson County at Old Hickory and Percy Priest lakes, Radnor and Marrowbone lakes and Long Hunter State Park, or at the Hermitage, Traveler's Rest, and Tulip Grove, nor did it include dozens of athletic fields and recreation programs operated by the city's schools, colleges, and universities.

With that many parks and recreation opportunities, both public and private, available within Nashville, it is small wonder that the city has become a green-jeweled tourist mecca and that it consistently ranks tops in the nation among comparably sized cities in the quality of its urban environment. Nashvillians in 1985 truly lived in the city's golden age of recreation.

An assessment of the future of Nashville's park system was essayed in 1983 by Mayor Fulton's Commission for Community Excellence, composed of 230 civic leaders divided into eight groups studying various features of the urban milieu. The blue-ribbon panel chaired by John Ed Miller of South Central Bell Telephone intensely studied the city's future recreation needs, reaching several conclusions and proposing a number of improvements. It concluded, for instance, the costs of operating the park system were substantially less than would be the costs of juvenile delinquency and resulting damages to community life if the city's youth were without recreation opportunities. It declared the recreational styles of Nashvillians were in transition as a result of their increased sensitivity to the natural environment and widespread adoption of walking, jogging, hiking, and bicycling in efforts to achieve greater personal fitness.[11]

According to the committee, new recreational patterns demanded new planning responses, and it specifically recommended the "linear park" as supplement to the fixed park system, consisting of natural corridors along the Cumberland River and its tributaries and along the rugged Highland Rim Escarpment in the northwestern sector of the county, to provide paths for walkers, hikers, runners, and joggers without conflicting with vehicular traffic. That recommendation leads to the amusing reflection that Nashville's parks and playgrounds were developed early in the century to get children off the streets, and a half century later those same children, now honored senior citizens, were back on the streets, walking and jogging to extend their lives, and it had again become necessary to devise a park system that would get them off the streets.[12]

Along with linear parks, environmental preservation areas, and a number of other recommendations for improving the city's recreational opportunities, the Recreation Committee for Community Excellence proposed that the undeniable connection between the city's park system and its economic prosperity receive full recognition, specifically recommending that Nashville businesses "Adopt a Park" for sponsorship, similar to the "Adopt a School" program then in progress. If businessmen enjoyed and profited from the existence of a nearby park, it seemed logical that they should give the development of that park their special attention. According to the conclusion reached by the committee:[13]

> Finally, we recognize that Nashville is blessed with a relatively clean and aesthetically pleasing physical environment, and a healthy economic environment. They need not be incompatible! A pleasing natural setting complements and enhances a strong economic base.
>
> As we look to further strengthen our economy, we must accept the principle that, over the long term, a healthy economy is inextricably connected to and dependent upon a healthy and pleasing environment, the preservation of which will not occur automatically.

Though the Nashville park system by 1985 featured such attractions as a sea serpent, an ocean surf pool, a locomotive, a sailboat marina, and a steeplechase, the Parthenon of 1897 had not lost its historic status as the park system's centerpiece, and in fact a distinct revival of interest in the building occurred as a stage for drama and a setting for new art. Drama reminiscent of Sidney Hirsch's 1913 "The Fire Regained" returned to the Parthenon in 1983 with productions of James Goldman's "The Lion in Winter" and of "Oedipus the King," the ancient Greek drama by Sophocles. As part of the park system's Family Outing Series, E. Teresa Choate and Theatre Parthenos continued the series with "Medea" in 1984; and it appeared the award-winning productions might become another Nashville park tradition, adding to its reputation as "The Athens of the South."[14]

Except a small replica of the huge statue of the goddess Athena which had adorned the interior of the original Parthenon, the central room of Nashville's Parthenon had remained barren since 1931, and for many years people had urged the creation of a full scale Athena to display therein. Sculptor Puryear Mims proposed in 1974 to create such a statue, but funding then was insufficient and the Park Board placed a donation box in the Parthenon for people who wished to contribute toward the project. Public donations had grown to $50,000 by 1982 and, after reviewing proposals from several sculptors, the Board selected that of Alan LeQuire of Nashville to sculpt a thirty-nine-foot replica of the Athena Parthenos by Phidias of fiberglass-reinforced concrete to be mounted atop a ten-foot base.[15]

Board chairman George Reichardt said the Board had wished to begin the Athena project for many years, and the Park Board took intense interest in it, often meeting informally to discuss the work and monitoring the sculptor's progress at his Bass Street warehouse. Former Commissioner Anne Roos helped the sculptor secure corporate sponsorship with labor and materials; and when the initial funding was exhausted Anne Roos orchestrated a private fund-raising effort to assure the project's completion. By 1985, various sections of the replica were beginning to resemble the long-lost original Athena, and the Park board members were eagerly awaiting its advent as an addition to the historic features of the park system.[16]

Perhaps the coming advent of Athena on the cultural stage of the "Athens of the South" warrants the publication of a poem written in 1926 by Tennessee historian John Trotwood Moore after a study of the Parthenon's history:

THE PARTHENON AT NASHVILLE

I saw Athens on a bluegrass hill,
  Artemis and Aphrodite in her train.
  Hephaestos forged his thunders in the rain
And mists of Lemos. Beside his salty rill
Poseidon sat and all the air was still.
  Awed, in dumb wonder, Zeus sat amain
  Gazing at his brain-child on the plain
Sun-crowned—resplendent on this bluegrass.

And so, Athena came to Tennessee
  With youth immortal; and Grecian skies
Are here—the Acropolis—the plain beneath:
Again the winds blow only for the free.
  And dreams fall down on far-off children's eyes—
Beauty is birthless and it has no death.

John Trotwood Moore
Nashville, May 1, 1926

NOTES

CHAPTER 1. THE CENTENNIAL EXPOSITION AND PARKS

1. *Banner,* October 30-31, 1897.
2. Louis L. Davis, "The Parthenon and the Tennessee Centennial: The Greek Temple that Sparked a Birthday Party," *Tennessee Historical Quarterly* 26 (1967):335-53.
3. Herman Justi, ed., *Official History of the Tennessee Centennial Exposition* (Nashville: Brandon Printing, 1898), pp. 465-69.
4. Ibid.
5. Ibid., pp. 13-34, 465-69.
6. Ibid.
7. Ibid.
8. Ibid.
9. Ibid.
10. Ibid.
11. Ibid.
12. Ibid.
13. Ibid.
14. Ibid. Other items casting light on the history of the Centennial are: Josephine Murphey, "Centennial Exposition: Wonder of the Nineties," *Nashville Tennessean Magazine,* Jan. 27, 1946; Alfred Leland Crabb, "Romance at the Centennial," *Nashville Tennessean Magazine,* Sept. 21, 1958; Jesse C. Burt, "Gayest Day of the Nineties," *Nashville Tennessean Magazine,* Sept. 16, 1954; Wilbur F. Creighton, *The Building of Nashville* (Nashville: Ambrose Printers, 1968), pp. 138-51.
15. *Banner,* Oct. 31, 1897; *American,* Nov. 11, 1897.
16. *American,* Nov. 11, 1897.
17. *Banner,* Oct. 28-30, 1897: Justi, ed., *Official History,* p. 448.

18. H. J. Demoss, "Nashville, Tennessee: Its Post Office and Postmasters" (manuscript, Nashville Public Library), p. 103.
19. *Tennessean*, April 1, 1930, prints Head's obituary.
20. Robert White, ed., *Messages of the Governors of Tennessee, 1899–1907*, Vol. VIII (Nashville: Tennessee Historical Commission, 1972), pp. 39, 61, 76.
21. Ibid.; *Banner*, Feb. 4–5, 19, 1898.
22. J. M. Head, "Message of the Mayor," Jan. 15, 1901, in Municipal Reports Collection, Nashville Public Library.
23. A printed copy of the law of April 3, 1901, Chapter 114, Senate Bill No. 414, is pasted inside the front cover of Volume I of the *Minutes of the Nashville Board of Park Commissioners, 1901–1984*, consisting of 20 consecutive bound volumes now maintained by Board Administrative Assistant Pauline Rigsby in the vault of the Centennial Park office building. These handwritten and typescript minutes of the Board, upon which this history is principally based, are cited hereafter as: *Mins.*, followed by the volume and page numbers.

CHAPTER 2: NASHVILLE PARKS BEFORE 1901

1. M. O. Stone, "Our Public Pleasure Grounds, " *Review of Reviews* 26 (October 1902): 458–60; Allen R. Coggins, "The Early History of Tennessee's State Parks, 1919–1956," *Tennessee History Quarterly* 43 (Fall 1984): 295–315.
2. Frederick Law Olmsted, "The Justifying Value of Public Park," *Journal of Social Science* 12 (December 1880):147–64.
3. Ann Harwell Wells, "Lafayette in Nashville, 1825," *Tennessee History Quarterly* 34 (Spring 1975):28. South Field became the site of the 1880 Nashville Centennial Celebration, and now is occupied by Federal office buildings.
4. *Nashville Scene*, July 24, 1984, quoted with permission of Mr. Boyles.
5. Herschel Gower and Jack Allen, eds., *Pen and Sword: The Life and Journals of Randal M. McGavock* (Nashville: Tennessee Historical Commission, 1959), pp. 363, 467. A private amusement park in Nashville in 1834 was Vauxhall Garden, owned by John Decker and located on Eighth Avenue South. It had an auditorium, walkways, and dining facilities, and a miniature railroad ride with cars propelled by turning cranks by hand.
6. Charles B. Thorne, "The Watering Spas of Middle Tennessee," *Tennessee Historical Quarterly* 29 (1970:321–59; Josephine Murphey, "Springs Party," *Nashville Tennessean Magazine*, July 18, 1948.
7. Nashville *Daily Gazette*, March 26 and 30, 1856.
8. Ibid.
9. *Nashville: An Illustrated Review of Its Progress and Importance* (Nashville: Enterprise Publishing Co., 1885), pp. 92–93; F. M. Williams, "You'll Never See the Likes Again," *Nashville Tennessean Magazine*, Sept. 1, 1968. The baths at Sulphur Springs were in use as early as 1834.
10. Margaret Lindsley Warden, "Ghosts that Trot and Pace," *Nashville Tennessean Magazine*, Sept. 14, 1947; Margaret Lindsley Warden, "A Dark Horse Came Up from Behind," *Nashville Tennessean Magazine*, April 27, 1969; Andrew Morrison, *The City of Nashville* (St. Louis: George W. Englehardt, 1892), p. 42. An eyewitness account of the Frank James race at West Side Park is William B. Marr, "A Sports Thrill," *Nashville Tennessean Magazine*, May 1, 1949.
11. "The Trolley Park," *Cosmopolitan* 33 (1902):265–72; Andrew Morrison, *The City of Nashville*, p. 16, 42.
12. *Nashville: An Illustrated Review of Its Progress and Importance*, p. 29; John Thompson, "The Edgefield Story," *Nashville Tennessean Magazine*, June 19, 1949.
13. *Banner*, March 1, 1951; *Tennessean*, June 18, 1972, June 15, 1980, Jan. 9, 1985; James E.

Caldwell, *Recollections of a Life Time* (Nashville: Baird-Ward Press, 1923), pp. 108–09; Nashville *Daily American*, June 29, 1890.
14. Allen Pettus, "A Taste of Rapid Transit," *Nashville Tennessean Magazine*, Dec. 5, 1948; *Banner*, June 9, 1913; John Lipscomb, "Indian Tombstone," *Nashville Tennessean Magazine*, July 2, 1950; Karl I. Faust, *Campaigning in the Philippines* (San Francisco: Hicks-Judd Co., 1899), p. 3.
15. Pettus, "A Taste of Rapid Transit," p. 24; "The Trolley Park," pp. 265–72: *Daily American*, June 29, 1890.
16. Pettus, "A Taste of Rapid Transit," p. 24. Population statistics from U.S. Census records supplied by Laura H. Rehmert, Nashville Room, Nashville Public Library.
17. *Fifteenth Census of the United States*, Vol. I, 8–9, 18–19; Alfred Runte, *Preservation Heritage: The Origins of the Park Idea in the United States* (Indianapolis: Indiana Historical Society, 1983), pp. 1–55.
18. For Olmsted, see Elizabeth Stevenson, *Park Maker: A Life of Frederick Law Olmsted* (New York: Macmillan Co., 1977); Albert Fein, *Frederick Law Olmsted and the American Environmental Tradition* (New York: George Braziller, 1972); and Virginia L. Fitzpatrick, "Frederick Law Olmsted and the Louisville Park System," *Filson Club History Quarterly* 59 (January 1985): 54–65.
19. Andrew Crawford, "The Development of Park Systems in American Cities," *Annals of the American Academy of Political and Social Sciences* 25 (March 1905):218–34.
20. "The Park System of American Cities," *Annals of the American Academy of Political and Social Science* 23 (May 1904):555–61; Charles Brown, "The Park Movement in Madison, Wisconsin," *Annals of the American Academy of Political and Social Science* 35 (March 1910):297–303; Henry Oyen, "Beautification and Business," *World's Work* 12 (July 1911):14614–15.
21. Steven Fox, *John Muir and His Legacy: The American Conservation Movement* (Boston: Little, Brown and Co., 1981), pp. 115–16; Wilbur F. Creighton and Leland R. Johnson, *Boys Will Be Men: Middle Tennessee Scouting Since 1910* (Nashville: Middle Tennessee Boy Scout Council, 1983), pp. 1–15.

CHAPTER 3: THE FIRST NASHVILLE PARK BOARD

1. James M. Head, "Message of the Mayor," Jan. 9, 1902, in Nashville Municipal Reports, Nashville Room, Nashville Public Library.
2. See the McWhirter obituary, *Banner*, Jan. 14, 1914, and Dudley obituary in *Banner*, Dec. 22, 1924. Fedora S. Frank, *Beginnings on Market Street: Nashville and Her Jewry, 1861–1901* (Nashville: Jewish Community of Nashville, 1976), pp. 120–21, reviews the career of Lindauer. J. S. Reeves & Company in 1920 purchased the Herman and Lindauer firm.
3. Alfred Leland Crabb, "Major Eugene Castner Lewis," address to Old Oak Club, March 17, 1967, transcript in Tennessee State Library and Archives; "Presentation of Loving Cup from the People of Nashville to Major Eugene Castner Lewis," July 7, 1913, program in possession of Lallie Richter, Research and Planning Division, Metro Board of Parks and Recreation.
4. Champion's obituary is in *Mins.*, I. 179.
5. *Mins.*, I, 1.
6. *Mins.*, XI, 337; *Tennessean*, July 16, 1972; Josephine Murphey, "For the Business of Life," *Nashville Tennessean Magazine*, Oct. 7, 1945. Watkins also funded the Watkins Institute. When Wilbur Creighton, Jr., constructed the housing project adjacent to Watkins Park, which was located atop the fill in the old rock quarry, he found entire boxes of Civil War ammunition in the foundation excavations. He states that after the Battle of Nashville, Confederate prisoners were interned inside the quarry and food scraps tossed down to them by the Union Soldiers.

7. *Mins.*, I, 3; *Banner*, April 26, 1901; "Report of Park Commission, 1901," in Nashville Municipal Reports, Nashville Room, Nashville Public Library.
8. *Mins.*, I, 27, 34, 48, 96, 139, 143, 147, 154. Wills's donation is mentioned in *Mins.*, I, 24.
9. *Mins.*, I, 3.
10. *Banner*, Jan. 27. 1902.
11. *Mins.*, VII, 434, contains a history of Centennial Park by J. Glenn Skinner; *Mins.*, I, 7.
12. *Mins.*, I, 8; *Banner*, Jan. 28–29, Feb. 4–5, 1902.
13. J. M. Head, "Message of the Mayor," Jan. 15, 1901, in Nashville Municipal Reports, Nashville Room, Nashville Public Library.
14. *Banner*, May 18 and Oct. 14, 1901.
15. *Banner*, Oct. 14, 1901. The new transfer station opened on June 14, 1902.
16. *Banner*, May 17, 1901.
17. *Banner*, Oct. 8–11, 1902; *Mins.*, I, 20, 321. The city parks actually received the title to Centennial Park on December 22, 1902; the deed is registered in Book 281, p. 23, Registers Office.
18. The independent Park Board concept apparently grew out of the support given by Major E. B. Stahlman to ownership of public parks by a nonprofit corporation. Mayor Head was married to Minnie Cherry.
19. *American*, Nov. 23 and Dec. 30, 1902, Jan. 2 and April 30, 1903.
20. Jesse C. Burt, Jr., "Whitefoord Russell Cole: A Study in Character," *Filson Club History Quarterly* 28 (Jan. 1954):31–32; Louise Davis, "Sycamore and 'Major' Lewis," *Nashville Tennessean Magazine*, Aug. 2, 1953. Hugh Walker's opinion concerning the incident is found in *Tennessean*, Sept. 2, 1984. The 1913 comment is from E. C. Lewis to editor, June 15, 1913, unidentified clipping in Photograph Box, Vault, Centennial Park administration building. The Jere Baxter statue completed in 1907 was moved many years later to Baxter School on Gallatin Road. Claudius C. Smith, a Nashville native, recalls distinctly seeing in Centennial Park a stone block bearing the metal letters MURREL.
21. *Mins.*, I, 19.
22. "Presentation of Loving Cup from the People of Nashville to Major Eugene Castner Lewis," July 7, 1913, Program, in possession of Lallie Richter, Research and Planning Division, Metro Board of Parks and Recreation.

CHAPTER 4: MANAGEMENT OF THE FIRST PARKS

1. *Mins.*, I, 26, 36–37, 52, 66, 83.
2. *Mins.*, I, 37–42, 47, 136.
3. *Mins.*, I, 136, 149, 163–65, 244, 256–58, 313–14, 318, 320, 330, 337. Borum was appointed chief of the patrol in 1909, J. H. Matthews in 1912. Park patrolmen in 1912 were: T. G. Payne, Ben F. O'Barr, J. K. Graves, Charles Cook, W. H. Wright, and W. A. Wynne. John Borum probably was related to Davidson County Sheriff Sam Borum, a gunslinger on the order of Wyatt Earp who deserves a biographical study.
4. *Mins.*, I, 31, 75, 150, 178, 183.
5. *Mins.*, I, 206, 233, 235; *ibid.*, p. 188, reports the gift of two Belgian horses by Robert Mitchum; *Banner*, May 31, 1905.
6. *Mins.*, I, 55–56, 99, 131, 134, 235; *Banner*, April 5, 1904.
7. *Mins.*, I, 64, 304, 371; *Banner*, May 23, 1904. The Dentici and Catagnani families generally held the concessions contract at Centennial and other parks until after the Second World War.
8. *Mins.*, I, 55–56, 99, 134, 304, 371.
9. *Mins.*, I, 66, 76; *Banner*, July 4, 6, 10, 25, 1903.
10. *Mins.*, I, 47, 96, 117, 120.
11. *Mins.*, I, 44, 53, 78, 86; *Banner*, July 6, 1903; *American*, Oct. 11–12, 1903.

12. "Report of the Park Commission, 1904," in Nashville Municipal Reports, Nashville Room, Nashville Public Library.
13. "Report of the Park Commissions, 1905," in Nashville Municipal Reports, Nashville Room, Nashville Public Library.
14. *Mins.*, I, 108, 134, 189, 232, 267.
15. *Mins.*, I, 84, 179–80; *ibid.*, III, 136; *Banner*, July 28, 1927.
16. *Mins.*, I, 145, 212; *Banner*, June 19, 1905; Captain Alfred T. Levine of the Nashville Grays received permit to camp in Centennial Park in 1906.
17. *Mins.*, I, 184; *Engineering News* 55 (Feb. 15, 1906): 188, 224, 250, prints obituary of Thomas and a biography of E. C. Lewis; *Tennessean*, June 19–20, 1909.
18. W. F. Creighton, "A Reinforced-Concrete Band Stand," *Engineering News* 59 (May 28, 1908):577; Wilbur F. Creighton, "Centennial Park Bridges," in possession of Wilbur F. Creighton, Jr., are his father's original design and construction notes; *Mins.*, I, 205–06, 276. The figurehead of the *Tennessee* previously had been on exhibit at The Seattle, Washington, Exposition of 1909 and was given to Nashville on the recommendation of Admiral Albert Gleaves. The first concrete bridge in the United States was constructed at Fairmount Park in Philadelphia in 1892.
19. "Annual Report of the Park Commission, 1908," n.p., in the files of Lallie Richter, Research and Planning Division, Metro Board of Parks and Recreation, contains the budget summary and quotation.

CHAPTER 5: THE PLAYGROUND MOVEMENT

1. "Public Parks and Playgrounds: A Symposium," *Arena* 10 (July 1894): 284–86, quoting Walter Voorman, founder of the New York Society for Parks and Playgrounds for Children.
2. *Mins.*, I, 9; *Banner*, May 18–20, 1901; Henry T. Tipps, *A History of McKendree Church* (Nashville: Parthenon Press, 1984), pp. 143–45; *Mins.*, I, 27.
3. Clarence E. Rainwater, *The Play Movement in the United States: A Study of Community Recreation* (Chicago: University of Chicago Press, 1922), pp. 1–65; John Nolen, "The Parks and Recreation Facilities in the United States," *Annals of the American Academy of Political and Social Science* 35 (March 1910): 225.
4. Rainwater, *The Play Movement*, p. 71; "A Brief History of the Playground Movement in America," *Playground* 9 (1915–16): 2–11; Roosevelt quoted in note in *Playground* 12 (March 1919): 527–28.
5. *Mins.*, I, 136, 166–67; Charlotte A. Williams, *The Centennial Club of Nashville: A History from 1905–77* (Nashville: Centennial Club, 1978), pp. 11–13.
6. Williams, *The Centennial Club*, pp. 29–31; "Annual Report of the Park Commissioners, 1908," n. p. (copy at Research and Planning Division, Metro Board of Parks and Recreation).
7. Williams, *The Centennial Club*, p. 27-31; *Mins.*, I, 216. In their 1908 Annual Report, the Park Commissioners also wrote: "We should have sites in the thickly populated sections of the city where the small boy and girl can go for fresh air and recreation under the competent supervision of instructors who can also look after their morals."
8. "Annual Report of the Park Commission, 1908," n. p. (copy in Research and Planning Division, Metro Board of Parks and Recreation).
9. *Banner*, May 30, 1905; *Tennessean*, Jan. 7, 1946, prints Brown's obituary.
10. *Mins.*, I, 229, lists an instance in which the entire Board voted against the Mayor.
11. John Lipscomb, "Indian Tombstone, " *Nashville Tennessean Magazine*, July 2, 1950; *Banner*, June 9, 1913; *Mins.*, I, 193, 195, 197, 207, 212, 258, 267.
12. *Mins.*, I, 67, 71, 224, 228, 234, 236–37, 323; Louise Davis, "Too Many Short Graves," *Nashville Tennessean Magazine*, Jan. 24, 1960; Williams Kinsbury, "The City's Stepchild,"

Nashville Tennessean Magazine, Sept. 23, 1945; National Register of Historic Places nomination form for City Cemetery. An account of his design of the City Cemetery walls was related by Major Foster to Wilbur Creighton and passed on to the author.
13. *Mins.,* I, 59; *ibid.,* VII, 436; *Banner,* July 15, 1912, and June 9, 1913. See Plat Book 21, p. 32, Davidson County Registers Office. Cornelius A. Craig in 1940 sought to rename Elizabeth Park in honor of Dr. J. W. Bauman, a community leader near the park, but the Board decided to seek to identify Elizabeth before making the change. They did not succeed in the identification, nor has the author. Arther, Jane, and other family names were used as names of streets in the McGavock addition, and David McGavock who settled in Nashville in 1786 was married to Elizabeth McDowell McGavock. David McGavock, builder of Two Rivers mansion, married Willie Elizabeth Harding and they had a daughter named Elizabeth who died as an infant in 1870. See Leona T. Aiken, *The McGavocks of Two Rivers* (Kingsport: the author, 1975), p. 4.
14. *Mins.,* I, 245-46, 250-55.
15. *Mins.,* I, 271-73, 277; *Banner,* June 9, 1913; *Tennessean,* Nov. 6, 1916; Cecil Jones, "Watering Place," *Nashville Tennessean Magazine,* July 28, 1946; H. B. Teeter, "Strong Drink Aplenty," *Nashville Tennessean Magazine,* July 12, 1953.
16. *Mins.,* I, 309, 319, and II, 127, 138, relate the history of Gunfactory Playground; *ibid.,* I, 308, and II, 391, concern the Fillmore Street Playground; and ibid., II, 42, 107, and III, 4, 26, 41, 55 concerns Dudley Park. The accident occurred when a train hit the Dudley touring car at Glidden, Iowa, seriously injuring Mr. and Mrs. Dudley and causing the deaths of their daughters.
17. *Mins.,* I, 249-50, 257, 279, 287, 294, 299, and III, 24, 39, 54-55, 85; see also the *Annual Report of the Park Commission for 1912.*
18. *Mins.,* III, 11, 25, 27, 31.
19. *Mins.,* I, 312-14, 369.
20. *Mins.,* I, 353-54, and II, 100, 105, 166, 196, 334.
21. *Mins.,* II, 99, 114, and III, 11.

CHAPTER 6: PARK EXPANSION, 1910-1916

1. Williams, *The Centennial Club,* pp. 41, 46; *Mins.,* I, 158, 294.
2. *Tennessean,* May 18, 1913; *Banner,* April 11, 1913.
3. *Mins.,* II, 19, 21, 26, 32.
4. *Banner,* June 9, 1913; *Mins.,* II, 29, 36, 107, 111, 320, and III, 32. Morton B. Howell, son of the Rev. R. B. C. Howell of First Baptist Church, was born about 1834, became mayor of Nashville in 1874, and died in 1909.
5. *Mins.,* II, 111, 142, 165, 196, and IV, 15. The city reservoir broke on Nov. 5, 1912, without causing loss of life but resulting in considerable property damage along Eighth Avenue; it was repaired and returned to service.
6. *Mins.,* I, 58, 138, 161, 197; Nell Savage Mahoney, "Mansion Called Fatherland," *Nashville Tennessean Magazine,* May 13, 1951.
7. *Mins.,* I, 222, 260, 262, 265, 268, 275-76, 299, 301.
8. *Mins.,* I, 303, 309, 314, 369; *Banner,* June 9, 1913 and Dec. 24, 1914; Board of Park Commissioners, *Twelfth Annual Report, 1912* (Nashville: Park Board, 1912), n. p.
9. Bill Holder, "Fire to the East," *Nashville Tennessean Magazine,* March 19, 1950; *Banner,* March 23 24, 1916.
10. *Banner,* March 29-30, 1916; *Mins.,* II, 254, 258, 261, 274, 302, 321; *Tennessean,* May 26, 1916.
11. Bobby L. Lovett, ed., *From Winter to Winter: The Afro-American History of Nashville, Tennessee, 1870-1930* (Nashville: Tennessee State University, 1981), pp. 63-64; *Banner,*

Sept. 4, 1981; Wilbur Creighton and Leland Johnson, *Boys Will Be Men: Middle Tennessee Scouting Since 1910* (Nashville: Parthenon Press, 1983), p. 109.
12. Lovett, *From Winter to Winter,* pp. 167, 172–73, 181, 184; *Banner,* Sept. 4, 1981; *Mins.,* I, 335, 339, 343; *Nashville Globe,* June 28 and July 12, 1912. The reporter for the *Globe* assumed the park was named for the Hadley family which owned the park land during the 19th century, and that may well be the case. Major Lewis did not identify which Hadley he meant to honor in his resolution naming the park, however, and it is possible that he intended to honor Dr. W. A. Hadley, a pioneer black physician in Nashville with whom Lewis had worked during planning for the 1897 Centennial Exposition. Older park employees have for many years believed the park was named for the physician. Isaiah T. Creswell, interviewed by the author, September 12, 1985.
13. *Tennessean,* July 5, 1912; Board of Park Commissioners, *Twelfth Annual Report, 1912,* n. p.; Charles W. Crawford, "A History of the Memphis Park System (unpublished manuscript, Memphis Park Commission), p. 14.
14. *Mins.,* I, 360, and II, 345.
15. *Mins.,* II, 135, 144; *Banner,* June 9, 1913.
16. *Mins.,* II, 24, 72, 74, 87, 316, 267, 388; Jesse C. Burt, Jr., "Whitfoord Russell Cole: A Study in Character," *Filson Club History Quarterly* 28 (Jan. 1954): 28–54; *Tennessean,* Dec. 5, 1940, prints Loventhal's obituary. The Loventhal story was related to the author by Wilbur F. Creighton, Jr., elder emeritus of First Presbyterian Church. According to Robert McGaw, Loventhal played in 1892 on the first basketball team in Nashville; he graduated at Vanderbilt University in 1896.
17. *Mins.,* IV, 81; *Tennessean,* Feb. 5, 1931, prints John Lewis's obituary; Josephine Murphey, "World Authority," *Nashville Tennessean Magazine,* Sept. 9, 1945, is a biography of George B. Moulder.
18. *Mins.,* II, 62, 66, 82, 121, 184, 186, 229, 235.
19. *Mins.,* I, 340, 348, and II, 48, 126, 321, 337–38, 368.
20. Board of Park Commissioners, *Twelfth Annual Report, 1912,* n. p.; *Mins.,* I, 364, and II, 62, 301, 304. A trolley car for children was in Centennial Park by 1916, when the Board voted to move it to the playground; see *Mins.,* II, 323.
21. *Mins.,* II, 238, 355.

CHAPTER 7: RECREATIONAL AND CULTURAL EMPHASIS
1. Foster Rhea Dulles, *A History of Recreation: America Learns to Play* (2nd ed.; New York: Appleton-Century-Crofts, 1965), pp. 9–12; George Martin to Rev. Robert Bunting, Oct. 6, 1868, Archives of First Presbyterian Church, Nashville (Martin settled in Nashville in 1799 and was describing to Bunting the socioreligious conditions in the city at that time).
2. See the discussion of racetracks at Nashville in Chapter 2. The duels and caneings arising from racing are amply illustrated in the Papers of Andrew Jackson, Vols. I and II, now being published by editors Harold Moser and Sharon MacPherson. The Tennessee legislature in 1985 gave serious consideration to legalizing racing and parimutuel betting in the state.
3. See Martin to Bunting, October 6, 1868, cited in note 1 above, and the history of the Cottage Sunday School mission also in Archives of First Presbyterian Church. Alfred Hume and A. W. Putnam were founders of the mission, after observing the riotous ball games in 1850 at the corner of Ewing and Bass streets. J. D. Brown, "Gun Totin' at 81," *Nashville Tennessee Magazine,* April 21, 1946, is a biography of Sam Houston Borum, the Davidson County Sheriff, 1908–1912, who in 1910 arrested about a hundred participants at a Sunday game at Sulphur Dell; the case went to the Tennessee Supreme Court which decided Sunday games did not violate state laws.

4. Dulles, *History of Recreation*, pp. 193–96; "American Croquet," *Nation* 3 (Aug. 9, 1866):113–15; Bill Holder, "Scorcher," *Nashville Tennessean Magazine*, Sept. 22, 1946, is a biography of Herrick.
5. E. D. Mitchell, "The Contribution of the Recreation Movement to Physical Education," *Recreation* 25 (1931–32):90. On the origins of team sports in Nashville, see the "Among Us Fans" columns by John Bibb in the *Nashville Tennessean Magazine* during the 1950s, especially the contributions by Samuel A. Weakley who was eyewitness to the baseball and football games of the 1890s.
6. *Mins.*, I, 34, 77, 86, 95, 102, 112, 175, 193–94, 199, 201. F. E. Kuhn and T. J. Tyne represented the Nashville Baseball Club in negotiations with the Board; representatives of the Nashville Tennis Club in 1903 are identified in the records only as Farrell, Jr., and Walker. The land was leased from Mrs. F. D. Elliston.
7. *Mins.*, II, 49, 57, 88, 185, 190, 199, and VII, 434; *Mins.*, II, 229, indicates the Board extended permission to the Barnum and Bailey Circus to use the Elliston tract on Oct. 11, 1915, for a fee of $150. Use of that area for circuses and similar activities continued until the Second World War.
8. *Mins.*, I, 304; *Banner*, April 19, 1912, and the quotation in the July 5, 1911, issue.
9. *Mins.*, I, 288–89, 292, 294, 297, 300–01; *Banner*, Aug. 3, 1912.
10. *Mins.*, II, 1–2, 4, 17, 74; Louise Davis, "Glory that Was Greece," *Nashville Tennessean Magazine*, July 6, 1952, prints photographs of the 1913 pageant. The author has interviewed participants in the 1913 pageant such as Helen Frank and has conducted an extensive search for the film made of the pageant without success.
11. Ed Huddleston, *Big Wheels and Little Wagons* (Nashville: Banner, 1959), pp. 58–59, 65, 77; Dulles, *History of Recreation*, pp. 292–94; *Mins.*, II, 104, 138, 274; *Tennessean*, March 5, 1984. St. Louis, Mo., began showing free movies in its parks in 1915. John Siegenthaler's enjoyment of the movies came much later than 1915, and apparently after 1932 when talkies were first shown in Nashville parks.
12. *Mins.*, II, 365, 369, 383, and III, 73, 226, and IV, 34.
13. Oliver C. Tidwell, Jr., *Belle Meade Park* (Nashville: author, 1983), pp. 75–79; *Mins.*, III, 22, 27, 31, 85, 88, 153, 157; Dulles, *History of Recreation*, pp. 241–42, states golf was introduced to the United States in 1888 at St. Andrews Country Club in New York and in 1894 the U.S. Golf Association formed.
14. *Mins.*, III, 157; John Bibb, "Strictly for the Kids," *Nashville Tennessean Magazine*, June 6, 1954. Winners of the Schoolboy Tournament included Luther Hickman and Louis Graham. The tournament was the second oldest in the city in 1954, the City Amateur being the oldest, but has since become the oldest and the sixtieth annual tournament was held in 1985. Blinkey Horn was a sports reporter for the *Tennessean*.
15. *Mins.*, III, 36, 43, 48, 58, 114, 121, 152, 181, 218; Frederick W. Cron, *The Man Who Made Concrete Beautiful: A Biography of John Joseph Earley* (Ft. Collins, CO.: Centennial Publications, 1977), *passim*. Several excellent histories of the Parthenon replica and its reconstruction exist, and should be consulted for further details: George B. Moulder, *The Parthenon at Nashville, Tennessee, U.S.A.* (Nashville; author, 1931); Benjamin F. Wilson, III, *The Parthenon of Pericles and Its Reproduction in America* (Nashville: Parthenon Press, 1937); Wilbur F. Creighton, *Building of Nashville* (Nashville: Ambrose Printing, 1969); and Wilbur F. Creighton, *The Parthenon: Pearl of the Centennial* (Nashville: Ambrose Printing, 1968). Several of these may be purchased at the bookstore inside the Parthenon building.
16. Cron, *The Man Who Made Concrete Beautiful, passim*; *Mins.*, III, 118, 121, 124.
17. An undated news clipping pasted in *Mins.*, Vol. III, provides complete details concerning the plans advocated by Mrs. Bradford; *Mins.*, III, 194, 292–03, 286, 288, 333, 373. The Board had contributed an aggregate of $29,911.69 to the Nashville Art Association

from 1914 to 1927, and on that basis laid claims to the paintings purchased by the Association and moved them to the Parthenon in 1941.
18. *Mins.*, III, 306, 344, 371–73, and IV, 8, 84, 200. At the recommendation of interior decorator A. Herbert Rodgers, George Moulder in February 1931 built the pedestals and installed the Elgin Marbles copies in the Parthenon. Ben Wilson became custodian of the Parthenon building on June 3, 1931.
19. *Mins.*, III, 157, 194, 228; Philip LeBoutillier, "Educating the Public," *Playground* 22 (December 1928):513; Mary Stahlman Douglas, "Recreation Week in Nashville," *Playground* 19 (Sept. 1925):381–82, 393–95.
20. *Mins.*, II, 199; *Banner*, March 23, 1939, quotes McCabe. McCabe also was responsible for a change in the dress code permitting women to wear shorts while riding bicycles in the parks.

CHAPTER 8: MANAGEMENT AND EXPANSION, 1917–1930

1. Tidwell, *Belle Meade Park*, pp. 90–93; *Mins.*, II, 341, 374, 386, 383.
2. *Mins.*, III, 22, 221, 348, and VII, 437, and IX, 439. The square was returned to the state in 1969.
3. *Mins.*, III, 69; see Chapter X following concerning the monuments built with WPA funding during the 1930s.
4. Louise Davis, "The House that Dautless Built," *Nashville Tennessean Magazine*, May 9, 1948, is a biography of Connell. *Mins.*, IV, 165, indicates that the Board in 1932 allowed the Iris Association to use 25 acres of Warner Park for the cultivation of iris bulbs.
5. *Mins.*, III, 157; Sadie A. Frank, "A Japanese Garden in Tennessee," *Garden Magazine & Home Builder* 40 (Nov. 1924):197–98; *Tennessean*, June 9, 1935; John Lipscomb, "Drowning Buddha," *Nashville Tennessean Magazine*, June 15, 1947.
6. *Mins.*, III, 85, 160, 229, 232. Edgehill Park was traded to the city housing authority when it was replaced with E. S. Rose Park; Bass Park continues in operation behind the fire hall on Holly Street, and is still maintained by Captain Mack Johnson and Engine Company No. 14.
7. *Mins.*, III, 178, 231–32, 284.
8. Among several sources concerning the life of Percy Warner, see the speech of Mayor Hilary Howse at the dedication of Warner Park gate on April 26, 1932 found in *Mins.*, IV, 170.
9. For Brown and the "Four Horsemen," see "A Home Town Job," *Nashville Tennessean Magazine*, Sept. 28, 1947.
10. H. J. DeMoss, "Nashville, Tennessee: Its Post Office and Postmasters," p. 108.
11. George Barker, "The Rogers Caldwell Story," *Nashville Tennessean Magazine*, Oct. 20, 27, Nov. 3, 1963.
12. *Mins.*, III, 240, 243, 246.
13. Dulles, *History of Recreation*, pp. 312–13, 319; *Mins.*, III, 243; Leland R. Johnson, *Memphis to Bristol: A Half Century of Highway Construction* (Nashville: Tennessee Road Builders Association, 1978), recounts the history of motor vehicle and highway construction in the state.
14. *Mins.*, III, 251. No copy of the 1926 report is now in possession of the Park Board.
15. *Mins.*, III, 117, 276, and IV, 3.
16. *Mins.*, III, 308, 323. It is perhaps important here to emphasize that the bidding was competitive, that Caldwell and Company did place a bid, and that the bonds were awarded to the competing J. C. Bradford Company, which was not controlled by Caldwell.
17. Tidwell, *Belle Meade Park*, pp. 11, 17, 19, 94–95; *Mins.*, III, 253.
18. Tidwell, *Belle Meade Park*, pp. 94–95. After hearing Lea's motives for the gift ques-

tioned, the author discussed the subject with several financiers, notably Melville Barnes, Sr., who agreed that Lea could have profited considerably by keeping the land, or even by selling it in 1926 when land prices were relatively high.
19. *Mins.*, III, 262; *Banner*, May 13, 1976, prints an objection to Warner parks by a member of one of the families forced to relocate.
20. *Mins.*, III, 298–99, 304, 328, 338, and IV, 9, 17; *Banner*, June 14, 1938, quotes McCabe.
21. Nick Sullivan, "Warner Parks . . . A Pocket of Wilderness in the City," *Tennessean*, July 31, 1983; Louise Davis, "Those Wonderful Warner Parks—Forever Yours," *Nashville Tennesse Magazine*, July 21, 1963; *Banner*, June 14, 1938, quotes Warner.
22. *Banner*, July 14, 1938; Ewell Costello, interview by author, Dec. 5, 1984: *Mins.*, IV, 30.
23. Tidwell, *Belle Meade Park*, pp. 95–97, 102–03; *Mins.*, IV, 120, 169–73, 191, 198.
24. *Mins.*, III, 290, 319, 325, 346, and V, 54. When the Board of Education in 1934 sought to purchase Elmington Park, the Park Board responded that the land had cost $110,000, of which it had supplied $65,000 and the citizens of that part of town gave $45,000 toward the purchase; they therefore were under a moral obligation to keep the park. The persons who contributed the $45,000 are not identified in Park records.
25. *Mins.*, II, 36, and III, 237, 352; *Tennessean*, Oct. 18 and 30, Nov. 16, 1928. The Board issued "Fort Negley Bonds" for $20,000 at 4.5 percent to purchase the fort from the Fargason family of Memphis.
26. Leland R. Johnson, *Engineers on the Twin Rivers: A History of the Nashville District, Corps of Engineers* (Nashville: U.S. Army Engineer District, 1978), pp. 89–100; Dixon Johnson, "Silent-Gunned Fort," *Nashville Tennessean Magazine*, May 5, 1946.

CHAPTER 9: BOOM TO BUST IN THE PARKS

1. *Mins.*, III, 44, 189, 210, 348, 366, and IV, 2, 14, 94.
2. Ewell Costello, interviewed by author, Dec. 5, 1984; Bowser Chest, "I'll Always Remember," *Nashville Tennessean Magazine*, Oct. 3, 1948; Roy E. "Pat" Striegel Scrapbook, Red Binns, Hermitage, TN; *Mins.*, IV, 22.
3. *Mins.*, III, 289, and IV, 20–21; Ewell Costello, interviewed by the author, Dec. 5, 1984.
4. Ewell Costello, interviewed by the author, Dec. 5, 1984; *Mins.*, III, 47, 68, 74, 93, 117, 151, 295.
5. *Mins.*, III, 19, 73, 102, 141, 219, and VII, 296.
6. *Mins.*, III, 281, 285, 368, 374, and IV, 19.
7. Parthenon Galleries, *The Parthenon: Nashville, Tennessee, 50th Anniversary, 1931–1981* (Nashville: Anniversary Exhibition brochure, 1981), *passim; Mins.*, IV, 102 and undated news clippings at IV, 400.
8. *Mins.*, III, 366, and IV, 27, 95, 113. The author discussed the effects of the 1930 collapse with Melville Barnes, Sr., who states that depositors in the Fourth and First National Bank recovered their funds because the bank was taken over by First American National Bank.
9. *Mins.*, IV, 86, 89. See discussion of Whitfield Park in a subsequent chapter herein.
10. *Mins.*, IV, 121, 123, 204, 298, and VI, 125; *Tennessean*, Nov. 15, 1931, and Jan. 8, 1932.
11. *Mins.*, IV, 108, 128, 161, 174, 207, 262, 287, and VI, 84–86.
12. *Mins.*, IV, 242; *Tennessean*, July 21, 1935.
13. Ewell Costello, interviewed by author, Dec. 5, 1984; Dulles, *History of Recreation*, p. 363; Bob Krause, "Sissy Game? No!" *Nashville Tennessean Magazine*, Aug. 18, 1946.
14. *Mins.*, V, 166, 3005, VI, 83, 93–94, and VII, 210, 321; Krause, "Sissy Game? No!," *passim*.
15. Krause, "Sissy Game? No!" *passim*. Ewell Costello, interviewed by the author, Dec. 5, 1984.

16. *Mins.*, IV, 187, 201, and V, 80. The Southern Archery Association held its tournament in Centennial Park on Sept. 3–5, 1932.
17. *Tennessean*, April 13, 1968, prints the memoirs of Pickens; *Mins.*, V, 56; George Barker, "The Night the Roof Fell Up," *Nashville Tennessean Magazine*, March 13, 1960.
18. *Mins.*, 167, 217. Patrol Chief W. C. Scott retired as Shelby Park maintenance foreman in 1963. The patrolmen in 1937 were C. M. Boner at Morgan Park, A. W. Vester at Centennial, J. A. VanHook at Centennial, M. E. Grissom at Centennial, Adrian Troutt at Centennial, J. D. Arnett at Shelby, T. W. Mayhew at Shelby, C. W. Fox at Shelby, Joe Hitt at Warner, Walter Parson at Richland, H. G. Hailey at McFerrin, W. K. Bush at South, T. R. Luster at Dudley, John Fuller at Elizabeth, Ben Wilson at Hadley, and Noah F. Templeton at Reservoir. John Siegenthaler recounted his decoration of Thomas statue in *Tennessean*, March 5, 1984.
19. *Mins.*, IV, 180, 203.
20. *Mins.*, V, 4, 35, 45, 235, and VII, 438.
21. *Mins.*, V, 344, and VI, 126, 247, 356, 367; Isaiah T. Creswell, interviewed by the author, September 12, 1985.
22. *Mins.*, V. 199, VI, 84, and VII, 46. In 1964 the Board named the new community center in Coleman Park in honor of George Lawrence Dudley, citizen of Woodbine who devoted his life to the area's youth.
23. *Mins.*, VI, 366, VII, 9, 32, 294, and VIII, 59, 330, 375.

CHAPTER 10: FEDERAL ASSISTANCE BEGINS

1. *Mins.*, IV, 267, 353, and V, 209, 212, 307; *Tennessean*, June 7–8, 1935.
2. *Mins.*, V, 13, 34, 96, 115, 247, 263.
3. James A. Burran, "The WPA in Nashville, 1935–1943," *Tennessee Historical Quarterly* 34 (Fall 1975):293–306; George Barker, "Digging Up $21 a Month," *Nashville Tennessean Magazine*, Dec. 11, 1960.
4. Ewell Costello, interviewed by the author, Dec. 5, 1984.
5. Barker, "Digging Up $21 a Month," *passim*; *Mins.*, V, 263.
6. *Mins.*, V, 308, and VI, 86, 126, 258. The author discussed the Shelby Park riprap revetment project in 1968 with Samuel Weakley, Johnny Hicks, G. Reid Bethurum, and other Corps of Engineers personnel who administered the project.
7. Ewell Costello, interviewed by the author, Dec. 5, 1984; *Banner*, June 1, 1938; *Mins.*, VI, 654, 247, and VII, 148, 193.
8. Ewell Costello, interviewed by the author, Dec. 5, 1984; *Banner*, June 1, 1938; Burran, "The WPA in Nashville," p. 297; Johnson, *Memphis to Bristol*, pp. 50, 110.
9. *Mins.*, VI, 1; *Banner*, June 1, 1938.
10. See undated news clipping in Park File, Tennessee State Library and Archives, for list by Scales; *Mins.*, VI, 184.
11. *Mins.*, VII, 96, 122, 128, 131, 146, 183, and VIII, 222.
12. *Mins.*, V, 318, and VI, 93, 219; Burran, "The WPA in Nashville," pp. 303–04.
13. *Mins.*, VI, 56, 228, 296, 310, 356, and VII, 211; Tidwell, *Belle Meade Park*, pp. 97–101; *Banner*, May 3, 1941.
14. U.S., Congress, House, Committee on Appropriations, *Investigation and Study of the Works Progress Administration*, 76th Cong., 1st Sess., 1939, pp. 970–88; Barker, "Digging Up $21 a Month," *passim*.
15. *Mins.*, VII, 184, 196, and VIII, 218, 220.
16. Margaret Lindsley Warden, "Most Sporting of the Horse Sports," *Nashville Tennessean Magazine*, May 8, 1949.
17. Bob Steber, "On Again Off Again!" *Nashville Tennessean Magazine*, May 5, 1946; Tidwell, *Belle Meade Park*, 97–101.

18. *Mins.*, VI, 369, and VII, 11, 363.
19. *Mins.*, VII, 9, 122, 233, 279; *Banner,* May 24, 1946.
20. *Mins.*, VII, 11, 32–33, 59.
21. *Mins.*, VII, 32–33, 42, 295–96.
22. *Mins.*, VII, 128, 198, 211, 243, 266, 419.
23. *Mins.*, VIII, 223; Institute for Training in Municipal Administration, *Municipal Recreation Administration* (Chicago: International City Managers Association, 1945), pp. 39–40.

CHAPTER 11: THE PARKS DURING WARTIME

1. *Mins.*, VII, 4, 257, 307, and VIII, 39.
2. *Mins.*, VII, 308, 360, 365, and X, 165. Major John H. Suther commanded the military police patrolling the parks in 1943.
3. *Mins.*, VIII, 136; Jack Stanton, "Without a Catch," *Nashville Tennessean Magazine,* Oct. 14, 1945.
4. Stanton, "Without a Catch," *passim.* Wilbur Creighton and Leland Johnson are preparing a documentary history of First Presbyterian Church which will supply information concerning use made of the Downtown Presbyterian Church building during the Second World War.
5. *Mins.*, VIII, 95. Craig selected dead and dying walnut trees, from which 54,668 board feet of walnut lumber was obtained.
6. *Mins.*, VIII, 113, 121, 133, 219, and IX, 53. Farming in Warner parks ended in 1947 except for crops needed to feed work animals.
7. *Mins.*, VIII, 95, 153, 320–21.
8. *Mins.*, VIII, 114, 122, 130, 136, 364. The board received $16,916.69 from the Whiskey and Wine Fund in 1943 and $37,500 in 1944. In 1943 there were 121 retail and 5 wholesale liquor stores in Nashville.
9. *Mins.*, VIII, 155, IX, 311, 330, and X, 342–43. The Corps of Engineers ended its moorage lease at Shelby Park after Old Hickory Dam and Lake was completed in 1952, moving its fleet to the new lake near the lock.
10. *Mins.*, VIII, 320–21.
11. *Mins.*, VIII, 219, X, 285; Louise Davis, "Pickens Park Posies," *Nashville Tennessean Magazine,* Aug. 21, 1949.
12. *Mins.*, X, 144, 162, 165. The Board apparently received also the salvage value of the buildings on the campsite.
13. *Mins.*, VII, 146, 182–83, 196, VIII, 155, 271, and IX, 266–67, 297.
14. *Mins.*, IX, 5, 38, 51, 92, 105, 174, and XII, 6, 70, 178. Jane Hinshaw, *Sevier Park: Eighteenth Century Trading Post or Nineteenth Century Settlement?* (M.A. thesis, Vanderbilt University, 1976), concluded on the basis of archaeological excavations that the cabins behind the mansion are not French trading posts, but Mr. and Mrs. Jack Spore and others disagree with the Hinshaw thesis and are continuing their historical research on the subject.
15. *Mins.*, IX, 105, and XII, 6, 70, 178; *Banner,* June 7, 1948; Bill Woolsey, "Private Life in a Public Park," *Nashville Tennessean Magazine,* Oct. 3, 1948.
16. John J. "Jack" Spore, interviewed by the author, Oct. 15, 1984; see also Spore biography in *Nashville Tennessean Magazine,* Oct. 23, 1960.
17. John J. "Jack" Spore, interviewed by the author, Oct. 15, 1984; *Mins.*, X, 308.
18. *Mins.*, IX, 223, 311–13. In 1948 the Board adopted official uniforms for playground supervisors composed of white uniforms with one-quarter length sleeves bearing a red emblem.
19. *Mins.*, IX, 164, 225, 316, and X, 30; Creighton and Johnson, *Boys Will Be Men,*

pp. 106–07; Allen Pettus, "Victimless Battle," *Nashville Tennessean Magazine*, June 6, 1948. The most serious accident in Nashville park history occurred on May 27, 1945, when four teenagers drowned in Lake Sevier at Shelby Park after their boats overturned.
20. *Tennessean*, Aug. 17, 1947; *Mins.*, X, 71, 91, 228, 266, 341, XI, 3, and XIV, 315.
21. *Mins.*, IX, 399, X, 141, 470, XIII, 175, 242; Bob Steber, "Whacking Good Times," *Nashville Tennessean Magazine*, May 23, 1948.
22. *Banner*, July 14, 1945; *Mins.*, IX, 35–36, 230, 353, 468, 433.
23. Louise Davis, "Museum for the Future," *Nashville Tennessean Magazine*, Aug. 19, 1945; *Mins.*, IX, 310, and X, 32, 43.
24. *Mins.*, IX, 433.
25. *Mins.*, X, 27, 122, 224, 474, and XII, 3–4.
26. *Mins.*, X, 280, 364–65; Bill Crouch, interviewed by the author, Nov. 15, 1984.
27. *Mins.*, X, 296–97, and XI, 10; *Banner*, April 26, 1951, prints Skinner's memoir of his service to the park system.

CHAPTER 12: PARKS IN THE WEST ADMINISTRATION
1. *Tennessean*, Nov. 3, 1947; *Mins.*, IX, 389, 402, and X, 67.
2. *Tennessean*, Nov. 30, 1947, and March 12, 1967.
3. *Mins.*, IX, 469, and X, 167.
4. Isaiah T. Creswell, interviewed by the author, September 12, 1985.
5. *Mins.*, X, 131, 153, 296, 314, 364, 469, XI, 299, and XIII, 1396, 139.
6. *Mins.*, XI, 83, XII, 207, 359, 378, 397, 461, and XIII, 66. The Cumberland course was renamed in honor of Rhodes on Aug. 13, 1969, and a new clubhouse dedicated on May 26, 1976, by Dr. Reichardt and Vice Mayor David Scobey.
7. George Barker, "Man Behind the Move," *Nashville Tennessean Magazine*, April 16-23, 1961, is a biography of Looby; *Mins.*, XI, 313, 342; *Banner*, Feb. 10, 1956; *Tennessean*, Feb. 14, 1956.
8. *Tennessean*, Jan. 26 and Feb. 14, 1956; *Mins.*, XIV, 146.
9. *Banner*, May 24, 1946, *Tennessean*, Jan. 11, 1950, Feb. 6, 1979; *Mins.*, XI, 35–36, 107, 439, 481, and XII, 87.
10. Wilbur F. Creighton, Jr., supplied the biography of Jones; *Mins.*, 279, 298. Historical materials concerning the locomotive and many other features of the park system are found in Park Board Correspondence Files (alphabetical files in vault, Centennial Park administration building, maintained by Administrative Assistant Pauline Rigsby). Roy Stewart, Ken Commander, and Chester Whitaker in 1980 received permission from the Board to repair and maintain the locomotive.
11. *Mins.*, XIII, 34, XV, 380, XVII, 197, XX, 204, 266. The aircraft was moved to its present location in 1981–82 and maintained by 118th Aircraft Maintenance Squadron, Tennessee Air National Guard.
12. *Mins.*, XII, 291, 346, and XVII, 15; *Tennessean*, Dec. 14, 1983. The critic quoted was Don Shoemaker of the *Miami Herald* who once lived in Nashville.
13. *Mins.*, XII, 331, XIII, 3, 14, 32, 364, and XVI, 11, 40; *Tennessean*, March 5, 1984; John Fetterman, "Music Swells the Breeze," *Nashville Tennessean Magazine*, June 6, 1954.
14. *Mins.*, XII, 355, XIII, 15, 33, 270, XIV, 234.
15. *Mins.*, XI, 104, XII, 284, 374, XIII, 465, XIV, 433; Margaret Lindsley Warner, "Bound to Be a Winner," *Nashville Tennessean Magazine*, Aug. 22, 1954; George Barker, "Ramrod of the Dudes," *Nashville Tennessean Magazine*, Oct. 16, 1960. Lt. William E. Holder of the Navy and the East Nashville Exchange Club in 1960 built a concrete model of a navy aircraft carrier at the Warner Park model airfield.
16. *Mins.*, XII, 1, 300; Bill Woolsey, "Little Ones' Kingdom," *Nashville Tennessean Magazine*, July 13, 1952.

17. John J. "Jack" Spore, interviewed by the author, Oct. 15, 1984; *Banner*, June 16, 1959; *Tennessean*, Oct. 23, 1960.
18. *Mins.*, XIII, 440, and XIV, 175; Johnson, *Engineers on the Twin Rivers*, pp. 150–53, 218–21.
19. *Mins.*, XIV, 152, 176.
20. *Mins.*, XII, 391, XIII, 213, 271–72, 370, 487; *Banner*, Feb. 13, 1956.
21. *Mins.*, IX, 388, XIII, 272, 487.
22. *Mins.*, XIII, 133, 446; *Tennessean*, June 14–15, 1956.

CHAPTER 13: ENDING THE CITY SYSTEM

1. Spore's report on the Oct. 29, 1956, meeting is in *Mins.*, XIII, 484.
2. *Mins.*, XIII, 485.
3. National Recreation Association, *A Study of Recreation and Parks in Nashville and Davidson County, Tennessee* (New York: National Recreation Association, 1957), *passim*.
4. *Ibid.*, pp. ii-vi.
5. *Mins.*, XIV, 187, 191, 193–94.
6. *Mins.*, XIV, 60, 80, 384: XV, 21. To coordinate architect and engineering services for the projects approved in the bond issue, the Board employed John Charles Wheeler and E. A. Papuchis.
7. *Mins.*, XIV, 451, XV, 117, 144, 305, and XVI, 39, 55. See also undated news clippings in Vols. XIV and XV.
8. Bill Woolsey, "Landlord to 5000," *Nashville Tennessean Magazine*, July 27, 1952; Louise Davis, "Our Capitol Hill: Reform of a Shady Lady," *Nashville Tennessean Magazine*, Sept. 18, 1966.
9. *Mins.*, XIII, 134, 240; XIV, 360.
10. *Mins.*, XV, 412, XVI, 95–96, 324.
11. *Mins.*, XVI, 84, 142, 164, 270.
12. *Mins.*, XVI, 218, 237, 280.
13. *Mins.*, XIII, 174, 273, XIV, 77, 216, 407, and XVI, 148.
14. *Mins.*, XIII, 36, 48, 66, 94, XVI, 10, 163, 242–44; *Tennessean*, Oct. 28, 1962.
15. *Mins.*, XV, 377, 440, 464; Lallie Richter, interviewed by the author, Sept. 21, 1984; Mrs. Pauline Rigsby, interviewed by the author, Sept. 20, 1984. Memphis public parks were fully integrated in 1963 as result of the Supreme Court decision.
16. National Recreation Association, *A Study of Recreation in Nashville*, p. 20, 67; *Mins.*, XI, 210, 221, 251, and XVI, 24, 165.
17. *Mins.*, XVI, 165, 259, 260.
18. *Mins.*, XVI, 175. The city Board took no action of record at its last meeting.
19. From a 1957 but otherwise undated column by Dick Battle filed in *Mins.*, XIV; Bill Crouch, interviewed by the author, Nov. 15, 1984.

CHAPTER 14: THE METROPOLITAN PARK CHALLENGE

1. "Mayor Asks Staff to First Session," *Metropolitan* 1 (May 1963):1; Metropolitan Board of Parks and Recreation, *Annual Report, 1964* (Nashville: Board of Parks, 1964), n.p.; George Barker, "The Race for Inner Space," *Nashville Tennessean Magazine*, May 3, 1964.
2. *Tennessean*, Aug. 27, 1971; Metropolitan Board of Parks and Recreation, *Annual Report, 1964*, n.p., quotes Briley on his mandate for the park system.
3. *Mins.*, XVI, 207; George W. Reichardt, interviewed by the author, May 6, 1985.
4. *Mins.*, XVI, 207.
5. *Mins.*, XVI, 207, 217, 231; Lallie Richter, interviewed by the author, Sept. 21, 1984.
6. *Mins.*, XVI, 207, 236, 263; see records of Madison Community Park Association, 1956-1963, in Park Board Correspondence File, Centennial Park Office Vault.
7. The City Cemetery and Fort Nashborough were transferred by Executive Order No.

12, June 15, 1963, from the Department of Public Works to the Park Board; see *Mins.*, XIX, 155, 166, XX, 114, 127, 222, concerning cemetery operations and *Banner*, Dec. 4, 1981. In 1976 Mayor Fulton transferred the County Cemetery at 18th and Jennings avenues to the Park Board. Brochures published by the Park Board concerning the history of the City Cemetery and Fort Nashborough are available at each site and at the Centennial Park office.
8. *Mins.*, XVI, 217, 231; Bill Crouch, interviewed by the author, Nov. 15, 1984.
9. *Mins.*, XVI, 272, XVII, 118, 128.
10. "Board of Parks and Recreation," *Metropolitan* 1 (June 1963):6; George Barker, "The Race for Inner Space," *Nashville Tennessean Magazine*, May 3, 1964; Metropolitan Board of Parks and Recreation, *Annual Report, 1964*, n.p., quotes Dr. Reichardt.
11. *Mins.*, XVI, 294; Metropolitan Board of Parks and Recreation, *Annual Report, 1964*, n. p.
12. *Mins.*, XVI, 80. The new Douglas Park Community Center was dedicated on Sept. 10, 1964, and the Cleveland Park Center on Jan. 30, 1964. A plaque memorializing C. T. Kirkpatrick is located at the school.
13. *Mins.*, XVI, 271, XVIII, 42, XIX, 131, relate to Tony Rose Park, which the Country Music Association took on December 1, 1965; the board on Sept. 3, 1975, named Music Square Park in honor of country music fans and assigned the name Tony Rose to the park on Hawkins Street to fulfill a commitment made to the Rose family. Governor Gordon Browning finally arranged for delivery of the title to Victory Square to the Park Board in 1953; in 1962 the Board approved a city request to build a parking garage under Victory Square and on Aug. 13, 1969, it approved returning the square to state government. See *Mins.*, XII, 208, XIV, 287, 292, XVI, 37, XVII, 90.
14. *Mins.*, XVI, 112, 175, 256–57.
15. Metropolitan Planning Commission, *Recreation Space, 1980* (Nashville: Planning Commission, 1965), *passim:* George Barker, "The Race for Inner Space," *Nashville Tennessean Magazine*, May 3, 1964.
16. *Mins.*, XVI, 274–76, XVIII, 11, 25. Cedar Hill Park was first referred to as Old Center Park because Old Center school was located near it; Dr. Reichardt referred to it as "Buck Heights." The Cedar Hill Park lands were purchased from J. O. Covington, W. L. Horn, and Ralph Fensterwald. The Charlotte Park property was owned by John Hanley and M. L. Levitan; the park received its name from the subdivision, which in turn acquired its name from Charlotte Pike, which ran to Charlotte, Tennessee. For South Inglewood Park, see *Mins.*, XVIII, 66, and XIX, 12.
17. *Mins.*, XVI, 248, 257, 278, 298, 301, 314, XVII, 235, XVIII, 10, 162.
18. *Mins.*, I, 296, XVI, 322, 338, XVIII, 177.
19. Metropolitan Planning Commission, *Recreation Space, 1980, passim*; George Barker, "The Race for Inner Space," *Nashville Tennessean Magazine*, May 3, 1964.
20. *Mins.*, XVII, 23, XVIII, 177.
21. *Mins.*, XVIII, 59, 77, 139, 155, 157; Craig Guthrie, "Painful Pinch in the Park," *Nashville Tennessean Magazine*, April 9, 1967.
22. *Mins.*, XVII, 47, 113, 134, 204.
23. *Mins.*, XVII, 115, 117, 152, XVIII, 170, 176, 210; Metropolitan Board of Parks and Recreation, *Annual Report, 1964*, n.p., lists Mr. Pickens' yearly tasks. Mrs. Lillian Lambert retired in 1968 after 50 years as a recreation supervisor, and Noah F. Templeton retired in 1969 after 40 years as a park patrolman.
24. Bill Crouch, interviewed by the author, Nashville, August 19, 1985.

CHAPTER 15: PARKS FOR AN AFFLUENT SOCIETY
1. *Mins.*, XVI, 289, 305, 309, 339.
2. Bill Crouch, interviewed by the author, Nov. 15, 1984.

3. *Mins.*, XVIII, 50, 73, XIX, 155, XX, 52, 83.
4. *Mins.*, XVII, 166, 226, 239, XVIII, 220, XIX, 10.
5. Lallie Richter, interviewed by the author, Sept. 21, 1984; *Mins.*, XIX, 69, 165, 169, 170.
6. Max York, "Cleanest Mind in Town," *Nashville Tennessean Magazine*, Sept. 13, 1964; *Mins.*, XIX, 144, 148, XXI, 46. After the 1984 "Keep America Beautiful" Award was presented, Dr. Reichardt commented that winning had become routine for the park system.
7. *Mins.*, XV, 205, XVI, 163, 302. Wesley Paine succeeded Malcolm Parker as Director of the Parthenon in 1979. The building in 1963 was declared a Civil Defense fallout shelter. The Parthenon was the setting on Aug. 30–31, 1974, of the filming of the finale of the movie "Nashville."
8. *Mins.*, XVII, 7, XIX, 71, 179, XVIII, 3, 52, 195; "Cultural Recreation: What Is It?" *Art Lines* 1 (Winter 1984): 1.
9. *Mins.*, XVII, 6, 56, 67, 94, 141, 145, 156, 179, 186, 198, 203, and XIX, 9.
10. *Mins.*, XVII, 23, 104, 141. The author witnessed both the rock concerts and flower-children activities in the parks and observed that many of the so-called "hippies" became respected members of the community two decades later while a few of the guitar-strummers earned national acclaim in the creative arts.
11. Steven Fox, *John Muir and His Legacy: The American Conservation Movement*, provides an excellent analysis of the environmental preservation movement. Federal legislation resulting from the movement include the National Environmental Policy Act (NEPA) of 1970, the Historic Preservation Act (Muskie Bill) of 1974, and the Clean Water Act of 1977. The Scenic River Act and other Tennessee legislation also reflect the influence of the environmental movement. Park Commissioner B. R. Allison represented environmental interests during Board deliberations.
12. *Mins.*, XVII, 3, 8, 42, 156, 174, 232, XVIII, 103, 113, 118, 187, XX, 88, 241; *Banner*, March 30, 1979; *Tennessean*, March 25, 1979; Louise Davis, "Two Lives of 'Two Rivers,'" *Nashville Tennessean Magazine*, July 3, 1955; Jeanette C. Rudy, *Historic Two Rivers: A Pictorial Review of Two Rivers Mansion* (Nashville: Blue & Gray Press, 1973), p. 28; Leona T. Aiken, *The McGavocks of Two Rivers* (Kingsport, author, 1975), p. 44; Hugh Walker, "Two Rivers Park," in Park Board Correspondence File, Centennial Park Office Vault. Dr. Reichardt met with Mrs. Spence McGavock several times during the early 1960s to urge her to participate in the creation of a public park that would preserve the mansion and estate.
13. *Mins.*, XVII, 41, 48, 123, XIX, 118, 137, XX, 48, 173; *Suburban News*, March 8, 1978; Charles Spears to Bill M. Wise, March 11, 1975, in Park Board Correspondence File, Centennial Park Office Vault.
14. *Mins.*, XVII, 54, 140, 173, XVIII, 105, 174, XIX, 123, XX, 227, 291. A discussion of the founding and early history of the Children's Museum is provided in Chapter XI.
15. *Mins.*, XVII, 174, 179, XIX, 168, 182; *Tennessean*, Jan. 28, 1971. F. M. Williams, "You'll Never See the Likes Again!" *Nashville Tennessean Magazine*, Sept. 1, 1968, recites the history of Sulphur Dell. The Greer Stadium became the home of the Nashville Sounds, which in 1985 became a Triple A franchise.
16. Bob Parrish and Sandy Bivens, "Nashville's Warner Parks," *Tennessee Conservationist* 50 (May-June 1984):12–15; Pat Embry, "Warner Parks are Historical Places," *Banner*, July 19, 1984.
17. *Mins.*, XVII, 56, 137, 142–43, 147, 230, XVIII, 152, 158, XIX, 56, 68, XX, 106; *Banner*, June 8, 1968. Robert M. "Bob" Heriges, 1921–1967, was manager of Breeko Industries.
18. *Mins.*, XX, 67; *Tennessean*, Jan. 27, 1985.
19. Notes on Board meeting of April 5, 1985, made by the author who attended.
20. *Mins.*, XIX, 80, 134, 145, XX, 73, 94, 303; *Suburban News*, March 8, 1978.

21. *Mins.*, XVII, 171, 178, XVIII, 184.
22. *Mins.*, XVII, 37, 40, 169, XIX, 147, 164.
23. *Mins.*, XVI, 243, 265, 306, XVII, 111, 114; George W. Reichardt, interviewed by the author, May 6, 1985.
24. *Mins.*, XVI, 247, 281, XVII, 92, 217, XVIII, 20, 26, XIX, 27, 131, 140, XX, 145. Mayor Fulton opened the marina on June 4, 1980. For histories of the Corps of Engineers projects, see Leland R. Johnson, *Engineers on the Twin Rivers, passim.*

CHAPTER 16: PARK MANAGEMENT IN THE 70's

1. *Mins.*, XVII, 219–20, 229; Bill Crouch, interviewed by the author, Nov. 15, 1984.
2. *Mins.*, XVII, 219, 240, XIX, 121; *Nashville Scene*, May 8, 1984, Mildred DuBois served the park system from 1966 to her death in 1984, and became public information specialist in 1977.
3. *Mins.*, XVII, 125, 134, 140, 148.
4. Although the park budget increased to as much as $9 million during the 1980s, Director James H. Fyke believes the peak budgets for the system actually occurred during the 1970s if the figures were translated into constant dollar values.
5. *Mins.*, XVII, 234, 241, XX, 256, 266; Mrs. Ruth Burkitt, interviewed by the author, April 10, 1985, was personally acquainted with Mr. Crawford.
6. *Mins.*, XIX, 187, XX, 1, 21, 196; *Tennessean*, Sept. 9, 1980; *Banner*, Dec. 26, 1980. The park was first referred to as the Cavert-Eakin Park. Frank S. Curran to Charles Spears, April 27, 1978, Park Board Correspondence File, Centennial Park Office Vault, stated that Fannie Mae Dees was a medical technician who lived on Capers Avenue and led the Eakin Community Council in opposition to urban renewal; she died on March 4, 1978, and the park was named in her honor because of her "deep concern for the welfare and safety of children in the Eakin community."
7. Richard Fulton to B. R. Allison, Oct. 31, 1975, in Park Board Correspondence file, Centennial Park Office Vault; *Mins.*, XIX, 147, 161, 178, XX, 29; James Fyke to Philip Sadler, Oct. 9, 1981, in Park Board Correspondence File, Centennial Park Office Vault, relates the history of Ezell Park.
8. *Mins.*, XVII, 115, XVIII, 146, 174, XIX, 101, XX, 32.
9. *Mins.*, XVII, 108, XIX, 122, 187, relate to Pitts Park; *ibid.*, XIX, 43, 187, to Paragon Mills Park; *ibid.*, XIX, 33, to Parkwood Park; *ibid.*, XIX, 165, to Maplewood Park; *ibid.*, XX, 288, to Willow Creek Park; and *ibid.*, XX, 170, to Barry Zeitlin's gift in Bordeaux. Most of these small parks are part of PUD, or Planned Unit Development.
10. Bill Crouch, interviewed by the author, Nov. 15, 1984.
11. *Ibid.*; see also Craig Guthrie, "Painful Pinch in the Park," *Nashville Tennessean Magazine*, April 9, 1967.
12. *Mins.*, XVII, 42, 106, XIX, 176, 181, 189, 193, XX, 11, 30, 66, 98. During the 1960s the Board had studied opening an ice rink at the old Shelby Park swimming pool.
13. Tom Wood, "Softball Season Gets Under Way," *Tennessean*, April 7, 1985; *Mins.*, XVII, 10, 30, 174, XIX, 30, 34, 82, XX, 103, 183.
14. *Mins.*, XVII, 55, XX, 104, 143, 208, 211, 274; Tony Cavender to James Fyke, March 30, 1983, in Park Board Correspondence File, Centennial Park Office Vault. The Nashville Boys Club and Sheriff Fate Thomas sponsored boxing competition, and there were other boxing programs in the city producing boxers with national rankings.
15. *Mins.*, XX, 15–16, 29–30, 32.
16. Metro Council Ordinance 78-929 permitted political rallies in the parks; *Mins.*, II, 145, XX, 92. The modern Park Board probably was unaware of the 1914 policy, which no doubt resulted from some incident involving either a fight with watermelon rinds or some immense mess left in a park after a watermelon feast.

17. *Suburban News*, Sept. 6, 1978, prints a memoir by Spears of his service with the Nashville park system.

CHAPTER 17: PARK MANAGEMENT IN THE GOLDEN AGE

1. *Mins.*, XX, 200.
2. *Mins.*, XX, 283; *Tennessean*, Oct. 7, 1984, Feb. 3, 1985. The Memphis park figures come from Crawford, "A History of the Memphis Park System," p. 20. After the park service reductions of 1984–85 ended, the *Banner*, April 29, 1985, printed an editorial paying tribute to Director Fyke's efforts to avoid a budgetary deficit, which concluded: "What Mr. Fyke did was not surprising. It is called good management, and his is a well-managed department that provides beneficial services to many thousands of Nashvillians. The same solution should have occurred to other department heads who have since trooped into the council chambers, hat in hand, asking for money to cover budget deficits." Director Fyke in 1981 testified before a Congressional committee in opposition to federal funding reductions for urban park systems.
3. *Tennessean*, April 2, 1984, printed a statement in opposition to sale of the Wave pool; George W. Reichardt, interviewed by the author, May 6, 1985. The hearings concerning the sale were tape recorded, and the tape is in the Public Information Office, Centennial Park Office.
4. *Mins.*, XX, 281–82; *Tennessean*, March 3, 1985; James R. Sutton, "Mounted Ranger Proposal," 1985, copy furnished the author.
5. *Mins.*, XX, 73, 82, 200, 253, 256, 258, 266, 274, 293; *Banner*, May 30, 1979; *Tennessean*, Oct. 22, 1979, July 9, 1981; James Fyke to Charles O. Frazier, Oct. 14, 1981, in Park Board Correspondence File, Centennial Park Office Vault (these files also contain miscellaneous correspondence concerning each park in the system).
6. *Mins.*, XIX, 155; *Tennessean*, June 8, 1983; *Banner*, Oct. 14, 1983.
7. *Mins.*, XVII, 214, 245, XVIII, 209, XIX, 195, XX, 51, 80, 109, 171; *Tennessean*, Jan. 16, 1972, Feb. 11, 1974.
8. *Banner*, July 6 and 11, 1983, Dec. 7, 1984; *Tennessean*, July 24, 1983; U.S., Cong., House, Committee on Appropriations, *Energy and Water Development Appropriations for 1984*, 98th Cong., 1st Sess., 1983, pp. 1835–36.
9. *Tennessean*, July 4 and 8, 1984.
10. *Banner*, April 8, 1983, prints a tribute to Dr. Reichardt's twenty years of service to the park system which contains the comparative figures.
11. *Banner*, Jan. 12, 1983; Mayor's Committee for Community Excellence, Recreation Subcommittee, "Final Report," 1983, 1–10 (copy supplied author by Wilbur F. Creighton).
12. Mayor's Committee for Community Excellence, Recreation Subcommittee, "Final Report," pp. 1–10.
13. *Ibid.*; see also report summary in *Banner*, Jan. 3, 1983.
14. *Mins.*, XX, 268; *Tennessean*, Feb. 11, 1983; *Banner*, Aug. 6, 1983.
15. *Mins.*, XIX, 72, XX, 222, 227, 231, 236; *Tennessean*, May 7, 1982.
16. *Banner*, Sept. 19, 1984. The author attended Board meetings when the progress of the Athena statue was discussed.
17. A copy of Moore's poem was found inserted in the Park Board's minutes for 1928.

BIBLIOGRAPHY

ARTICLES
"A Brief History of the Playground Movement in America." *Playground* 9 (1915–16):2-11.
"A Home Town Job." *Nashville Tennessean Magazine*, September 28, 1947.
"American Croquet." *Nation* 3 (August 9, 1866):113–15.
Barker, George. "The Night the Roof Fell Up." *Nashville Tennessean Magazine*, March 13, 1960.
⸻. "Ramrod of the Dudes." *Nashville Tennessean Magazine*, October 16, 1960.
⸻. "Digging Up $21 a Month." *Nashville Tennessean Magazine*, December 11, 1960.
⸻. "Man Behind the Move." *Nashville Tennessean Magazine*, April 16-23, 1961.
⸻. "The Rogers Caldwell Story." *Nashville Tennessean Magazine*, October 20, 27, and November 3, 1963.
⸻. "The Race for Inner Space." *Nashville Tennessean Magazine*, May 3, 1964.
Bibb, John. "Strictly for Kids." *Nashville Tennessean Magazine*, June 6, 1954.
"Board of Parks and Recreation." *Metropolitan* 1 (June 1963): 6.
Brown, Charles. "The Park Movement in Madison, Wisconsin." *Annals of the American Academy of Political and Social Science* 35 (March 1910):297–303.

Brown, J. D. "Gun Totin' at 81." *Nashville Tennessean Magazine*, April 21, 1946.
Burran, James A. "The WPA in Nashville, 1935–1943." *Tennessee Historical Quarterly* 34 (Fall 1975):293–306.
Burt, Jesse C. "Gayest Day of the Nineties." *Nashville Tennessean Magazine*, September 16, 1954.
―――――. "Whitefoord Russell Cole: A Study in Character." *Filson Club History Quarterly* 28 (January 1954):28–54.
Casas, William B. de las. "The Boston Metropolitan Park System." *Annals of the American Academy of Political and Social Science* 35 (March 1910):280–86.
Chest, Bowser. "I'll Always Remember." *Nashville Tennessean Magazine*, October 3, 1948.
"Cities and Parks." *Atlantic* 7 (April 1861):416–29.
Coggins, Allen R. "The Early History of Tennessee's State Parks, 1919–1956." *Tennessee Historical Quarterly* 43 (Fall 1984):295–315.
Crabb, Alfred Leland. "Romance of the Centennial." *Nashville Tennessean Magazine*, September 21, 1958.
Crawford, Andrew W. "The Development of Park Systems in American Cities." *Annals of the American Academy of Political and Social Science* 25 (March 1905):218–34.
Creighton, Wilbur F. "A Reinforced-Concrete Band Stand." *Engineering News* 59 (May 28, 1908):577.
"Cultural Recreation: What Is It?" *Art Lines* 1 (Winter 1984):1.
Davis, Louise L. "Museum for the Future." *Nashville Tennessean Magazine*, August 19, 1945.
―――――. "The House that Dauntless Built." *Nashville Tennessean Magazine*, May 9, 1948.
―――――. "Picken's Park Posies." *Nashville Tennessean Magazine*, August 21, 1949.
―――――. "Glory That Was Greece." *Nashville Tennessean Magazine*, July 6, 1952.
―――――. "Sycamore and 'Major' Lewis." *Nashville Tennessean Magazine*, August 2, 1953.
―――――. "Two Lives of 'Two Rivers.'" *Nashville Tennessean Magazine*, July 3, 1955.
―――――. "Too Many Short Graves." *Nashville Tennessean Magazine*, January 24, 1960.
―――――. "Those Wonderful Warner Parks—Forever Yours." *Nashville Tennessean Magazine*, July 21, 1963.
―――――. "Our Capitol Hill: Reform of a Shady Lady." *Nashville Tennessean Magazine*, September 18, 1966.
―――――. "The Parthenon and the Tennessee Centennial: The Greek Temple

that Sparked a Birthday Party." *Tennessee Historical Quarterly* 26 (1967): 335–53.
Douglas, Mary Stahlman. "Recreation Week in Nashville." *Playground* 19 (September 1925):381–82, 393–95.
Embry, Pat. "Warner Parks are Historical Places." *Nashville Banner*, July 19, 1984.
Fetterman, John. "Music Swells the Breeze." *Nashville Tennessean Magazine*, June 6, 1954.
Fitzpatrick, Virginia L. "Frederick Law Olmsted and the Louisville Park System." *Filson Club History Quarterly* 59 (January 1985):54–65.
Frank, Sadie A. "A Japanese Garden in Tennessee." *Garden Magazine and Home Builder* 40 (November 1924):197–98.
Guthrie, Craig. "Painful Pinch in the Park." *Nashville Tennesseean Magazine*, April 9, 1967.
Head, James M. "Municipal Construction Versus the Contract System." *Arena* 31 (April 1904):337-52.
Holder, Bill. "Scorcher." *Nashville Tennessean Magazine*, September 22, 1946.
———. "Fire to the East." *Nashville Tennessean Magazine*, March 19, 1950.
Johnson, Dixon. "Silent-Gunned Fort." *Nashville Tennessean Magazine*, May 5, 1946.
Jones, Cecil. "Watering Place." *Nashville Tennessean Magazine*, July 28, 1946.
Kingsbury, William. "The City's Stepchild." *Nashville Tennessean Magazine*, September 23, 1945.
Krause, Bob. "Sissy Game? No!" *Nashville Tennessean Magazine*, August 18, 1946.
LeBoutillier, Philip. "Educating the Public." *Playground* 22 (December 1928):513.
Lipscomb, John. "Drowning Buddha." *Nashville Tennessean Magazine*, June 15, 1947.
———. "Indian Tombstone." *Nashville Tennessean Magazine*, July 2, 1950.
Mahoney, Nell Savage. "Mansion Called Fatherland." *Nashville Tennessean Magazine*, May 13, 1951.
Marr, William B. "A Sports Thrill." *Nashville Tennessean Magazine*, May 1, 1949.
"Mayor Asks Staff to First Session." *Metropolitan* 1 (May 1963):1.
Merwin, H. B. "Park-Making as a National Art." *World's Work* 1 (January 1901):293–303.
Mitchell, E. D. "The Contribution of the Recreation Movement to Physical Education." *Recreation* 25 (1931–32):90–92, 100.
Murphey, Josephine, "World Authority." *Nashville Tennessean Magazine*, September 9, 1945.

———. "For the Business of Life." *Nashville Tennessean Magazine*, October 7, 1945.

———. "Centennial Exposition: Wonder of the Nineties." *Nashville Tennessean Magazine*, January 27, 1946.

———. "Springs Party." *Nashville Tennessean Magazine*, July 18, 1948.

Nolen, John. "The Parks and Recreation Facilities in the United States." *Annals of the American Academy of Political and Social Science* 35 (March 1910):217–28.

Olmsted, Frederick Law. "The Justifying Value of a Public Park." *Journal of Social Science* 12 (December 1880):147–64.

Oyen, Henry. "Beautification and Business." *World's Work* 12 (July 1911): 14612–18.

Parrish, Bob, and Sandy Bivens. "Nasvhille's Warner Parks." *Tennessee Conservationist* 50 (May-June 1984):12–15.

Peden, Peggy. "Inner City Escapes." *Nashville* 12 (July 1984):40–43.

Pettus, Allen. "Victimless Battle." *Nashville Tennessean Magazine*. June 6, 1948.

———. "A Taste of Rapid Transit." *Nashville Tennessean Magazine*, December 5, 1948.

"Public Parks and Playgrounds: A Symposium." *Arena* 10 (July 1894):274–88.

Robbins, Mary C. "The Art of Public Improvement." *Atlantic* 78 (December 1896):742–51.

Stanton, Jack. "Without a Catch." *Nashville Tennessean Magazine*, October 14, 1945.

Steber, Bob. "On Again Off Again!" *Nashville Tennessean Magazine*, May 5, 1946.

———. "Whacking Good Times." *Nashville Tennessean Magazine*, May 23, 1948.

Stone, M. O. "Our Public Pleasure Grounds." *Review of Reviews* 26 (October 1902):458–60.

Sullivan, Nick. "Warner Parks—A Pocket of Wilderness in the City." *Nashville Tennessean*, July 31, 1983.

Teeter, H. B. "Strong Drink Aplenty." *Nashville Tennessean Magazine*, July 12, 1953.

"The Park System of American Cities." *Annals of the American Academy of Political and Social Science* 23 (May 1904):555–61.

"The Trolley Park." *Cosmopolitan* 33 (1902):265–72.

Thompson, John. "The Edgefield Story." *Nashville Tennessean Magazine*, June 19, 1949.

Thorne, Charles B. "The Watering Spas of Middle Tennessee." *Tennessee Historical Quarterly* 29 (1970):321–59.

Warden, Margaret Lindsley. "Ghost that Trot and Pace." *Nashville Tennessean Magazine*, September 14, 1947.
??????. "Most Sporting of the Horse Sports." *Nashville Tennessean Magazine*, May 8, 1949.
??????. "Bound to Be a Winner." *Nashville Tennessean Magazine*, August 22, 1954.
??????. "A Dark Horse Came Up from Behind." *Nashville Tennessean Magazine*, April 27, 1969.
Wells, Ann Harwell. "Lafayette in Nashville, 1825." *Tennessee Historical Quarterly* 34 (Spring 1975):19–31.
Williams, F. M. "You'll Never See the Likes Again." *Nashville Tennessean Magazine*, September 1, 1968.
Wood, Tom. "Softball Season Gets Under Way." Nashville *Tennessean*, April 7, 1985.
Woolsey, Bill. "Private Life in a Public Park." *Nashville Tennessean Magazine*, October 3, 1948.
??????. "Little One's Kingdom." *Nashville Tennessean Magazine*, July 13, 1952.
??????. "Landlord to 5000." *Nashville Tennessean Magazine*, July 27, 1952.
York, Max. "Cleanest Mind in Town." *Nashville Tennessean Magazine*, September 13, 1964.
Zolnay, George J. "The Reconstruction of the Nashville Parthenon." *Art and Archaeology* 12 (August 1921):75–81.

BOOKS

Aiken, Leona T. *The McGavocks of Two Rivers*. Kingsport: the author, 1975.
Board of Park Commissioners, Nashville. *Eighth Annual Report, 1908*. Nashville: Marshall & Bruce Co., 1908.
??????. *Twelfth Annual Report, 1912*. Nashville: Park Board, 1913.
Caldwell, James E. *Recollections of a Life Time*. Nashville: Baird-Ward Press, 1923.
Creighton, Wilbur F. *Life Story of Robert Thomas Creighton*. Nashville: Ambrose Printers, 1965.
??????. *The Parthenon: Pearl of the Centennial*. Nashville: Ambrose Printers, 1968.
??????. *The Building of Nashville*. Nashville: Ambrose Printers, 1968.
Creighton, Wilbur F., and Leland R. Johnson. *Boys Will Be Men: Middle Tennessee Scouting Since 1910*. Nashville: Parthenon Press, 1983.
Cron, Frederick W. *The Man Who Made Concrete Beautiful: A Biography of John Joseph Earley*. Fort Collins, CO: Centennial Publications, 1977.
Doyle, Don H. *Nashville in the New South, 1880–1930*. Knoxville: University of Tennessee Press, 1985.

Dulles, Foster Rhea. *A History of Recreation: America Learns to Play.* 2nd ed.; New York: Appleton-Century-Crofts, 1965.
Faust, Karl I. *Campaigning in the Philippines.* San Francisco: Hicks-Judd Co., 1899.
Fein, Albert. *Frederick Law Olmsted and the American Environmental Tradition.* New York: George Braziller, 1972.
Frank, Fedora S. *Beginnings on Market Street: Nashville and Her Jewry, 1861-1901.* Nashville: Jewish Community of Nashville, 1976.
Fox, Steven. *John Muir and His Legacy: The American Conservation Movement.* Boston: Little, Brown & Co., 1981.
Gower, Herschel, and Jack Allen, eds. *Pen and Sword: The Life and Journals of Randal W. McGavock.* Nashville: Tennessee Historical Commission, 1959.
Hinshaw, Jane. *Sevier Park: Eighteenth Century Trading Post or Nineteenth Century Settlement?* Nashville: Vanderbilt University Department of Anthropolgy Thesis, 1976.
Historical Commission of Nashville-Davidson County. *Nashville: Conserving a Heritage.* Nashville: Historical Commission, 1977.
Huddleston, Ed. *Big Wheels and Little Wagons.* Nashville: Banner, 1959.
Institute for Training in Municipal Administration. *Municipal Recreation Administration.* Chicago: International City Managers Association, 1945.
Johnson, Leland R. *Engineers on the Twin Rivers: A History of the Nashville District, U.S. Army Engineers.* Nashville: U.S. Army Engineer District, 1978.
_____. *Memphis to Bristol: A Half Century of Highway Construction.* Nashville: Tennessee Road Builders Association, 1978.
Justi, Herman, ed. *Official History of the Tennessee Centennial Exposition.* Nashville: Brandon Printing, 1898.
Lovett, Bobby L., ed. *From Winter to Winter: the Afro-American History of Nashville, Tennessee, 1870-1930.* Nashville: Tennessee State University, 1981.
McLean, Christine, and Dennis Hermanson. *Leisure Services: the Measurement of Program Performance.* Nashville: Urban Observatory, 1974.
Metropolitan Board of Parks and Recreation, *Annual Report, 1964.* Nashville: Board of Parks and Recreation, 1964.
Metropolitan Planning Commission. *Recreation Space, 1980: A Community Facilities Plan for Park and Recreation Areas, Metropolitan Nashville and Davidson County, Tennessee.* Nashville: Planning Commission, 1965.
Miller, Wihry and Lee, Inc. *Fort Negley Park: A Study for the Metropolitan Historical Commission.* Nashville: Miller, Wihry and Lee, Inc., 1980.
Mode, Robert L., ed. *Nashville: Its Character in a Changing America.* Nashville: Vanderbilt University Publication, 1981.

BIBLIOGRAPHY   229

Morrison, Andrew. *The City of Nashville*. St. Louis: George W. Englehardt, 1892.
Moulder, George B. *The Parthenon of Nashville, Tennessee, U.S.A.* Nashville: the author, 1931.
Nashville: An Illustrated Review of Its Progress and Importance. Nashville: Enterprise Publishing Co., 1885.
Nashville Parks & Playgrounds at the Turn of the Century. Nashville: Blue and Gray Press, 1971.
National Recreation Association. *A Study of Recreation and Parks in Nashville and Davidson County, Tennessee*. New York: National Recreation Association, 1957.
Parthenon Galleries. *The Parthenon: Nashville, Tennessee, 50th Anniversary, 1931–1981*. Nashville: Anniversary Exhibition Brochure, 1981.
Presentation of Loving Cup from the People of Nashville to Major Eugene Castner Lewis. Nashville: program, 1913.
Rainwater, Clarence E. *The Play Movement in the United States: A Study of Community Recreation*. Chicago: University of Chicago Press, 1922.
Rudy, Jeanette C. *Historic Two Rivers: A Pictorial Review of Two Rivers Mansion*. Nashville: Blue and Gray Press, 1973.
Runte, Alfred. *Preservation Heritage: the Origins of the Park Idea in the United States*. Indianapolis: Indiana Historical Society, 1983.
Stevenson, Elizabeth. *Park Maker: A Life of Frederick Law Olmsted*. New York: Macmillan Co., 1977.
Tidwell, Oliver Cromwell, Jr. *Belle Meade Park*. Nashville: the author, 1983.
Tipps, Henry T. *A History of McKendree Church*. Nashville: Parthenon Press, 1984.
U.S. Congress. House. Committee on Appropriations. *Energy and Water Development Appropriations for 1984*. 98th Cong., 1st Sess., 1983.
―――――. *Investigation and Study of the Works Progress Administration, Hearings on H. Res. 130*. 76th Cong., 1st Sess., 1939.
White, Robert, ed. *Messages of the Governors of Tennessee, 1899–1907*. Vol. VIII. Nashville: Tennessee Historical Commission, 1972.
Williams, Charlotte A. *The Centennial Club of Nashville: A History from 1905–77*. Nashville: Centennial Club, 1978.
Wilson, Benjamin F., III. *The Parthenon of Pericles and Its Reproduction in America*. Nashville: Parthenon Press, 1937.

ARCHIVES AND MANUSCRIPTS

Binns, John E. "Red," Roy E. "Pat" Striegel Scrapbook. Collection of news clippings and memorbilia by a coach containing considerable information about early sports in Nashville located at Mr. Binns' home in Hermitage.

Board of Park Commissioners. Minutes, 1901–1985. Twenty bound volumes in the vault of the Centennial Park administration building maintained and updated by Mrs. Pauline Rigsby.

──────. Payroll, 1903–1908. One bound volume in Reach and Planning Division, Centennial Park administration building.

──────. Correspondence File. Two file drawers of miscellaneous correspondence pertaining to historical subjects in the vault of the Centennial Park administration building maintained and updated by Mrs. Pauline Rigsby.

──────. Photograph Collection. One box containing about 200 photographs, various news clippings, and a scrapbook in the vault of the Centennial Park administration building.

Crabb, Alfred Leland. "Major Eugene Castner Lewis." Address to the Old Oak Club, March 17, 1967, in Tennessee State Library and Archives, Nashville.

Crawford, Charles W. "A History of the Memphis Park System." Brief manuscript account of the system at Memphis Park Commission, Memphis, Tennessee.

Creighton Papers. Two boxes of notes, clippings, and personal memorbilia relating to the 1897 Centennial, the Parthenon, and Nashville parks in general in possession of Wilbur F. Creighton, Jr., Nashville, Tennessee.

Demoss, H. J. "Nashville, Tennessee: Its Post Office and Postmasters, 1796 . . ." Manuscript in the Nashville Room, Nashville Public Library.

First Presbyterian Church, Nashville, Archives. One trunk of materials in the church library on Franklin Road which contains considerable information concerning the socioreligious life of Nashville.

Gale, Smith & Company. Engineering Report: Board of Park Commissioners. A 1942 inspection of structures in the parks for insurance requirements with photographs of the buildings in Research and Planning Division, Centennial Park administration building.

Mayor's Committee for Community Excellence. Recreation Subcommittee. Final Report, 1983. Manuscript draft in possession of Wilbur F. Creighton, Nashville, Tennessee.

Nashville Room, Nashville Public Library. Municipal Reports Collection. Bound copies of city department reports of the late 19th and early 20th centuries.

──────. Nashville Parks File. Two bound volumes of newspaper clippings and miscellaneous materials relating to the history of the Nashville park system.

Tennessee State Library and Archives. Nashville, Tennessee. Parks File. Manila folders containing news clippings and miscellaneous materials concerning the history of various parks in the state.

INTERVIEWS

Burkitt, Ruth (Mrs. Jack). Interviewed by the author. Nashville, April 10, 1985.
Costello, Ewell. Interviewed by the author. Nashville, December 5, 1984.
Creighton, Wilbur F., Jr. Interviewed by the author. Nashville, September 10, October 25, December 16, 1984, February 11 and March 25, 1985.
Creswell, Isaiah T. Interviewed by the author. Nashville, September 12, 1985.
Crouch, Bill L. Interviewed by the author. Nashville, November 13, 1984, and August 19, 1985.
Fyke, James H. Interviewed by the author. Nashville, May 7 and August 14, 1985.
Northern, Isaac. Interviewed by the author. Nashville, May 9, 1985.
Reichardt, George W. Interviewed by the author. Nashville, May 6, 1985.
Richter, Lallie. Interviewed by the author. Nashville, September 21, 1984.
Rigsby, Pauline. Interviewed by the author. Nashville, September 20, 1984.
Spore, John J. "Jack." Interviewed by the author. Nashville, October 15, 1984.
Wright, Rena. Interviewed by the author. Nashville, August 6, 1985.

APPENDIX A

Historical Resources Inventory of the Metropolitan Nashville and Davidson County Parks and Recreation System

BASS PARK. 16th Street and Holly Street in East Nashville. 0.2 acres. A playground purchased by citizens of East Nashville and presented to the Park Board on December 12, 1921. Located next to a fire hall, the park apparently was named for Fire Chief Herman Bass who maintained and supervised the playground during the 1920s. It is the smallest park in the system.

BATTLE ROAD PARK. Battle Road at Burkitt Road in the southeastern corner of Davidson County. 280.60 acres. The Metro Council in 1972 appropriated $250,000 for the purchase of a large park in the southeastern sector of the county, which was matched in 1976 by a Bureau of Outdoor Recreation grant for land acquisition and development. The park was named for the road which borders it. Barge, Waggoner, Sumner, and Cannon prepared the master plan for park development which Mayor Richard Fulton released to the public in June 1983. The plans included four softball diamonds, eight tennis courts, soccer and rugby fields, and a jogging trail, with most of the park land reserved as a natural area.

BELLEVUE PARK. 656 College Jeanne Road and Highway 70 South in Southwestern Davidson County. 7.94 acres. Once the site of Bellevue Junior High

School, the Metro Board of Education declared the site surplus in 1982 and it was transferred to the park system. On September 1, 1982, the Metro Council approved the construction of a multipurpose community center in the park which was completed in 1984.

BICENTENNIAL PARK. 170 First Avenue North on the bank of the Cumberland River downstream of Fort Nashborough. 4.4 acres. Under the five-year capital improvement program of 1968-74, the Nashville Housing Authority acquired the park site as part of the central loop urban renewal project. The Metro Beautification Commission and the Park Board began coordinated planning for the park in 1971. The sculpture of James Robertson and John Donelson by Puryear Mims was moved in 1979 from inside Fort Nashborough to the center of the park at the request of the Horticultural Society of Davidson County, and the site was named Bicentennial Park to commemorate the celebration of Nashville's Bicentennial in 1979-80.

BORDEAUX GARDEN PARK. Snell Road near County Hospital. 12.7 acres. At the request of the people of Bordeaux represented by Councilmen Arch Carney and James Bates, the County Hospital leased the land to the Park Board in 1964. Funding from a 1964 bond issue was used to construct a playground and ball diamond in the park.

BORDEAUX-TIMOTHY DRIVE PARK. In Bordeaux on Timothy Drive south of Kings Lane. 16.44 acres. Barry Zeitlen, a real estate developer, gave the park to the Board in November 1980. Plans called for making it a playground-park, but the park was still undeveloped in 1985.

BOYD PARK (R. H. BOYD-PRESTON TAYLOR PARK). Clifton Avenue and 39th Avenue North. 14 acres. Located between McKissack School and the Preston Taylor Homes, the park was obtained in 1947 through a land exchange of 8.3 acres of city property at Albion and 37th Avenue North for the park land, then owned by McKissack and McKissack, Architects. At the request of Calvin McKissack, the park was named in honor of Richard Henry Boyd (1843-1938). Boyd, born a slave in Mississippi, became a Texas rancher after the Civil War, attended Bishop's College in Texas, and became an ordained minister and education director of the Texas Baptist Convention. Moving to Nashville in 1896, he founded the National Baptist Publishing Board, published the *Nashville Globe* and fourteen books, served as trustee of Fisk University and Meharry College, and was president of Citizen's Bank and Trust Company. Boyd was a close friend of Preston Taylor for whom the homes adjacent to the park was named and of Moses McKissack for whom the school was named. McKissack and McKissack were architects for the Boyd Community Center in the park, built during the early 1970s with federal Model Cities program funding.

BRICK CHURCH PARK. Brick Church Pike near Haynie Avenue. 27.48 acres. This park, which takes its name from the pike bordering it, was acquired in 1983 as part of a land exchange with the Oman Construction Company, which received in return the land called Rucker Park on the site of Brick Church Pike opposite that of the present park. Park development had not begun in 1985.

BUENA VISTA PARK. Tenth Avenue North and Cass Street. 76.8 acres. Buena Vista Springs was a popular mineral water spa during the 19th century. The Spanish name, which loosely translates as "good view," probably honors the 1847 American victory at the Battle of Buena Vista in Mexico. W. J. Arrington, owner of the springs, first offered to sell the site to the Park Board in 1902, but funding was inadequate at that time. The Park Board on May 16, 1934, purchased the first tract of the park from the Buena Vista Springs Company, and began development of recreation facilities with labor supplied by a 200-man camp of the Tennessee Transient Bureau located in the park to supply emergency work relief and subsequently by the Works Progress Administration. The U.S. Army leased the park for special field maneuvers from September 30 to November 15, 1942. Through a land exchange with the developers of the Metro Center complex during the early 1970s, the size of the park was increased from 37 to 76.8 acres. The park in 1985 had a community center, playground, ball diamond, swimming pool, and library.

CANE RIDGE PARK: see CRAWFORD PARK.

CEDAR HILL PARK. Near Goodlettsville on Dickerson Road at Old Hickory Boulevard. 224.89 acres. First called Old Center Park because Old Center School was located near the park, it was purchased in 1964 with Federal Open Space funding from J. O. Covington, W. L. Horn, and Ralph Finsterwald for $386,700 and officially named Cedar Hill Park on August 4, 1965, because the hilly park was covered with native cedar trees. It has a four-diamond softball complex centered around a concessions building, which the director of the Amateur Softball Association terms "the finest softball facility in the nation." Ground was broken on October 15, 1975, and the park opened to the public on August 28, 1977. In September 1977, the National Men's Fast-Pitch Softball Tournament took place at the park. A "softball hall of fame" honoring local contributors to the sport was established in the central building in 1979; those honored before 1985 included Fred N. Hazlewood, Rose "Skip" Way, Stan Cioccia, Ellis Cook, and Paul "Peanut" Spears. In addition to ball diamonds, the park in 1985 had picnic shelters, a lake, tennis courts, hiking trails, and a playground.

CEMETERIES: see notes at the end of this alphabetical listing of parks.

CENTENNIAL PARK. West End and 25th Avenue North. 132.3 acres. This park was the site of the 1897 Tennessee Centennial Exposition. It previously had been a farm purchased in 1783 by John Cockrill, the brother-in-law to James Robertson, then became the state fairgrounds after the Civil War and from 1884 to 1895 became a racetrack known as West Side Park. Construction of the buildings for the 1897 Centennial began in 1895 with the laying of the cornerstone for the

Parthenon replica on October 8, and a large number of elaborate structures were built to serve the 1.8 million visitors to the Exposition from the President down. When the Exposition closed on October 30, 1897, its leadership called for preservation of the Parthenon replica and the Centennial grounds as a public park, initiating the city park movement in Nashville. As the result of a litigation settlement with city government, Percy Warner and the Nashville Railway and Light Company purchased the first 72 acres of Centennial Park for $125,00 and gave it to the Park Board on December 22, 1902. The Park Board built a swimming pool, stocked Lake Watauga with fish, planted flower gardens and shrubs, built drives and walkways, and opened the park to the public in 1903, scheduling Gilbert and Sullivan operettas for cultural recreation purposes and also providing art exhibits in the Parthenon. During 1903, the monuments paying tribute to James Robertson and to the leaders of the 1897 Centennial Exposition were erected in the park, becoming the first of many monuments and memorials placed throughout the park. (Details concerning each are provided in the Inventory of Monuments, Memorials, and Artifacts which follows this Inventory of Park History) In 1903 the Park Board leased the Elliston Tract across 25th Avenue from the park as the site of ball diamonds, tennis courts, and a football field; it purchased the tract in 1911 and named it the Centennial Athletic Field. Land exchanges with the railroad north of the park and purchases of residential properties around the periphery of the park gradually expanded the park area to its present size. The first community center in the park was constructed in 1916, with a trolley car located in the playground at its side. The steam locomotive was placed in the park in 1953 and the fighter plane in 1961. The Sunken Gardens in 1897 was a pond called Lily Lake and from 1922 to 1949 was a Japanese Water Garden displaying aquatic plants. The bridge between the Sunken Gardens and Lake Watauga was constructed in 1906 and is the first reinforced concrete bridge built in Tennessee. The Centennial Park swimming pool, built in 1932, was reconstructed as the Centennial Art Center in 1972, with the site of the pool becoming a sculpture garden. Ice Centennial was built in 1978. The Parthenon replica of 1897 was reconstructed of concrete from 1921 to 1931 and received a minor renovation in 1962. The Centennial Croquet Club was constructed in 1963, although croquet courts had occupied the site many years before. The Confederate powder wheels were moved into the park from Sycamore Mills during the 1897 Centennial and are probably the most prominent artifact of the Exposition in the park, though many others are scattered functionally and unobtrusively throughout the park. (See the list in the Inventory of Monuments, Memorials, and Artifacts following this Inventory of Park History)

CHARLOTTE PARK. Deal Avenue and Eastboro Drive. 25.5 acres. Located at the Charlotte Park subdivision, which acquired its name from the Charlotte Pike leading to Charlotte, Tennessee, the park was purchased from John Hanley and M. L. Levitan for $53,225 in 1964 under the Federal Open Space program. It has a small community center, ball diamonds, tennis courts, a playground, and a picnic shelter. The name Charlotte honors Charlotte Reeves Robertson, wife of James Robertson.

CHEROKEE PARK. The park no longer exists. Located on Louisiana Avenue in West Nashville, it was established in 1887 as an 83-acre trolley park by the Nashville Land Improvement Company and the Nashville and West Nashville Railway Company on the Mark Cockrill farm and had amusement facilities similar to those at Glendale Park. It served as the training camp in 1898 by the First Tennessee Regiment commanded by Colonel William C. Smith prior to service in the Philippines. The Nashville Realty Company subdivided and sold most of the park in 1903, leaving a one-block park area on which the Cockrill Sulphur Springs were located for public use. After Nashville annexed West Nashville, the city council turned Cherokee Park over to the Park Board for operation in 1909. The park included the "Treaty Oak," under which James Robertson negotiated a treaty with Chickasaw Chief Piomingo, but the land was swampy and was developed only as a playground by the Park Board. (Efforts to preserve the dying oak tree after the Second World War failed). At the request of Mayor Ben West, the Board in 1952 transferred the park to city government in exchange for the 26-acre West Park on Morrow Road.

CITY CEMETERY: see the end of the alphabetical list of parks.

CLEVELAND PARK. In East Nashville near the Cleveland Street viaduct. 18.03 acres. The park takes its name from Cleveland Street, which presumably honored President Grover Cleveland. The park was part of the Nashville Housing Authority's East Nashville Urban Renewal program, and was given to the Park Board for operation in 1963. The park's community center was dedicated on January 30, 1964. In addition to the community center, the park has ball diamonds, tennis courts, a playground, and a small swimming pool.

CLIFTON PARK. The park no longer exists. Occupying four city blocks, or about ten acres, at Indiana Avenue and North Sixth Avenue, it was acquired like Cherokee Park in 1908 after Nashville annexed West Nashville and was initially laid out by the developers of West Nashville. The Park Board fenced the park and laid out ball diamonds on it, but undertook no extensive development because it was located only two blocks from Richland Park. At the request of Mayor Thomas Cummings, the Park Board gave Clifton Park to the city in December 1938 to become the site of a public school in exchange for the land which became McCabe Park.

COLEMAN PARK. (William Coleman Park) Thompson Lane and Nolensville Road. 10.4 acres. Mrs. William Coleman gave the park on April 27, 1935, to the Park Board in memory of her late husband, a local community leader. Park facilities initially were developed with Works Progress Administration labor and opened to the public on June 11, 1939. The modern community center was constructed in 1964 and named in honor of George Lawrence Dudley, a citizen who had devoted much of his life in service to the youth of Woodbine. In addition to the community center, the park has ball diamonds, a playground, and a swimming pool.

CRAWFORD PARK (Cecil Rhea Crawford Park). Old Hickory Boulevard and Cane Ridge Road in the southeastern sector of Davidson County. 7 acres. First known as Cane Ridge Park because the 2.8 acres on which the Cane Ridge School, (an old one room schoolhouse) sits, was declared surplus by the School Board and taken over by the Park Board. The additional 4.2 acres is land once owned by Cecil Rhea Crawford and given to the Park Board by Crawford in December 1971 on the condition that the gift remain a secret until after his death. A native of Oklahoma, Crawford taught music in the Cane Ridge community for many years, often scheduling recitals by his students in the old schoolhouse which was being used as the Cane Ridge community center. After his death on April 1, 1982, the Board named the park in his honor. He left most of his estate to endow a trust fund for the future maintenance of the park.

DALLAS H. NEIL PARK: see NEIL PARK.

DEES PARK. (Fannie Mae Dees Park) Blakemore Avenue and 24th Avenue South. 7.6 acres. Informally referred to as Cavert-Eakin park because it is located near those two schools, it was also referred to as Sunset Park after the Sunset playground that once operated near the site. The Park Board purchased the park because of its excellent location near the schools, and at the recommendation of the Eakin Community Council on May 4, 1978, named it to honor Fannie Mae Dees, a local civic leader, for her "deep concern for the welfare and safety of children in the Eakin community." The park has three tennis courts and modern playground apparatus, and it is distinguished by the sea serpent sculpture of Pedro Silva. With a grant from the Tennessee Arts Commission, Silva was brought to Nashville from New York to design the park's centerpiece, funded by grants from Vanderbilt University and businesses and by contributed materials and labor. Individual artists undertook the various graphics in the mosaic design adorning the serpent's coils, and a portrait of Fannie Mae Dees can be seen on the loop nearest its tail, which serves as seating. The sculpture was dedicated on April 25, 1981. This park is one of few containing equipment and furnishings for use by the severely physically handicapped. Much of this was developed in cooperation with the staff at Harris-Hillman School.

DOUGLAS PARK (Fred Douglas Park). North Seventh and Howerton streets in East Nashville. 24.11 acres. For $2,500, the Park Board purchased the first Douglas Park, a 7.13-acre plot on Fite Avenue, in early 1935. The origin of the name is obscure; at its meeting of May 17, 1935, the Board named it "Douglas Park," as shown in the typed minutes, but someone with an ink pen inserted "Fred" in front of Douglas, probably at the next Board meeting when the minutes were read. No Fred Douglas prominent in Nashville or East Nashville history has been identified, and the Park Board may well have intended to honor Frederick Douglass (1817?-1895), the famous black leader, journalist, and statesman. The original Douglas Park was developed as a Works Progress Administration project, and the land was taken by the Nashville Housing Authority during the East Nashville Urban renewal program of the 1950s. The present Douglas Park was opened in 1963 next to the Meigs School and a new community center was dedicated on September 10, 1964. The present park has ball diamonds, a swimming pool, a playground, and tennis and croquet courts.

DUDLEY PARK (Louise and Rebecca Dudley Park). Chestnut Street and Third Avenue South. 6.7 acres. When purchased in 1913, it was known as the Chestnut Street Park and served as a playground for that park of South Nashville. The Board renamed it the Louise and Rebecca Dudley Park in 1914 in memory of the two daughters of Park Commissioner Robert M. Dudley, who died when a train hit the family car at Glidden, Iowa. A swimming pool, bathhouse, bandstand, and ball diamond were built in the park in 1920, and it became a site of the annual park baseball championship tournaments during the 1920s. The Works Progress Administration renovated the park during the 1930s and completed there the second community center with gymnasium built in the park system, using materials donated by city government from wrecked public buildings. In addition to a community center, the park now has ball diamonds and tennis courts.

EAST PARK. Woodland Street and South Sixth Street. 10.26 acres. The founding of this park marked the first successful effort by the Park Board to combine park and school development programs and to participate in urban renewal. The East Nashville fire of March 22, 1916—the greatest disaster in Nashville history—destroyed 648 homes, churches, and schools, taking one life. On March 29, the Board conducted a public hearing in the Christian Church at Russell and Ninth streets, where they learned that East Nashvillians wanted Warner School rebuilt and the area near it converted into a public park. In accordance with that public demand, the Board in May 1916 purchased the land between Woodland and Russell streets and Sixth and Seventh streets for $48,750 from Whitefoord R. Cole, president of the Nashville, Chattanooga, and St. Louis Railway. The Board originally called it the "Edgefield Park," but in December 1916 officially named it East Park. Park Commissioner Robert T. Creighton prepared the original park plans, complete with central bandstand, fountain, walks, trees, and flowerbeds. The bandstand or pavilion was removed in 1956 shortly after a Quonset hut was placed in the park to serve as a community center. At the petition of East Nashvillians, in 1955 the Board placed a plaque in the community center honoring R. N. Chenault, for many years the principal of nearby Warner School. In addition to a community center, East Park in 1985 had ball diamonds, tennis courts, a playground, and a swimming pool.

EASTLAND PARK. 1501 Douglas Avenue. 2.4 acres. The site of old Eastland School, the park was given to the Park Board in 1953 by the Board of Education, which also leased the school building to the park system as a community center for $1 a year. It has a ball diamond and a playground, and during the 1980s the Tennessee Police Athletic League renovated the community center as the site of its boxing and sports program for the youth of the community.

EDGEHILL PARK: see ROSE PARK.

EDMONDSON PARK (William Edmondson Park). Charlotte Avenue and 17th Avenue South adjoining the John Henry Hale Homes. 0.9 acre. Opened on June 1, 1979, this green buffer zone between the homes and Charlotte Avenue was a joint project of the Metro Beautification Bureau, Park Board, Public Works Department, and Mayor Richard Fulton's Office. The park has no facilities other then the monument dedicated on July 8, 1981, to the memory of William Edmondson, for whom the park is named. Edmondson (1883-1951), who lived in the vicinity of the park, was a stone carver specializing in tombstones and garden ornaments honored in 1938 with the first one-man show by a black artist at New York's Museum of Modern Art. His valuable sculpture has been displayed in Paris, at the Smithsonian Institution, and various art centers.

EDWIN WARNER PARK: see WARNER PARK (Edwin).

ELIZABETH PARK. Arthur Street and Eleventh Avenue North. 1.62 acres. This triangle known before 1909 as Elizabeth Place was laid out when the McGavock Addition was platted in 1887 by Frank McGavock, administrator of the estate of Hugh W. and Mary McGavock, as an open space for people living in the vicinity. Mayor James S. Brown and the city council transferred the triangle to the Park Board on February 8, 1909. A. G. and Caroline A. Seibert gave a small addition to the park in 1911. (While the identity of Elizabeth for whom the park was named has not been established, when Frank McGavock family—Jane and Arthur streets, for instance—and Elizabeth may well have been Elizabeth McDowell McGavock, wife of pioneer David McGavock who settled in Nashville in 1786.) The park was initially developed as a playground, with swings and a paved circle for roller skates. With Works Progress Administration labor and materials salvaged from wrecked public buildings, the Elizabeth Park community center was constructed during the late 1930s and opened on January 12, 1940. The center was extensively used, especially for Golden Gloves boxing programs. The community center was completely renovated with $274,000 of Community Development funds and dedicated in May of 1982. The park has a playground and outdoor basketball courts.

ELMINGTON PARK. West End and Bowling Avenues. 13.34 acres. The Park Board purchased this park on November 1, 1927. It and the nearby Richland golf course were part of the "Elmington" estate of Edwin Warner. The Board paid $65,000 to the Harding Realty Company for the park while unidentified citizens donated an additional $45,000 toward the $110,000 purchase price. West End School was built adjacent to the park in 1935 and the park was developed with Works Progress Administration labor. It has a ball diamond, playground, and tennis courts.

E. N. PEELER PARK: see PEELER PARK.

E. S. ROSE PARK: see ROSE PARK.

EZELL ROAD PARK. Ezell Road at Mill Creek. 65.2 acres. The Park Board leased this park for $10 a year in 1976 from the State of Tennessee on part of Central State Hospital (DeBerry Correctional Institute) property. The Board subleased the park to the Junior Pro Football League which invested substantial sums in building ten football fields and related facilities in the park. An additional 19.1 acres was leased and subleased to the Antioch Youth Athletic Association for youth baseball. The park, named for the road which borders it, opened on August 5, 1978.

FANNIE MAE DEES PARK: see DEES PARK

FATHERLAND PARK. This park no longer exists. The city council in 1909 gave a 150-foot vacant lot at Fatherland and Tenth streets in East Nashville to the Park Board for use as a neighborhood playground. The Board installed play equipment and lights in 1910 and operated the park until 1920, when it returned the property to city government for other uses.

FEDERAL PARK. This park no longer exists. It was located on the lawn of the Federal Customs House at Eighth and Broad streets from 1902 until 1917 when wings were added to the Customs House, eliminating its lawn and the park. Postmaster Andrew W. Wills arranged for the public use of this park—the second public park in Nashville—and maintained it. With donated materials, the Park Board in 1902 installed a fence, walks, flowerbeds, and water fountain in the park. In 1905, a large Spanish cannon, captured by Admiral George Dewey at Manila in 1898, was moved from Fogg School into Federal Park for display and mounted upon a donated concrete foundation. The original park concept involved providing a resting place for citizens who picked up their mail once a week, usually on Sundays, at the Customs House, but being the only public park land in the vicinity it became crowded with children during the weekdays.

FILLMORE STREET PARK. This park no longer exists. The Park Board in May 1911 purchased for $1,500 the 150' by 170' lot owned by the Omohundro family at the corner of Fillmore and Decatur streets in South Nashville near Lipscomb School, placing play equipment and benches in it. After South Park opened, the Board closed Fillmore Park in 1918 and in 1920 turned the property over to city government for other uses.

FORT NASHBOROUGH. On the bank of the Cumberland River at First Avenue North in Riverfront Park with Bicentennial Park adjoining it on the north, this representation of the fort built in 1780 when Nashville was founded serves as a "Living History Museum" in which the life of the pioneers is reenacted. The stockade with five log cabins, representing the much larger original fort which was located on the bluff, was initially constructed during the 1930s by the Daughters of the American Revolution led by Lizzie Elliott and with architect

Joseph Hart as consultant and has been remodeled several times to better serve the public. Executive Order No. 12 in 1963 transferred the fort to the Metropolitan Board of Parks and Recreation's management. In 1979, the Puryear Mims sculpture of James Robertson and John Donelson was moved from within the stockade to the center of nearby Bicentennial Park.

FORT NEGLEY. Chestnut Street and Ridley Avenue in South Nashville. 63.34 acres. Designed by Captain James St. Clair Morton, built in 1862 by Union Army Engineers, and named for Union General James S. Negley, the original Fort Negley was part of a chain of fortifications ringing Nashville to protect it from Confederate attack. The fort's guns were fired twice, once when General Nathan B. Forrest's cavalry entered the outskirts of the city in 1862 and again during the Battle of Nashville in December 1864. The fort was abandoned at the end of the Civil War and the stone used in its construction was removed in 1889 for use in building the city reservoir atop a nearby hill. Efforts during the early 20th century to make the fort a national park failed, and in 1928 the Park Board purchased it and St. Cloud Hill on which it is constructed for $20,000 from the Fargason estate. During the 1930s, the Works Progress Administration reconstructed the Union Army fortification and the National Youth Administration built a playground and ball diamonds at the base of the hill near Chestnut Street. The park once was the site of the city's Golden Gloves boxing matches and of its Little League championship games. At various times, the park was considered for use as the site of a Civil War museum, city zoo, National Guard armory, and vocational school, The Board in 1967 leased part of the park as the site of the Cumberland Museum and Science Center and in 1976 leased another portion as the site of Herschel Greer Stadium, the home of professional minor league baseball in Nashville. The fort in 1975 was listed by the Tennessee Historical Commission on the National Register of Historic Places.

FRED DOUGLAS PARK: see DOUGLAS PARK

GAY STREET PARK: see LINDAUER PARK

GLENDALE PARK. This park no longer exists and never was a public park. Located on 64 acres near the intersection of Caldwell and Lealand Lanes, it was a trolley park established about 1887 and operated until 1932 as the most popular park in the city. It was initially known as Woodstock Park and was established by the Waverly Land Development Company and Overland Railway, a "dummy" streetcar line which became the Glendale line. Percy Warner established a zoo in the amusement park in 1912, which Clare Lovett managed until 1932. During its years of operations, it has such attractions as a roller coaster, balloon ascensions, vaudeville, and concerts. Several Nashville leaders have been credited with founding the park and streetcar line, but note that the Nashville *Tennessean*, November 15, 1931, states that the park and the line were built by Frederick W. Hunter of Philadelphia. When the park closed at the end of 1931, the Tennessee Electric Power Company which then owned it offered to lease it to the city park system for $1 a year, but the Park Board lacked the financial resources needed to continue its operation at the time.

GRANBERY SCHOOL. Hill Road and Wakefield Drive west of Granbery School. 7.01 acres. The land was given to the park system on September 19, 1979, by James T. Granbery, Jr., and Charles L. Cornelius, Jr., and had not been developed as park as of 1985.

GREEN HILLS PARK. Lone Oak Road and Belmont Park Terrace. 16.5 acres. The Park Board during the 1960s planned to establish a large regional park in the Green Hills community, using Federal Open Space funding from the Department of Housing and Urban Development to acquire the land. Because of rapidly escalating real estate prices in the Green Hills area, the plan for a large park was abandoned in 1971 and through cooperation with the Board of Education the present Green Hills Park was established adjacent to the John Trotwood Moore School. The park land was obtained through legal condemnation proceedings on December 20, 1973, with sixty percent of the purchase price paid by the Board of Education and forty percent by the Park Board.

GREENWOOD PARK. This park no longer exists and never was a public park. Located between Elm Hill Pike and Lebanon Road near the present Greenwood Cemetery, philanthropist Preston Taylor established the park for the black community in 1905 at the end of the Fairfield Street car line. About 17 acres in area, it included a ball park, swimming pool, picnic facilities, and amusements, serving not only as a park but also as the site of the black state fair and Boy Scout summer camp. Preston Taylor, a minister, left the park to the national convention of the Disciples of Christ Church which closed it about 1949. Efforts of the black community and the Park Board to acquire it as a public park at the time it closed failed.

GUNFACTORY PLAYGROUND. This park no longer exists. Located at Mulberry Street and Third Avenue South, this playground for the children of South Nashville operated from 1912 until 1914. The Park Board purchased the 131' by 135' foot vacant lot from Will and Louisa Nelson for $4,000 in July 1914 and installed play equipment on the lot. Because of "ruffianism," the Board closed the playground in 1914 and in 1920 turned the property over to city government for other uses.

HADLEY PARK. 28th Avenue North and Centennial (John Merritt) Boulevard. 34 acres. At the request of President George Gates of Fisk University and other leaders of the North Nashville community, the Park Board purchased the park in May 1912 for $20,000 which was furnished by Mayor Hilary Howse and the city council and dedicated it on July 4, 1912. Purchase records identify the park as the "Harding property," but it contained the home of the Hadley family whose plantation became the site of Tennessee State University at about the time the park was purchased. Mayor Howse in 1912 described Hadley Park as the first public park for black citizens established by any city in the world, and that hyperbole probably is accurate insofar as it relates to the Tennessee and the South. Major E. C. Lewis named it Hadley Park, but did not identify the Hadley he intended to honor. The city's black newspaper at the time assumed Lewis meant the Hadley family, John L. Hadley specifically, a white, slave-owning family which had lived on the site and which had helped former slaves adjust to freedom. That assumption probably was accurate, but it is possible that Lewis intended to honor Dr. W. A. Hadley, a pioneer black physician with whom Lewis had worked during the 1897 Centennial. The Board in 1912 approved the use of the park as the site of a public library, converted the Hadley house into a community center, installed benches and play equipment, and employed Benjamin Carr, Jr., as caretaker with Lucille Lacour becoming the first playground supervisor. The Works Progress Administration during the 1930s built the park entrance gates and improved recreational facilities, and the Park Board in 1943 built shower facilities for the use of black servicemen. In 1952 a swimming pool and new community center designed by McKissack and McKissack opened in the park, and in 1963 a new bandshell was constructed. Community Development funds were used in October of 1983 to renovate the swimming pool and used again in 1985 to renovate the community center. The park in 1985 also had ball diamonds, tennis courts, picnic shelters, and a playground.

HAMILTON CREEK PARK. Ned Shelton Road at J. Percy Priest Lake. 790 acres. As the J. Percy Priest Dam and Lake neared completion in 1965, the Park Board planned in cooperation with the Nashville District, U. S. Army Corps of Engineers, a public park on the east side of the lake, which is named in honor of a congressman from Nashville. The master plan for park development was approved in 1965 and in 1972 the Board leased the 790 acres of park land from the Corps of Engineers. In 1975 the Board agreed on a cost-sharing basis to participate in the construction of a sailboat marina at the Hamilton Creek embayment, which opened on June 4, 1980. In addition to the marina, the park in 1985 had a beach, boat-launching ramp, bicycle motocross track, and other public facilities.

HARPETH KNOLL PARK. Harpeth Knoll Road and Goodpasture Terrace. 10 acres. Leased from Board of Education. As a playground park in January, 1972.

HARTMAN PARK (Richard W. Hartman Park). 2801 Tucker Road in Bordeaux. 24.5 acres. The initial land for this park was transferred from the Metropolitan Convalescent Hospital grounds to the park system in 1964. At the request of Councilmen James Bates and Arch Carney, the park was named in honor of Richard W. Hartman, who for many years worked with the youth of Bordeaux. The Park Board transferred a portion of the park in December 1982 to the Metro Police for use in police training, and on March 2, 1983, Mayor Richard Fulton opened the new community center in the park. The park has ball diamonds, tennis courts, a playground and a picnic shelter. The park land is part of a 150-acre tract purchased by the city in 1911 from Albert W. Shaves and James W. McConnell.

HOWELL PARK (Morton B. Howell Park). This park no longer exists. A two-acre park at Third Avenue South and Peabody Street in South Nashville, it was the site of the University of Nashville Medical School and was purchased, along with South Park, in May 1913 from the trustees of the University, which had moved west to become George Peabody College. The Board named it in honor of Morton B. Howell (1834-1909), a businessman and Mayor of Nashville in 1874. The Board installed play equipment at the park and in 1920 built a community center with reading room and bandstand. During the 1930s, the Tennessee Transient Bureau with emergency work relief funding renovated the park and reopened it to the public on June 7, 1935. When the area changed from residential to industrial, the Board declared the park surplus and transferred it to city government in 1967. The Metro Council in 1980 made it part of the Rutledge Hill Redevelopment District and the park became the site of Reece Smith, Jr.'s 40-unit condominium development.

J. C. NAPIER PARK: see NAPIER PARK.

KIRKPATRICK PARK. Sevier and South Ninth Street in East Nashville. 8 acres. The Nashville Housing Authority's East Nashville Urban Renewal Project of the 1950s created Kirkpatrick Park which opened in 1963. It serves chiefly as a playfield for the adjacent Kirkpatrick School, from which the park takes its name. C. T. Kirkpatrick was a teacher and principal in the city school system from 1900 to 1940.

LINDAUER PARK (Ben Lindauer Park). This park no longer exists. First known as the Gay Street playground because it was located on that street, it was renamed Ben Lindauer Park in 1916 after the death of Park Commissioner Lindauer, president of the city council, charter member of the Park Board, and supervisor of the playgrounds established in 1909. At the request of the Council of Jewish Women, the Board moved the playground in 1919 to a 163' by 180' lot on Fifth Avenue North between Gay and Jo Johnston streets where it became the playground for the Fensterwald Settlement House. When the settlement house became the Fisk University Social Center in 1937, Lindauer Park became a black park, serving until 1954 when it was taken by the Nashville Housing Authority as part of the Capitol Hill Redevelopment project.

LOCK ONE PARK. Lock Road at Seminary Street in Bordeaux. 5.8 acres. This park marks the site of Cumberland River Lock and Dam 1, built by the Nashville District, U.S. Army Corps of Engineers during the 1890s for the benefit of steamboat commerce. Called the lock "reservation," it was the site of homes built by the Engineers for the use of the lockmaster and assistant lockmaster alongside the lock wall. When the modern Cheatham and Old Hickory Locks and Dams were constructed during the 1950s, the old locks and dams became surplus and were removed. The Corps of Engineers leased the Lock 1 reservation to the Park Board for use as a public park in 1969. The old series of locks had an unusual identification system: from Lock 1, the locks were numbered in upstream order to Lock 8 near Carthage, while below Lock 1, starting with Lock A, the locks were lettered from A to F at Eddyville, Kentucky.

LOCK TWO PARK. Lock Two Road at the apex of Pennington Bend. 8.6 acres. Lock 2 was the first lock upstream of Lock 1 described above. The Nashville District, U.S. Army Corps of Engineers, demolished the lock and dam, declared the lock reservation surplus, and in 1956 leased the reservation to the Park Board for use as a public park. A playground and picnic facilities opened at the park in 1957. The houses used by the lockmasters still stood in the park in 1985.

LOUISE AND REBECCA DUDLEY PARK: see DUDLEY PARK

MCCABE PARK. Murphy Road at 46th Avenue North. 209.6 acres. City government purchased most of this park in 1927 on which the Nashville Airport was constructed and named McConnell Field in honor of Lieutenant Brower McConnell, a Tennessee Air National Guard pilot killed in a 1927 air crash. When construction of the new city airport near Donelson began, McConnell Field was no longer needed and at the request of Mayor Thomas Cummings the airfield was transferred to the park system in exchange for Clifton and South Parks which were needed as the sites of schools; in 1938 therefore, the Park Board traded the city the 10-acre Clifton Park and 16 acres of South Park for 131.6 acres of the McConnell Airfield. The Board subsequently purchased tracts adjoining the park and in 1944 Mayor Cummings transferred 56.9 acres of land to the park which formerly had been the site of the Municipal Children's Home. The Board named the park in honor of Charles McCabe, the Nashville Park Commissioner and Postmaster who died in 1939. The first playground, athletic field, and nine-hole golf course were constructed with Works Progress Administration labor. C.E. Danis and Edwin Warner laid out the first nine, which opened to golfers on July 11, 1942. When the second nine-holes were constructed in 1947, several Indian graves were discovered on the course and were excavated by archaeologists from the Children's Museum. Park Commissioner Alvin G. Beaman presented the new McCabe Park Community Center to Mayor Ben West when it was dedicated on May 8, 1960. McCabe Park in 1985 had a ball diamond, tennis courts, and a playground, and a total of 27 holes of golf.

MCFERRIN PARK. Berry Avenue and Meridian Street in East Nashville. 11.12 acres. This park began as the Meridian Street playground when the Park Board in June 1909 purchased for $5,500 the Maney property at Meridian Street and Grace Avenue. It consisted of two lots measuring 150' by 300' in area, on which the Board installed a playground, built a small shelter pavilion, and planted trees, shrubs, and a privet hedge. At the request of the Northeast Nashville Improvement Club, the Board in 1920 purchased the D.C. Scales and adjoining lots across Meridian Street from the playground for $1,500. The new park was located on what once had been the farm of prominent Nashvillian John B. McFerrin, a Methodist Church leader, and the old McFerrin home still stood in the park in honor of its former owner. As part of the Nashville Housing Authority's East Nashville Urban Renewal Project, McFerrin Park was expanded in area to its present size in 1962, and a Quonset hut was placed in the park to serve as community center. A new community center was built and dedicated in March of 1963. The park in 1985 had a ball diamond, basketball court, playground, swimming pool, and community center.

MCKISSACK PARK. Torbett Street and 28th Avenue North in North Nashville. 1.52 acres. The park was the site of the McKissack School Annex, named in honor of Moses McKissack. Mayor Beverly Briley and the Board of Education in 1969 transferred the abandoned schoolyard to the park system. With Community Development funds, the Park Board removed the old school building and established a playground on the site, acquiring two more lots in 1982 to expand the size of the playground.

MADISON PARK. Delaware Avenue and Dupont Street in Madison. 30.5 acres. This was the first park acquired by the Metropolitan Board of Parks and Recreation established in 1963; the Board accepted the park at its first meeting. Madison civic clubs purchased the park from Miss Opha Bixler for $9,000, raising funds for the purchase and park development through a campaign starting in 1956. Colonel Tom Parker, the promoter best known as the manager of Elvis Presley, contributed $7,000 toward the park development. contributions from the civic clubs, from local businessmen, and from the proceeds of the annual Madison Hillbilly Day funded the work in the park, which was managed by Madison Community Park, Inc., a nonprofit corporation chartered for the purpose in 1957. Realtor J. R. Coarsey served a president of the park corporation, James Pigue as its executive secretary, and its first directors included Harris Vaughn, A. J. Coleman, Ronald Coleman, Bernard Odum, Herman DePriest, Ray Garrett, Carlos Brawner, Ben Cunningham, and E. E. Marlin. The park had ball diamonds, a playground, and a crafts center when the Park Board purchased it for $16,500 from the corporation and also agreed to build a community center in the park. In 1985, the park also had picnic shelters and tennis courts.

MAIN STREET PARK. This park no longer exists. Located at Main Street and Seventh Street in East Nashville, the small playground was transferred to the Park Board by Mayor Hilary Howse in August 1910. The Mayor agreed to have the public works department grade the vacant lot, after which the Park Board installed swings and play equipment. The playground was used until after 1914, when it was returned to the city for other uses.

MEMORIAL SQUARE PARK: see VICTORY SQUARE.

MERIDIAN STREET PARK: see MCFERRIN PARK.

MONROE STREET PLAYGROUND. Monroe and Scovel streets at Eleventh Avenue North in North Nashville. 0.5 acre. This park was purchased and developed using community development funds. The site in 1985 had play equipment and a basketball court.

MORGAN PARK. Hume Street and Fifth Avenue North in North Nashville. 7 acres. The Park Board purchased Frederick Laitenberger's German beer garden occupying the block between Hume and Fifth Avenue in 1909 to provide a park for the working-class neighborhood surrounding the Warioto Cotton Mills and the Morgan-Hamilton Bag Company (now the Werthan mills). At the request of Major E. C. Lewis, the Board named the park in honor of Samuel Dold Morgan (1789-1880), "The Merchant Prince of Nashville," who had founded the nearby textile mills and had owned similar mills at Lebanon, Huntsville, and other cities. Morgan had served as president of the state commission which supervised construction of the State Capitol building and was interred in the wall of that building. He was the uncle of Confederate General John Hunt Morgan and during the Civil War he manufactured munitions for the Confederacy. The Park Board developed the park as a playground and arranged for the piping of mineral water to the park from the 2,933-foot deep well drilled in 1889 at the nearby textile mills. The mineral (sulphur) water was provided without charge to the public, and many Nashvillians visited the park frequently to fill jugs with the water for home use. Maintenance of the fountain in the park ceased about 1955 and the mineral water outlet was relocated to Taylor Street. The park has a new community center completed in 1984, plus basketball courts, a ball diamond, and a playground.

MORTON B. HOWELL PARK: see HOWELL PARK.

MUSIC SQUARE PARK. Division Street and Music Square East. 0.6 acre. Mayor Beverly Briley dedicated this park on August 27, 1975; it was his last official act as mayor. The Metropolitan Housing and Development Agency planned the park as part of urban renewal in the Music Row area; the park was designed by Carter and Burgess of Texas and constructed by Alman Construction Company of Nashville. It was given its name by the Park Board in tribute to country music fans, who contribute substantially to the city's economic base and who use the park while visiting the Country Music Hall of Fame and other attractions in the park's vicinity.

NAPIER PARK (J. C. Napier Park). Fairfield Avenue and J. C. Napier Street between Lebanon and Murfreesboro roads in South Nashville. 2.5 acres. Located next to Napier School named for Alonzo Napier, the park is named for Alonzo's brother James Carroll Napier, the son of a Nashville blacksmith and freedman. He attended Wilberforce and Oberlin colleges and Howard University, becoming an attorney and banker and serving on the Nashville City Council. He had charge initially of the black achievements exhibits at the 1897 Centennial exposition and earned a national reputation as U.S. register of the Treasury during the administration of President William H. Taft. Napier promoted playgrounds in the city to serve the black community, and In 1913 the Park Board purchased for

$1,500 a vacant lot adjoining Napier School and there built the playground which was named Napier Park and which subsequently was expanded in size. The park has a large community center, which replaced a Quonset hut used earlier for the purpose. The center has one of the larger swimming pools in the system. Other facilities in 1985 included a ball diamond and a playground.

NAPIER MINIPARK (J. C. Napier Minipark). Fain Street and Maury Street. 0.4 acre. This playground was acquired with Community Development block grant funding under the Community Development Act of 1974.

NEIL PARK (Dallas H. Neil Park). Wedgewood Avenue at Eighth Avenue South. 0.88 acre. The Metropolitan Development and Housing Agency transferred this small park to the Park Board in 1981. At the request of Andrew B. Gibson, the Board named the park in honor of Dr. Dallas H. Neil, a prominent local civic leader.

NORTH FISK PARK. Burch and Osage streets at 25th Avenue North. 7.6 acres. The Metro Council on June 30, 1982, approved Ordinance 82-933 authorizing the Park Board to acquire property for the development of this park with Community Development funding. Planning for the park began in 1976, it opened in 1983, and in 1985 had a ball diamond, basketball court, shelter, and restroom facility.

OAKWOOD PARK. Oakwood Avenue and Bethwood Drive in East Nashville between Dickerson Road and Ellington Parkway north of Trinity Lane. 26.55 acres. In 1977 Manuel Cypress and Alfred Sheppard donated 3.26 acres and The Park Board purchased the rest of the land for the park. Master plans were initiated in 1981. Councilman Richard Adams secured the initial funding for park development from the Metro Council, while Director James Fyke sought funding from the Land and Water Conservation program. The park opened in 1983 with a ball diamond and two playgrounds.

OLD HICKORY BEACH. Cinder Road at Old Hickory Lake near the navigation lock and dam. acres. The beach was constructed by the Nashville District, Corps of Engineers, when it built the Old Hickory Lock and Dam during the 1950s. The lake borders the town of Old Hickory, and both are named in honor of President Andrew Jackson, who was called "Old Hickory" because of the strength of his character. William G. Redmon, project resource manager for the Corps, met with the Park Board on October 2, 1963, to request it to assume management of the beach and to establish a public park there under a leasing arrangement with the Corps and the nearby E. I. DuPont Corporation. The Board leased the beach in 1964 and established an adjacent public park with a playground, boat-launching ramp, and public conveniences.

PARAGON MILLS PARK. Benita Drive and Scotwood Drive in the Paragon Mills community near Interstate 24 in southeast Nashville. 35.69 acres. Located at the abandoned Radnor wastewater treatment plant, the park was acquired in 1973 when a real estate developer offered to donate several acres of land at the site to the park system if the Park Board would purchase more. The Board accepted the offer on March 7, 1973 and applied to the Bureau of Outdoor Recreation for a grant to fund the purchase. Kevin Tucker and Associates were employed to undertake the master plan for the park in 1977, and during the 1980s funding for park development was added to the capital improvement budget on an incremental basis. Two ball diamonds and a basketball court were completed by 1984.

PARKWOOD PARK. Vailview Drive and Brickdale Lane off Ewing Lane between Interstates 24 and 65 north. 10.26 acres. This park was acquired from a real estate developer in that community in 1972 and its development funded by a grant from the Bureau of Outdoor Recreation. The name derives from the Parkwood community around it. In 1985 it had a ball diamond, tennis courts, a playground, and basketball court.

PEELER PARK (E.N. Peeler Park). At the end of Neely's Bend Road in Madison bordering the Cumberland River. 273.61 acres. The Park Board in November 1963 took an option to purchase the E.N. Peeler farm for $750 per acre, then applied for matching funding from the Federal Open Space program of the Department of Housing and Urban Development. Lallie Richter presented the master plan for the park in 1965, which then included a golf course although construction of the course was deferred to avoid competing with a nearby private golf course. From Homer Chance, the Board acquired the Sun Valley Swim Club adjacent to Peeler Park in 1969 for $65,000, about fifty percent of its appraised value. The park in 1985 had a ball diamond and swimming pool and would be further developed in the future.

PERCY WARNER PARK: see WARNER PARK.

PITTS PARK (William A. Pitts Park). Tusculum Road near Packard Drive. 27.4 acres. In 1969 a Tusculum area real estate developer offered to donate fifteen acres adjacent to an apartment complex and the Park Board accepted, expecting to develop the park in cooperation with the Woodbine Junior Chamber of Commerce. In 1975, at the request of Mayor Beverly Briley and Metro Planning Commission Director Farris Deep, the Board named the park in honor of William A. Pitts, who joined the County Planning Commission in 1950 and subsequently served as Director of Planning for the City-County Commission, as the county's first Director of Public Works, and as the first Metropolitan Director of Codes before his death on September 17, 1964. The master plan for park development was completed in 1977, a softball diamond was completed by 1985, and other facilities were planned for future construction.

RESERVOIR PARK. Argyle Avenue and Eighth Avenue South. 16.8 acres. The city reservoir built in 1889 is located on the site of a Union Army fortification built during the Civil War, and the reservoir walls were initially constructed with stone taken from Fort Negley atop a nearby hill. The reservoir wall failed on November 5, 1912, sending a damaging flood down Eighth Avenue but causing no loss of life, and it was repaired and restored to service. At the request of City Commissioner Robert Ellicott, the Board in 1914 agreed to establish a public park at the reservoir if city government graded the land to repair the damages caused by the 1912 flood. The grading was accomplished and the Board opened a playground on the site, although the title to the property remained with the public works department which had charge of the reservoir. In 1932 the Board contracted with J. E. Campbell to construct a community center in the park for $10,000. The building was used for meetings of local civic groups, for arts and crafts and sewing classes, and in 1941 the sewing club there headed by Mrs. H. W. Lavender fabricated "Bundles for Britain." The community center was remodeled during the 1970s and in 1979 renamed the Senior Citizens Building to better reflect its purpose. The park in 1985 had a ball diamond, tennis courts, picnic shelters, and a playground.

R. H. BOYD PARK: see BOYD PARK.

RICHARD W. HARTMAN PARK: see HARTMAN PARK.

RHODES (Ted Rhodes) PARK. Metro Center Boulevard and Mainstream Drive. 161.2 acres. Known originally as Cumberland Golf Course, this park first opened on July 10, 1954. When 150 black golfers asked in 1950 that facilities for their game be provided, the Park Board asked city government to donate the land for the purpose at the old detention home in North Nashville near the Cumberland River. Councilman Robert Lillard sponsored the legislation in the Metro Council providing the requested land and funds for development of the golf course. Work on the course began in 1953, and Mayor Ben West named it Cumberland Municipal Park. Joe Hampton became the first golf pro at the course and in 1984 completed thirty years service at the course, which began as a segregated course but was integrated shortly after its opening. At the request of Councilman Lillard in 1969, the Board renamed the park in honor of Theodore "Ted" Rhodes, a renowned black golf professional from Nashville. When the nearby Metro Center complex with a levee along the riverfront was constructed during the early 1970s, the area of the park was increased through a land exchange negotiated with the developers of Metro Center. The modern Ted Rhodes Golf Clubhouse in the park was dedicated on May 26, 1976. The park in 1985 also had three tennis courts.

RICHLAND PARK. Charlotte Avenue and 46th Avenue North. 10.69 acres. After the City of Nashville annexed West Nashville, Richland Park, which had been laid out during the 1890s on the plat of West Nashville by the land development company, was added to the city park system along with Cherokee and Clifton parks. The land development company sought to maintain control of Richland Park, and in late 1906 the Park Board sued in chancery court to secure full title to the property. The court entered its decree in July 1907, turning the park over to the Board and requiring the Board to pay the company $250 for a house located in the park. The Board had the livestock driven out of the park, installed a playground, and planted flowers and shrubs. A community center was built in the park in 1932 by contractor J. E. Campbell. In 1961 a library was built on the property and dedicated by Mayor Ben West. The park in 1985 had ball diamonds, tennis courts, a playground, croquet courts, and a swimming pool.

RIVERFRONT PARK. Broad Street and First Avenue North on the left bank of the Cumberland River. 7.5 acres. When plans for the Ryman Landing development between the Thermal Plant and Fort Nashboro faded, the Park Board requested Mayor Fulton to use the land to create a riverfront park as a historical project commemorating the Nashville Bicentennial. On November 5, 1980, Sandra (Mrs. Richard) Fulton and Betty Brown co-chairmen of a Century III special project committee, presented plans developed by the committee for a riverfront park and requested the assistance of the Park Board in securing federal funding assistance with park development. The Nashville District, U.S. Army Corps of Engineers, on December 17, 1981, entered into an agreement with city government on a cost-sharing basis for development of the park, the plan costing about $4.2 million. This cost was shared by the federal government and community development funds, with a small amount coming from the Department of Conservation's Tennessee Land and Conservation Fund. The three-phase park construction program proceeded, and the first phase was completed and opened with a gala riverfront celebration on July 10, 1983. Third phase construction, including a boat dock, was approved at the end of 1984, and was in progress in 1985.

ROCK CITY PARK: see SOUTH INGLEWOOD PARK.

ROSE PARK (E. S. Rose Park). Edgehill Avenue and Tenth Avenue South between Rose School and Carter-Lawrence School. 22.31 acres. The Park Board in 1926 bought a 212' by 410' lot between Edgehill and Vernon streets and Eleventh Avenue South as a playground for the Edgehill community, naming it Edgehill Park. Park Commissioner James G. Stahlman in 1946 recommended that a new Edgehill park be developed at the abandoned rock quarry called "Rockcrusher Hill," but funding for the project was unavailable until 1959 when Mayor Ben West persuaded the Park Board to issue bonds for the purpose. The principal public advocates of the new Edgehill park were Judge Benson Trimble of the South Street Community Center organization and Rev. E. S. Rose of the Southwest Nashville Civic Club. In 1960, the rock quarry, eight acres in area and fifty feet deep, was filled with materials excavated for the interstate highway construction, and the new park established atop the fill and named for the Rev. E. S. Rose, pastor for many years of the Bethel African Methodist Episcopal Church who died in 1956. Barge, Waggoner, and Sumner performed the engineering for the park. In 1962, the Park Board turned the old Edgehill Park playground over to the Nashville Housing Authority and contracted for the construction of a community center with swimming pool in Rose Park, which was named the Easley Memorial Center in honor of Rev. T. H. Easley, the pastor of the New Hope Baptist Church for twenty-five years before his death in 1954. It was the first Park-School complex completed by the Park Board, the park serving as playfield for the two schools at the ends of the park. In addition to the community center and pool, the park in 1985 had ball diamonds, tennis and basketball courts, picnic shelters and a playground.

ROSE PARK (Tony Rose Park). Music Circle East and Hawkins Street in the Music Row area. 2.3 acres. This is the second park to bear the name of Tony Rose, a renowned musician whose band often played Sunday concerts at Glendale Park early in the century. The Board acquired the first Tony Rose Park at Sixteenth Avenue South and Division Street in 1940 as part of a land exchange with Director of Public Works Robert Lawrence, who received in exchange for the park land permission to build a polling place in Morgan Park. At the request of the Women's Political Union, the Board in 1940 named the park in honor of Tony Rose and developed it as a playground for neighborhood children. It purchased an adjoining lot in 1944 to increase the park area to 1.3 acres. By 1964 the playground was engulfed by surrounding commercial development and the Board declared it surplus property for use in the urban renewal of the Music Row area. In 1966 the Country Music Association started construction of the Country Music Hall of Fame on the site of the playground. As compensation for the loss of the playground, the Park Board received two new small parks in the neighborhood, tiny Music Square Park across Sixteenth Avenue from the Hall of Fame which opened to the public in 1975, and a 2.3 acre plot on Hawkins Street which was given the name Tony Rose Park but which had not been developed with park facilities in 1985.

RUCKER PARK. This park no longer exists. It was located at Rucker Avenue and Interstate 65 North and consisted of 31.5 acres given to the park system by the Hercules Powder Company. The land was traded to the Oman Construction Company in 1983 in exchange for Brick Church Park which was better situated for public access.

SEVEN OAKS PARK. School Lane and McGavock Pike in the Glenbine community near Berry Field. 76 acres. The Board purchased this park in 1963 from C. H. and Margaret Waldron, paying $44,517 with the balance funded under the Federal Open Space program. Records do not indicate the origin of the park name, which may have come from a historic home on the land or perhaps be derived from a cluster of oak trees in the park. The park in 1985 had ball diamonds, tennis and basketball courts, picnic shelters, and a playground.

SEVIER PARK. Lealand Lane and Clayton Avenue in South Nashville. 20.36 acres. The Board purchased this park in 1945 for $50,328 from the estate of Colonel Granville Sevier, a retired Army officer and descendent of a brother to the first Governor of Tennessee. Sunnyside Mansion in the park was the home before the Civil War of Mrs. Jesse Benton, whose husband was the brother of

Thomas H. Benton. The Benton brothers had a memorable encounter with General Andrew Jackson on Nashville's Public Square in 1813, and Thomas Benton later represented both Tennessee and Missouri in Congress. The mansion bears the marks of the Battle of Nashville in 1864 and has two log structures at its rear with a controversial history—local tradition holds they served as trading posts with the Indians during pioneer times. The park was dedicated by Mayor Thomas Cummings on June 7, 1948. The second floor of the mansion became the home of the families of John J. "Jack" Spore and John Fuller, employed by the Park Board, and the first floor served during the 1950s as the offices of the Recreation Division of the park system. The J. B. Regen Construction Company built the small swimming pool in the park in 1954. The park in 1985 had picnic shelters, a ball diamond, tennis courts, a playground, a basketball court, and a community center, which was built in 1963.

SHELBY PARK. Shelby Avenue and South 20th Street on the Cumberland River. 361.5 acres. The park was once owned by John Shelby, who built the Fatherland and Boscobel mansions in East Nashville during the 19th century; born in 1786, Shelby was the first white child born in Sumner County. It was called Shelby Park by a real estate development company which owned it at the turn of the century and operated an amusement park in it. When that company bankrupted in 1903, the Park Board investigated its purchase as a public park, but deferred action as a result of opposition from East Nashvillians. In 1909 the Board purchased the first 151 acres of the park from the creditors of the bankrupt land company for $40,000 and initiated negotiations with J. R. Meredith for his eighty acres, acquiring the Meredith property in 1911. Additional land adjoining the park was subsequently purchased as the need and opportunity arose. Though public support existed for naming it Riverside Park, the original name was retained by the Board. The park was opened to the public on July 4, 1912, and Major E. C. Lewis prepared the plans for park development, designing the Sycamore Lodge which opened on August 24, 1912, the Mission House, several log cabins, and various other park features. A Dutch windmill was built on a promontory overlooking the park and a unique boathouse resembling a steamboat at the side of Lake Sevier. A rock quarry was opened in the park and seven bridges were constructed over ravines. A mule stable and tool shed was constructed in Meredith Grove for park maintenance. The original intention of the Board was to maintain the park largely in its scenic natural condition, but public demands for golf courses, athletic fields, playgrounds, and other recreation facilities eventually forced use of most space in the park. In 1923 the Board purchased the 50-acre Hinds tract to build thereon the first municipal golf course in Nashville, which opened in 1924, and in 1927 it purchased the 60-acre Tillman tract to expand the course to eighteen holes and the total park acreage to about its present size. In 1915, Dr. A. S. Keim of the YMCA organized the first city park baseball league with eight teams which played on Saturdays at diamonds in Shelby Park. The Shelby Park swimming pool was constructed in 1932 and served until 1961 when it closed. During the Second World War, the pool was used by the Army for river assault boat training and the park riverfront was used as moorage by the U.S. Coast Guard and the Army Corps of Engineers. The U.S. Naval Reserve office, shaped like the prow of a ship, was constructed from 1946 to 1949 on land leased in Meredith Grove from the Board. The most serious accident in park history occurred on May 27, 1945, when four young people drowned in Lake Sevier after their boat overturned. The City of Nashville annexed all of Shelby Park into its corporate limits in 1954. The baseball diamonds in the park were named in honor of Oscar Capps of the Jess Neeley Athletic Association in 1974. Shelby Park in 1985 had 10 ball diamonds, 4 of which were completely reconstructed in 1981, a community center, six picnic shelters, tennis and basketball courts, and playgrounds, along with 27 holes of golf including the Riverview golf course.

SOUTH PARK. Lindsley Avenue in South Nashville adjacent to old Howard School and offices of Metropolitan government. 4.6 acres. The Park Board purchased this park in May 1913 from the trustees of the University of Nashville, which had used the park as the site of Montgomery Bell Academy, for $22,500 at the same time it purchased nearby Howell Park for $10,000. The park was located on the tax-exempt 100 acres granted in 1785 by the State of North Carolina (which then included Tennessee) to Davidson Academy; Davidson Academy in 1806 became Cumberland College and in 1826 became the University of Nashville, which in turn became George Peabody College in 1912. The park was first named Montgomery Bell Park and was renamed South Park by the Board in December 1916. The Board built playgrounds and a community center in the park, and Mrs. Nannie W. Eagan directed a public library in the community center until it burned in 1942. The park facilities were renovated and improved by transient labor employed by the Works Progress Administration during the 1930s. During the First World War, the Surgeon General of the U.S. Army leased the building in the park as a military hospital. In 1947, the Board of Education, Children's Museum, and Park Board entered into an agreement for joint use of South Park by all three agencies, and the Board of Education constructed the swimming pool for the use of Howard School and the park system. The pool has since been removed and replaced with tennis courts. The Metro Council in 1980 created the Rutledge Hill Redevelopment District which included Howell and South parks, and Reece Smith constructed a $2.1 million residential complex in South Park on the east side of Howard School. When the Children's Museum relocated in the 1970s to the Cumberland Museum and Science Center in Fort Negley Park, office of Metropolitan government were relocated onto South Park.

SOUTH INGLEWOOD PARK. Cahal Avenue at Rebecca Avenue in East Nashville. 19.1 acres. Known originally as Rock City Park because that street runs into the park, the park is on the site of an old rock quarry. The Board established the park at the request of an East Nashville Civic League in 1966 under a Federal Open Space grant. At the request of the civic league, the Board changed the name of the park to South Inglewood Park in July 1972. In 1985 the park had a playground, two lighted ball diamonds and a small community center.

SPRING PARK. This park no longer exists and never was a public park. Bounded by Fatherland, Holly, Thirteenth, and Fourteenth streets in East Nashville, it was the only park in the city in 1885 and was sold and subdivided during the 1890s. Operated by a streetcar line, it had a monkey cage, bandstand, and a spring-fed lake.

TED RHODES PARK: see RHODES PARK

THOMPSON LANE AND MILL CREEK PARK. Along the left bank of Mill Creek between Thompson Lane and Briley Parkway near Seven Oaks Parks. 23.8 acres. 11.9 acres of this park were given to the park system in 1980 by Chester Atkins, Homer L. Randolph, and Floyd Cramer, the famous Nashville musicians, and 11.9 acres were purchased. Located in the creek's floodplain, the park had not been developed in 1985.

TONY ROSE PARK: see ROSE PARK.

TRINITY HILLS PARK. South of Aldrich Lane between Brick Church Pike and Whites Creek Pike north of the Trinity Hills Village community. Fifty acre park area was purchased in February of 1975 as part of the planning of the Trinity Hills Village community sponsored by federal government agencies, but access to the land is difficult and the park has not been developed as of 1985.

TWO RIVERS PARK. Briley Parkway and Two Rivers Parkway at McGavock Comprehensive High School. 384.8 acres. The Park Board in 1966 purchased this park from the estate of Mrs. Spence (Louise Bransford) McGavock with Federal Open Space matching funding. Mayor Beverly Briley announced the purchase for $995,000 on October 20, 1966, noting that one strip of the estate would be used for the construction of the Briley Parkway, other acreage would go to the Board of Education for use in building the McGavock comprehensive high school, and the remainder of the estate would become Two Rivers Park, as one of the city's cooperative Park-School complexes. The estate had been owned by the McGavock family since pioneer times, and during the 19th century the family had occasionally allowed use of the estate riverfront for park purposes—steamboats had transported Sunday School classes from Nashville upriver to the McGavock estate for picnics. Working with the Metropolitan Historical Commission, which wished to preserve the 1859 Italianate Two Rivers mansion and the older home built in 1802 behind the mansion, the Board employed historian Hugh Walker to investigate the mansion's history and report upon its preservation. The master plan for park development was completed in 1969 and five-phase development began with funding from the Bureau of Outdoor Recreation. During construction of the golf course, archaeological sites were discovered and explored on the course. The Two Rivers mansion was restored, with public conveniences added, and its interior redecorated with volunteer assistance and contributions from the Stones River Women's Club and other citizens. The Metro Council in 1978 (Ordinance 78-860) funded the construction of a swimming pool in the park with a mechanism capable of producing waves, which the Board named "Wave Country" and which became an extremely popular attraction of the park. The recreation facilities provided in the park in cooperation with the Board of Education's comprehensive McGavock High School constituted the fourth joint Park-School dual use program within the park system. The Two Rivers Mansion and the 1802 house adjacent thereto have been placed on the National Register of Historic Places. In addition to the restored mansion, wave pool, and schools, the park in 1985 had an eighteen-hole golf course, five ball diamonds, six tennis courts, five picnic shelters, a playground, hiking trails, and a recreation center. A new horticultural center (greenhouse) for the park system was under construction in this park in 1985.

VICTORY SQUARE (War Memorial Park). This park no longer exists within the city park system. It was located at the east side of the War Memorial Building in the downtown business district near the State Capitol building and now is known as the Legislative Plaza, a state-owned paved area atop a state office complex which has become the site of the annual Summer Lights Festival. The Tennessee General Assembly in Section 2, Chapter 122, Public Act of 1919, authorized the creation of this park as a memorial to the veterans of the First World War, providing funding for its development and maintenance and directing that the title to the property be given to the City of Nashville for use as a public park to be known as Victory Square. The park site was rocky, and during the 1920s the Park Board had the rock excavated, the site covered with soil, walks constructed, and flowers and shrubs planted. By 1936 the state appropriation for park development and maintenance was exhausted, but the Park Board continued minimum maintenance at its own expense. State authorities refused to relinquish the title to the property until Governor Gordon Browning ordered that it be given to the Park Board in 1953. The park became the central transfer point for city bus transport, and during the 1950s was maintained by the Nashville Horticultural Society with the cooperation of the city transit authority. During the downtown urban renewal efforts of the 1960s, the Board returned the title to the park to city government, which planned construction of a subterranean parking garage beneath the park. The title was returned to state government in 1969, which constructed a state office complex on the site, naming the roof of the complex the Legislative Plaza. Victory Square was the sole park given to the city park system by state government, although during the 1970s the state leased several of its properties to the system for use as parks.

WARNER PARK (Edwin Warner Park). Vaughn Road and Old Hickory Boulevard. 606.7 acres. This park is named in honor of Edwin Warner who succeeded his older brother Percy on the Park Board in 1927, served as Board chairman from 1939 until his death in 1945, once served briefly without pay as Superintendent of Parks, devoted half of each working day to park system development, and gave not only his time but also his personal funds and property to the parks. On April 7, 1930, he gave the Park Board $20,000 to initiate development of the park southwest of Old Hickory Boulevard through the purchase of the 267.7 acre

E. H. Woolwine farm; the balance of the gift was used for construction of an entrance gate into the new park. The Board purchased additional properties adjoining the initial acreage, bringing the park to near its present area by November 18, 1937, when it named the park in honor of Edwin Warner. Other members of his family also have made donations to the park system: Mrs. Edwin Warner in 1946 donated a tract of land near the entrance to Percy Warner Park and in 1954 Mrs. William (Milbrey Warner) Waller contributed 2.5 acres near the Page and Chickering Road intersection which she had inherited from Edwin Warner. Initial park development was completed as a Works Progress Administration project, using rock for drives and construction material excavated from the quarry in Edwin Warner Park. The park in 1985 contained two ball diamonds, a playground, hiking trails, thirteen picnic shelters, a polo field, soccer field, model airplane field, and the park nursery. The junior baseball diamond in July 1967 was named in honor of Robert M. "Bob" Heriges (1921-1967), who devoted much of his life to the youth of the area and who was instrumental in the construction of the diamond. Development of the model airfield began in 1946 and of the polo field in 1973. The Warner Park Nature Center was established in 1973 for environmental recreation and education, including the C. E. Farrell natural history museum and gardens; the Nashville Garden Club in 1985 contributed funds toward the construction of a library and other facilities in connection with the Nature Center.

WARNER PARK (Percy Warner Park). Belle Meade and Old Hickory Boulevards. 2,058.1 acres. This park for about a decade after it was established in 1926 was the largest public park of any type in Tennessee, and it remains one of the largest city parks in the nation. Park Board chairman Percy Warner in 1926 directed the first professional efforts to devise a comprehensive park plan for the city, and those plans called for ringing the city with large parks linked together by a system of boulevards. He discussed the plans with his son-in-law, Senator Luke Lea, a hero of the First World War who published the Nashville *Tennessean* and owned the company which was developing the Belle Meade community. Senator Lea, who had seen the large Rock Creek Park in the District of Columbia and Swope Park in Kansas City, understood the value of large parks and on September 17, 1926, donated 868 acres of his Belle Meade property to the park system. Four days after the death of Percy Warner, the Board on June 22 1927 named the park in his honor; on November 25, 1927, it named the highest point in the park Luke Lea Heights (Lea Summit) in honor of the park donor. With the proceeds of a 1927 bond issue, the Board purchased farms adjacent to the original tract, rapidly expanding the park area. Mrs. Percy Warner in 1930 donated $20,000 for the construction of the entrance gates to the park, which were designed by Edward Dougherty, built by Oman Construction Company, and dedicated on April 26, 1932. Bryant Fleming in 1931 designed the steps, or allée, leading up the hill behind the entrance gates. Many of the scenic drives, bridges, picnic shelters and other features were constructed as Works Progress Administration projects during the 1930s, generally under the personal supervision of Edwin Warner, who had succeeded his older brother on the Park Board.

The two most interesting WPA projects in the park are the steeplechase course and the monument to the First Tennessee Infantry, which had assembled in the park in 1917 before departing for France. The Percy Warner golf course opened in 1938 and the Harpeth Hills golf course in 1965. In addition to the facilities mentioned, the park in 1985 had a small lake, a playground, hiking trails, twelve picnic shelters, equestrian facilities and riding trails. The park is listed on the registers of natural wonders and of historic places, and is perhaps best known for the Iroquois Steeplechase and other equestrian events sponsored by the Volunteer Horseman's Association.

WATKINS PARK. Jo Johnston Avenue and Seventeenth Avenue North. 8.2 acres. This was the first public park in Nashville, transferred to the Park Board at its first meeting in 1901 and given to the city by Samuel Watkins in 1870. Watkins (1794-1882), an orphan from Virginia, served during the War of 1812 under Andrew Jackson, and became a brick-maker and construction contractor. He quarried stone for the State Capitol building during the 1840s in the vicinity of Watkins Park, and in 1876 he funded the creation of Watkins Institute. Before the Civil War, Watkins Park was known as "Watkins Grove" and served as the site of political barbeques, school commencement exercises, and concerts. Union Army soldiers cut the trees and pastured mules in the park, ruining it for park purposes at the time. Confederate soldiers captured at the 1864 Battle of Nashville were interned down in the rock quarry near the park. Watkins deeded the park to the city in June 1870 and the title was registered in 1880. Park Board chairman E. C. Lewis planned the development of Watkins Park in 1901, building an entrance gate and fence, walkways, flowerbeds, and benches with materials donated by citizens. The Centennial Club in 1906 took charge of the park and opened the first children's playground in the city at the site, with swings, a skating pavilion, and a "merry-go-round," and as a result of that example the Park Board in 1909 opened children's playgrounds on vacant lots throughout the city, initiating the Board's recreational programming. The park was improved as a Works Progress Administration project during the 1930s and in 1936 became a black park. The park in 1985 had a ball diamond, a community center, three tennis courts, a basketball court, a playground, and a picnic shelter.

WEST PARK. Morrow Road and 61st Avenue North. 26 acres. This park was transferred by city government at the request of Mayor Ben West in 1952 to the Park Board in exchange for Cherokee Park. The Board named the park in honor of the Mayor, opened recreational facilities, building a small swimming pool in 1954 and opened a Quonset hut community center. In 1985, the park also had five ball diamonds, basketball courts, and a playground, and a new community center that replaced the Quonset hut.

WHITES CREEK PARK. Old Hickory Boulevard and Lickton Pike in northwestern Davidson County. 10 acres. This park was established during the 1970s as part of the Park-School cooperative program in connection with the construction of Whites Creek comprehensive high school. The park in 1985 included an indoor swimming pool, a community center, ball diamonds and tennis courts. Planning for the park had begun in 1975 and the community center and swimming pool opened on December 6, 1978.

WILLIAM COLEMAN PARK; see COLEMAN PARK.

WILLIAM EDMONDSON PARK: see EDMONDSON PARK.

WILLIAM PITTS PARK: see PITTS PARK.

WILLIAM WHITFIELD PARK. Edmondson Pike and Brewer Drive at the Ellington Agricultural Center. 11.4 acres. Mayor Richard Fulton, Councilman Carney Patterson, Senator Douglas Henry, and Director Charles Spears negotiated a lease on this park land in 1975 with B. R. Allison, Tennessee Commissioner of Conservation and his deputy M. T. Estes. The park is located on the former Brentwood Hall estate of Park Commissioner Rogers Caldwell which became the Ellington Agricultural Center. At the request of Councilman Patterson, the Board named the park in honor of William D. Whitfield, a leader of Little League baseball in Nashville who died on January 17, 1976. The park opened officially on July 14, 1978, and had ball diamonds, and a playground.

WILLOW CREEK PARK. Westchester Drive north of Ewing Creek at the Willow Creek subdivision. 13.51 acres. Metro Council Ordinance 83-57 in 1983 accepted this donated park from Willow Creek Properties (Billy DeVasher), which constructed the subdivision. Park development had not been initiated in 1985.

CEMETERIES: The Park Board is the caretaker for the City Cemetery on South Fourth Avenue and Oak Street and for the County Cemetery on Jennings Avenue and Eighteenth Avenue North. The City Cemetery, 28.2 acres, became a Park Board responsibility on June 15, 1963, by direction of the mayor, and the 5.7-acre County Cemetery was assigned to the Park Board in June 1976. The City Cemetery is of great historical interest, including among its 23,000 interments the graves of many Tennessee pioneers, of Confederate generals, of the original Fisk Jubilee Singers, and of Captain William Driver who named the American flag "Old Glory." The first interment took place in 1813 and it became the official city cemetery in 1822, serving as such until 1885 when the city council decreed that no further interments would be permitted except from the families already owning lots and the number of interments thereafter dwindled. The cemetery served briefly as a public park in the 1908-1912 period, when the city council gave the Park Board funds to repair the drives, build walkways, right the stones, and construct a fence and entrance gate. The four-foot high fence was designed and built by contractor Wilbur F. Foster. Major E. C. Lewis designed the entrance gates which were constructed with funding donated by the South Nashville Women's Federation headed by Mrs. Stephen Driver in 1911. After the 1908 appropriation was exhausted, cemetery maintenance responsibility returned to the city's public works department. The city in 1947 constructed a $2,500 office building at the cemetery maintenance responsibility returned to the city's public works department. The city in 1947 constructed a $2,500 office building at the cemetery, and in 1958 the city provided $75,000 to install a lighting system, drives, walks, and 21 historical markers. State government has on occasion contributed small sums for the restoration of selected markers. The Park Board in 1981 gave cemetery management responsibility to the Metropolitan Historical Commission.

APPENDIX B

Inventory of the Monuments, Memorials and Markers in the Parks of Metropolitan Nashville and Davidson County

INVENTORY METHODOLOGY

With a list of monuments, memorials and markers mentioned in the minutes of the Park Board since 1901, the author drove from park to park during August 1985 photographing the monuments and copying the legends inscribed thereon to create a record which would permit restoration of the monuments in the events of future deterioration or vandalism. Some monuments mentioned in park records, notably the water fountain in Hadley Park honoring Park Commissioner Lee Loventhal, were not found, and several monuments not mentioned in park records were found during walking tours of the parks. The many monuments, memorials, and markers located in the City Cemetery were not inventoried because it is administered at present by the Metro Historical Commission. Certain structures, such as the Children's Coach in Centennial Park and the serpent sculpture in Dees Park, were included in the inventory because they possess a monumental character although they lack historical inscriptions.

Among the total of sixty monuments, memorials and markers inventoried are many unusual and unique structures with interesting histories. The parks contain four monuments and markers—at Centennial Park, City Cemetery, and two at Fort Nashborough—honoring General James Robertson, and none—except perhaps the Natchez Trace monument—honoring General Andrew Jackson. Monuments to Charlotte Robertson and Ann Robertson Cockrill also exist, but there are none honoring Rachel Jackson. There are no monuments honoring mayors of Nashville as such, and surprisingly only West Park bears the name of a mayor (Morton B. Howell Park no longer exists.) Several monuments and structures provide the park system with a unique nautical flavor; the system contains a wave pool, a sea serpent, a sailboat marina, and three fake ships—the gunboat *Tennessee* prow in Centennial Park, the shiplike configuration of the U.S. Naval Reserve Center in Shelby Park, and the model aircraft carrier at the model aircraft field in Percy Warner Park (some of these are not listed as monuments in this inventory).

The count of military monuments is interesting. The parks contain no monuments to veterans of the Revolutionary War, although a number of those veterans are listed at the Founders Monument in Bicentennial Park and some are buried in the City Cemetery. No monuments except the Natchez Trace monument in Centennial Park honor veterans of the War of 1812, nor are there monuments to veterans of the Mexican War. The Confederate Private Monument in Centennial Park and Fort Negley honor veterans of the Civil War, but none memorialize veterans of the Spanish-American War except perhaps the gunboat *Tennessee* figurehead or the William C. Smith plaque in Centennial Park. The parks contain four monuments to veterans of the First World War—two in Centennial Park and two at Percy Warner Park—but only one, located at Morgan Park, to veterans of the Second World War. No monuments in the system honor veterans of the Korean and Vietnam conflicts, although that neglect may in the future be remedied.

Monuments concerning technology include the power-grinding wheels, Children's Coach, Locomotive 567, the door of the Nashville,

Chattanooga, and St. Louis Railway, the F-86 Aircraft, and perhaps the John Thomas statue, all located in Centennial Park. Although the system has several fake ships, it surprisingly includes no monuments relating to steamboat or automobile transport.

Considering their various ages, all monuments, memorials and markers within the system are in relatively good condition except the Fort Negley monument placed in 1936 by the WPA which had weathered to the point of being illegible and the Dudley-Creighton Memorial flagpole base now in storage near the Centennial Park Office.

BATTLE OF NASHVILLE MARKER. Centennial Park. Standard state metal marker located at roadside about 100 feet west of the Parthenon and bearing the identification number N1-3. Legend:

BATTLE OF NASHVILLE
FEDERAL DEFENSES

The hill to the west was a strong point in the system of permanent Federal defenses, started in 1862, which extended to the river on both sides of the town. Artillery was emplaced here from time to time.

TENNESSEE HISTORICAL COMMISSION

BRADLEY MARKER. Music Square Park. Metal plate attached to low concrete foundation located adjacent to the walkway near the fountain. On January 3, 1979, Judson Collins requested that Owen Bradley be honored in Music Square Park because of the years of leadership he provided to the city's music industry, and the Board directed that a plaque for that purpose be placed in the park. Legend:

In recognition of
OWEN BRADLEY

for his leadership and vision as one of the pioneers who paved the way for music to become a major industry in this city.
1979

CHENAULT MEMORIAL. East Park. Small metal plate mounted on a wall near the entrance to the newer East Park Community Center building. On May 27, 1955, 183 residents of East Nashville petitioned the Park Board to place a plaque in the East Park Community Center in honor of R. N. Chenault, principal for many years of Warner School adjacent to the park, and the Board approved. Legend:

IN RECOGNITION OF THE
SERVICE AND LEADERSHIP
OF
R. N. CHENAULT
CHAIRMAN OF EAST PARK
COMMUNITY COUNCIL
JULY 31, 1955
WARNER SCHOOL
PARENT-TEACHER ASSOCIATION

CHILDREN'S COACH. Centennial Park. The brightly painted trolley car located at the side of the Centennial Art Activities Center serves as play equipment. Few historical sources mention the history of the coach, but apparently it has been renovated for maintenance purposes on many occasions and it may not be the original trolley which was used by children in the park as early as 1916. It is probable that the original trolley was a gift from Percy Warner and the Nashville Railway and Light Company.

CITY CEMETERY MARKER. City Cemetery. Metal plate number 3A-35 placed by the Tennessee Historical Commission on the stone gate entrance at the northeast corner of the cemetery next to Fourth Avenue South. Legend:

CITY CEMETERY

First established in 1822, the remains of many early settlers were then brought here for permanent burial. Among the more than 20,000 persons buried here are Gen. James Robertson, Gov. William

Carroll, Sec. of Treasury George W. Campbell, Lt. Gen. Richard S. Ewell, Brig. Gen. Felix K. Zollicoffer & Capt. William Driver.

TENNESSEE HISTORICAL COMMISSION

CHARLOTTE ROAD MONUMENT. Richland Park. A three-foot high concrete block with attached metal plate located at the edge of the park near Charlotte Pike. The monument was located at another site from 1935 to 1962 when, at the request of Mrs. John Ambrose of the DAR, the Board approved moving it into the Richland Park because the widening of Charlotte Pike had taken its previous site. Legend:

CHARLOTTE ROAD

ROUTE OF EARLY SETTLERS TO CHARLOTTE, MEMPHIS, AND THE SOUTHWEST, OPENED ABOUT 1800. TOWN AND ROAD BEAR THE NAME OF CHARLOTTE REEVES ROBERTSON, WIFE OF GENERAL JAMES ROBERTSON.

GEN'L JAMES ROBERTSON CHAPTER D.A.R. 1935

COCKRILL MONUMENT. Centennial Park. Granite boulder about four feet high with attached metal plate located at roadside about 500 feet north of the entrance to the park from West End Avenue. Francis B. Warfield on October 18, 1945, requested the Park Board to permit the Tennessee Historical Society to place a monument to Ann Robertson Cockrill near the site of her home in Centennial Park and near Cockrill Spring. Above the legend on the metal plate is a bas-relief picture of a pioneer woman with book in hand teaching children under a tree outside Fort Nashborough. Legend:

ANN ROBERTSON
COCKRILL

NEAR THIS SPOT STOOD THE HOME OF JOHN COCKRILL AND HIS WIFE, ANN ROBERTSON COCKRILL, SISTER OF GENERAL JAMES ROBERTSON. BORN IN NORTH CAROLINA ON FEBRUARY 10, 1757, ANN ROBERTSON CAME TO THE CUMBERLAND SETTLEMENTS WITH THE DONELSON FLOTILLA EARLY IN 1780. HERE SHE ORGANIZED A SCHOOL FOR THE PIONEER'S CHILDREN, THUS BECOMING NASHVILLE'S FIRST SCHOOL TEACHER. ALSO SHE ORGANIZED AND TAUGHT NASHVILLE'S FIRST SUNDAY SCHOOL CLASS. SHE DIED HERE ON OCTOBER 15, 1821, AND IS BURIED IN THE CITY CEMETERY.

ERECTED BY THE SCHOOL CHILDREN OF NASHVILLE AND DAVIDSON COUNTY AND THE TENNESSEE HISTORICAL COMMISSION. 1946

COCKRILL SPRING MARKER. Centennial Park. Standard metal marker located at the southern edge of the park next to West End Avenue. Legend:

COCKRILL SPRING

The house of John Cockrill, an early settler, stood about 60 yards north, near a large spring, whose water ran northeast into Lick Branch, which emptied Great Salt Lick, around which Nashville was founded. A blacksmith shop stood under the great oak tree nearby. The spring was a stopping place for travelers along Natchez Trace.

TENNESSEE HISTORICAL COMMISSION

CONCRETE BRIDGE. Centennial Park. Located at the northwest end of Lake Wautauga, with the Sunken Garden (Lily Lake) at one side, and still in use as a roadway, the bridge when constructed in 1906-07 by Wilbur Creighton, Sr., attracted considerable attention from the engineering profession because it was the first concrete arch bridge constructed in Tennessee and perhaps in the South. (The first such bridge in the United States was built in Fairmount Park, Philadelphia, in 1892.) Its history is detailed by Creighton's civil engineering thesis at Vanderbilt University. In 1985 no informational marker concerning its history existed.

CONFEDERATE PRIVATE MONUMENT. Centennial Park. Sometimes called the "Sam Davis" monument, this heroic sculpture by George Zolnay stands on a concrete base about five hundred feet southwest of the Parthenon. Park Commissioners S. A. Champion and E. C. Lewis joined with Theodore Cooley in 1903 to plan the monument to the heroism of the Confederate private soldier. Its cornerstone was placed in June 1904 during a Confederate Army reunion in the city, and some 10,000 people attended the ceremony. Funds for its construction were raised by the Frank Cheatham Bivouac, United Confederate Veterans, and by the First Tennessee Regiment Chapter of the Daughters of the Confederacy, led by Mrs. Reau E. Folk. Confederate veteran units commanded by Maj. B. M. Hord, Capt. F. A. Hager, and Capt. I. J. Howlett attended the dedication ceremony on June 19, 1909, in uniform, and cheered sculptor George Zolnay when little Winston Pilcher Folk, grandson of Capt. M. B. Pilcher, unveiled the monument by removing a large Confederate flag covering it. The concrete monument base bears inscriptions on each of its four sides and a list of members of the Frank Cheatham Bivouac on the metal plate. The four inscriptions on the base are:

SOUTH SIDE:

DUTY DONE HONOR WON
1861-1865

EAST SIDE:

TO THE HEROISM
OF THE
PRIVATE CONFEDERATE SOLDIER

NORTH SIDE:

FAITHFUL TO THE END

WEST SIDE:

ERECTED 1908
BY
FRANK CHEATHAM BIVOUAC
NUMBER 1
ASSOCIATION OF
CONFEDERATE SOLDIERS
CAMP NUMBER 35
UNITED CONFEDERATE VETERANS
NASHVILLE, TENNESSEE

The list of names if inscribed on the metal plate at the monument's west side in eight columns. The names are:

COLUMN ONE: ABBAY, S. W., ADKEISON. T. J., AIMISON, W., ALEXANDER, J. ALEXANDER, J. O., ALEXANDER, J. T., ALLEN, A. J., ALLEN, A. S., ALLEN, G. T., ALLEN, J. O., ALLEN, J. B., ALLEN, W. H., ALLISON, T. F. P., ALSON, J. B., ANDERSON, F., ANDERSON, J. H., ANDERSON, T., JR., ANDREWS, J. J., ARMISTEAD, G. W., ATKINSON, F. M., ATWELL, W. H., AVERELL, E. W., BAILEY, P. R., BAKER, A. J., BAKER, H., BARNES, M. M., BARNES, W. D., BARRY, W. A., BASKETTE, G. H., BASS, J. O., BASS, S. D., BATE, H. C., BATE, W. B., BATEY, W. W., BAUGH, E. L., BAXTER, E., BAXTER, N., BELL, R. L., BELL, T. H., BENNETT, J. P., BENNETT, W. M., BETTERSWORTH, E., BINKLEY, B. F., BINKLEY, H. C., BINNS, J. E., BLAIR, C. T., BLEVINS, W. S., BLUE, W. N., BLUME, F. L., BOLTON, A., BOND, J. H., BOWER, A. B., BOWERS, A., BOWERS, J. C., BOWERS, J. L., BOWMAN, W. M., BRANDON, A. W., BREAST, J. K., BROTHERS, W. E., BROWN, A. S., BROWN, J. B., BROWN, J. C., BROWN, J. P. W., BROWN, J. T., BROWN, M. N., BRYSON, J. H., BUCHANAN, CR. R., BUFORD, ED.

COLUMN TWO: BUIST, J. R., BURKE, M., BURNS, J. W., BURRELL, H., BURTON, J. A., BUSH, I. F., BUSH, W. G., BYRNE, J. P., CAGE, JESSE, CALDWELL, S. J., CAMP, A. S., CAMPBELL, C. J., CAMPBELL, C. W., CARMACK, J. O., CARMICHAEL, C. W., CARSON, D. W., CARSON, J. T., CARTER, J. S., CARTER, J. W., CARVER, A. J., CAVE, R. L., CHANEY, D. M., CHASE, I. K., CHEATHAM, M., CHEATHAM, R. A., CISCO, J. C., CLAIBORNE, THOS., CLARK, C. S., CLARK, J. I., CLARK, S. C., CLARK, W. B., CLARKE, W. L., CLAY, D. D., CLAYBROOKE, S. P., CLENDENNING, W. A., COCKRILL, M. S., COGGIN, J. J., COLE, J. C., COLLEY, S., COLLINS, R. E., COOK, B. F., COOLEY, C. B., COOLEY, THEO., COOPER, G. W., COOPER, J. L., CORBITT, J. M., COWAN, J. C., CRAIG, W. S., CRUTCHFIELD, J. L., CUMMINGS, T. W., CUNNINGHAN, S. A., CURREY, J. H., DALLAS, T. B., DARSEY, W. H., DAVIS, H. B., DAVIS, J. K., DAVIS, T. W., DEARMAN, L. L., DERRICKSON, J. M., DIBRELL, G. C., DIGGONS, G. A., DILLAHUNTY, J. B., DILLARD, W. H.,

DILLEHAY, W. C., DISMUKES, J. L., DOAK, A. S., DOAK, H. M., DODD, T. L.

COLUMN THREE: DONALDSON, S. B., DONALDSON, W. R., DOUGLASS, A. H., DOUGLASS, D., DOUGLASS, T. J., DRIVER, W. O., DUDLEY, R. H., FUMM, E. A., DURRETT, W. T., EAKIN, S., EASTMAN, C. H., EATON, A. J., EDMUNDSON, H., EDMUNDSON, J., EDWARDS, S. W., EDWARDS, W. T., ELAM, T. A., ELLISON, S. H., ELY, JESSE, EPPERSON, S. A., ERSKIN, J., ESLICK, L., ESTES, J. T., EWING, O., FAIN, R. W., FARRELL, N., FIELDS, J. W., FISHER, J. R., FLETCHER, W. H., FLIPPEN, A. B., FORD, A. B., FORSTER, W. F., FREEMAN, M. A., FRY, G. W., FRYAR, J. F., FULKERSON, W. W., FULLTON, J. H., FERGUS, J. T., FAINES, F. W., GALE, W. D., GAMBILL, J. T., GARDNER, E. M., GARNER, J. K., GARRETT, R. C., GEE, M. M., GEE, Q. R., GIBSON, J., GIBSON, T., GILBERT, A., GILL, J. Y., GILMAN, J. W., GILMORE, M. S., GLASGOW, L. A., GOOCH, N., GOODLOE, B. R., GOODRICH, M. B., GOODWIN, J. A., GORDON, J. P., GRANT, J. F., GREEN, F. W., GRIFFIN, P. M., GRIZZARD, M. T., GROSS, A. H., GUILD, G. B., GUNN, L. C., HAGAN, L. P., HAGER, C. F.

COLUMN FOUR: HAILEY, J. G., HALBERT, W. H., HALL, J. A., HAMBLEN, J. K. P., HAMILL, H. M., HAMILTON, W. A., HAMPTON, N. J., HANCOCK, E., HANDLEY, C. R., HANDLY, J. R., HARDISON, H. A., HARDISON, R. C., HARDISON, W. T., HARLIN, S. M., HARPER, J. B., HARRIS, F. S., HARRIS, N. C., HARRIS, T. W., HARRIS, W. B., HARRISON, H. V., HEIGHT, H., HENRY, O., HENRY, OWEN., HERBERT, D. C., HESSEY, L. C., HEVERIN, H., HICKMAN, J. P., HIGH, S. S., HIGHTOWER, R. P., HILL, J. L., HINSON, W. J., HOGAN, G. W., HOLLOWAY, J. J., HORD, B. M., HORN, H. H., HOUSE, T. B., HOUSE, W., HOWARD, S. M., HOWLETT, I. J., HOWES, G. H., HOWSE, S. H., HUGGINS, A. L., HUGHES, J. B., HUGHES, R. B., HUME, WM., HUNTER, WM., IRELAND, H. C., IRWIN, J. W., IRWIN, THOS., IVIE, H. J., JACKSON, M. R., HACKSON, W. H., JACKSON, GEN. W. H., JENKINS, G. S., JOHNS, W. N., JOHNSON, C. S., JOHNSON, TIM, JOHNSTON, G., JONES, G. W., JONES, I. N., JONES, J. W., HONES, R. W., JONES, T. J., JONES, T. W., JOPLIN, T. M., KEEBLE, J. M., KELLEY, D. C., KELLEY, JAS.

COLUMN FIVE: KELLEY, T., KELLEY, W. D., KEMPER, W. A., KENDRICK, F. B., KENNEDY, H. S., KENNEDY, J. B., KEY, J. T., KEY, T. J., KIRKPATRICK, S., KOGER, JAS., LANE, R. S., LASLEY, W. H., LAURENT, ED., LEAKE, B. B., LEASCHER, G., LEE, Z. P., LILLARD, W. G., LINDSEY, A., LINDSEY, J. W., LITTON, C. S., LITTON, I., LOCKE, C. A., LOFTIN, B. F., LOFTIN, C. A., LOFTIN, E. C., LOFTIN, I. C., LONG, G. R., LONG, J. N., LONG, W. M., LOWERY, WM., LUCKEY, W. H., LYON, A. A., MALONE, T. H., MANEY, D. D., MANEY, GEO., MANEY, T. H., MANEY, W. B., MANLOVE, P. H., MANSON, H. W., MARCH, J. C., MARCH, W. F., MARGART, C. M., MARKS, A. S., MARTIN, H. D., MARTIN, J. S., MARTIN, M. J.M MARTIN, W. D., MATHIS, W. J., MATTHEWS, H. C., MATTHIAS, W. J., MAY, B. F., MENESS, H. B., MEREDITH, T. H., MERRITT, A. G., MILAM, W. W., MILLIRON, J., MITCHELL, H. B., MITCHELL, W. H., MOODY, W. H., MOORE, J. H., MOORE, J. H., MOORE, V. B., MORRIS, R. L., MORROW, A. G., MORROW, WM., MORTON, G. H., MULLER, C. P.

COLUMN SIX: MUNROE, W. T., MURRAY, S., MURRAY, WM., MCARTHUR, J. L., MCCABE, B., MCCABE, J. A., MCCANN, B. W., MCCARLEY, G. W., MCCARTHY, B. J., MCCLANAHAN, J. A., MCCONNELL, J. W., MCCONNICO, G. H. K., MCDANIEL, J. G., MCDANIEL, J. R., MCDOWELL, J. H., MCFARLAN, J. P., MCCONICAL, J., MCGUIRE, J. P., MCIVER, E., MCKAY, W. L., MCLEAN, R. O., MCLIN, J. D., MCMILLIN, T. P., MCMURRAY, W. J., MCNEILL, A. J., MCWHIRTER, A. G., NANCE, C. P., NANCE, J. B., NASH, G. R., NEAL, R. J., NEELLEY, W. M., NEIL, J. B., NELLUMS, D. A., NICHOL, B., NICHOL, J. E., NOLAND, C., OAKLEY, C. A., O'BRYAN, J. B., OLIVER, F. S., OZANNE, J. M.,

PARDUE, D. C., PARKER, W. T., PARKES, THOS., PARKS, H., PATTERSON, E. M., PATTON, W. M., PEEBLES, JAS., PENUEL, J. N., PETWAY, B. W., PHILLIPS, J, PHILLIPS, A. J., PHILLIPS, W. H., PICHARD, P. P., PILCHER, M. B., POLK, R. K., POLLARD, W. J., POWELL, J. M., PRICE, N., PRICE, P. G., PRICE, J. T.

COLUMN SEVEN: PROCTOR, A. W., PRYOR, J. J., PYRON, S. B., RANDALL, W. H., RANDOLPH, W. W., RAWLEY, J. W., REECE, ED., RICE, N. B., RICHARDSON, E. R., RICHARDSON, J. B., RICHARDSON, N. D., RIDGE, I. S., RIDLEY, C. L., RIDLEY, J. A., RIDLEY, S. J., RIVES, N. G., ROBERTS, D. J., ROBERTS, E. H., ROBINSON, S., ROSE, H., ROTHROCK, R. G., RUSSELL, L. W., SADLER, J. R., SANDERS, J. P., SAVAGE, J. R., SAWRIE, W. S., SCALES, D. C., SCALES, R., SCOGGINS, S., SCRUGGS, W. J., SEAY, G. W., SEAY, S., SETLIFF, A., SHARPE, T., SHEARON, S. B., SHELTON, J. T., SHIELDS, J., SHUMATE, J. C., SHUMATE, T. W., SIMRALL, J. F., SIMS, H. G., SIMS, JAS., SINNOTT, H. T., SKEGGS, C. H., SLOAN, J. A., SLOAN, J. E., SMITH, BAXTER, SMITH, I. E., SMITH, J. B., SMITH, J. M., SMITH, J. M., SMITH, L. W., SMITH, R. L., SMITH, W. C., SMITH, W. H., SPAIN, A. B., SPAIN, G. W., SPARKS, M. S., SPEIER, A., SPENCE, W. C., SPURR, M. A., STEELE, S. W., STEGER, T. M., STEWART, G. W., STONE, S. H., STOWERS, J. T.

COLUMN EIGHT: STRATTON, M., JR., SUIT, J. M., SULLIVAN, J. E., SUMMITT, D., SUTTON, J., TALBOT, J. B., TANT, P. G., TARKINGTON, J. H. C., TAYLOR, T. B., THOMAS, W. T., THOMPSON, C. W., THOMPSON, J. A., THOMPSON, J. H., THOMPSON, J. W., TINDALL, J. A., TINNIN, R. M., TIPPS, W. P., TONEY, W. B., TOWNS, R. T., TRACEY, C. T., TRAWICK, A. M., TREANOR, J. D., TROUSDALE, W. F., TURNER, J. S., TURNEY, P., UTLEY, J., VANDIFORD, C. R., VANDIVER, W. C., VAULX, J., VERNON, E. R., VERNON, T. C., VIVRETT, J. L., WALKER, J. S., WALLACE, J. F., WARD, J. H., WARMACK, J. P., WATKINS, W. E., WEAKLEY, R. W., WEAKLEY, T. P., WELLS, L., WEST, J. B., WEST, J. H., WHARTON, A. D., WHEELING, C. E. C., WHELESS, J. F., WHITE, F. N., WHITE, J. B., WHITSETT, J. B., WHITSETT, P., WILKERSON, J. W., WILKES, J. H., WILLIAMS, B. B., WILLS, WYLIE, WILSON, S. F., WINFREY, A. J., WINKLER, P. H., WOMACK, J. P., WRAY, W. A., WRIGHT, J. T., WRYE, J. M., YATES, T. J., YEARGIN, W. A., YOUNG, J., YOUNG, J. S., YOUNG, W. H., YORK, J. W.

DONELSON MARKER. Fort Nashborough. A large metal plate attached to the outside of a cabin's stone fireplace within the stockade. Legend:

IN APPRECIATION OF
THE SERVICES OF
COLONEL JOHN DONELSON
BORN IN DELAWARE, 1718.
DIED IN KENTUCKY, 1786.

DISTINGUISHED IN EARLY LIFE IN VIRGINIA AS A CIVIL, INDUSTRIAL AND MILITARY LEADER.

MEMBER OF THE HOUSE OF BURGESSES, IRON MANUFACTURER, LIEUTENANT COLONEL OF PITTSYLVANIA COUNTY, AND DEVOTED VESTRYMAN OF CAMDEN PARISH.

NOTED SURVEYOR OF STATE BOUNDARIES, MAKER OF TREATIES WITH THE INDIANS, AND REVOLUTIONARY PATRIOT. EMIGRATED WEST IN 1779-1780, A LEADER AND "DIARIST" OF THE SETTLERS GOING BY WATER IN:

"THE GOOD BOAT ADVENTURE FROM FORT PATRICK HENRY TO THE FRENCH SALT SPRING ON CUMBERLAND RIVER."

FOUNDER OF DONELSON'S STATION ON STONE'S RIVER, 1780.

ONE OF THE COMMISSIONERS HOLDING TREATY WITH THE CHICKASAW INDIANS NEAR NASHBOROUGH, 1783.

MEMBER OF "THE TENNESSEE LAND

COMPANY" PROJECTING A SETTLEMENT IN THE "GREAT BEND" OF TENNESSEE RIVER, 1785.

LOST HIS LIFE—SUPPOSED TO HAVE BEEN MURDERED BY THE INDIANS— NEAR BIG BARREN RIVER, KENTUCKY, 1786.

"DISTINGUISHED NOT ONLY IN
THE ESTIMATION
OF HIS FELLOW-CITIZENS, BUT
MORE EXCELLENT
AT HOME IN THE FAMILY CIRCLE."
(PUTNAM)

DUDLEY-CREIGHTON MEMORIAL. Morgan Park. Concrete flagpole base about three feet high with a metal plate attached. It was located in Morgan Park, but the concrete has deteriorated and it was stored in 1985 in the parking lot on the side of Flagpole Hill near the Parks Administration Building in Centennial Park. The Nashville Kiwanis Club in 1927, shortly after the deaths of Robert M. Dudley and Robert T. Creighton, raised funds to construct a small swimming pool in Morgan Park, and it placed the flagpole base memorial next to the pool. The speakers at the 1927 dedication were B. W. Landstreet, who headed the Kiwanis Club committee in charge of the project, E. T. Seay, president of the Kiwanis Club, and Charles McCabe of the Park Board. Legend:

ERECTED TO THE MEMORY OF
ROBERT M. DUDLEY
ROBERT T. CREIGHTON
NASHVILLE KIWANIS CLUB
A D 1927

DUDLEY MARKER. Centennial Park. Standard metal marker located at the south edge of the park next to West End Avenue. Legend:

ANNE DALLAS DUDLEY
1876-1955

Anne Dudley played a significant role in the ratification of the Nineteenth Amendment by the State of Tennessee. A native of Nashville, she served as president of the Nashville Equal Suffrage League, 1911-15; president of the Tennessee Equal Suffrage Association, Incorporated, 1915-17; and as vice president of the National American Woman Suffrage Association 1917. May 1, 1916, Anne Dudley walked from downtown Nashville to Centennial Park to demonstrate her support for the right of women to vote.

TENNESSEE HISTORICAL ASSOCIATION

DUDLEY MEMORIAL FOUNTAIN. Dudley Park. Water fountain (no longer operable) at the rear of the Dudley Park Community Center building, having a raised concrete foundation, a concrete roof supported by four columns, and bronze memorial plates attached to the east and west ends of the roof. The Park Board on May 5, 1914, voted to change the name of Chestnut Street Park to Dudley Park and to place in it a bronze memorial plate for Louise and Rebecca Dudley, the daughters of Commissioner Robert M. Dudley, who died in a 1914 automobile accident. Records do not detail the history of the fountain's construction, but it probably was funded in part by contributions from the Dudley family and completed in 1915. The legend on the metal plates reads:

LOUISE AND REBECCA DUDLEY
PARK

LOVELY AND PLEASANT IN
THEIR LIVES
AND IN THEIR DEATH THEY WERE
NOT DIVIDED

EAST PARK MARKER. East Park. Metal plate atop a low concrete foundation located near the steps leading into the southwest corner of the park, placed in 1983 after renovation of the park. Legend:

EAST PARK

ORIGINALLY CALLED
EDGEFIELD PARK,
THIS PARK WAS DEVELOPED AS A
RESULT OF THE GREAT 1916 FIRE.

REDEDICATED FOR THE USE OF THE
CITIZENS OF NASHVILLE AND
DAVIDSON COUNTY
BY
MAYOR RICHARD H. FULTON

MAY 14, 1983

EDMONDSON MONUMENT. Edmondson Park. A carved stone monument about three feet high which was unveiled on July 8, 1981, to honor a skilled stone carver who had once resided in the vicinity of the park and who was the first black artist honored with a one-man show at the Museum of Modern Art in New York. A dove with an olive branch in its beak is carved in the stone above the legend:

> THIS PARK IS DEDICATED
> TO THE MEMORY OF RENOWNED
> NASHVILLE SCULPTOR
> WILLIAM EDMONDSON
> ABOUT 1883-1951

F-86 AIRCRAFT MONUMENT. Centennial Park. Located in the northwest sector of the park near the locomotive and croquet court, the jet fighter was secured by Mayor Ben West and Councilman Charles Bramwell as Air Force surplus in July 1961 and the Park Board paid $1,000 to move it from the airport to the park. It served as play equipment for children initially, but in 1981 was moved to its present site and placed on a stand by the 118th Aircraft Maintenance Squadron, Tennessee Air National Guard, which also repaired and refurbished it for display purposes. In 1985, no informational marker explained its history.

FIRST TENNESSEE INFANTRY MONUMENT. Percy Warner Park. A granite monument about ten feet high with metal plates attached on two sides and located about one thousand feet inside the main entrance gates to the park. This monument to the First Tennessee Infantry, which became the 115th Artillery, located at the field where the regiment mobilized in 1917 was constructed in 1936 at a cost of $2,497 by the Works Progress Administration at the direction of Colonel Harry S. Berry, previously an officer of the 115th Artillery. The metal plates on both the front side facing the driveway and the back side facing the hill are inscribed with the following legends:

> FRONT SIDE:
>
> TO THE MEN OF THE
> FIRST TENNESSEE INFANTRY
> WHO SLEEP IN HONORED GLORY

> THE MUFFLED DRUM'S SAD ROLL HAS
>   BEAT
>   THE SOLDIER'S LAST TATTOO,
> NO MORE ON LIFE'S PARADE SHALL
>   MEET
>   THAT BRAVE AND FALLEN FEW.
> ON FAME'S ETERNAL CAMPING
>   GROUND.
>   THEIR SILENT TENTS ARE SPREAD,
> AND GLORY GUARDS, WITH SOLEMN
>   ROUND,
>   THE BIVOUAC OF THE DEAD.
>
> NOR SHALL YOUR STORY BE FORGOT
>   WHILE FAME HERE RECORD
>   KEEPS,
> OR HONOR POINTS THE HALLOWED
>   SPOT
>   WHERE VALOR PROUDLY SLEEPS.
> NOR WRECK, NOR CHANGE, NOR
>   WINTER'S BLIGHT,
>   NOR TIME'S REMORSELESS DOOM,
> SHALL DIM ONE RAY OF GLORY'S
>   LIGHT
>   THAT GILDS YOUR DEATHLESS
>   TOMB.

> ON THIS FIELD, APRIL 25, 1917 THE
> FIRST TENNESSEE INFANTRY,
> RECENTLY RECALLED FROM THE RIO
> GRANDE, MOBILIZED FOR SERVICE
> WITH THE AMERICAN
> EXPEDITIONARY FORCES IN FRANCE.
> THE REGIMENT WAS ASSIGNED TO
> THE THIRTIETH DIVISION AND
> PARTICIPATED IN THE BATTLES OF
> YPRES, BELLICOURT, ST. QUENTIN,
> TROYON, ST. MIHIEL, AND THE
> ARGONNE.
>   1916-1919
>
> BACK SIDE INSCRIPTION:
>
> WE ARE THE DEAD, SHORT DAYS AGO
>   WE LIVED, FELT DAWN, SAW
>   SUNSET GLOW
>   LOVED AND WERE LOVED, AND
>   NOW WE LIE
>   IN FLANDERS' FIELD

PVT. VICTOR L. ANGEL
COOK THOMAS C. ANTON

LIEUT. HENRY G. ARMSTRONG
PVT. WILLIAM A. BALLARD
PVT. JOHN R. BAKER
PVT. CHARLES L. BARTON
PVT. FRANK H. BEASLEY
PVT. MIKE J. BECKER
LIEUT. SHIRLEY D. BOHANNON
LIEUT. CLYDE O. BRATTON
CORP. MACK D. BUSSEY
LIEUT. ALLEN CAMPBELL
CORP. WILLIAM A. CHAMERS
PVT. HUGH C. CLABO
PVT. ALBERT CLARK
LIEUT. RODERICK DHU COE
PVT. SEWELL J. CRABTREE
SGT. WILLIAM E. DALTON
PVT. WALLACE A. DAVIS
SGT. CHARLES W. EATON
PVT. BURD R. ERWIN
PVT. ED EVANS
LIEUT. JAMES D. EVERETTE
CORP. EMERY C. FARVER
LIEUT. NAL B. FINLEY
PVT. WILLIAM P. FULCHER
PVT. JOSHUA O. GATLIN
SGT. SAMUEL O. GIVENS
PVT. LINZY A. GOODWIN
PVT. GEORGE W. GORDON
CORP. HERBERT L. GRIFFIN
SGT. JAMES C. GUTHRIE
PVT. LIDA M. HACKWORTH
PVT. DEWEY HARRIS
PVT. DEWEY L. HARRIS
CAPT. LEONARD K. HART
WAG. WALTER HENSLEY
PVT. CHARLES L. HICKS
PVT. JOHN P. HIGGS
PVT. RICHARD HILL
PVT. GEORGE H. HINES
PVT. JAMES T. HINKLE
CORP. HEBERT H. HODGE
PVT. WILSON D. HOLMAN
SGT. BUFORD W. JACKSON
CORP. EDDIE L. JONES
LIEUT. FRANK S. LATHAM
PVT. LEE LEWIS
PVT. RAYMOND D. LYONS
PVT. GEORGE L. MOORE
SGT. JOE H. MOREHEAD
LIEUT. VIVIAN K. MOUSER
SGT. ROGER E. MURRY
PVT. KARL L. MCGEHA
PVT. HOWARD O. MCWHIRTER
PVT. WILLIAM R. NEWMAN
PVT. EDWARD NOLEN
PVT. ARLIE H. OGLE

LIEUT. SAMUEL K. ORR
PVT. EUGENE T. PARKS
WAG. ROBERT S. PARKS
LIEUT. JAMES A. PIGUE
WAG. CHARLES J. POWERS
PVT. HERMAN RAY
LIEUT. GEORGE REED, JR.
LIEUT. LLOYD G. E. REILLY
LIEUT. MATHEW J. REYNOLDS
PVT. FRANK B. RICKEY
CORP. LESTER T. SIGLER
CORP. GRADY S. SILER
PVT. ALONZO K. SMITH
PVT. ISHAM B. SMITH
LIEUT. TILLMAN H. SMITH
LIEUT. WILLIAM B. STUART
SGT. WYLIE SULLIVAN
LIEUT. THOMAS S. TATE
LIEUT. HERBERT J. TAYLOR
PVT. JOHN J. TEMPLE
PVT. ELLIOT F. TROUT
CAPT. ROBERT B. UNDERWOOD
PVT. RALEIGH WALDRON
SGT. ROBERT WARREN
PVT. CHARLIE WEBB
PVT. JOSEPH WYERMAN
SGT. KARL G. WYMER

FORT NASHBOROUGH MARKER. Fort Nashborough. Standard metal marker on First Avenue outside the replica stockade. Marker number 3A-33.

FORT NASHBOROUGH

The original stockade fronted on the river slightly north of here, covering an area of about two acres. In that enclosure, on May 13, 1780, representatives of this and other settlements met and adopted the Cumberland Compact for the government of the new settlement. About 500 yards west, April 2, 1781, settlers assisted by dogs, drove off the Indians in the Battle of the Bluffs.

TENNESSEE HISTORICAL COMMISSION

FORT NASHBOROUGH MARKER. Fort Nashborough. Large metal plate attached to a six-foot high granite boulder inside the stockade. Legend:

FORT NASHBOROUGH

Named in memory of General Nash of

North Carolina, who fell at Germantown, Pennsylvania, October 4, 1777, in the War of the Revolution.

Erected on the bluff near this location, by the pioneers of the Cumberland settlement in the year 1780, as a central fort of defense against Indian attacks.

Was the scene of many noted historical events, especially the Indian attack of April 2, 1781, known as
"The Battle of the Bluff."

This representation of the original fort was built by appropriations from the State of Tennessee, the County of Davidson and the City of Nashville, through the patriotic work of the Tennessee Society Daughters of the American Revolution and the persevering efforts of the four Nashville chapters: viz:
Cumberland, General James Robertson Campbell, and Colonel Thomas McCrory.

Erected in 1930—the one hundred and fiftieth anniversary of the settlement of what is now the City of Nashville.

FORT NEGLEY MARKER. Fort Negley Park. Standard metal historical marker at the entrance to the park, 150 feet west of the stone entrance gates. Legend:

FORT NEGLEY SITE

The guns of Fort Negley, commanding three turnpikes to the South & Southeast, opened the Battle of Nashville, December 15, 1864. This site was selected by Capt. J. S. Morton as the key strongpoint in the Federal line around the city. The European style fort, named for General James S. Negley, was built of stone, logs, earth & railway iron.

THE HISTORICAL COMMISSION OF
METROPOLITAN NASHVILLE AND
DAVIDSON COUNTY

No. 55   Erected 1975

FORT NEGLEY MONUMENT. Fort Negley Park. A three-foot high stone monument located about 100 feet inside (uphill) of the stone entrance gates to the park.

Weathering has made the legend on the monument nearly illegible. Legend:

FORT NEGLEY
BUILT
BY FEDERAL FORCES
1862
RESTORED BY WPA
1936

FOSTER MARKER. Centennial Park. Standard metal marker on east side of Lake Watauga honoring the engineer who employed his business partner Robert T. Creighton as Engineer in Charge of the 1897 Centennial Exposition, who laid the foundation of the Parthenon Building in 1895, and who built under contract several structures in the park system, notably the stone wall around the City Cemetery. Legend:

MAJOR WILBUR FISK FOSTER
1834–1922

Chief Engr. Army of Tenn. C. S. A.; Construction Engineer on first R. R. Bridge in Nashville; City Engineer of Nashville and Member of American Society of Civil Engineers; Director of Works at the Tennessee Centennial Exposition, 1897 & Co-Founder of Foster & Creighton Co.; Elder, First Presbyterian Church; 33rd Degree, Scottish Rite Mason.

THE HISTORICAL COMMISSION OF
METROPOLITAN NASHVILLE
AND DAVIDSON COUNTY
No. 52   Erected 1975

FOUNDERS MONUMENT. Bicentennial Park. This Puryear Mims sculpture of James Robertson and John Donelson, leaders of the land and water groups of pioneers who founded Nashville, was sculpted in 1962 and first placed inside the stockade of Fort Nashborough, where it remained until 1979 when it was moved to the center of Bicentennial Park adjacent to the fort. A metal plaque on the base of the sculpture placed in 1962 noted that if space were available the names of every signer of Cumberland Compact would have been listed, and in 1980 the Metropolitan Historical Commission remedied that neglect by adding a second metal plaque, lying on the ground at the monument base, with the names inscribed. The legends are as follows:

PLATE ATTACHED TO THE SIDE OF THE MONUMENT BASE:

THE FOUNDING OF NASHVILLE

ON MONDAY, APRIL 24, 1780, TWO PIONEERS, JAMES ROBERTSON AND JOHN DONELSON, SHOOK HANDS UPON THE COMPLETION OF A REUNION AT THE SITE ON WHICH YOU NOW STAND. EACH MAN, ONE BY LAND, THE OTHER BY WATER, PLAYED OUT HIS PART IN A TWOFOLD PLAN FOR A NEW SETTLEMENT THAT GREW INTO PRESENT-DAY NASHVILLE. ROBERTSON, AT THE HEAD OF HIS MOUNTED BAND OF 226 FRONTIERSMEN, TRAVERSED THE LONG, CIRCUITOUS OVERLAND ROUTE THROUGH KENTUCKY AND TENNESSEE DOWN TO THE GREAT SALT LICK. HIS GROUP ARRIVED ON CHRISTMAS DAY, 1779, ABOUT THE TIME THAT DONELSON'S FLOTILLA LEFT FORT PATRICK HENRY, AND AT ONCE SET ABOUT PREPARING A PLACE FOR THE BOATMEN, WOMEN, AND CHILDREN WHO WERE TO JOIN THEM LATER. ROBERTSON, AS ONE OF THE EARLIEST AND MOST RESOURCEFUL FRONTIERSMEN OF EARLY TENNESSEE HISTORY, HAD LONG REALIZED THAT THE ROLLING COUNTRY AND RICH BOTTOM-LAND OF MIDDLE TENNESSEE WOULD BE AN IDEAL LOCATION FOR A SETTLEMENT. ALTHOUGH MUCH WARFARE AND VIOLENCE WERE INEVITABLE, IT WAS HIS ABILITY TO DEAL WITH THE INDIANS AND THEIR MUTUAL RESPECT AND ADMIRATION FOR HIM THAT MADE THIS VENTURE POSSIBLE. HE SAID, "WE ARE THE ADVANCE GUARD; OUR WAY IS WESTWARD ACROSS THE CONTINENT." BUT CIVILIZATION COULD ONLY BEGIN WITH THE RIVER-BORNE FAMILIES THAT WERE TO COME IN THE SPRING. IN FOUR MONTHS THESE FAMILIES FLOATED THE ENTIRE EXTENT OF THE TENNESSEE RIVER, THEN TURNED NORTH TO THE OHIO AND CAME UP THE CUMBERLAND TO THE GREAT SALT LICK—A 1000-MILE TRIP UNEQUALLED IN THE ANNALS OF AMERICAN HISTORY. THIS FLOTILLA WAS HEADED BY THE COURAGEOUS COLONEL JOHN DONELSON ON HIS FLAGSHIP ADVENTURE. HE TRIUMPHED OVER FREEZING WEATHER, THE TREACHERIES OF A RIVER AT THE HIGHEST IN ITS HISTORY, PESTILENCE, AND SAVAGE INDIANS TO REACH HIS APRIL RENDEZVOUS. THIS ACHIEVEMENT HAS IMMORTALIZED HIS NAME, FOR HE MANAGED IT SO WELL THAT NO MAN COULD HAVE DONE IT BETTER. HIS RESPONSIBILITIES WERE GREAT BECAUSE HE HAD IN HIS CHARGE A LARGE PERCENTAGE OF NON-COMBATANTS.

IN THIS MEMORIAL GROUP EACH MAN STANDS AS A REPRESENTATIVE OF THE HARDY SOULS HE LED TO FULFILL A MAGNIFICENT DESTINY; IN THIS HISTORIC HANDSHAKE EACH BRAVE PIONEER FINDS HIS PLACE IN HISTORY. NO CITY SHOULD BE INDIFFERENT TO ITS FOUNDING, NO PEOPLE TO ITS HISTORY OF NASHVILLE. IF SPACE WERE AVAILABLE THE NAME OF EVERY SIGNER OF THE CUMBERLAND COMPACT SHOULD BE HERE: THESE TWO MEN STAND WITNESS TO THEIR TOIL AND DEVOTION.

THIS STATUE COMMISSIONED BY MAYOR BEN WEST IN 1962, WAS ERECTED HERE IN THE FORT WHERE THEY MET THAT FLOWERING SPRING DAY OF LONG AGO. THIS STATUE IS INTENDED TO KEEP THEIR MEMORY GREEN AND OUR LOVE FOR THEM TENDER AND PROFOUND. THESE MEN ARE THE TREES; WE ARE THEIR FRUIT.

HORIZONTAL PLATE AT GROUND LEVEL AND THE MONUMENT BASE:

SIGNERS OF THE CUMBERLAND COMPACT
NASHBOROUGH 13 MAY 1780

Richd. Henderson
Nathl. Hart
Wm H Moore
Samuel Phariss
Jno Donelson C.
Casper Mansker
John Caffery
Jno Blakemore Senr
John Blakemore Junr
James Shaw
Samuel Deech
Samuel Martin
James Buchanan
Solomon Turpin
Isaac Rentfro
Robert Cartwright
Hugh Rogan
Joseph Morton
William Woods
David Mitchell
David Shelton
Spill Coleman
Saml. McMurray
Henderson
Edward Bradley
Edw Bradley Junr.
Jas. Bradley
Michael Stoner
Joseph Mosely
Henry Guthrie
Francis Armstrong
Robert Lucas
Js. Robertson
George Freland
James Freland
John Tucker
Peter Catron
Philip Catron
Francis Catron
John Dunham
Isaac Johnson
Adon. Kelar
Thos. Burgess
Wm Burgess
Bartner Hainey
Richd. Sims
Titus Murray
James Hamilton
Henry Daugerty
Zacha White
Burgess White
William Calley

James Ray
William Ray
Perly Graves
Samuel White
Daniel Hogan
Thos. Hines
Robert Goodloe
Thos W. Alston
Wm Barret
Thomas Shannon
James Moore
Edward Moore
Richd. Moore
Saml. Moore
Elijah Moore
John Moore
Demsey Moore
Andrew Ewin
Ebenezer Titus
Mark Roberson
John Montgomery
Charles Campbill
William Overall
John Turner
Nathaniel Overall
Patrick Quigley
Josias Gamble
Saml. Newell
Joseph Reid
David Maxwell
Thos. Jefriss
Joseph Dunnagin
John Phelps
Andrew Bushong
Daniel Ragsdell
Jno. McMyrty
William Green
Moses Webb
Abselom Thomson
John McVay
James Thomson
Charles Thomson
Robert Thomson
Martin Hardin
Elick Thomson
Andrew Thomson
Wm Leaton
Edward Thomson
Isaac Drake
Jonathan Jenings
Zachariah Green
Andrew Lucas

James Patrick
Richd. Gross
John Drake
Daniel Turner
Timothy Terel
Isaac Lefever
Thomas Fletcher
Sam'l Barton
James Ray
Thomas Denton
Thomas Hendricks
John Holloday
Frederick Stump
William Hood
John Boyd
Jacob Stump
Henry Hardin
Richard Stanton
Sampson Sawyers
John Hobson
Ralph Wilson
James Givens
Robert Givens
Jas. Harrod
James Buchanan El.
William Geloch
Saml. Shelton
John Gibson
Da. Williams
John McAdames
Samson Williams
Thomas Thompson
Martin King
Wm. Logan
John Allstead
Nicholas Counrod
Evin Evins
Jonathan Evins Thomas
Joshua Thomas
David Rounsavall
Isaac Rounsavall
James Crocket
Andrew Crocket
Russell Gower
John Shannon
David Shannon
Jonathan Drake
Benjamin Drake
John Drake
Meraday Rains
Richd. Dodg
James Green

274 APPENDICES

James Cooke	Joseph Jackson	John Pleak
Daniel Johnston	Daniel Ragsdil	Willis Pope
Geo. Miner	Michael Shaver	Silas Harlan
George Green	Samuel Willson	Hugh Leeper
William More	John Reid	Harmon Consellea
Jacob Cimberlin	Joseph Daugherty	Humphrey Hogan
Robert Dockerty	George Daugherty	James Foster
John Crow	Chas. Cameron	Wm Morris
William Summers	W. Russell Junr	Nathaniel Bidlw
Name Undecipherable	Hugh Simpson	A. Tatom
Ambs Mauldin	Samuel Moore	William Hinson
Morton Mauldin	Joseph Denton	Edmund Newton
John Dunham	Arthur McAdoo	Jonathon Greer
Archelaus Allaway	James McAdoo	John Phillips
Saml. Hayes	Nathl Henderson	George Flynn
Nathl. Hayes	John Evans	Daniel Jarrett
Isaac Johnson	Wm. Bailey Smith	John Owens
Thomas Edmeston	Peter Luney	James Frelan
Ezekl Norris	Jon. Luney	Thos. Molloy
Robert Espey	James Cain	Isaac Lindsey
George Espey	Danl. Johnston	Isaac Bledsoe
William Gowen	Danl. Jarrot	Jacob Castleman
John Wilson	Jesse Maxey	George Power
James Espey	Noah Hawthorn	James Lynn
Michael Kimberlin	Charles McCartney	Thomas Cox
John Cowan	John Anderson	Edward Lucas
Francis Hodge	Matthew Anderson	Philip Alston
William Fleming	Wm. McWhorter	James Russell
James Leeper	William Purnell	
George Leeper	Wm. McMurrey	These names have been
Daniel Mungle	John Cordry	deciphered as accu-
Patrick McCutchan	Nicolas Tramal	rately as possible from
Saml. McCutchan	Haydon Wells	the signatures on the
Wm Price	Daniel Ratlett	original document
Henry Kerbey	John Callaway	

PRESENTED BY
THE METROPOLITAN HISTORICAL COMMISSION
IN OBSERVANCE OF NASHVILLE'S CENTURY III CELEBRATION
13 May 1980

GOLD STAR MONUMENT. Centennial Park. This memorial to members of the armed forces from Davidson County who lost their lives during the First World War was sculptured by George Zolnay in 1922. Funded by the Nashville Kiwanis Club during the years immediately following the war, the concrete base of the sculpture has inscriptions in the concrete on its north and south sides and metal plates listing the dead on its east and west sides. Alfred E. Howell, chairman of the Kiwanis Club memorial committee, secured permission from the Park Board on March 1, 1921, to place the monument to Gold Star heroes in the park corner near the intersection of West End with 25th Avenue North. Wilbur Creighton restored and refurbished the monument in 1967. Legends:

SOUTH SIDE INSCRIPTION:

I GAVE MY BEST
TO MAKE A BETTER WORLD
1917–1918

NORTH SIDE INSCRIPTION:

ERECTED
BY THE CITIZENS OF
DAVIDSON COUNTY TENNESSEE.
1923
NASHVILLE KIWANIS SPONSOR

NAMES LISTED ON EAST SIDE PLATE:

Private William P. Akard   Air Service
Sergeant Horace L. Alexander   Medical Corps
Corporal Edgar B. Anderson   114th Field Artillery
Sergeant H. B. Anthony   362nd Infantry
Private Thomas Antonopoulas   115th Field Artillery
1st Lieut Oliver Winston Bailey   47th Infantry
Seaman Robert Edgar Arnold   U S Navy
Captain Robert Baker   56th Pioneer Infantry
Private Wilkie S. J. Banks   371st Infantry
Private Alexander Battle   304th Stevedores
Private Dewitt Bennett   149th Infantry
Cook Hugh D. Biggs   332nd Infantry
Private Harold Frederick Blackwood   5th USMC
1st Lieut Shirley D. Bohannon   120th Infantry
Private William Herschell Booth   57th Pioneer Inf.
Carlos Boyd   (no unit listed)
Private Walter L. Bracey   117th Infantry
Corporal Ernest H. Bradley   Quartermaster Corps
Private Leslie Branch   801st Pioneer Infantry
1st Lieut Arthur Stuart Brown   143rd Infantry
PVT Frank E. Burke   114th Machine Gun Battalion
Private Alexander Bush   801st Pioneer Infantry
Sergeant James M. Byram   865th Air Squadron
Candidate Dandridge Wentworth Caldwell   ROTC
Sergeant William Smith Caldwell   419th Telg BN SC
1st Lieut Paul C. Calhoun   124th Infantry
1st Lieut H. Alvin Cameron   365th Infantry
Sergeant William C. Carlyle   5th Infantry
CPL Overton Carter   325th Field Battalion SC

Private John Casey   17th Engineers
2nd Mate William Orman Chest   USN Air Service
Sergeant Carl Atmore Chilson   59th Infantry
Private William R. Chechorne   114th Field Artillery
Captain Paul Clements   Medical Corps
Private Frank Buford Cochran   105th Engineers
Private James Conry   158th Depot Brigade
Private Gus A. Cooper   6th U S Marine Corps
Private Guy L. Cooper   109th Infantry
Private Joseph H. Cudworth   119th Infantry
Private Willie Davis   158th Depot Brigade
Corporal Will L. Davis   372nd Infantry
Private George R. Dismukes   Infantry
Private George L. Dixon   52lst Battalion Engin-ezs
Private William J. Donohue   50th Infantry
Private Emmanuel Dotson   30th Depot Brigade
Private Abner B. Douglas   812th Air Squadron
Seaman Carlos B. Dowell   U S Navy
Captain Charles B. Duncan   77th Field Artillery
Private Eugene Earls   61st Infantry
Private Marvin E. Edmondson   6th U S Marine Corps
Seaman Horace Clinton Elliott   U S Navy
Private Earl Evans   Infantry
1st Lieut James Dixie Everett   54th Infantry
Corporal Tobey Farmer   365th Infantry
PVT Charles M. Ferguson   814th Pioneer Infantry
2nd Lieut Hilary R. Frazier   117th Infantry
Captain Meade Frierson Jr.   125th Infantry
Private Thomas R. Frith   16th Infantry
Private Willie L. Gardner   370th Infantry
Private James L. Garland   57th Pioneer Infantry
Private Joshua O. Gatlin   114th Field Artillery
Private George R. Gerard   6th Machine Gun Battalion
Private Arthur B. Gilliam   50th Infantry
Sergeant Earnest Gilliam   438th Air Squadron
Oiler William Alexander Goff   U S Navy
Private Marke Goods   11th Infantry

1st Lieut Richard H. Graham   360th Infantry
Private Aubrey Grant   327th Infantry
Sergeant Walter Ward Greer   1st Corps Artillery
Corporal Orman P. Greer   6th U S Marine Corps
Coppersmith Schuyler Gregory   U S Navy
Corporal John O. Griffith   Infantry
Corporal William Allen Grubb   126th Infantry
Corporal Doss B. Haas   18th Infantry
Private Clarence E. Hackthorn   126th Infantry
Private George William Hager   3rd U S Marine Corps
Private Albert S. Harper   55th Infantry
Private Johnnie S. Hart   Engineers
Captain Leonard K. Hart   4th Ammunition Train
Private Fred S. Hathaway   OSC
Sergeant John W. Head   Quartermaster Corps
Private Richard Hill   115th Field Artillery
Sergeant Thomas J. Hindman   6th U S Marine Corps
Corporal Arthur J. Hindes   6th Infantry
Private James T. Hinkle   115th Field Artillery
Private Fred Hitner   363rd Infantry
Private Leighton Hodges   Infantry
PVT Charles Jackson Holman   5th U S Marine Corps
Cook Wilson D. Holman   114th Field Artillery
Private Henry Horton   372nd Infantry
1st Lieutenant Raymond F. Houston   47th Infantry
Sergeant H. L. Hudson   Signal Corps
Private Otto J. Hughes   8th Infantry
Bugler Buford W. Jackson   3rd Field Artillery
PVT Earl W. Jacobs   141st Machine Gun Battalion
Private J. C. Jenkins   11th Infantry
Private Frank Johnson   11th Infantry
Private Joseph Johnson   Medical Corps
Private Robert N. Johnson   411th Engineers
Private Henry Jordan   372nd Infantry
2nd Lieutenant James Britt Journey   30th Infantry
Private Roy E. Joyner   154th Depot Brigade

NAMES LISTED ON WEST SIDE PLATE:

Private Joseph Keeling   368th Infantry
Private Frank A. Kerrigan   5th U S Marine Corps
Corporal George G. Kidd   157th Depot Brigade
PVT Thomas M. Kirwin   114th Machine Gun Battalion
Private William Newton Knox   6th US Marine Corps
Private Sam Lamberson   (no unit listed)
Seaman William I. Lanier   U S Navy
Private Owen B. Layne   114th Machine Gun Battalion
Private Louis E. Lee   5th U S Marine Corps
Private Henry Lehning Jr.   305th Engineers
Private John Lewis   368th Infantry
1st Lieutenant George W. Long, Jr.   58th Infantry
Private Alcie M. Lovelace   114th Field Artillery
Bugler Richard M. Luter   9th Infantry
Private Frank McCall   23rd Infantry
Private Arthur Lee McCampbell   117th Infantry
Private Frank C. McClanahan   2nd Engineers
Private Waldo F. McFollin   57th Pioneer Infantry
Private Owen H. McKinnon   225th Air Squadron
Private Abner Mabe   Medical Corps
Bugler Ernest Maddux   114th Machine Gun Battalion
1st Lieutenant Emmett M. Manier   12th Escadrille
Private Jesse R. Mannis   6th U S Marine Corps
PVT Christian Frank Mayers   Coast Artillery Corps
Pharmacists Mate Carter Milan   U S Navy
Private John Mitchell   442nd Engineers
Private Lambert H. Mocker   20th Engineers
Captain Charles E. Monk   105th Field Battalion SC
Private George A. Moore   166th Infantry
Sergeant J. Louis Moore Jr.   Medical Corps
Sergeant James Moran   11th Infantry
Seaman James Watkins Moran   U S Navy

APPENDICES 277

Private Johnnie L. Morris   368th Infantry
2nd Lieutenant James McC. Newell   Infantry
Private John H. Nichols   158th Depot Brigade
Private Rile Horace Nixon   372nd Infantry
Private John H. Nollner   10th Field Artillery
Private John Farris Norton   6th U S Marine Corps
Private Guy Olney   11th Infantry
Chief Machinists Mate Thomas Freeman Ormsby   USN
Private Louis B. Orr   125th Infantry
1st Lieutenant Samuel K. Orr   122nd Infantry
1st Lieutenant John W. Overton   6th U S Marine Corps
Wagoner Elias Homer Parker   57th Infantry
Private James H. Patterson   114th Field Artillery
Seaman Edward T. Patton   U S Navy
Corporal Charles J. Payne   Quartermaster Corps
Private Alex W. Perry   Coast Artillery Corps
Wagoner James H. Persley   372nd Infantry
1st Lieutenant James A. Pigue   117th Infantry
Sergeant Donald Pons   533rd Engineers
Private Herman Ray   115th Field Artillery
Corporal Leroy Ray   10th Field Artillery
Private Claude C. Raymer   36th Infantry
CORP Ernest P. Rickets   75th Coast Artillery Corps
Private Henry G. Ring   6th U S Marine Corps
Private Horton Allen Riter   114th Machine Gun Battalion
2nd Lieut. Joseph H. Rosenthal   Quartermaster Corps
Private Dee Ross   541st Engineers
Sergeant James Elisha Seaton   117th Infantry
Fireman Dudley Ray Shawl   U S Navy
PVT William Lawrence Shores   872nd Air Squadron
Private Angelo Silverman   25th Field Artillery
Private Raymond Skerritt   Unassigned
Private Irving Small   138th Field Artillery
Fireman Howard B. Smith   U S Navy

Private King J. Smith   327th Infantry
Private Simi Smith   159th Depot Brigade
Private Robert Snyder   165th Infantry
Corporal Thomas G. Speck   18th Infantry
SERGT William John Spire Jr.   5th U S Marine Corps
Private Romi Steel   350th Infantry
1st Lieut Clay G. Stephens Jr.   20th Air Squadron
Corporal William H. Stephens   51st Infantry
PVT Charles Lofton Stevens   5th U S Marine Corps
Private William T. Taylor   7th Infantry
Sergeant Paul Terry   5th Field Battalion SC
PVT William Reed Terry Jr.   114th Machine Gun BN
Private Herman Thomas   810th Trains
2d LT James Simmons Timothy   6th U S Marine Corps
Private J. W. Turbeville   327th Infantry
Private Samuel Vaughn   320tg Engineers
Private Richard Wainright   372nd Infantry
Private Lawrence A. Wair   Unassigned
Private E. J. Walsh   168th Infantry
Private Lycurgus M. Walton   Ordnance Dept.
Sergeant Joseph B. Warren   6th U S Marine Corps
SERGT Robert Buist Warren   115th Field Artillery
Private Dan Wasserman   3rd Infantry
Private Allen Watkins   Engineers
PVT Henry Watterson III   7th BN Canadian E F
Private Private Robert P. Webb   158th Depot Brigade
Private John W. Weber   141st Infantry
Corporal John F. Weis   308th Infantry
Corporal Alpheus N. White   11th Infantry
Private John H. White   368th Infantry
Private John H. White   801st Pioneer Infantry
Candidate Charles H. Wilbur   ROTC
Private Joseph W. Wilkinson   317th Field Artillery
Sergeant Edgar O. Williams   14th Infantry
Private George H. Williams   383rd Bakery Company
1st Lieut Walter Spain Yarbrough   355th Infantry

GUNBOAT *TENNESSEE* MONUMENT. Centennial Park. This concrete replica of a ship's prow bearing the figurehead of the gunboat *Tennessee* was accepted by the Park Board on March 8, 1910, and was located at the main entrance to the park from Elliston Place. It originally had a golden color and has the form of an eagle and thirteen stars in the scrollwork. Because of its beauty, it was displayed at the Seattle World Fair of 1909 and brought to Nashville through efforts of Admiral Albert Gleaves and J. T. Howell. Major E. C. Lewis directed construction of the concrete ship's prow to hold the figurehead during 1910. In 1985 it had no informational marker concerning its history.

HADLEY PARK GATES MEMORIAL. Hadley Park. The stone columns at each side of the main entrance to the park next to the public library building contain a memorial listing of black soldiers from Davidson County who died during the First World War. On March 25, 1937, the Park Board approved WPA plans to construct the gates, with McKissack and McKissack, Architects, providing the design and American Legion Post 6, the H. A. Cameron Post, Dr. H. H. Walker commanding, supplying the memorial list for each column. The legends are:

LEFT GATE:

DEDICATED
TO THE
COLORED SOLDIERS OF DAVIDSON
COUNTY WHO WERE KILLED DURING
THE WORLD WAR

OVERTON CARTER
H. A. CAMERON
CHARLIE FERGUSON
HENRY JORDAN
HENRY HORTON
JOHN ED DAVIS

RIGHT GATE:

DEDICATED
TO THE
COLORED SOLDIERS OF DAVIDSON
COUNTY WHO WERE KILLED DURING
THE WORLD WAR

WILLIE GRAY
JESSE SHERIDAN
OTTO BILLHONUS
JAMES MENDERSON
ED TAYLOR

HERIGES MARKER. Edwin Warner Park. Standing metal marker between Old Hickory Boulevard and the ball diamonds in Edwin Warner Park.

BOB HERIGES
MEMORIAL FIELD

Dedicated to the Memory of
Robert M. "Bob" Heriges (1921-1967)

His devotion and desire
Will always be an inspiration
to those who knew him.
He was a sportsman, athlete and
friend of boys.

Bob believed that not all boys become baseball players but all boys become men.

LEA MONUMENT. Percy Warner Park. A five-foot high granite boulder with attached metal plate located 300 feet inside the Warner entrance gates and at the foot of the allé. The Park Board granted permission to officers of the 114th Field Artillery to place this monument to their commanding officer during the First World War and the monument was unveiled on April 16, 1950, by Governor Gordon Browning, who had served in the 114th. Legend:

IN MEMORY OF
COLONEL LUKE LEA
1879-1945

SO THAT POSTERITY MIGHT ENJOY
THE BENEFITS OF A PUBLIC PARK
PRESERVED IN ITS NATURAL BEAUTY,
IN 1927 COLONEL LUKE LEA GAVE
THE ORIGINAL TRACT OF 868 ACRES
OF THIS LAND TO THE CITY OF
NASHVILLE REQUESTING THAT THE
PARK BEAR THE NAME OF HIS
FATHER-IN-LAW, THE LATE PERCY
WARNER.

ERECTED BY OFFICERS WHO SERVED
UNDER COLONEL LEA IN THE 114TH
FIELD ARTILLERY DURING THE FIRST
WORLD WAR

LEA'S SUMMIT MARKER. Percy Warner Park. Standard metal marker located at the crest of Lea's Summit, highest point in Percy Warner Park. Legend:

LEA'S SUMMIT
elevation 922 feet

Luke Lea Heights, now known as Lea's Summit, was named in 1927 by the Park Board to honor Col. Luke Lea (1879-1945). He and his wife, Percie Warner Lea, donated the original 868 acres of this park. This point overlooks Belle Meade, which he had a major role in developing. Founder of the Nashville Tennessean in 1907, U.S. Senator 1911-1917, he organized the 114th Field Artillery in WWI

THE HISTORICAL COMMISSION OF METROPOLITAN NASHVILLE AND DAVIDSON COUNTY

No. 79   Erected 1985

LEWIS MARKER. Centennial Park. Bronze tablet of Greek design honoring Major Eugene Castner Lewis located in the wall of the gift shop in the basement of the Parthenon. Sarah Polk (Mrs. J. C.) Bradford requested and received permission from the Park Board on February 26, 1926, to raise funds for the placement of a memorial to Major Lewis in the Parthenon. The Greek design tablet, signifying the bestowal of laurels, was created by Leopold and Belle Kinney Scholz and unveiled on June 10, 1934, by Rumsey Lewis, grandson of Major Lewis. The tablet bears the legend:

IN MEMORIAM • MAJOR EUGENE CASTNER LEWIS • 1845-1917 • DISTINGUISHED CITIZEN • ENGINEER • PATRON OF THE ARTS • DIRECTOR GENERAL OF THE TENNESSEE CENTENNIAL EXPOSITION IN 1897 • IT WAS HE WHO CONCEIVED THE IDEA OF THIS EXACT REPLICA OF THE PARTHENON AT ATHENS GREECE • THIS BUILDING HAS MARKED A PERIOD IN THE ART HISTORY OF THE COMMONWEALTH OF TENNESSEE.

L. F. Scholz . . . Belle Kinney
Sculptors

LOCOMOTIVE MARKER. Centennial Park. Metal plate attached to the side of Locomotive 576 forward of its right drive wheels. Legend:

N. C & ST. L. RAILWAY LOCOMOTIVE NO. 576

PRESENTED IN 1953 ON BEHALF OF THE N. C. & ST. L. RAILWAY TO THE CITY OF NASHVILLE BY W. S. HACKWORTH, PRESIDENT OF THE N. C. & ST. L. AND ACCEPTED FOR PERMANENT EXHIBIT IN CENTENNIAL PARK BY MAYOR BEN WEST, EDWIN CRUTCHER, CHAIRMAN OF THE PARK COMMISSION, AND WRENNE C. PHELPS, COUNCILMAN, FOURTH WARD.

BUILT IN 1942 LOCOMOTIVE NO. 576 WAS ONE OF THE MOST MODERN STEAM ENGINES IN SERVICE ON AMERICAN RAILROADS AND WAS ONE OF A LARGE FLEET OPERATED ON THE N. C. & ST. L DURING WORLD WAR II IN THE MOVEMENT OF MILITARY PERSONNEL AND WAR MATERIAL.

AT THE END OF 1952 DIESEL-ELECTRIC MOTIVE POWER HAD COMPLETELY REPLACED STEAM ENGINES ON THE N. C. & ST. L.

LOVENTHAL MEMORIAL FOUNTAIN. Hadley Park. On April 20, 1944, Mrs. Lee J. Loventhal proposed to install a memorial drinking fountain in Hadley Park with a legend honoring her late husband who served many years as Park Commissioner. Careful inspection of the park in 1985 revealed two concrete foundations which may have been the site of the fountain, but the fountain itself was not found. It may have been removed because of the deterioration or perhaps to make room for other facilities.

MORGAN PARK MEMORIAL FIELD MARKER. Morgan Park. A four-by-four-foot concrete block with a metal plate located adjacent to the ball diamond. On February 2, 1949, the North Nashville Men's Club requested permission to place a plaque at the Morgan Park ball diamond in honor of the boys of North Nashville who lost their lives during the Second World War; the Board approved and the memorial ball field was dedicated on April 10, 1949. Legend:

MORGAN
PARK
MEMORIAL
FIELD

TO THOSE BOYS OF
NORTH NASHVILLE
WHO IN LIFE'S EARLY AFTERNOON
LEFT THE RED WINE
OF ATHLETIC COMPETITION
FOR THE RED BLOOD OF WAR—
TO GET A JOB DONE,
THIS FIELD IS REVERENTLY DEDICATED
APRIL 10, 1949

MURRELL MONUMENT. Centennial Park. Long established oral tradition, first repeated in print about 1954 by Jesse Burt in his history of the Nashville, Chattanooga and St. Louis Railway, asserts that Major E. C. Lewis became irritated when Nashvillians erected a statue in 1907 honoring Jere Baxter of the Tennessee Central Railroad and declared that if the city could build a monument to a "railroad thief" he would build one to a horsethief, namely the notorious John Murrell. Nashville historian Hugh Walker asserts that Lewis actually scratched Murrell's name on a sundial in the park, and that is confirmed by long-time park employees who point to a sundial base in the park as the monument to Murrell. Although minus any trace of the name Murrell and in fact missing the sundial, the base composed of two stone blocks is surrounded by a hedge and located about 300 feet northwest of the Parthenon, or 300 feet south of the Park administration building.

NASHVILLE, CHATTANOOGA & ST. LOUIS RAILWAY MONUMENT. Centennial Park. The doorway of the railway office at 930 Broadway in Nashville contained a transom with a bas-relief depicting two types of steam locomotives. The Louisville and Nashville Railroad during the 1970's removed the doorway and placed it as a monument in Centennial Park on the north side of Locomotive 576. Legend:

THE
NASHVILLE, CHATTANOOGA
& ST. LOUIS RAILWAY

DOORWAY OF HOME OFFICE BUILDING
IN NASHVILLE
REPRODUCED AND PRESENTED TO
THE CITY OF NASHVILLE

BY

LOUISVILLE AND NASHVILLE
RAILROAD COMPANY

TO COMMEMORATE THE N. C. & ST. L. RAILWAYS 107 YEARS OF RAILROAD TRANSPORTATION SERVICE. THE TERRA COTTA TRANSOM DEPICTING BOTH EARLY AND LATER TYPES OF N. C. & ST. L. STEAM LOCOMOTIVES WAS REMOVED FROM THE OFFICE BUILDING FOR PRESENTATION IN THIS MEMORIAL.

"The N. C. & St. L. Railway, built in 1851, was an important factor in the historical, economic and social development of Tennessee and other Southern States."

TENNESSEE HISTORICAL COMMISSION

NATCHEZ TRACE MONUMENT. Centennial Park. a five-foot high granite boulder with attached metal plate located in the southwest corner of the park near West End Avenue. On August 6, 1912, Mrs. Maggie Hicks of the DAR requested permission from the Park Board to install this monument near Cockrill Spring as the point from which General Andrew Jackson and his army started their march over the Natchez Trace a century earlier. The Board approved the monument design and granted approval, provided the DAR paid for the monument. Legend:

NATCHEZ TRACE

Nashville, Tenn.—Natchez, Miss.
Five Hundred and One Miles

———

Erected by
Cumberland, Campbell & McCrory
Chapters
Daughters of the American Revolution
1912

APPENDICES 281

PARTHENON MARKER. Centennial Park. Metal plate on a vertical concrete foundation located next to the walkway about 50 feet from the west entrance to the Parthenon. Frank Atchley of the Metropolitan Historical Commission (and also Park Maintenance Administrator) on February 14, 1979, requested and received permission to install this marker for the information of visitors to the Parthenon.

THE WORLDS ONLY REPLICA OF THE PARTHENON, EPITOME OF GREEK CULTURE, WAS THE CENTRAL BUILDING AT TENNESSEE'S CENTENNIAL EXPOSITION, MAY 1 THRU OCTOBER 31, 1897. THE ORIGINAL TEMPLE, DEDICATED TO ATHENA, GREEK GODDESS OF WISDOM, OCCUPIED THE MOST SACRED AREA IN ANCIENT GREECE, THE CREST OF THE ACROPOLIS, A HILL OVERLOOKING ATHENS.

MAJOR EUGENE C. LEWIS, DIRECTOR GENERAL OF THE CENTENNIAL, BELIEVED THAT A REPRODUCTION OF THE GREEK MASTERWORK TO SERVE AS A GALLERY OF FINE ARTS WOULD INSPIRE A LOVE OF BEAUTY AND A SPIRIT OF EXCELLENCE. COLONEL WILLIAM C. SMITH SERVED AS ARCHITECT AND GEORGE J. ZOLNAY, SCULPTOR. CONTRACTOR FOR THE BUILDING WAS EDWARD LAURENT WITH FOSTER AND CREIGHTON CONTRACTING FOR THE FOUNDATION.

THE RECEPTION OF THE CENTENNIAL—IT WAS THE FIRST EXPOSITION IN THE NATION TO BE BOTH AN ARTISTIC AND FINANCIAL SUCCESS—AND PUBLIC RESPONSE TO THE PARTHENON INDICATED THAT, ALTHOUGH IT WAS MADE OF TEMPORARY MATERIALS, IT SHOULD BE RECONSTRUCTED ON A PERMANENT BASIS. CONSTRUCTION WAS STARTED IN 1921, THE EXTERIOR COMPLETED IN 1925, BUT DUE TO THE LACK OF FUNDS, IT WAS NOT UNTIL MAY 20, 1931, THAT THE PARTHENON AS IT STANDS TODAY WAS OPENED TO THE PUBLIC.

HART, FREELAND AND ROBERTS, WITH WILLIAM B. DINSMOOR CONSULTING, SERVED AS ARCHITECTS: GEORGE J. ZOLNAY, LEOPOLD SCHOLZ AND BELLE KINNEY SCHOLZ, SCULPTORS. FOSTER AND CREIGHTON WERE GENERAL CONTRACTORS. OTHERS WHO CONTRIBUTED TO THE WORK INCLUDED JOHN J. EARLY COMPANY, GENERAL BRONZE CORPORATION, JOHN BOUCHARD AND SONS, HERBRICK AND LAWRENCE, H. E. PARMER, J. J. HUTCHISON AND SON, J. O. KILPATRICK, CHARLES A. HOWELL, ART MOSAIC AND TILE COMPANY AND A. T. KANADAY.

BOARD OF PARK COMMISSIONERS

Robert M. Dudley
M. T. Bryan
Lee J. Loventhal
W. R. Cole
Robert T. Creighton
Charles M. McCabe
Percy Warner
Rogers Caldwell
J. P. W. Brown
Edwin Warner
C. A. Craig

PARTHENON MARKER. Centennial Park. Standard metal marker located at the southern edge of the park next to West End Avenue. Legend:

THE PARTHENON

Erected as the central structure of the Tennessee Centennial Exposition, 1897, this is the only full-scale reproduction of the fifth century B.C. Athenian temple and is exact in almost every detail to the original. The idea of reproducing this magnificent building was conceived by Major E. C. Lewis, Director General of the Exposition. The building served as a gallery of fine arts during the commemoration.

TENNESSEE HISTORICAL COMMISSION

POAG GARDEN MEMORIAL MARKER. Hadley Park. Metal plate standing on support in the triangle near the entrance to the park and the public library building. On February 4, 1976, the Park Board approved the placement of this marker by the Green Thumb Garden Club in memory of Dr. Thomas E. Poag, a prominent citizen who made outstanding contributions to community cultural activities. Legend:

THOMAS E. POAG
MEMORIAL GARDEN
BY
THE GREEN THUMB
GARDEN CLUB
1977

POWDER-GRINDING WHEELS MARKER. Centennial Park. Standard metal marker located next to the wheel display in the northeast corner of the park. As indicated in old pictures of the park, the powder wheels have since 1897 been rolled from one point in the park to another, but apparently have occupied their present site since 1968. Legend on the marker:

POWDER-GRINDING WHEELS

These wheels used by the Confederacy to grind gunpowder at Augusta, Ga. in 1863-1864 were made in Woolwich, England and were shipped on the blockade runner "Spray," via Mobile. After the war Gen. Miles purchased them for use at Sycamore Powder Mills, Cheatham County. They were exhibited at the Tennessee Centennial Exposition in 1897.

THE HISTORICAL COMMISSION OF
METROPOLITAN NASHVILLE AND
DAVIDSON COUNTY
No. 15   Erected 1968

PULLEN MARKER. Hadley Park. Metal plate attached to the wall of the bandshell located in 1980 at the request of Councilman Willis McAllister and others. Don Q. Pullen, organizer and director of the Sunday concerts at Hadley Park for twenty years, had retired in 1979. Legend:

IN HONOR OF
DON "Q" PULLEN
COMPOSER,
BAND DIRECTOR,
AND PRODUCER
FOR YEARS OF DEDICATED
SERVICE TO THIS
COMMUNITY
IN THE DEVELOPMENT OF
MUSICAL CONCERTS
IN
METROPOLITAN PARKS
1981

ROBERTSON MARKER. City Cemetery. Metal plate attached to the metal gate at the northeast entrance to the City Cemetery next to Fourth Avenue North. Though not mentioned in Park Board records, this marker was placed during the renovation of the cemetery accomplished by the Board after 1908. Legend:

ERECTED
NOVEMBER 21, 1909
IN MEMORY OF
JAMES ROBERTSON
THE FOUNDER OF NASHVILLE
CHARLOTTE REEVES
HIS WIFE
AND
THE OLD CITIZENS
AND
CONFEDERATE SOLDIERS
BURIED WITHIN
THIS SACRED ENCLOSURE

ROBERTSON MARKER. Fort Nashborough. Large metal plate inside the fort stockade attached to the outside of a cabin's stone fireplace. Legend:

IN HONOR OF
COLONEL JAMES ROBERTSON
Born 1742 in Virginia
Died 1814 in Tennessee

He came from eastern North Carolina to the Watauga settlement in what is now eastern Tennessee 1769-1770, where he was a leader in civil and Indian affairs.

Conducted the "Land Party" of settlers to the French Lick in 1779-1780, built this Fort Nashborough and defended it in all the various Indian attacks. Remained with the colony when many had forsaken it during a period of great stress, suffering and discouragement, and gave to it a whole life-time of patriotic service.

The Verdict of history well entitles him to the name of:
  "The Father of West (now Middle) Tennessee" and the
  "Founder of Nashville."

―――

"He possessed to an eminent degree the confidence and esteem of all his contemporaries, and merited all the

eulogium and affection which the most ardent of his countrymen have ever bestowed upon him. His services in peace and war are gratefully remembered."
(Haywood)

ROBERTSON MONUMENT. Centennial Park. A fifty-foot high granite shaft and base weighing a total of 105,000 pounds with metal plaques on all four sides of the monument. The granite shaft was quarried at Stone Mountain, Georgia, by Venerable Brothers of Atlanta and shipped to Nashville for display during the 1897 Centennial Exposition. Oral traditions says a portion of the shaft broke off during transit to Nashville. Major Lewis purchased the shaft for $200 in 1902 and Commissioner S. A. Champion resolved that it be erected in the park as a monument to the memory of James Robertson. With a tripod made of three large oak logs and block and tackle, Major Lewis raised the shaft into position and then constructed the foundation beneath it. The monument was dedicated on October 11, 1903, with more than one hundred descendants of General Robertson present; Dickson Wharton Robertson, great-great-grandson of the General, unveiled the plaques. The legends on the four plaques are:

NORTH SIDE:

JAMES ROBERTSON
BORN IN BRUNSWICK COUNTY,
VIRGINIA, JUNE 28, 1742
MOVED TO NORTH CAROLINA IN 1750
CAME TO TENNESSEE IN 1769
SETTLED NASHVILLE IN 1780
DIED IN TENNESSEE, SEPT. 1, 1814

REINTERRED IN THE CITY CEMETERY
AT NASHVILLE, 1825
UNDER AUTHORITY OF THE
TENNESSEE LEGISLATURE

WEST SIDE:

JAMES ROBERTSON
FOUNDER OF NASHVILLE

"WE ARE THE ADVANCE GUARD OF CIVILIZATION. OUR WAY IS ACROSS THE CONTINENT."
ROBERTSON—1779

SOUTH SIDE:

A WORTHY CITIZEN OF BOTH VIRGINIA AND NORTH CAROLINA. PIONEER PATRIOT AND PATRIARCH IN TENNESSEE. DIPLOMAT, INDIAN FIGHTER, MAKER OF MEMORABLE HISTORY. DIRECTOR OF THE MOVEMENT OF THE SETTLERS REQUIRING THAT HAZARDOUS AND HEROIC JOURNEY SO SUCCESSFULLY ACHIEVED FROM WATAUGA TO THE CUMBERLAND. FOUNDER OF NASHVILLE. BRIGADIER GENERAL OF THE UNITED STATES ARMY. AGENT OF THE GOVERNMENT TO THE CHICKASAW NATION. HE WAS EARNEST, TACITURN, SELF-CONTAINED, AND HAD THAT QUIET CONSCIOUSNESS OF POWER USUALLY SEEN IN BORN LEADERS OF MEN. "HE HAD WINNING WAYS AND MADE NO FUSS." (OCONNOSTOTA) HE HAD WHAT WAS OF VALUE BEYOND PRICE—A LOVE OF VIRTUE, AND INTREPID SOUL, AN EMULOUS DESIRE FOR HONEST FAME. HIS WORTH AND SERVICES IN PEACE AND WAR ARE GRATEFULLY REMEMBERED. AMIABLE IN PRIVATE LIFE, WISE IN COUNCIL, VIGILANT IN CAMP, COURAGEOUS IN BATTLE, STRONG IN ADVERSITY, GENEROUS IN VICTORY, REVERED IN DEATH.

EAST SIDE:

CHARLOTTE REEVES

WIFE OF JAMES ROBERTSON. BORN IN NORTH CAROLINA, JAN. 2, 1751. MARRIED TO JAMES ROBERTSON, 1768. DIED IN NASHVILLE, JUN. 11, 1843. BURIED IN THE CITY CEMETERY. MOTHER OF THE FIRST MALE CHILD BORN AT NASHVILLE. SHE PARTICIPATED IN THE DEEDS AND DANGERS OF HER ILLUSTRIOUS HUSBAND: WON HONORS OF HER OWN AND ALONG HIS PATH OF DESTINY CAST A LEADING LIGHT OF LOYALTY, INTELLIGENCE AND DEVOTION.

ROSE ARBOR. Centennial Park. The rose arbor with stone columns supporting wooden trellis framework near the children's playground was initially constructed for the 1897 Centennial Exposition, arcing around a fountain and sculpture of Athena. The wooden framework has been replaced from time to time, but at least some of the supporting columns are the originals. In 1985 no information marker existed to explain its history.

SHELL SPRING. Centennial Park. This unusual reinforced concrete structure over a spring in the southeast sector of the park near the Lick Branch Sewer was designed and constructed under the direction of Major E. C. Lewis sometime between 1906 and 1912. Park records do not mention it, nor have newspaper accounts of its history been located. Major Lewis found a beautiful shell on a Florida beach and brought it to Nashville as a model for the design. No marker concerning its history existed in 1985.

SERPENT MONUMENT. Fannie Mae Dees Park. This sculpture may also be considered a monument. Park Commissioner Ann Roos secured the services of Pedro Silva with multiple funding sources for this artistic endeavor. Hundreds of Nashvillians had a role in forming the mosaic designs decorating the sculpture, which was dedicated on April 25, 1981. It had no identifying and informational marker in 1985.

SMITH MEMORIAL. Centennial Park. Stone tablet in the Parthenon basement over the south doorway into the art display rooms. On March 2, 1903, H. M. Brunicke of the Nashville chapter, American Red Cross, requested permission to place a memorial to Colonel William C. Smith at the Parthenon. The gray marble tablet, then set on the east front of the Parthenon building, was unveiled on July 5, 1903, by Mrs. Hart Blanton, the daughter of Colonel Smith. Mrs. Smith, along with Confederate veterans, soldiers who had served under Smith's command in the Philippines, and a crowd of 2,000 attended the unveiling ceremony, where Tully Brown and Governor Benton McMillin were the principal speakers. Smith was born in Virginia in 1837, served in the Virginia infantry throughout the Civil War, moved to Nashville after the war to become an architect and commander of the First Tennessee Volunteer Infantry.

He was the architect of the temporary Parthenon constructed in 1895-1897, master of the Corinthian Lodge F&AM, and died of apoplexy while leading the First Tennessee into battle at Santa Mesa outside Manila in 1899. Legend:

The Architect of This Building
WILLIAM CRAWFORD SMITH
Colonel commanding First Regiment of Tennessee Volunteer Infantry;
BORN at Petersburg, Va. Nov. 26, 1837:
Died at the head of this command on the firing line in front of
Manila, Philippine Islands,
February 5, 1899
A soldier in the Army of the Confederate States, May 1861 to April 1865.

SUNKEN GARDEN MARKER. Centennial Park. Metal marker atop a low concrete foundation located next to the stone bridge in the Sunken Garden. The site of the Sunken Garden had been Lily Lake during the 1897 Centennial Exposition; during the 1920s Park Superintendent George Moulder converted the pond into a Japanese Water Garden; and after the Second World War the pond was drained and it was converted during the 1950s into a sunken floral garden under the direction of the park system personnel listed on the marker placed in the garden in 1974. Legend:

IN APPRECIATION OF

F. W. PICKENS   SUPERINTENDENT PARKS
Z. N. DOBBS   HORTICULTURIST
CLIFFORD KING   GARDNER
METRO PARKS & RECREATION

FOR DEDICATED SERVICE TO THE
CITIZENRY OF
NASHVILLE & DAVIDSON COUNTY
FOR THEIR ROLE
IN THE DEVELOPMENT OF
THIS GARDEN
CONSTRUCTION PERIOD 1951-1959

SUNNYSIDE MARKER. Sevier Park. Standard metal marker installed at roadside near the front of Sunnyside Mansion in Sevier Park by the Historical Commission of Metropolitan Nashville and Davidson County in 1970. Legend:

APPENDICES 285

SUNNYSIDE

Home of Mrs. Jesse Benton, widow of Jesse Benton who left Nashville after a feud with Andrew Jackson. Built in the 1840's, restored in the 1920's by Col. Granville Sevier. Two log cabins east of the home, reported to have been built by the French for trade with the Chickasaw and Choctaw Indians, may be the oldest structures in Metropolitan Nashville.

The Historical Commission of Nashville and Davidson County

No. 22   Erected 1970

TENNESSEE CENTENNIAL EXPOSITION MONUMENT. Centennial Park. Metal plate laid atop a flat stone on the west bank of Lake Watauga. Major E. C. Lewis purchased the stone for $10 in 1903 from the company in Georgia which displayed it at the 1897 Exposition; during the Exposition, the stone served as the base for the granite shaft which was moved in 1903 to become part of the Robertson monument elsewhere in the park. The metal Centennial Memorial Tablet attached to the stone was unveiled on May 21, 1904, by Governor James Frazier, former Governor J. P. Porter, and General Gates P. Thurston of the Tennessee Historical Society. In his speech, Governor Porter stated the stone slab had come from Guilford County, North Carolina, perhaps indicating that it had come from a quarry in North Carolina owned by the Georgia firm. The large metal tablet is divided by raised metal lines into several sections containing the following legends:

TENNESSEE CENTENNIAL
EXPOSITION—May 1, to
November 1, 1897
William McKinley, President of
the United States
Wm. M. McCarthy, Mayor of Nashville
Robert L. Taylor, Governor of Tennessee
Norman Farrell, Mayor of Centennial City

THIS TABLET PLACED IN THE
YEAR 1904, COMMEMORATES
THE WISE, PATRIOTIC, PLEASING
AND SUCCESSFUL ORGANIZATION
CREATION, ADMINISTRATION
AND DIRECTION OF THE
TENNESSEE CENTENNIAL EXPOSITION

WHICH WAS HELD ON THESE
GROUNDS IN THE YEAR 1897,
IN CELEBRATION OF THE ONE
HUNDREDTH ANNIVERSARY OF
THE ADMISSION OF THE STATE
OF TENNESSEE INTO THE
FEDERAL UNION

"THE EXPOSITION WHICH REPRODUCED THE PARTHENON, WHICH STAKED ITS WHOLE ARTISTIC EFFORT UPON THE SUBORDINATION OF EVERYTHING TO THAT FLAWLESS CENTRAL JEWEL NEEDS NO DEFENCE ARTISTICALLY. NOTHING BUILT ON THIS CONTINENT EVER EXCELLED IT IN BEAUTY."
Nathaniel Stephenson

John W. Thomas   President of the
    Tennessee Centennial Exposition
Charles E. Curry   Secretary
W. A. Henderson, Van Leer Kirkman,
John Overton   Vice Presidents
E. C. Lewis   Director General
W. L. Dudley   Director of Affairs
R. T. Creighton   Engineer in Charge
A. W. Wills   Commissioner General
S. A. Champion   General Counsel
W. P. Tanner   Treasurer
Frank Goodman   Auditor

EXECUTIVE COMMITTEE
John W. Thomas, Chairman

Tully Brown	Van Leer Kirkman
E. E. Barthell	E. C. Lewis
G. H. Baskette	H. H. Lurton
J. W. Baker	S. M. Murphy
H. W. Buttorff	Jno. J. McCann
E. W. Cole	J. H. McDowell
S. A. Champion	J. C. Neely
M. J. Dalton	John Overton
W. L. Dudley	H. E. Palmer
J. H. Fall	A. H. Robinson
T. D. Fite	W. P. Tanner
W. A. Henderson	John W. Thomas, Jr.
W. H. Jackson	J. Van Derventer
S. J. Keith	B. F. Wilson

Luke E. Wright

ARCHITECTS

W. C. Smith	G. W. Thompson
B. J. Hodge & Bro.	
Sara Ward Conley	F. W. Krider
E. C. Lewis	Gibel & Gabler
S. A. Asmus	J. G. Zwicker
Frederick Thompson	

WOMAN'S BOARD

Mrs. Van Leer Kirkman	President
Mrs. Robert Weakley	Treasurer
Miss Ada Scott Rice	Secretary
Miss Mary B. Temple	
Mrs. Florence K. Drouillard	Vice
Mrs. Charles N. Grosvenor	Presidents
Mrs. John W. Thomas	

DEPARTMENTS

Agriculture	T. F. Allison	Chief
Admission	J. N. Brooks	Chief
Bureau of Publicity	Herman Justi	Chief
Commerce and Manufacture	J. H. Bruce	Chief
Children	W. T. Davis	Chief
Concessions	S. B. Wadley	Chief
Education	W. L. Dudley	Chief
Electricity	J. W. Braid	Chief
Electrician	J. W. Pentecost	Chief
Foreign	Sen. A. Macchi	Chief
Florist	W. F. Josolyne	Chief
Fine Art	T. Cooley	Chief
Forestry	A. E. Baird	Chief
Geology	James M. Safford	Chief
Grounds & Buildings	R. T. Creighton	Engineer
Hygiene, Medicine and Sanitary	J. D. Plunkett	Chief
Installation	E. F. Blodgett	Chief
Military	Charles Sykes	Chief
Machinery	George Reyer	Chief
Negro	Richard Hill	Chief
Transportation	A. H. Robinson	Chief
Commissioner of Awards	G. G. Hubbard	

THOMAS MONUMENT. Centennial Park. On May 15, 1906, the Park Board granted permission to employees of the N. C. & St. L. Railway to place a monument to the memory of President John W. Thomas at the former site of the flagstaff. Enid Yandell sculpted the statue of Thomas, which was unveiled in 1907. The base of the statue has metal plates on all four sides, three with symbolic figures in bas-relief and the fourth with the legend. The concrete foundation has eight benches, two to a side, forming a balustrade, with words cut into each bench. The words on the outside of the benches are: (north) LAW, TRAFFIC; (west) MECHANICAL, TRANSPORTATION; (south) ROADWAY, ACCOUNTING; (east) ADMINISTRATION, EXECUTIVE. The words on the inside of the benches are: (north) JUSTICE, CHARITY; (west) DEVOTION, PROMPTNESS; (south) INTEGRITY, COURAGE; (east) PATRIOTISM, WISDOM. The legend on the metal plate at the east side of the statue base is:

JOHN W. THOMAS
1830–1906

A native of Nashville,
Forty-eight years in the service
of the Nashville, Chattanooga &
St. Louis Railway;
President for twenty- two years.
President of the
Tennessee Centennial Exposition,
which resulted in securing
to Nashville this Park.
A worthy man in all the lines of life.
An efficient man of affairs.
An upright and eminent citizen.
A Christian and a gentleman.
A friend and a brother.

This memorial is erected by the employees of the Nashville, Chattanooga & St. Louis Railway.
———1907———

TIMOTHY MONUMENT. Centennial Park. A three-foot high concrete slab with a bronze plate attached located at roadside about 1000 feet north of the entrance to the park from West End. Legend:

THIS TREE WAS PLANTED
MAY 24th, 1919 BY THE
CATHOLIC CHILDREN OF NASHVILLE
IN GRATEFUL MEMORY OF
LIEUTENANT JAMES SIMMONS
TIMOTHY OF THE
80th COMPANY, 6th REGIMENT U.S.M.C
WHO WAS KILLED IN ACTION AT
BELLEAU WOOD, FRANCE
JUNE 14th, 1918, AGED 25 YEARS

HE WAS FIRST WOUNDED WHILE
SERVING WITH THE FRENCH IN THE
VERDUN SECTOR, MAR. 22, 1918. ON
THE DAY OF HIS DEATH HE TOOK HIS
COMPANY OF TWO HUNDRED MEN
"OVER THE TOP" AND RETURNED
WITH ONLY FIVE. LATER IN THE DAY
HE WAS KILLED BY AN ENEMY SHELL.

LIEUTENANT TIMOTHY WAS THE
FIRST TENNESSEE OFFICER TO MAKE
THE SUPREME SACRIFICE IN THE
GREAT WAR FOR JUSTICE AND
HUMANITY. HIS LAST WORDS WERE,
"INTO THY HANDS, O LORD, I
COMMEND MY SOUL."

STRONG IN FAITH, NO FEARS
HE KNEW,
THIS GALLANT KNIGHT OF GOD
SO TRUE:
PURE, COURAGEOUS, GRAND
WAS HE—
OUR HERO SON OF TENNESSEE.

TWO RIVERS MANSION MARKER. Two Rivers Park. Standard metal marker on McGavock Pike at the entrance to Two Rivers Mansion. Legend:

TWO RIVERS MANSION

Built in 1859 by David H. McGavock, this mansion stands on lands inherited by McGavock's wife, Willie, from her father, William Harding. The smaller house to the left was built in 1802. Dr. James Priestley's Academy, established about 1816, was located on the 1,100 acre farm 1 mile from the mansion on the Cumberland River bluff.

THE HISTORICAL COMMISSION OF
METROPOLITAN NASHVILLE AND
DAVIDSON COUNTY
No. 10   Erected 1968

WARNER GATE MARKER. Percy Warner Park. Metal plate attached to the Percy Warner Gate at the entrance to the park from Page Road.

PERCY WARNER
1861   1927

THAT THROUGH THIS ENTRANCE
THERE MAY PASS THE MULTITUDES
OF THE FUTURE TO ENJOY THE
BEAUTY OF WOOD AND FIELD AND
FLOWER THE GATEWAY TO THIS PARK
HAS BEEN ERECTED IN MEMORY OF
HIM WHOSE VISION BEHELD ITS
SPLENDOR AND WHO WROUGHT
THAT IT MIGHT BE YOURS

APPENDICES   287

MRS. PERCY WARNER
AND DAUGHTERS
SADIE WARNER FRAZER
MARGARET WARNER WHITE
MARY LOUISE WARNER LEA
MARY TOM WARNER MALLISON
PERCIE WARNER LEA

1931

WARNER MARKER. Edwin Warner Park. Standard metal marker located inside the stone gate entrance to the park on Old Hickory Boulevard. Legend:

EDWIN WARNER PARK
606.7 acres

Edwin Warner (1870-1945) succeeded his brother Percy on the Park Board in 1927 and served for eighteen years. He personally directed the acquisition of most of the Warner Park acreage and supervised WPA development of the property. Warner organized a major Victory Garden program in the park during WWII. Park land west of Old Hickory Blvd. was renamed in his honor in 1937.

THE HISTORICAL COMMISSION OF
METROPOLITAN NASHVILLE AND
DAVIDSON COUNTY
No. 80   Erected 1985

WARNER MARKER. Percy Warner Park. Standard metal marker located outside the stone gates on the median at the Page Road entrance to Percy Warner Park. Legend:

PERCY WARNER PARK
2058.1 acres

Percy Warner (1861-1927) was a pioneer in electric utilities and hydroelectric development in the South. As chairman of the Park Board, he expanded Nashville's park system. Preservation of this natural area was one of his greatest civic projects. Named in his honor by the Park Board in 1927, this land constitutes the largest municipal park in Tennessee.

THE HISTORICAL COMMISSION OF
METROPOLITAN NASHVILLE AND
DAVIDSON COUNTY
No. 78   Erected 1985

WARNER MARKER. Edwin Warner Park. Metal plate attached to right column of stone entrance gate to the park. The memorial was unveiled on November 26, 1948, by Edwin Warner Bass and Edwin Warner Dean, grandsons of Edwin Warner. Legend:

EDWIN WARNER PARK

A part of this beautiful area embracing 597 acres of woodland, field and stream was presented by Mr. and Mrs. Edwin Warner to the City of Nashville and dedicated by them to the perpetual use and enjoyment of its citizens.

    Board of Park Commissioners
    of the City of
    Nashville, Tennessee

WATKINS MARKER. Hadley Park. Metal plate attached to a low concrete foundation located adjacent to the tennis courts in Hadley Park. On October 5, 1978, Councilman John L. Driver and the Hadley Park Tennis Club requested the Park Board to install a marker at the tennis courts honoring the contributions of James H. Watkins. Legend:

In honor of

JAMES H. WATKINS

for the insight and vision he manifested through the years of tireless, selfless devotion to the development of tennis in this community.   1979

WOMAN'S MONUMENT. Centennial Park. A twelve-foot high stone monument located about 400 feet southwest of the Parthenon near the children's play area and Centennial Art Activities Building. It consists of a vertical rectangular shaft with a metal plate attached and surmounted by a granite sphere with a diameter of nearly four feet. The sphere probably is the one sent to the 1897 Centennial Exposition by the Southern Marble Company of Marblehill, Georgia. In 1903 the Park Board turned the former site of the Woman's Building at the 1897 Exposition over to the ladies who had directed the exhibits in that building for development as they saw fit, and in 1904 the monument was placed on the site. The monument was moved from its original site in 1928 when the roads in the park were relocated. Legend:

THIS MONUMENT
APTLY MARKS THE SITE OF
THE WOMAN'S BUILDING
AT THE
TENNESSEE CENTENNIAL
EXPOSITION
HELD IN THIS PARK
IN THE YEAR 1897

"THAT THAT IS ROUND CAN BE
NO ROUNDER"

WOMAN'S DEPARTMENT

Mrs. Van Leer Kirkman	president
Mrs. John W. Thomas	
Mrs. John W. Thomas	
Miss Mary B. Temple	vice presidents
Mrs. Florence K. Drouillard	
Mrs. Charles N. Grosvenor	
Mrs Robert Weakley	treasurer
Miss Ada Scott Rice	secretary

WOMAN'S WORK

WHATEVER MAY BE NECESSARY TO
PRESERVE THE SANCTITY OF THE
HOME AND ENSURE THE FREEDOM
OF THE STATE.

KATE KIRKMAN

APPENDIX C

Members of the Nashville Board of Park Commissioners and the Metropolitan Board of Parks and Recreation

NASHVILLE BOARD OF PARK COMMISSIONERS

Eugene C. Lewis	1901-1913
Fountain P. McWhirter	1901-1914
Ben Lindauer	1901-1916
Samuel A. Champion	1901-1906
Robert M. Dugley	1901-1925
M. T. Bryan	1906-1923
Robert T. Creighton	1913-1926
Whitfoord R. Cole	1914-1926
Lee J. Loventhal	1916-1940
Charles M. McCabe	1923-1939
Percy Warner	1925-1927
J. P. W. Brown	1926-1939
Rogers Caldwell	1926-1931
Edwin Warner	1927-1945
C. A. Craig	1931-1951
James G. Stahlman	1939-1950
Vernon Tupper	1940-1946
Bascom F. Jones	1940-1963
Tony Sudekum	1945-1945
Edwin Crutcher	1946-1963
William Hume	1947-1950
Richard N. Coolidge	1949-1963
Newman Cheek	1950-1963
C. Madison Sarratt	1950-1955
Alvin G. Beaman	1955-1963

METROPOLITAN BOARD OF
PARKS AND RECREATION

Dr. George Reichardt	1963
Bascomb F. Jones	1963-1972
A. J. Roper	1963-1979
Mose J. Davie	1963-1976
Ernest Hardison	1963-1964
Charles F. Mager	1963-1980
B. R. Allison	1964-1973
Annette S. Eskind	1963-1976
Bill L. Crouch	1972-1975
I. T. Cresswell	1976-1980
Doug Holloway	1975
A. J. Kreitner	1976
Anne Roos	1976-1984
Tom Keysaer	1979-1983
Ruthelia L. Buchi	1980
Barbara Mann	1980-1982
Fred Russell	1983
Isaac Northern, Jr.	1983
James Vance	1984

APPENDIX D
Biographical Sketches of the Director and Park Board Members of the 1980s

BUCHI, RUTHELIA L. (Mrs. Ernest), appointed to the Board in 1980, is a native of Nashville and has strongly supported the active sports recreation program in the park system. She also serves on the boards of the Cumberland Museum and the Arts Commission.

FYKE, JAMES H. The Director of Parks and Recreation for the Board is a native Nashvillian. He joined the park system staff in 1965 as Sports Supervisor in the Recreation Division, subsequently serving as Special Services Division Administrator and in 1978 becoming the Director. The park system has experienced a major expansion under his direction and its annual budget has more than doubled.

HOLLOWAY, A. D. "Doug," appointed to the Board in 1975, was born in Clinton, Ky., and has lived in Nashville 54 years. Very active in Scouting and the Civitan Club, he donated the land for the Una Recreation Center and also serves on the boards of the Merci-Home and Arlington Memorial Methodist Church.

KEYSAER, THOMAS C., served on the Board from 1979 to 1983. A resident of Nashville 56 years, he was the Director of Youth, Inc., providing meaningful recreation for Nashville's boys and girls. As supervisor and commissioner of basketball officials in Nashville and Middle Tennessee, he has exerted major influence on area athletic programs.

KREITNER, ALBERT JONES "Mickey," was appointed to the Board in 1976. He is famous in Nashville as a restaurateur and professional baseball player for the Nashville Vols, Chicago Cubs and other teams and takes great interest in the recreational sports program of the park system.

MANN, BARBARA E., who served on the Board from 1980 to 1982, was born in Mobile, Alabama, and has resided 27 years in Nashville. She also served on the Metro Board of Education, has been president of the Nashville League of Women Voters, and has served on the boards of Grace M. Eaton Day Home, Martha O'Bryan Community Center, and Leadership Nashville.

NORTHERN, ISAAC J. "Ike," appointed to the Board in 1983, is a native of Nashville. He was elected to the Metro Board of Education, is a leader in several community organizations, and is very active in Little League football programs.

REICHARDT, GEORGE W., appointed to the Board in 1963, has served as Chairman of the Metro Board since its inception. Born in St. Paul, Minnesota, he has resided in Nashville 43 years. Active in the Red Cross and Rotary Club, holder of Scouting's Long Rifle and Silver Beaver Awards, he has twice been elected Tennessee's Chiropractor of the Year and has been president of the Commissioners and Board Branch of the National Recreation and Parks Association.

ROOS, ANNE F. (Mrs. Charles E.), served on the Board from 1976 to 1984 as representative of the Metro Planning Commission. She serves on the Metro Historical Commission, Metro Arts Commission, and on boards of the Cumberland Museum, Friends of the Alexander and Jean Heard Library, Blair Academy, Tennessee Performing Arts Center, Dede Wallace Mental Health Center, Human Services Corporation, and others.

RUSSELL, FRED, appointed to the Board in 1983, is a Nashville native known throughout the United States as a sports reporter and editor. He joined the staff of the *Nashville Banner* in 1929 and is its Vice President. He has served as national president of the Vanderbilt University Alumni Association.

VANCE, JAMES, appointed to the Board in 1984 as representative of the Metro Planning Commission, is an attorney and Civitan Club leader.

Active in the development of the metropolitan concept of government, he has served on the Metro Planning Commission since May 1, 1984.

www.ingramcontent.com/pod-product-compliance
Lightning Source LLC
Jackson TN
JSHW041917141225
94742JS00010B/12/J